Foredoomed is my Forest

The Diary of a Zimbabwe Farmer

Richard F. Wiles

© Copyright 2005 Richard F. Wiles.
All rights reserved. No part of this publication may be reproduced, stored in a retrieval system, or transmitted, in any form or by any means, electronic, mechanical, photocopying, recording, or otherwise, without the written prior permission of the author.

Note for Librarians: A cataloguing record for this book is available from Library and Archives Canada at www.collectionscanada.ca/amicus/index-e.html
ISBN 1-4120-5584-9

Offices in Canada, USA, Ireland and UK

This book was published on-demand in cooperation with Trafford Publishing. On-demand publishing is a unique process and service of making a book available for retail sale to the public taking advantage of on-demand manufacturing and Internet marketing. On-demand publishing includes promotions, retail sales, manufacturing, order fulfilment, accounting and collecting royalties on behalf of the author.

Book sales for North America and international:
Trafford Publishing, 6E–2333 Government St.,
Victoria, BC v8t 4p4 CANADA
phone 250 383 6864 (toll-free 1 888 232 4444)
fax 250 383 6804; email to orders@trafford.com
Book sales in Europe:
Trafford Publishing (uk) Limited, 9 Park End Street, 2nd Floor
Oxford, UK ox1 1hh UNITED KINGDOM
phone 44 (0)1865 722 113 (local rate 0845 230 9601)
facsimile 44 (0)1865 722 868; info.uk@trafford.com
Order online at:
trafford.com/05-0482

10 9 8 7 6 5 4

To Beth
My wife and later my
Guardian Angel
Without her this could never have been written

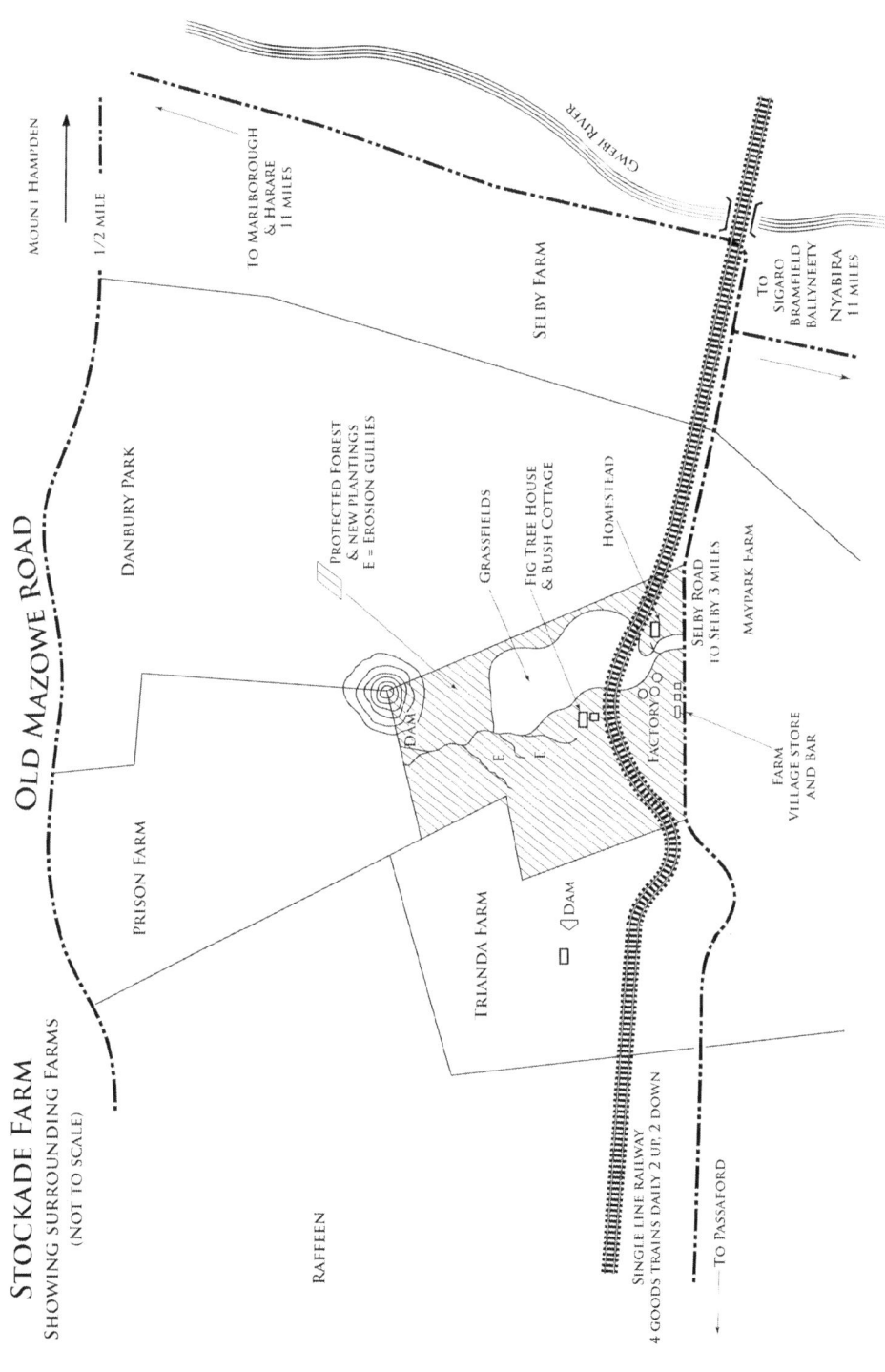

With Beth in the pigsties in earlier, happier times.

Preface

There was an ominous beginning to the new millennium in Zimbabwe. In the first months of the year 2000, in a move that was clearly preconceived and put into effect by the government itself, white-owned farmlands were invaded by militant activists of the ruling party.

Those steady, efficient and productive white farmers were to be shocked and traumatized when Mugabe, as President with complete political power, let loose lawless and brutal elements of his own making a full 20 years after Zimbabwe had obtained independence in 1980. He had proclaimed a policy of reconciliation and in return the farmers had continued to work their lands, agricultural production was sustained and national food security ensured. Simultaneously there was increased investment in subsidiary land usage such as the conservation and management of wildlife and tourist attraction. Had Mugabe wished to introduce land reforms, he could easily have done so during those 20 years of relative stability in a fair and peaceful way. Countless transfers of property took place over those 20 years but government never showed interest in taking up its right of first refusal. Why now was land such an emotional and urgent matter for the ruling party? Why suddenly did Mugabe turn the matter of white-held farms into an emotive and burning issue?

In retrospect, an answer can be found. By 2000 Mugabe had lost popular support and his ZANU PF party had no prospect of winning a free and fair general election. Since the beginnings of history, a well-worn stratagem used by demagogues, when they wish to draw attention away from their own failings, is to identify a scapegoat. To succeed passion must be roused; the scapegoat is publicly vilified and demonstrably thrown down. The choice was made and the finger pointed at the white farmer. The government plan, demonically executed, came upon me as it did others like a bolt from the blue.

Rhodesia, later to be called Zimbabwe, was renowned for its highly productive farms and earned the epithet; "The breadbasket of Africa". My farm Stockade, in and around which the actions recorded in my diary take place, was in the district known as Mazowe. This is a farming district of fertile, well-watered valleys threading through picturesque, wooded hills often studded with massive rocky outcrops. The water of the Mazowe River and its many tributaries flows north to the great Zambezi.

Stockade, 400 hectares in extent, was perhaps small in relation to the rather splendid farms in the area and when my wife and I moved on in 1963, we were told that it would be hard to make a living. It took all our savings and another 16 years to pay off our bonds. At last we could call the land our own. For a farmer and his wife, the farmland becomes an intimate extension of their home, and home is where the heart is. Here, definitely, Beth and I agreed we would see out our days.

The farm was indeed rather small, and an additional drawback was that half the land on Stockade was classified as non-arable; this being broken and steep forest land much of it with shallow or stony soils. Albeit, the farm's arable land bore heavy crops and this enabled me to raise and feed cattle and pigs and to grow Burley tobacco. We had spent ten years dairy faming in Nyasaland before this, so we had much to learn. By working hard we managed well enough. Beth was my tireless helpmate. Paradoxical though it may seem, during my legal battle to keep my property, it was the non-arable which gave me the most intense personal concern and which became the centre of a running dispute with government; a dispute which went on to the bitter end. This was because I had turned the whole of that sector into a nature sanctuary and government itself had proclaimed it a Protected Forest in perpetuity.

My relationship with the forest was one of passionate involvement. Some background notes will follow to make this important issue clear. They may induce an understanding of the reason why I fought so tenaciously for nature and wildlife against the cold, impassive force which was aligned against me.

The first entries in my diary were made in May 2000 and I continued making entries up until the end of 2003—nearly three years later. Upon scanning through the pages, I realized that I had not been nearly as methodical as I had righteously intended to be, especially at the beginning. I was away from the farm for more than two months in June to August 2000, but thereafter I saw that I had left quite long gaps in the ongoing narrative. This in no way implies that my lapses occurred during days of peace and tranquillity. The reverse is true. At the end of a strenuous and stressful day, I would feel too fatigued to sit up writing notes. Letters written to police officers or to the District Administrator [DA] have been inserted and may help to maintain continuity.

It may also help if I explain something of the farm-based factory, which is often referred to in the early pages. The factory was a business owned and run by my son, Martin. It manufactured clothing and hats, employing up to a hundred employees. Some of the factory workers lived in the farm village, but most commuted to work from their urban homes. The factory had an office and sales outlet in Harare.

It will be seen that because of continual harassment and the threat to the safety of all concerned, the factory was eventually closed. Before this it received marked attention from the activists. At the time of the closure, Martin moved his family off the farm.

Apart from my own homestead, two other houses are often mentioned. Martin, his wife Jean and the two girls, Holly and Renee, both of school age, lived in a house which I had built in 1977. I think it looked quite smart with a dark green roof and whitewashed walls set in a pretty garden with lush green lawns. I had designed, supervised, and done much of the building work myself.

This was the home referred to as Fig Tree House, so named due to a group of huge wild fig trees in the garden. These wild figs attracted a multitude of birds of many kinds such as Glossy Starlings, gorgeously coloured Oriels and Turacos, or noisy, tell-tale "Goaway" birds. I had chosen the site carefully and the house enjoyed a fine panoramic view overlooking the wooded slopes of the forest to distant blue hills. I think of it now with nostalgia.

Bush Cottage is another residential house; built in 1993 it is sited on the same ridge as Fig Tree House. I named it Bush Cottage because I took great care to conserve all the surrounding indigenous trees—it nestles in the bush. Beyond the trees is an open grass field. Here at sundown or early morning, duikers and reedbuck moved freely. Both houses are about a mile away from any other buildings.

Members of the Zimbabwe War Veterans Association are generally known throughout the land as War Vets or simply Warvets. They are central to my story. At the time of the Rhodesian Bush War, the Warvets were persons who fought with the guerrilla forces and who were trained, armed, and indocrinated by Russia, China, and other communist regimes during the Cold War. Hence they take the title of "Comrade" and refer to themselves as such.

Pror to their recall, and nearly twenty years after the end of hostilities, all Warvets were given a lump sum gratuity by Mugabe. They continue to receive a monthly wage from government. It is said that this is one reason for the collapse of the Zimbabwean economy. When they were mobilized for the "land reform" exercise, their leader was a volatile activist known as Hitler Hunzvi and it was he who led the first farm invasions. He became a ZANU PF M.P., drove a large Mercedes, and eventually died of AIDS.

It is thought that many of the Warvets are spurious—this was certainly the opinion among the farm workers.

The Warvet cadres were deployed throughout Zimbabwe; control was centred in Harare; and there was supposedly a chain of command by way of area and district bases. In practice, it seemed each Warvet was his own commander. Stockade became a district base and the commander, Simukayi, you will meet!

In newly-fledged African countries, political parties have long-winded titles which nobody remembers or uses. The locals all use the acronyms and in this diary so have I. Thus ZANU PF stands for Zimbabwe African National Union—Patriotic Front. This is Mugabe's ruling party. The opposition party is simply: MDC. This is short for Movement for Democratic Change. Needless to say, democratic change is the last thing the incumbent party will allow so woe betide anyone accused of being an MDC sympathizer.

Whenever the Warvets shouted, "You are MDC!" this was as good as a death threat.

I should explain references to Tredar or Tredar guards. Tredar was an acronym for the Trelawny and Darwendale Farmers' Associations. Many years before, the farmers in these two districts got together to form their own security organization. They paid for the scheme themselves. Initially it was a great success and it expanded to other farming districts. We found them invaluable in curbing crime and they did most of the groundwork for the regular police force. As time went on and farm invasions increased, their position became gradually untenable. No Warvet or Party activist could be arrested or charged and they were the very persons committing the crimes. Eventually government proscribed Tredar altogether and the farmers were left virtually defenceless.

When the Warvet cadres hit us, we were advised to keep a record of the events as they occurred. I suppose it was thought that the situation would change and law and order be re-established; the records would then be useful to identify wrong-doers. This proved to be an ingenuous belief. Nevertheless, I accepted the advice given and began writing a diary which covered this aspect so prominent in our lives. It has been a factual account of events written up close to the time of their occurrence. As such I have made no attempt to disguise the names of persons with whom I was dealing. In a very few instances I have thought it best to rename an innocent, who might feel at risk.

When reading this diary, it should not be thought that countering Warvet harassment was my only activity. Some farm work was carried out as best we could even when under duress and at most times work was going on in some part of the forest. I myself was for ever occupied raising tree seedlings and planting trees in the field. I was indeed keeping a parallel diary but the entries were mostly technical records.

During the first months, the incursions of the Warvet gangs could be described as probing forays. In July 2000, with the establishment of a Warvet headquarters on Stockade, the situation worsened dramatically. It will be told how the Warvets requisitioned a house and hoisted their flag in the centre of the farm village. In consequence my farm workers and their families came under direct surveillance and intimidation. This form of psychological violence is endemic to Africa. My workers, receiving instructions from me, the Warvets, and sometimes the Police or government officials, all in contradiction, never knew which way to turn. For the most part, they moved warily and silently—always fearful for their lives.

When I was writing, I often thought my tale was taking on the likeness of a Greek legend. A demonical ogre ravages the gentle land and terrorizes the innocent inhabitants. Who will be its next victim? Alas, I lacked the strength of a Hercules or the guile of an Odysseus and one such never turned up to deliver us from the beast.

I should make it clear that the experiences which I have described in my diary are not in any way unique. Hundreds of white farmers have been subjected to similar harassment and have suffered ordeals of a thoroughly distressing nature. Some have been killed, others grievously assaulted. By comparison, my own afflictions were minor. I happen to have written them down on paper.

The Forest on Stockade

In recording the day to day struggles and episodes in my diary, there was an over-riding aspect which constantly guided my mind and purpose. In order to make this very clear, I need to tell about my forest.

I always called it "my" forest because it was my personal and passionate concern for over fifteen years. I use the personal pronoun only in the way a protective and loving guardian views the charges in his care. Please let it be understood, that far from a selfish outlook, the prime motivation for my protective compulsion had been my concern for the planet Earth! Yes. I owe her something—the Earth I mean—MY LIFE. If, with raised eyebrows, you were to liken this concept to a version of spiritual revelation, I would not argue with you. Such was my commitment.

As a farmer and landowner, I saw it was my duty to improve and protect the natural forest area on my property. In the world context, destruction of the tropical rain forests is the greatest concern. Albeit; I contend that temperate and sub-tropical woodlands assuredly play their role in local and planetary environmental stability.

In extent, the forested area of the farm amounted to some 250 hectares. This consisted of generally hilly, non-arable country and is in fact at the apex of two watersheds. Botanically the forest would be termed Miombo or Brachystegia woodland. Within this general description over eighty natural tree species are present. I identified and listed them all.

Over a period of fifteen years I was planting indigenous tree seedlings to augment and interplant existing stands. This involved the collection of seed; sowing, potting and watering seedlings for anything up to three years; digging large holes in the field and incorporating manure, compost and fertilizers. Finally the planting out was performed with piped water pumped from long distance or by tractor-drawn water-cart. Watering rounds continued during the first year of establishment. Many thousands of young trees were planted out in this manner. The addition of some 30 species, native to Zimbabwe but new to the farm, brought the total number of species to 110. This was surely a diverse collection of which I was very proud.

The costs for this work were met from farm revenue. If annual upkeep of 30 kilometres of firebreaks is added to the cleaning of the young plantings, it is clear that the monetary outlay was considerable.

As my project progressed, I could see that the forest would require permanent protection long after I was dead and gone. It was important for me to obtain government recognition for this by way of a statutory declaration giving it protected forest status. I applied to the Ministry for the Environment accordingly. The Minister in turn referred me to the Forestry Commission.

A senior extension officer was dispatched to examine the project. He was most enthusiastic and commented that I was doing work that the Commission itself should be doing but was not! He hoped the Commission would be able to use the forest for its own researches. Such an attitude delighted me because one of my desires was to set an example of natural forest management for others to follow.

So the experts came out and extolled my project and surveyors came out and pegged and measured. Things were moving. However; I had not had the experience of dealing with the slow-grinding machinery of government departments and this task tested my endurance and patience. For the present account I shall only say that by personal, dogged perseverance; allied I like to think with a degree of subtle charm, I was able to navigate my application through a multitude of interviews in a multitude of offices in just two years.

By Statutory Instrument 147 of 2001 the Minister of Environment and Tourism declared the non-arable parts of Stockade Farm a protected forest. It goes on to say that "this area of the farm which is unsuitable for cultivation has been converted into a nature sanctuary providing for as many species of indigenous plant and animal life as is reasonable to expect."

I had made it. The trees of course represented only a part of the exercise. Sure they are the dominant pillars in the system, roots anchored deep into the rocks and soil, the principal players in the carbon/oxygen exchange; but they also shelter, nurture, house and feed a myriad of microorganisms and thousands of larger ones; home to all creatures great and small. [In serious discussion it is called biodiversity and we think wisely of the bits which, if we conserve them, might be useful to mankind one day—the inevitable selfish argument we humans use.]

I already had in place a policy of no disturbance, no cattle grazing, and no extraction of wood. Wood for our workers was obtained from old eucalyptus plantations. Security scouts were employed to prevent poaching and the setting of snares. Wherever there was evidence of previous soil erosion, reclamation measures were put in place. These required the cartage by tractor and trailer of many tonnes of material into steep, almost inaccessible areas. It was often a hair-raising business.

My efforts had not been made for money, but I did foresee the need arising for additional revenue, so I looked to the prospect of ecotourism. Construction began on a large lodge to house parties of birders and the like. Bird life was prodigious and the walks I had made, varied and delightful. In discussions with the GM of the Forestry Commission and the Minister for the Environment, I offered my co-operation in the setting up of an education centre. Appalling degradation of the natural environment can be seen wherever one looks and only educated and enlightened youth will save Zimbabwe from being turned into a desert. For direct observation of good management, the forest was not too distant for students to visit and learn.

I had many fine, mature trees in the forest of course, but my policy was to encourage vigorous re-growth alongside these, making for natural replacement. It would take time and the establishment of new plantings would be a long and slow process. There was no way that I could have lived to see my work through to fulfilment. I always knew that. A tree outlives a man and I was growing old. The young trees that I had personally planted—so lovingly—I looked upon as my children. The child outlives the man. I visualized that in time others would welcome the challenge to continue the work.

In retrospect I see I was naïve. In human affairs political expediency will always come first. A concept such as mine formed no part in Mugabe's programme of land reform, which he set in motion by the use of his uncouth Warvet cadres and Marxist style Land Committees.

It is a bitter irony that in so-called land reform, it is the very land which suffers abuse and irrecoverable damage. The veld is burnt from end to end, trees axed down, wild animals are killed in their thousands. It seems that a lawless society becomes a destructive society and natural life takes the brunt of abhorrent human behaviour.

I fear that my many, many "children" will perish. As I write this, most, I expect, are already dead. In God's name, I tried my best for them—I really did.

List of persons whose names appear quite frequently in this book

Warvets

On Stockade: Simukayi, George, Mapolisa, Moffu, Chengerai Munatsi, Chauka.
On Danbury: Davite, Ghendi.
Itinerant: Chengerai a cripple.
Area commanders: I.C. Takawira
  2 I.C. Smart

The Warvets moved about a lot and some would disappear for weeks.

Police Officers

Marlborough
Insp.Mukungunugwa, ex BSAP, very tall, imposing. Curbed by political edicts. Insp.Mashamba, appointed in 2003, nice manner, helpful type but as above. Assistant Insp. Mupariano, stout, discovered to be incredibly two-faced.

Nyabira
Insp. Masuka, ex BSAP, good policeman in impossible position.
Insp, Sengwe, ex combatant, character will unfold.
Insp. Majoni, -ditto- pleasant but scared of putting a foot wrong.
Asst/Insp. Taswa, a cynic, he carried out his duties accordingly.
Sgt. Tezha, [later promoted Asst/Insp.] an odd mixture, but never decisive.

[The British South African Police, BSAP, relates to the British South Africa Company. The company, formed by Rhodes, was based in Britain's Cape Colony. It was given the Royal Charter to form the Pioneer Column which entered the land north of the Limpopo in 1890. Originally it was a mounted force. Most of its officers were recruited in the UK.]

The Ministry for the Environment and Tourism

The Minister	Francis Nhema
Personal Secretary	Helen
Ministry Secretary	Mr. Tavaya
Deputy Secretary	Mrs. Sangarwe
National Parks	
Deputy Director	Mr. Chadenga

[The Director is an Army Brigadier, a figurehead.]

Ministry of Agriculture and Lands

A senior assistant secretary   Mrs. Mandimika

Ministry of Youth Development, Gender and Employment Creation

Th Minister Elliot Manyika, ZANU PF Political Commissar; Acting Governor Mashonaland Central.

ZIMBABWE CURRENCY

Foreign currency is unobtainable for the average citizen; therefore the official rate of exchange is meaningless. Foreign currency can only be bought on the open market. This is called the parallel market and the exchange rate is based on the US dollar. Here and there I have referred to monetary figures which are in Zimbabwe dollar terms. For those who wish to relate them to their own currency, the following parallel exchange rates operative over the past 4 years will be a guide:

November	2001	400—1 usd
October	2002	1500—1 usd
February	2003	2100—1 usd
November	2003	6000—1 usd
January	2004	8700—1 usd
June	2005	25000—1 usd
July	2005	38000—1 usd

Annual inflation rate

2001	112 %
2002	not available
2003	598.7 %
2004	557.2 %
2005	597.2 %

It seems that annual inflation is being held at just under 600% per annum.

2000

Warvet incursion 26th. MAY 2000

Time: 1700 HRS. The incursion party consisted of 6 people who arrived on the farm in a blue Datsun pick-up Registration No. 509250 J. Our Farmers Association liaison man phoned to warn me that Warvets and ZANU PF supporters had mobilized and were moving into our district. We could expect a visitation. "These guys are out to antagonize you so the golden rule is; keep cool, don't lose your rag, avoid confrontation. Just refer them to the law. Rather than get heated, better walk away—clear out." Today the first raiders have come to Stockade. I admit I was nervous. It is in my nature to retaliate fiercely when provoked. I wasn't sure how I would re-act so when their vehicle drove in I kept out of sight. The following report was given by the Tredar security guard, who was on duty at the fenced premises of the Nola hat factory adjacent to the farm buildings.

The leader and chief spokesman of the group gave his name as Chamu also as Top Ten. The guard understood that the party had come from Pearson Farm. Of the six, 3 were men and 3 were female. I understood the latter were young and, from the guard's description, might be termed "nubile". The girls remained in the back of the open truck.

The three men were very drunk. Another witness observed that the driver remained in the cab, and was drinking beer from a bottle. A good number of beer bottles were seen within the vehicle. When the other two got out, the second Warvet staggered and fell. The guard, when relating the incident to me, said the man suffered a deformity of the legs—a rather novel description for the condition, I thought.

Chamu alias Top Ten approached the Tredar guard, accused him of being an MDC supporter and tried, unsuccessfully, to knock the guard's hat off. He then accused the guard of being a supporter of "The Farmers" and again attempted to knock off the man's hat. Once more he failed. It seems it was more through lack of co-ordination than of purpose that Top Ten was thwarted in his ambition to knock off the guard's hat.

The Tredar guard was told that they had come to see the Boss. Upon being told that the Boss was not there, they then demanded the keys to the factory because they wanted hats and items of clothing from inside. They were told that the keys were with the Boss. With that, the men returned to the truck promising to come back on Monday. They drove away and the drunken driver just managed to follow the general course of the road.

During this episode I was in fact at no great distance and had sight of it. On consideration, I have decided that I am temperamentally unsuited to conduct dialogue with beings of this sort. Magnanimously, Martin says he will accept the role of "The Boss". I shall be called "The Old Man" with the implication of advanced senility. I was told that the intruder's vehicle was owned and driven by the headmaster of the Pearson farm school, a school supported and largely funded by the Salvation Army. Does the headmaster with such a penchant for strong beer still have connections with The Salvation Army? Bless me!

30th May 2000

War Vets have established a cell on the neighbouring farm Danbury Park. Plainly the purpose has been to indoctrinate the resident workers. The workers and their families have been forced by the War Vets to attend ZANU PF meetings, these being held at night and continuing for many hours. I was informed that even children are obliged to attend—leastwise, they cannot be left at their homes unattended.

The leader of the Danbury War Vet band is known there as Davite. He has been described to me as being tall, about 40 years, and having an evil expression. From further information gathered, I learn that he was one of the parties who previously visited Stockade as a spearhead to the ZANU PF campaign of intimidation and extortion in this locality.

Jealosi Devison is a bricklayer who has worked for me on Stockade Farm for some weeks. He lives with a family on Danbury and thus falls under the control of the local War Vets. On Monday 29th. May, he did not come to work but arrived later in the day to explain his absence. Briefly, his account is as follows:

On Sunday night Jealosi arrived at his house in the darkness. He came upon the War Vet Davite at his home. Jealosi's wife, Murisha accused the War Vet of sexual harassment and assault. A fight ensued between the two men in the course of which, Davite sustained a battering about the head and face. The fracas was such that Tommy Bayley, the farm owner, was called to the compound. He decided to call in the police.

Two ZRP members from Mabelreign accompanied by a Tredar guard, appeared on the Monday morning to investigate. By this time the War Vet Davite was not to be found. The policemen took statements from the wife and two other women—all three claiming sexual harassment by the "War Vet". Apparently the Police agreed to take up the case.

On Tuesday 30th. May at 1430, a brown pick-up No 543878 W, was driven on to Stockade. There were 9 men in the band. The man Davite was among them; our Tredar guard recognised Davite because he had come into the factory the previous Saturday and been very abusive to Mr. John Aird, Martin's manager. The men left the truck and walked past the guard ignoring him. They proceeded without permission to the building site where the guest lodge is being constructed. The men were looking for the builder Jealosi, who upon seeing them had quickly hidden. When they could not find him, the gang returned to their pick-up and drove away.

The episode had the hallmarks of an intended revenge beating if not worse. Naturally enough Jealosi lives in fear of this and tells me he now stays elsewhere at night. The wife still awaits the Police but to date, 2nd. June, they have not returned.

The Member in Charge,	Stockade Farm
Z.R.P. Marlborough	30th. August 2000

Dear Sir,

I wish to draw your attention to a person known only by the name Simukayi. He leads a group of "War Vets" who, unbidden, took up residence on Stockade Farm in July and after the Election.

I was informed that Simukayi's status as leader was disputed by seniors in his organization who directed him to leave the farm. This he did, but then returned, since which time he has been the cause of unpleasantness, destabilization, disruption, cost and stress. A full record pertaining to these matters has been made and is available.

The direct dealings with Simukayi have been made through Martin Wiles, my son, and Mr. J. Aird both of whom direct the business operations taking place on the farm. [My son is away on leave for two weeks and Mr. Aird commutes and is resident in Harare].

From the information which has been passed on to me concerning his behaviour, it is my seriously considered opinion that Simukayi is suffering from a psychological disturbance and that it could well be a form of schizophrenia. Alternatively he could be taking drugs. Whichever the case, I wish to make it clear that I consider him to be of unstable mind and therefore a danger; particularly to myself because I am likely to be the target of his mental aberration.

It is my understanding that Police Districts have now been given authority to resume law enforcement duties especially as they pertain to unlawful farm incursions. To avoid the possibility of tragic consequences, I earnestly request your co-operation in the matter outlined above and that the man Simukayi [together with his followers] be removed permanently from the property.

Yours sincerely,

R.F. Wiles.
Attached are additional matters of complaint.

Simukayi—The intrusion on Stockade—Further Notes for ZRP

The group of Warvets under the leadership of Simukayi arrived to establish a permanent station on Stockade Farm on 6th. July last. An immediate demand for accommodation was made in a manner which was both uncompromising and aggressive. Workers' housing being fully occupied, a building within the farm work complex was given to them. Simukayi expressed strong dissatisfaction with this. Accordingly, farm workers were diverted to prepare a new house in the farm compound.

When the new house had been built, Simukayi refused it. His demand was for a better house with water and electricity. He said that if his demands were not met, he would forthwith move into a substantial house which is being constructed elsewhere on the property for the expansion of our business. Work on this house has been suspended until the political crisis has been resolved.

If this move was to take place, it was feared that damage would be done to expensive fittings. Consequently, Mr. Martin Wiles promised Simukayi that he would put his mind to an alternative arrangement. However, whilst Martin Wiles was off the farm attending to his business schedule, Simukayi chose a house in the compound for himself and ordered the occupants out; lying to them by saying that the Boss had ordered it. The evicted workers were told that they must double up with others; their household goods were thrown out.

Simukayi's next demand was that a water pipe be laid to the house he had commandeered, also an electricity line. When making these demands he issued threats that unpleasant repercussions would befall on us if we did not comply. In view of this, farm workers were diverted from their tasks to dig a trench and then water pipes were laid to within 25 metres of the house. 200 metres of electric cable was purchased and laid. This was expensive and further funds could not possibly be found to complete the work.

Since moving into the house, Simukayi has made "requests" for money and food including meat. Always the "requests" are coupled with a threat. The following threats have been made:

The immediate closure of the hat\clothing factory and the take-over of the premises by the Warvets.

The calling in of "Army" surveyors to peg the farm for redistribution.

The summoning of truckloads and busloads of squatters to occupy the farm.

Writing a report to President Mugabe in detrimental terms with regard to myself.

Farm workers were told that unless The Boss agrees to the Warvets demands, they will be made to suffer.

For security reasons, strangers are never permitted to enter the factory buildings where materials, equipment and machinery of considerable value are visible and thus present a temptation to criminals with intent to rob. Simukayi has ignored requests not to enter the factory. He has brazenly led his men all around the premises during the course of production. The threat in this case is to dare us to challenge him.

It is evident that one of Simukayi's objectives is to demean and lower the standing of ourselves, the owners and directors, in the eyes of the people we employ. He does this by flaunting his incontestable power and authority. Demands are made in the presence of company. There is usually a preamble of loud, hostile abuse, racial in character.

On occasions, Simukayi has sent a youth to Mr. Wiles at the factory, with the verbal message saying he must report to Simukayi who was waiting at "his" house. Martin Wiles once, with reluctance, complied with such a summons. Upon reaching the compound gate, he was stopped by the youth to be told that Simukayi had changed his mind and was not ready to see him. My son is a very busy person; it takes little imagination to see that Simukayi's ploy was to goad him into an angry confrontation.

The most recent threat to date was on 29th. August. Simukayi confronted Mr. Aird at the factory and, in his usual abrasive manner, demanded that the farm title deeds be brought to him. Upon production of the title deeds, sections of the farm would be signed away to himself and to three other Warvets. In addition he wanted three hats, beer and a bottle of brandy. Should the title deeds not be produced the factory would be closed down and not be allowed to re-open. This threat was issued twice; morning and evening. It was made forcefully enough for us to consider measures we should take in the eventuality.

In the event Simukayi failed to arrive to close the factory. Later however, he again referred to the title deeds saying that they must be produced before 4 Sept. He informed my son and Mr. Aird that on that date he would be returning to his post in the Army. In the Army, Simukayi told them, he held the rank of Lt. Colonel in the Presidential Guard.

We suppose Simukayi has chosen to spend his Army leave on Stockade. Or is he on secondment?

To avoid outright confrontation, certain measures were considered "cheap at the price" and Simukayi has received the following:

- One dozen Tee Shirts—Zimbabwe Bird & Star

- One dozen Caps—ditto
- Eight other assorted caps
- One bottle brandy, one bottle gin.

Because the Z.R.P. were not accepting reports of offences made by Warvets at the time, some background information, I feel, is not irrelevant to an understanding of our attitude towards present problems.

Roving bands of belligerent Warvets entered the farm and confronted us with demands of land. Under the immediate threat of burning the factory down, Mr. Wiles was forced, under conditions of great duress, to sign a paper purporting to deliver the farm over to the Warvets. I think the land was eventually ceded to three different parties each of whom claimed to have priority right.

In order to placate these roving bands, we distributed among them; 3 windcheaters, 3 hats, 6 caps, 2 Brandy, 1 crate cold drinks, 1 box biscuits, 2 X $500 cash for purchase of fuel. These roving bands were motorized and Simukayi was not among them.

Before the orchestrated campaign of land invasions, it seems likely that Simukayi was advised by superiors on tactics and methods to be deployed. That indoctrination of racial hatred formed part of the process seems evident because Simukayi is able to recite certain anti-white slogans and phrases with repetitive and rehearsed venom. However, after an initial outburst, he is unable to keep up the momentum whereupon his character alters. This suggests a limited capacity for original thought which is confined to the objective of obtaining immediate personal reward.

We supposed that he had no useful employment and that he was living on his Warvet pension and his commutation money. Reports received are that he spends most of the hours of the day and of the night drinking at the bar or at his house.

It might be said that to be held to ransom and to be stressed by a character such as has been described, is absurd—even ridiculous. However, the times we live in might also be described as absurd and ridiculous.

I repeat my belief that Simukayi is psychologically unbalanced and that in certain states of mental delusion he is a danger to those whom he has been trained to hate.

In making the request to the Zimbabwe Republic Police to effect the removal of the party of Warvets who have invaded Stockade, I feel that I must make some points clear.

My move has been greeted by those about me with a degree of scepticism and consternation. The concern is that we shall be the victims of instant and ugly reprisal. There are parties of Warvets on Danbury, Maypark and Trianda—all neighbouring farms and all subject to a central command. Unless the Police have the authority, the will, the manpower and the back-up, to clear all the farms in this area at one time, then we stand alone and will be mercilessly victimized. Such is fear; such is present reality.

I have, as requested, expanded on our own particular problem and trust that any action will be appropiate and effective for our immediate relief. That said, I am fully aware that the Z.R.P. have a huge countrywide task ahead of them to restore obedience to the law, and that from now on their performance will be watched with acute attention. This may be quite daunting for them!

For better or for worse, I sent the above to the local police inspector.

The Member-in-Charge,   Stockade Farm
Z.R.P. Marlborough   22nd. September 2000
Dear Sir,

Since my letter to you of 30th. August followed by personal visits, I was disappointed that you were unable to fulfil your promise to take follow-up action. Meanwhile the person referred to in the case, Comrade Simukayi, may have been transferred or gone on leave, because the quarters on the farm, which he had appropriated for himself, is now occupied by a cadre of three other Warvets. These too have become a cause for concern.

On Wednesday 20th. Sept. at 8 pm. two of these men left their house in the farm compound and proceeded to the work complex, where three Tredar guards are quartered. They whistled up the guards and spoke with them. The three guards reported the next morning that one of the cadre members was armed with a rifle.

On Thursday morning 21st. Sept. at 10 a.m., the same two Warvets walked up from the compound to the gates of the hat factory in full view of many factory and farm workers. Again one was carrying the weapon. The men did not speak but walked up the farm entry road where other workers were lifting garlic close by.

The security guards say they do not have the names of these Warvets but they know them well by sight and to be those staying on the property. The report by the Tredar guards is attached hereto.

On the same Thursday afternoon at approximately 4 pm. a Z.R.P. Landrover from Marlborough entered the farm and drove down to the factory gates. It seems the police detail was seeking information and directions in regard to a reported car accident in this vicinity and the police party had lost its way.

The sight of a Z.R.P. vehicle was so unexpected and so unusual that I hurried forward, welcoming the chance to express my concern about the armed man living on the farm.

The police vehicle was full of people, perhaps as many as sixteen, so it was not clear to me who was the senior person in charge, especially as most in the party wore no uniform. I therefore addressed the driver.

The Tredar guard was present and we reported the matter of the armed man to the constable. The driver's enigmatic reply was: "We know of no armed people in the Marlborough area." The innuendo contained in this reply certainly did not escape me.

The driver, in reply to my further query, went on to say: "If they are not interfering with the work, they should just be left alone." I asked if that meant that the Warvets had police authority to carry guns. If that was not the case was it in order for me to search for the weapon myself in their quarters. I was told emphatically not to do so.

Meantime, one of your sergeants had come forward from behind the Landrover and it was he who told me that your station would definitely react to a call from me but at another time. Right then they had to rush to the car accident. [This accident had occurred 5 hours earlier, the injured parties taken to a hospital, and I subsequently learnt that the car had mysteriously vanished!] All in all it was apparent to me that your junior ranks were unclear on how the law obtained and how to reply.

This matter raises a number of questions and I would be most grateful if you advise me on them.

1. Does the man, who may be readily identified, have legal authority and police permission to carry a firearm?
2. If not; are you in a position to search for and remove the weapon and to enter a charge of illegal possession?
3. It is plain that the deliberate exposure to view of the weapon to the guards and to numbers of workers is a considered psychological ploy to instil fear into me and into all the workers on the property. Is this not heinous intimidation?
4. Through intimidation, these people have taken one of our houses for themselves; now because of intimidation the long-standing residents of the farm live in fear. As the professional agency for law enforcement, are you able to expel the evil-doers from our property? If so, will you do so and can you protect our lives thereafter?

In the circumstances prevailing at this time, I considered it best for me to record my fears to you in writing. Should a tragedy occur then I feel that my own conscience will be clear.

I look forward to your understanding and co-operation.

Yours sincerely,

R.F. Wiles.

cc. CFU; Atherstone & Cook; et al.

Stockade Farm 11th. October 2000

Work was in progress in our irrigation land where a garlic crop had been lifted and preparations were being made to plant a following vegetable crop. A tractor was ploughing and farm workers were making ready the planting stations for butternut squash.

This work had been put in progress because we had the assurance that the Warvets [WVs] had no legal right to halt farm work. However, because they had issued threats that they would do so, Martin had driven to the ZRP Marlborough to request a police visit to Stockade in order that the WVs might be apprised of the facts and be dissuaded from taking action.

By mid-morning, a police Landrover from Marlborough arrived on the farm. In the vehicle were one police Asst. Inspector and one plainclothes policeman. In the back there was a group of WVs. In his own vehicle, Martin followed. They proceeded to the WV camp, which the WVs have established in the farm village. I was at the lands and close by the roadside.

Within 5 minutes 2 other vehicles came down the road towards me. The first was a small blue saloon car with 4 or 5 persons in it. I was told by my workers that these were well-known WVs. The car passed by me without stopping. Immediately behind the WV car there came another ZRP Defender. This vehicle stopped opposite to where I stood. It had "ZRP Mazowe" printed on its side.

In the front seat was a fairly corpulent man who identified himself with an ID card as Mr. Mubako of the Ministry of Local Government. He said he was from the DA's office in Concession and was the Asst. DA. The driver was a young person in police uniform and appeared to be the only policeman. The back was full of men who, I was told later, were all WVs.

Mr. Mubako seemed very affable and smiled broadly as did the constable. He saw a crop of Pigeon Pea growing nearby and asked me if he could have some seed which I gave him. One of the WVs in the back descended and took seed without asking my permission. They all seemed in high spirits.

I assumed that this was another party, who had been summoned to sort out the matter of our land preparation with the local WVs and to put the matter straight. If we were to be relieved of the constant confrontation and could continue with our farm work in peace, I could only be pleased. However, my happy expectations were soon to be dashed. It appeared that Mr. Mubako had come on another mission altogether.

The Asst. DA produced a list of farms listed for preliminary acquisition and noted that Stockade was on the list. He asked me if I was the owner and I told him that the owner of the property was a Trust. He said he supposed that

I would be able to tell the Trust that the farm had been selected for immediate resettlement.

I asked how this could be because, in timely accordance with the law, an appeal against acquisition had gone forward. Furthermore, we fell outside the criteria for acquisition as specified by the government itself. Mr. Mubako replied that the fact remained that the farm had been identified for acquisition and the process had now begun. "We shall be bringing people onto the farm very soon—within days".

I asked who would be responsible for paying my farm workers. He said that we would still have to pay them.

"How can we do that if we cannot utilize the land to earn our living and their living?"

To that question, Mr. Mubako went on to say that we could continue to prepare and plant the land that we always used, but must not plant up any "new" land. He pointed to a pasture nearby as an example of a "new" land. This astonished me, but I realized that because of his complete ignorance of farming and agricultural matters, he would not have known that this field was a valuable grass ley sown to Rhodes grass and the legume Desmodium and was mown annually for a nutritious livestock feed.

Never once, before or after listing, has this farming property been visited and assessed by an educated person qualified in the environmental sciences of ecology and appropriate land usage. Yet here was a woefully ignorant government spokesman, accompanied by a single police constable and a group of political provocateurs, informing me that I could expect an unspecified number of "settlers" with unknown [and probably non-existent] farming ability, to be placed on the farm within a few days!

By this time I realized with dismay that this mixed party were sailing under a false flag and using the ZRP Defender as a front of respectability to cover their wicked designs. Indeed there was a certain piratical cruelty in the gaiety of the group. I was the victim of their derisive amusement. Sensing this evil emanation, I turned away and the police vehicle drove on, going directly to the WVs camp.

Meanwhile, at the camp, 2 additional cars carrying WVs had driven in by another route. Thus Martin and the 2 officers from Marlborough were surrounded by about 30 WVs only to be added to by the DA's group then arriving. Outnumbered by the belligerent WVs not less than 10 to 1, there was little hope of resolving the land preparation dispute. The inspector acknowledged this to Martin in an aside. In the exchanges Martin was directly threatened that he would suffer ugly retribution if he allowed land preparation to continue.

The timely convergence of all these parties onto Stockade, clearly indicate co-ordination between the Police, the District Administrator, and the Warvet Command.

Mubaku, together with the Mazowe coningent left the farm about midday. I issued orders to my staff to continue with their work. This, they did.

At 2.30 in the afternoon I was informed by Johannes, the farm foreman, that the tractor which was working on our land, had been hi-jacked by the WVs and taken to their camp. The order to hi-jack was given by Comrade Mapolisa and carried out by young members of the local cadres. Two of these men were from government ministry offices at Gwebi Wood. The evidence of this event was described by the driver, Jack, and his statement is available. What the tractor driver did not say was that Mapolisa forced him to plough some land for the WVs by their camp. I only discovered this later. ZRP Marlborough was informed of the hi-jacking and an Asst. Inspector came out. He obtained the release of the tractor at about 5.30 pm. Cde. Mapolisa and the other members of the gang criminally took possession of the tractor but the police did not charge them.

During the afternoon the farm work was switched in order to avoid looming trouble. There had been a loss of half a day's work and a waste of diesel fuel.

Tuesday 17th. October 2000

It is apparent that Warvet tactics are to prevent or disrupt farming operations country-wide, with special regard to the preparation of fields for the coming season. The Warvets who have established themselves on Stockade have targeted our irrigation land for work stoppage.

I bought my farm legally 37 years ago and the laws have not changed to make my title deeds invalid. Government ministers, far remote, give instructions that unless and until proper legal procedures are carried through, farmers should continue planting crops without hinderence. The Warvets ignore both the instructions and the law because they have Presidential and Party support. The Police dither in the middle. This is administrative chaos amounting to anarchy.

On the farms the position for farmers becomes well-nigh intolerable. On Stockade I have to make a decision and it must be made TODAY. To survive financially, I must continue growing crops. If I succumb to the Warvets' intimidation I shall lose all. Besides, I have Right on my side and this moral aspect means much to me. And bullies make me angry.

I seek out Martin in the factory.

"Martin, I feel we must stand up to these bastards and keep on planting tomorrow come what may. I reckon they are not sure of their ground. I'm sorry that you're the one to take all the flak, but what do you feel yourself?"

"No, Dad. I agree. Maddening though it all is, we just have to keep calling in the Police. They do at least repond; however reluctantly."

At 5pm. The Warvets George, Simukayi and 2 younger men from Maypark came to the factory gate, entered the security area without permission, and approached Martin who was locking up the buildings. At this time Johannes the foreman was present as also was the Tredar security guard.

A discourse opened with a hostile demand by the Warvets to explain why we had ignored their orders not to prepare and plant our irrigation land. Ever patient, Martin told them that we were within our legal rights to do so and showed them several documents proving that this was so. This evidence was brushed aside as "nothing but pieces of paper". Martin then asked the Warvets to produce their written authority to stop us from doing our farm work. This they could not do and evaded the question with loud, angry and irrelevant interjections.

Because argument was pointless and could have been interminable, Martin ended the meeting saying that the farm work would continue the following morning. The Warvets were incensed by this and vowed they would prevent the planting. Like Simukayi, the Warvet George is a big aggressive man. He pointed the stick he always carries, first at the foreman Johannes and then at Martin. Speaking in Shona he said: "You will get trouble with your life!" [This was the interpretation given me by Johannes].

Wednesday 18th October 2000

In accordance with the decision to recommence land preparation and planting, I made some contingency plans. Martin had already notified the police that we had received threats and there was likelihood of trouble.

Bearing in mind that the foreman Johannes had been personally threatened and that other workers were unsuitable or too old for the challenge, I selected 3 men to work with me on the irrigation land—Divas, Bigg and Karissa. The others, under the charge of Johannes, went to "non-controversial" work far distant in the forest.

Because of, [a] previous examples of Warvet violence, [b] the real threats made the previous evening, [c] the racist, anti-white tenor of statements often made by these same Warvets, I considered that I would be their chief target should they use violent methods to prevent the planting. Further, I suspected that I would receive no help from the 3 farm workers if they were put under duress. In such circumstances, I felt I might well be roughed up or at least given some rough handling by the Warvets in order to stop me working. Not relishing this prospect I decided that 2 Tredar guards with dogs should be present with me in the field. I was not all that confident of them, but they had at least some training and now I needed them for my personal protection.

I gave the guards very specific instructions that should the Warvets come onto the field, they were to remain close by but silent and still. In no circumstances were they to make any move unless and until the Warvets began a physical assault.

About 7am, we began seed-planting along 4 rows, watering as we went. Shortly after, Martin had come up and was able to join the small team. The guards [who had entered the field rather irresolutely I thought!] stood with their dogs behind our line of advance and would therefore be at the back of us when the Warvets approached.

At 7.30 two Warvets appeared on the headland and walked up the rows towards us. The two were recognized as Comrade George, the local commander, and Munjoma. When they were about 12 yards off I commanded them to stop. George soon sent Munjoma away—doubtless to call up reinforcement.

The Warvet then began to speak with my workmen. I rapped an order to them not to reply and we worked on in silence. However, in due course, I became aware that it was only Martin and I who were working. Acutely aware of the tension, also that I was caught in a battle of wills, I purposely worked towards George planting my pumpkin seeds right up to his feet.

My 3 African workers had stopped work. Crouched down, they had become silent, miserable bystanders. Divas appeared to be looking for something in the ground; Karissa was searching for an escape route in the sky; Bigg, squatting under a tall pigeon pea plant in an adjoining row, took on the look of a scolded spaniel. I looked up briefly from my planting and asked him if he was afraid. "Yes" he could only mutter.

So my suspicion was proving correct. The Warvet had not moved and said no more than a few words but it was enough to have the men cowering and fearful. This Comrade George is a tall, imposing figure, but in addition to this, he is able to radiate an aura of power. This aura, coupled to the evil emanating with it, has a devastating effect on the mind of the ingenuous African. To me, this small incident explained a lot concerning the broader African political scene.

Martin and I continued planting for some time with the stationary Warvet on one side of us and the 2 guards and 2 dogs also stationary on the other. George began to speak to the guards but I cautioned them to silence. After a while we ran out of watering pipe and Martin had to start off his factory work so we were forced to call it a day.

Lest the Warvet should assume complete control of the petrified workers, I told them loudly to push off "NOW!"—Which they did at the run. Martin and I took our seed containers to the road edge but upon looking back found that the Tredar guards had not followed us. We spotted them eventually moving

Bigg and Divas watering the "hills" prior to planting pumpkin seeds.

The Madala Boss shows the way.

swiftly away. I called them back. It appeared that as we were leaving the planting rows, George had immediately called them to him. I asked them both what he had said to them. "For taking the side of the azungu [white men] you will both get a beating, is what he told us".

The upshot of this incident was that once more we should have to call in the ZRP. The police being usually short of transport, Martin left for Marlborough to collect them.

Warvet George meanwhile had mustered some of his gang and returned to the factory. There were now 6; George, Simukayi, Munjoma, Sydney, another man, and a woman called Kathrin. One of the young Tredar guards who had accompanied me earlier had returned to his quarters to kennel his dog and to change out of uniform. He was spotted by the Warvets. George and the female, Kathrin, strode across towards him brandishing sticks. Fearing a beating, the guard ran away into the trees.

The Warvets then turned their attention upon the other guards. They were abused and threatened because they had agreed to escort the "madala boss" [the old white man] into the field. They told the Tredar men that their O.C. must be called to give reason why they were interfering in the land dispute.

By this time the young guard, who had scampered off, had found enough courage to rejoin his fellows and presumably had been spared his beating. However, he was then sent up by the Warvets to my house with orders to tell me that I must report to them as they were waiting for me. In obedience to his instructions, this the guard duly did. My household staff called me to say that he was at the security gate, so I went to speak with him.

I saw a young man in a state of panic. He was sweating profusely and almost inarticulate. Out of his guard's uniform, he looked a thin, pathetic figure. He spluttered out the Warvets message and asked what he was to tell them. I said he should tell them that I had heard the message and that he had delivered it—no more. This seemed to upset him further. Perhaps he had been told that he mustn't return without me! Taking pity on him, I changed my mind and told him just to hide in the trees out of sight because the police would be arriving shortly.

Within 20 minutes Martin arrived on the farm with two ZRP members of non-commissioned rank. The police spoke to the Warvets and afterwards informed Martin that the Warvets understood the position and would not interfere further. The police however said that it would be advisable to give a little time for the Warvets to confirm the position with their chiefs. The six "Comrades" then trooped off to their camp.

The next arrival was Charles Chiwawa, 2 O.C. Tredar. He had come to assess the situation and told me that he had notified the police in Nyabira, which is the station closest to the Tredar camp. I had spoken to him earlier on the radio to inform him that his guards were getting a grilling from our Warvets. I asked Charles if he would be taking a statement from his guards to the effect that they had been seriously threatened. He thought this was really a matter for the police who had already taken statements from them.

I fully understood that this would be normal procedure but it would depend, I would think, if the aggrieved party wished to bring a charge. In the event the police never took a written statement from the guards. Once again we see that the Warvets are immune from prosecution on almost any count. And THIS is noted by EVERYONE. Small wonder the power they wield.

During the morning the Tredar base vehicle with their 2 IC, Christopher Moffat, drove in with 2 senior guards to replace the youngsters for whom I had been instrumental in exposing to a sort of baptism of fire. I expect they were relieved to be leaving their scene of torment!

At 1.30 pm. Insp. Masuka of the Nyabira station came onto the farm. I had a long talk with him and gave him a description of the events. He was accompanied by 2 plainclothes policemen, one of whom noted some of my personal particulars. This seemed a bit strange and unnecessary. The inspector proceeded to the factory area in order to ask some questions of the staff and also of the Tredar guards.

I followed shortly afterwards because I had forgotten to tell him that the Warvet George had been seen on two previous occasions carrying a weapon and it was thought that he still had it. The inspector replied that he would "look into all that" and I went to my house.

Later I learnt that Insp. Masuka had gone to the Warvets camp and spoken with them. He then returned to Nyabira without further communication with me. Thus it was only on the following morning that I learnt, through radio contact with Simon Hale and Hamish Turner, [farmer representatives for this district] that the inspector had told the Warvets that they were to allow us to continue farm work and should get confirmation of this by contacting their own leaders.

That evening there was another ZRP arrival. This time it was Insp. Mukungunugwa, the O.I.C. Marlborough. We understand that the inspector had previously had a meeting with the Provincial Governor at which it was confirmed that Warvets had no authority to interrupt farm work. I believe he said that the DA was also present at the meeting with the Governor.

The inspector informed Martin that he had given the Warvet cadre on Stockade all this information and in speaking to them he reiterated that work on the farm should be allowed to continue unhindered.

Thursday 19th. October 2000

There was no move by the Warvets to stop the farm work today. At 2pm. Chris Foot called in to say that the Warvets had halted work on Trianda and meanwhile he had found one of them, Mapolisa, poaching fish from his dam. This made him so angry that he resolved to continue with land preparation on the morrow come what may.

I was sorry to learn of Chris' aggravations. We enjoyed a less stressful day than of late. In the evening I strolled down to the private nature sanctuary, which I have enriched and nurtured over the years. Within the sanctuary is my wife's grave, so I hold it with special reverence. Here amongst natural things I can find peace. Indeed I can say it is, for me, a place of spiritual significance. I know every tree, every shrub, and every rock intimately. If Pan still seeks the quiet corners of the world, he must surely be found here.

This evening, to my chagrin and distress, I found 4 noisy Warvets fishing in the little pond which I have personally constructed. It is stocked with small fish obtained from Kariba. The only fishing permitted is by kingfishers, herons and reed cormorants. The Warvets involved were George, Simukayi, the female Kathrin, and with them was a young girl, who has recently joined the troupe, known as Jessica. They were being purposely loud and boisterous. I felt my anger rising but I dared not provoke a confrontation which I could only lose. Flushed and distressed I turned back.

Plainly this was an act of provocation and spite aimed at myself. "Checking out the land issue with their chiefs", as advised by the police, was far from their minds. Indeed, that line is nonsense from the start. Their communication and information gathering is swifter and better than ours. Furthermore, they have all the time in the world to plan their moves and they enjoy generous government funding to boot.

Tonight as I write, I feel distraught. The Warvets have discovered my weakness—my Secret Grove—I love it so much. Will they return to desecrate it? I am sick at heart.

Friday 20th. October 2000

The Trianda tractor came over to us at 5am. to plough. The section to be prepared for planting is close to the factory building and is visible from the compound.

The tractor driver had only completed the opening furrows when the woman Warvet, Kathrin, came across to him. She was carrying a burning brand with which she threatened the driver that unless he stopped ploughing she would burn him and the tractor. The driver, Jack, was the same man who had his tractor hi-jacked by the Warvets the previous week. He stopped his work and lost no time returning to Trianda.

Upon learning of the Warvet action of stopping the tractor from working, Martin decided to report the matter to ZRP Marlborough. He went there in person. The Asst. Inspector to whom he spoke was reluctant to move on this issue, so Martin left to go to his office.

Meanwhile, however, the Warvets had come up in force from their quarters on the farm and stopped the entire work force from continuing with the planting. Martin contacted the Officer-in-Charge, Marlborough. The latter collected the Warvet commander for the area, Takawira, and brought him to Stockade. We were told that our Warvets "now understood that they should not interfere with farm work". The whole day was lost. For how long does the charade go on?

Monday 16th October 2000

This morning it was discovered that 32 pockets of garlic had been stolen from the packing area over the weekend. The three Tredar guards, whose duty it was to secure the area, were very evasive and unconvincing with their explanations. Enquiries revealed that on Saturday night, in shocking neglect of duty, all three were drinking at the village bar in the company of the Warvets.

I notified Tredar base and their men came out bringing a ZRP constable from Nyabira and replacements for the offending guards. The policeman took some statements at the site of the theft and returned to Nyabira with Tredar.

It seems most likely that the garlic was carried by 2 or 3 people to be loaded on a vehicle, and that the theft took place on Saturday night. Two vehicles were present in the farm village on Saturday and both left for Harare late that night. One vehicle belongs to the bar keeper, the other [known because it has no number plate] to the Warvets. Either of these two vehicles could have been used to transport the garlic.

It is well known that the bar-keeper and her male partner, Douglas, are very friendly with the Warvets, especially Simukayi who lives and feeds at their house and drinks heavily at the adjoining bar. The other "Comrades" of our communist style cadre also spend much time at the bar where they doubtless receive favoured treatment. All in all, suspicion for the theft must be directed on the Warvets, the bar-keepers, the Tredar guards, or all parties acting together in collusion. The Tredar men will, I trust, be questioned rigorously. But will investigation extend to the bar-keepers and to the Warvets? We shall see.

The misdemeanour of the Tredar men is, of course, unpardonable; nevertheless it must be recognized that their subversion would have been the work of the unprincipled Warvets, whose goal is domination by any means. The Warvets move freely all over the property and enter working areas at any time of the day or night. The guards, who we employ for security, are instructed to avoid crossing them.

A ZANU PF. flag flies outside the Warvets requisitioned house to give the appearance of an administrative H.Q. One must acknowledge that their coercive tactics, though abominable, are brilliantly effective. Using them, they hold ruthless rule over the inhabitants of the village.

1st. November 2000

Farm work over the past 10 days has been uninterrupted by the Warvets. Preparation and planting has progressed. After 5 months of continuous harassment involving threats, extortion and insulting behaviour towards ourselves and blatant intimidation of farm workers, we seem to have won the last skirmish in the running battle. We have only managed to achieve this by making ourselves aware of our legal rights and very politely reminding the police of their role as law enforcement officers.

Given the climate of state promoted anarchy, we are fortunate that the police inspectors in charge of this area have responded positively to their proper duty, albeit with reluctance and a show of incredible pussyfooting. I think I understand their predicament and their unease.

These inspectors know their society far better than we do; they know the mind types of the ruling clique; they know that their own commanders are political appointees, who are subservient to that clique; they can expect the ruling hierarchy to be ruthless and revengeful should a policeman show greater respect for the law than for Party orders. And after all, the Party has pitted itself against the law. So far we have been lucky. God save us; we might have had a Mabunda of Karoi! Another Simukayi dressed in a police uniform!

It has been a relief to carry on work these last few days without open confrontation, but there is still much to be done. In a way, the lull seems ominous—something is hatching. There are agonizing conditions on farms elsewhere; nothing comes from government ministers except lies and spiteful rhetoric; the Warvets are in situ and cannot be moved. So, what next?

Indeed, what next? It could be any of the following:

1. A resumption of demands to stop land preparation and planting with accompanying threats and intimidation.

or

2. The invasion onto the farm by a motley crowd of "settlers" organized by the Warvets under the cover of a dubious government official.

or

3. A magnanimous offer by government to allow us to continue farming for this year in exchange for giving the poor Warvets and other "landless peasants" a part of the farm so that they can plant crops for themselves. "Government would take favourable note of farmers who actively assisted the new African settlers with the cost of their inputs." This would be the thrust of the message—the threat behind it thinly veiled.

We must be prepared to face up to any of these actions or a combination of them. A talk with the area police inspector yesterday, turned up a few hints. At a recent meeting of "Chefs" [high ranking office bearers] the last option apparently received favour. It is in keeping with this regime's method of fraudulent double-talk and Mugabe's cruel cynicism.

It would be the stick and carrot method; soften us up with all hell let loose followed by a well publicised appeal to reason and conciliation. The farmer gets on with his farming at which he is so able; the Warvets stay on the farms caring for the poor peasants—meanwhile holding everyone to political ransom using the particular skills at which they most excel. The nation is fed by the farmers and ZANU PF strengthens its hold on the rural communities in the time-honoured way. Mugabe is assured of the rural vote. It might induce him to smile.

No; if we swallowed that sop, we would suffer aggravation, provocation and positive fear every day of our lives. Most of us have areas of natural beauty and wildlife. It will be sickening to watch the animals being slaughtered to the last, the trees cut down, mutilated and burnt, the soils scarred and eroded. Under this iniquitous system of land settlement, IT WILL HAPPEN.

Our only recourse is the law and to ensure that, through the law, every trespasser and squatter on the property is evicted. It will be a tough battle because, as we all see, the present leaders scorn the law. Notwithstanding; there appears to be a note of desperation in their fast-track land grab. It is as if they are moving so rapidly because they fear the decision of the Supreme Court hearing next week.

5th. November 2000

Saturday 7am. Five Warvets led by Simukayi and George are at the farm entry gates. They are felling trees in order to block the roads into the farm. As they are axing the trees they are whooping and shouting to one another. In all they fell five trees including two tall and spreading acacia trees which I have been shaping and trimming over many years past. The roads are blocked very effectively so that no vehicles can get through.

Fortunately, it being Saturday, my granddaughters, Holly and Renee, are not going to school, so neither Martin nor Jean need be driving out of the farm right now. The Warvets must have been drinking heavily and are very noisy. The dreadful thuds of the axes are interspersed with deep-throated yells of triumph as the poor trees crash down on their sides

Later I found they had also felled a lovely lone-standing Jacaranda tree far from the road. This could only have been for the love of killing it; just as these savage brutes would enjoy killing an animal. I know the characteristic well. It makes one shudder!

Simukayi described himself as a "mean killer" when he made threats against my life on Wednesday. I can see it in the brutal nature of the man and many others like him.

I am really not sure what their motive was to block the roads. It seemed to be just a show of power. Later, down at the factory, they were shouting about how the farm was theirs. Martin decided to close the factory after this nasty incident so there was no production obtained at all. The workers had to return to their homes—mostly in Harare and involving them in a costly taxi-fare.

The Warvets went away after that and did not return. However; there was much trouble on a neighbouring farm so perhaps they went to join in that fracas. After all, that's what the government pays them for.

Insp. Mutsengi of ZRP Marlborough came out. He assured us that we should continue with our farm work and that should the Warvets stop us, to call them at the ZRP Marlborough station and they would come out. He also told me not to worry about Simukayi's death threats!

"They are meaningless—not worth making a charge. He'd never carry them out", the inspector said. "You'll have to get something on Simukayi more concrete than that."

The inspector may be right. Equally the inspector may be wrong. I have no wish to have it put to the test. Other farmers have been killed and their killers have gone free. Whatever; it seems to me that being a member of Mugabe's "elite regiment" is an assurance of immunity from prosecution.

Monday 6th. November 2000

We have been given so many threats by the Warvets and so many stoppages have been caused by them that forward planning has been made almost impossible. We need to prepare the main arable fields and to procure seed and fertilizers. At each step we are harassed by the enemy—and never was there a truer epithet. The enemy is foulness personified, which we can only counter by persistently adhering to statutory and moral law. I would like to compare it to a George and Dragon contest, but I'm afraid it's more of a David and Goliath one and David has little ammunition.

In the circumstances, Martin decided to go to the police this morning to obtain a measure of support—an assurance that they would intervene on our behalf, if our farm work was stopped yet again, and to sort out Simukayi and his outrageous threats.

No doubt, had the police inspector been alone, Martin would have received the quiet nod of affirmation. However to Martin's dismay, when he was at the station talking to Asst. Insp. Mutsengi, the O.I.C., Inspector Mukungunugwa, beckoned him into his office where he came face to face with the two Warvet leaders who control the whole of our area. Takawira and Smart are the names they operate under. Although Smart is the No.2 he is the more voluble and vicious of the two. It was the inspector's plan to have the two Warvets listen to Martin's complaints and to get them to curb Simukayi.

These then were the conditions in which Martin found himself when seeking a straightforward acknowledgment of our legal right to carry on with our work peacefully. Elsewhere, Martin has written out his own report of the day's happenings. In order to record events, I am summarizing them here.

In his habitual cool and polite manner, Martin stated his problem to the inspector. The two Warvets intervened with loud, aggressive, vituperation, the lean and ugly Smart losing self-control. The police inspector equivocated and rather than commit himself to the legal rights of our case took on the role of a negotiator. Finally Martin decided to leave, feeling very discomforted. Notwithstanding, he too is aware of the difficulties these policemen are in.

When a senior police officer has to negotiate with bandits, who even operate under assumed names, then it is further evidence of the protection these bandits receive from the very top of the ruling clique. They have been given fearful political clout.

The conditions of confused anarchy have in fact been carefully orchestrated. The confusion gives the impression of spontaneity. To coincide with this, Marxist-style slogans are trotted out [it is amazing how effective this claptrap can be even after all this time]: "Lack of resources makes it impossible to control a mass movement of discontent amongst the landless peasants" and so on. When it comes to cunning, Machiavelli had nothing on this lot.

Mid-afternoon a big group of Warvets entered the farm by way of the compound and the Warvets camp. Because the farm gates had been chained and locked, the party walked up to the factory. I was away on business concerning our forest and Martin was at the town office; thus it was the Tredar guard who received the group which numbered as many as 25. They were led by Takawira and Smart and included George. Simukayi was absent.

Immediately they were very hostile. Apparently they had heard that we had continued planting our field during the day. They were outraged that we had disobeyed their instructions not to do so. Smart said that Martin had agreed that very morning to instruct his farm workers to halt planting. [This was a blatant lie, but to lie is quite normal and expected in these people]. He demanded to see The Boss at once, but of course was told that the Boss was absent.

The guard entered the factory in order to radio the town office and to inform them of the onslaught of the Warvets. Smart, who had followed the guard into the factory, grabbed the transmitter mouthpiece from the guard and into it poured a string of invectives. His almost incoherent tirade was received in the company office by the imperturbable John Aird, who effectively dealt with Smart with stonewall answers.

The Warvet party, it was reported, had driven in from Berea, a farm some six kilometres distant which has already been targeted by the Warvets. I guess Oscar Neilson on Berea had been given a torrid time earlier today. The vehicle used to transport the big party was a police Landrover Defender. This vehicle, having delivered the Warvets to our factory, had been driven and parked at the top farm gate and in due course the group walked up the road to board it. Unfortunately, the police vehicle registration number was not noted.

After the main group had gone, George and Mapolisa, with another man, pulled up the "No Trespassers" notice. They brought it down to the factory and gave it to the guard. Mapolisa was in high temper and shouted to the guard that if we did not remove the chains and locks from the gates before tomorrow morning, they would smash the gates open and break them up. Later, on their way back to the compound, they pulled up the gatepost of the compound gate so making a vehicle opening that way.

One day they are felling trees to barricade us in; the next they threaten to break open our gates to allow their cars free entry.

The Warvets displeasure at the sight of the "No Trespassers" notice is interesting. Of course they are all trespassers; but can it be possible that people like this harbour a guilty conscience? That they dislike being reminded of the law?

Tuesday 7th. November 2000

Today we were left in peace so we could continue preparation for planting squash, pumpkins, beans and maize on the lower irrigation land. Workers have also been harvesting the pigeon peas and removing the woody haulms to make space for the onions which are presently in the seed beds. There has been some very useful rain over the past few days for which we are grateful, but to take best advantage of this we need to keep working without interruptions.

Yesterday, business connected with the farm took me to the offices of the Attorney General. When in talks with Mr. Dias of the Legal Drafting department, I learnt of a new piece of government legislation concerning land.

The government has agreed that if a white farmer cedes a part of his property for resettlement, he will not be listed for acquisition. If already served with a preliminary notice, then he will be delisted. I was informed that appropriate forms of agreement had been printed and were immediately available for signature.

For months on end, truly appalling harassment and intimidation has been dealt out to farmers by small groups of indoctrinated thugs—old-style communists still call them "cadres". They have been assigned local bases which are spread evenly throughout the farming districts. These cadre cells, under the direction and sponsorship of the ZANU PF government, have been given the directive to terrorize and soften up the white farming families. When necessary, their numbers can be augmented by paid ZANU PF supporters transported in government vehicles. With this scenario, the latest government "offer" should be read for what it is—out and out blackmail.

There is a cynical corollary to this bit of trickery. Repeatedly the President has said that whites will not be compensated for the land taken away from them—only the improvements. [Then only by the British!] So if the farmer, to avoid further persecution, cedes part of his land without buildings etc. in order to keep his home and to maintain his livelihood, the government takes the land for nothing. Not to take into consideration valuation of land types and fertility for compensation is so puerile that it can be deduced that the only motif is racial malice. Anyway, it is all meaningless rubbish.

Stockade Farm Report Wed. 8th. November 2000

Some excellent rainfalls have marked the start of the season and conditions look favourable for yet more rain. It was felt imperative that we proceeded quickly with the preparation of our main dry land arable fields. To this end we agreed to hire tractor power from a neighbour whilst there was a break in the weather. By mid-morning two tractors were employed heavy-discing and were making good progress.

At 2pm. three Warvets, Simukayi, George and Mapolisa, came down to the field and ordered the tractor drivers to stop work. They then climbed onto the tractors and directed the drivers to take their tractors to the Warvet camp. I had wondered why the two drivers had meekly obeyed the three Warvets and had not perhaps just driven their tractors off home. However; the witnesses, including the three Tredar guards, who watched the procession pass, state that Simukayi was holding an open Okapi knife to the back of his driver. The drivers were held for some hours but eventually released with instructions to tell their boss not send them here again if he wanted them to stay alive.

Meanwhile, I had notified Marlborough ZRP and Martin of the hi-jacking of the tractors together with the drivers. I was alarmed lest any damage be done to any of them. In due course Martin went to Marlborough and met with Insp.

Mukungunugwa who promised to come to the farm but explained that first he had to pay a visit to Danbury Farm. In a discussion with Martin, the Inspector made it clear that his hands were tied and that really there was little he could do to resolve these sorts of confrontations provided that violence was not initiated. He said clearly that there was no way he could arrest the Warvets for hi-jacking the tractors from the field. [I suppose hi-jacking at knifepoint doesn't constitute violence.]

The inspector suggested that we come to some kind of accommodation with the Warvets with regard to letting them have some land on a temporary basis until the whole land issue had been resolved. To compromise in such a way would be absolutely fatal. We would be milked dry in short time. I am sure the policeman knows this very well. It makes me wonder which side of the fence he is.

Martin returned disappointed with the reaction of the police officer but fortunately the two drivers and their tractors had been released by that time with no damage done. By 7pm. the police had not arrived so we returned to our homes—drained!

Friday 10th. November 2000 Stockade Farm

Land preparation for soyas, which was halted by the Warvets on Wednesday, has been postponed until we work out strategy. Planting of maize and beans by the farm workers was continued.

At 9 a.m., a message came to me that Johannes had been abducted by the Warvet Mapolisa, and taken to the Warvets camp. I didn't like the sound of this at all. If he escaped physical assault, the Warvets would at least give him a mental drubbing which could leave him shaken. ZRP was contacted and again the O.I.C said he would come out and in fact had planned to do so anyway.

Back on the farm, we were pleased when Johannes was released and appeared to be unruffled. He reported that the Warvets asked him why he had given the farm workers instructions to plant in defiance of their orders. Johannes replied, quite correctly, that he carried out the instructions as given him by the Azungu, because they were the ones who paid him his wages. Remarkably, the Warvets told him to carry on because they themselves were going fishing in the Trianda dam!

It is most noticeable that these Warvets have an enormous psychological hold over the ordinary rural people. It is perhaps true to say that the three principal Warvets that have been stationed here are particularly daunting. George and Simukayi are taller than average, hold themselves imperiously and are deep-voiced. Mapolisa makes up in breadth what he loses in height. He is thickset and bullish, has a fat belly that rolls obscenely over his trouser waist, and he stands with his legs astride to support the excess weight of his body. All three walk at a slow measured pace; all three abjure cultivated manners for abrasive insolence; all adopt a piercing intimidatory stare. Their very appearance signals danger. I expect thugs and ruffians the world over carry the same stamp.

At about 10a.m., the police inspector arrived in his Landrover. He came up to the factory from the compound and with him he had brought the top Warvet, Smart, and two others from their headquarter base at Glenara. He had also brought George, Mapolisa and the woman Katrina. Simukayi was not with them. I had the 2 dogs with me, which seemed to disturb the party particularly Mapolisa, so after greeting the inspector, I retired and left Martin to cope with the pending arguments.

I have avoided exchanges with these Warvets because I am ill-equipped to bridge the intellectual gap between us. They are ill-educated and limited to primitive thinking. George lives immovably within the confines of his early doctrinaire training; Mapolisa is the model of a Caliban; Simukayi, I am convinced, is a schizophrenic. [Because he could be dangerous, I have reported my suspicions in writing to the police three times, requesting he be taken in for psychiatric examination.]

Martin, being a graduate teacher, has been given the training to communicate with immature minds. Also, as a very experienced rugby referee, he is used to calming down volatile flare-ups by warlike rugby players! Of the two of us, he is obviously the man to face the Warvets, uncomfortable though the task is. Unluckily, he is invariably heavily outnumbered—on this occasion 6 to 1 with the inspector as intermediary.

Martin has written his own account of the meeting. However; it proved to be indecisive and from our point of view, disappointing. The inspector reiterated that he would not be involved in land disputes nor to say what was or was not the law. His role was to ensure that there was no violence and to tell "all parties" to refrain from violence. That was all.

At one point, Martin tells, Smart shouted at him the words: "If you carry on with planting, you will have to take the consequences!" Martin turned to the Inspector and asked him if this did not constitute a threat. The inspector repeated that we should negotiate and come to an understanding.

Martin persevered with the argument that we had to plant the crops in order to remain in business and to pay the worker's wages. He told the Warvets they should obtain written authority from government which forbade us to carry on with our crop production. As usual, this was brushed aside as being irrelevant.

The Warvets said that we were wasting our money planting our fields because they would be taking them anyway. Martin retorted that, in that case, we should be allowed to continue planting. When the government took the farm from us, they, the Warvets, would get the land and all the crops as well. They could only be winners. For some reason this didn't go down at all well. Finally Smart shouted: "In that case I shall tell my people to do whatever they like to stop you". Once more Martin asked the inspector if that didn't constitute a threat. He was unanswered. This pleased George, Mapoliza and Katrina no end. Puffed up with self-assurance they joined in the clamour.

The police inspector drove away taking Smart and the Glenara men with him. Within 10 minutes, our Warvets ordered the farm workers out of the field. The workers only returned to the field when they learnt the Warvets had gone fishing.

Sunday 12th. November 2000

Another week lies ahead; decisions have to be made; trouble can be anticipated whatever we do. In order to gauge the best plan of action for ourselves, we must attempt to size up the whole situation. With chaos prevailing throughout the farming areas, this is not easy.

Close to home, a lot of hostile activity has taken place on farms neighbouring us this weekend. Mayfield, which has been a target for the Warvets for months, again received attention. The D.A. proclaimed that half the farm was to be taken immediately for resettlement. Danbury and Selby farms were invaded on Saturday by numbers, estimated at 50 to 60, transported in a wide assortment of vehicles including minibuses, police cars, pick-ups, smart saloons and even an army staff car.

Ugly and violent scenes occurred at Glenara and Pearson farms. The following points, I think, are significant:

On all the farms NONE of the farm workers were involved in the disorder; thus confirming that the instigators find no support from that quarter and have to resort to bussing in ZANU PF "demonstrators". [An endeavour should be made to find out how much the latter get paid.] As usual, no written legal or governmental documents are produced to authorize the invasion of the properties.

In the absence of official authority, the invaders are encouraged to abuse and threaten the white owners of the farms. The main purpose of this form of intimidation is to halt farm production and to prevent the farmer from getting his seed in for the season now directly upon us. What then is the strategy of our enemy? For an enemy we surely have, and a ruthless and cunning one. Some thoughts come to mind.

For us, the situation is changing so rapidly that decisions on planting can only be made on a daily ad hoc basis. The government party may consider using draconian measures to stay in power and willy-nilly ride out their massive unpopularity amongst the population and the condemnation of the international community. To save their own skins, the leading clique will be prepared to plunge the whole country into destruction. Indeed, the historical record of dictatorships shows this to be the invariable pattern.

Martin with Beth in the factory 1994.

2 0 0 1

Stockade Farm
PO Box EH 95, Emerald Hill.

The District Administrator,
D.A.'s Office,
Concession   30th. January 2001

Dear Sir,

Malicious Injury to Property and Theft

I refer to my Fax to you [attention Mr. C Gurure] of 23rd. January and to the two letters of 29th. Dec. and 7th. Jan. addressed to the O.I.C., Z.R.P. Marlborough copies of which were given to you for information.

It will be seen from the letters that I anticipated legal action to be taken in this matter. However, in discussion with Mr. Gurure and the Police Inspector, it was apparent that they felt the case could be resolved without going to court.

Subsequently, the latter two gentlemen have met with the Warvet commander of the district on this farm. The result, as I clearly understand it, is that Simukayi was found to be seriously at fault in his actions. At the time of the meeting, I am told, he was irrational due to being drunk but his commander promised to "sort the matter out".

With regard to the 4 hectare soya field, Inspector Mutungunugwa pointed out to me that whilst Simukayi SAID he would take the crop, this was only a verbal threat and that technically he had not yet done so as it was still in the ground. At today's date, Simukayi has been employing workers to weed the soyas. It is manifest that he intends to steal the crop and that either he has not been given a directive by his commander or he is ignoring it.

In the matter of the Desmodium and Sunn Hemp seedlings which Simukayi destroyed; this small piece of land is within our irrigation perimeter and is therefore of high value for our purposes. The maize which Simukayi has planted for himself will yield a paltry amount and on much of it nothing at all.

We have been asked to co-exist with the invaders. I will remind interested parties of the following: there are only eighty hectares of arable fields on this farm and of these seventy hectares have been forcibly taken from us by the Warvets. Thus, co-existence for us means that Simukayi and others have had the use of 85% of the available cropping land. It is intolerable that they should continually intrude on our reduced and confined production base.

It is my understanding that you have fairly regular meetings with the Warvet command personnel. Further, they agree that we have been wronged. I would be most grateful if you would kindly take this matter up with them again and to give us a written assurance that the soya crop is the property of the farm and does not belong to Simukayi.

Also, may we have a written assurance that the one and a half hectare land rudely taken from us by Simukayi and turned to his own benefit, be restored to us forthwith.

I wish to record that I have had had very cordial discussions with your Mr. Gurure and I look forward to continued co-operation with your office.

Yours sincerely,
R.F.Wiles.
cc. ZRP Marlborough, Atherstone & Cook, CFU.

Stockade Farm
PO. Box EH 95 Emerald Hill

The District Administrator,   6th.February 2001
D.A.'s Office,
Concession.

Dear Sir,

Simukayi—Warvet & Psychopath

Over recent weeks it appears that we are being given the message, either through your administration or the Z.R.P., that we should accept the "settlers" who have been placed on the farm and must learn to co-exist with them in harmony. If this reflects a ministerial directive to ameliorate the out and out terror and intimidation of a previous period, then it has to be termed a relief.

An understanding of this kind presupposes a degree of cultural civility from the participants. In a person who is mentally deranged, as Simukayi obviously is, such a compact is meaningless. His manner is constantly aggressive and boorish. Rank threats and extortion are his sole stock in trade. To make matters worse, he is habitually drunk. His very presence on the farm can explode into unforeseen unpleasantness. I illustrate.

On Wednesday morning 31st.Jan. at around 8am, I was in the farm factory yard talking business with my son Martin [MW]. In my company was my dog Moppet, who is a highly intelligent and sensitive animal. The yard was busy with workers coming and going; the security guard was on duty; the yard sweeper was attending his flowerbeds; Moppet, not far from me, was idly watching the activity.

Unexpectedly, Simukayi arrived alone at the open factory gates. Here it must be born in mind that Simukayi is hated and feared by everyone on the farm and it follows that wherever he is present he induces tension—rather as the lion causes unease amongst the prey on which it feeds. To me, Simukayi is the personification of evil, and I have no doubt that upon seeing him, I also immediately tensed.

As you may well know, animals are extremely sensitive to a change in atmospheric tension. Moppet being the perceptive and intelligent dog she is, sensed the tautness in everyone in the yard and quickly identified the object of our fear, Simukayi, standing thirty metres off at the gates. She dashed past us all, set upon Simukayi and managed to bite him in the leg before we could call her away.

You can imagine the repercussions Moppet's plucky sally has brought. Simukayi demanded and was provided with transport to Parirenyatwa hospital. He was also given 1000 dollars for the clinic fees. The wound being slight, we think he never went to the hospital but pocketed the money provided instead.

Unfortunately that was not the end of the affair. The next morning at 7.30 Simukayi came again to the factory. He had been drinking heavily. Shouting like a madman, he forcefully drove the women workers back to their quarters; stopped three of the farm workers from doing their allotted task in the farm yard, ordering them back to the compound; instructed the security guards to lock the factory gates so denying the factory staff entrance.

Shortly afterwards Martin arrived at the factory to begin the day's work. Observing the lunatic behaviour of Simukayi, he endeavoured to calm him down and suggested they speak in the factory office. With that Simukayi shouted: "If I go with you into the office, I will kill you!" He kept on shouting; "I will kill you! I will kill you!" He also cried: "I will kill your Father and his dogs!"

In order to get the 60 workers into the factory and production started, Martin handed Simukayi a further sum of money. This was witnessed by the three security guards and Simukayi consented to the resumption of work. Notwithstanding; he continued assailing Martin with racial abuse, foul language and additional threats and demands.

Simukayi is obsessed with the thought of killing and the power that he has been given to threaten death is very real and meaningful to him. To watch him axe down a beautiful tree with obvious relish [as I have done] is a horrifying experience. He is a destroyer of life, a purveyor of death, a servant of Satan.

This then is the person with whom your, good Mr.Gurure, and indeed Inspector Mutungunugwa, requests us to come to an understanding. Simukayi is a habitual drunkard—that is generally known. I am told that he also smokes mbanje and that that is also well known at the bars. Withal, I have informed Authority over and over again that Simukayi's behaviour pattern indicates that he is insane; also that the form of his insanity is dangerous. There is no question that in a modern, enlightened society, he would be held in an institution for the mentally ill.

As a private citizen, I put this matter before you in your position as a responsible government authority and, in God's name; request that you take appropriate action.

Simukayi told my son that I should move off the farm in three days or he would kill me. Martin replied that he would have to see the D.A. about that. Thereon, Simukayi's words were:

"We have sacked the D.A. and it's no good going to the Governor either because we are going to sack him too."

On the chance that Simukayi may not be telling the truth and that you are still in office, I have decided to send this letter anyway.

Yours sincerely,
R. F. Wiles.

20th February 2001

The Supreme Court judgement on land acquisition has just been announced today. It has come out in our favour and it requires the law enforcement bodies to remove the Warvets within 48 hours. I understand that Mugabe has issued orders to the effect that the court order should be ignored.

The crunch has come—rather sooner than I expected. This Presidential directive to ignore the Supreme Court ruling shows a contempt that may well be interpreted as an invitation to general lawlessness. A wave of crime is almost certain to follow and still the police will not know where they stand. Their morale must already be low and their resolve questionable.

It could be at this point that there will be an outbreak of general unrest. This will give Mugabe the excuse to call in his army and continue to rule by force and fear. The prospect is grim indeed, and would mean the end of civilized standards in society. Unfortunately history too often repeats itself.

It seems to me, that our only hope lies in there being such a massive popular revolt, that the whole ZANU PF edifice collapses and that Mugabe's picked generals and police commissioners get scared and desert him. Meanwhile what can we do for ourselves on the farm? We must try to identify all persons involved in our persecution and record names, times and witnesses. Take photos if possible.

If Right prevails over Evil, the day of reckoning will come.

Not least; at all times we must look to our backs!

20th February 2001

The season has proceeded and we have no crops on our main arable fields. The Warvets refused us access to these fields and in consequence no land preparation could be done. Thus some 65 hectares were denied to us. This represents 85% of the farm arable and we have been confined to farming on 10 hectares of irrigation land. Even here we have been aggressively harassed every step of the way.

The Warvet Simukayi is one with whom it is not possible to deal with rationally because he is mentally deranged. His behaviour has been so threatening, vicious and obnoxious that his presence on the farm is proving to be literally intolerable. As a result, our decision has been to rapidly wind down operations. This means ceasing further farm work and closing down the factory, which was established on the farm some six years ago. Unhappily about 100 workers will be laid off.

22nd. February 2001

It is Martin who is nobly taking the brunt, the face to face confrontation with Simukayi and the other Warvets who trail along with him. He remains level-headed and outwardly patient in the face of extreme, calculated provocation. He acts as my front man, for which I thank my lucky stars. I am not a hot-tempered person, but faced with rude, boorish behaviour, I am easily goaded into fierce retaliation and will speak my mind. Martin restrains himself and keeps cool. Nevertheless, at the end of the day, he is often left shaken and strained. The relentless pressure is taking its toll. Stress can be dangerous, and he has Jean and his two girls to consider. There comes a breaking point. Well; that's Mugabe's strategy isn't it?

At recent meetings attended by the DA's representative, Mr.Guruve, the police inspector, and the Warvet leader Takawira, discussion was centred on the positive death threats Simukayi made against Martin and me and the coupled extortion. There were ample witnesses to this and appropriate statements were presented. It was agreed by all attending the meeting that Simukayi showed positive proof of insanity and that he should be removed for psychiatric treatment. Meanwhile, Simukayi was to be told to STOP INTERFERING with farm work.

At today's date this has not been put into effect. This, we are told, is due to logistic reasons; nevertheless, we rather suspect that the leader, Takawira, is scared of Simukayi and is frightened to handle the man by himself. Unfortunately this is of no help to ourselves who have to live with this dangerous psychopath on a daily basis. In the meantime Simukayi continues to confound ordered life on the farm.

A large, new tractor has been stationed on the farm for several weeks. It is parked at the quarters appropriated by Simukayi. The tractor belongs to the Agricultural Rural Development Authority [ARDA], a government body. Apparently it is for the use of the Warvets and squatters. On Tuesday 20th. February, 12 women farm workers with their supervisor were engaged cleaning a 1 acre section of our fields, removing the haulms of the previous horticultural crop in preparation for planting the next rotational crop of garlic. At 9 a.m., the ARDA tractor with Simukayi and the tractor driver at the wheel arrived at the field. Simukayi had been drinking heavily and had four litres of Chibuku beer with him in the cab. With raucous shouts, he ordered the women off the field. The field was now his and he was going to plough it and plant it for himself. With that he ordered the tractor driver to begin ploughing.

The driver commenced ploughing but the soil proved too wet and the tractor became bogged down. Rain had been falling daily for the past week. The land was gouged and compacted before the tractor was extracted. During this time Simukayi was swilling beer from the containers in the cab and passing the beer to the tractor driver who was also drinking merrily. Finally, the driver, showing off in front of the farm women, roared off at speed with Simukayi perched on the rear housing shouting above the noise that he would return in the afternoon.

It may seem incredible that a large, publicly owned and internationally assisted organization such as ARDA should place its expensive equipment at the disposal of a mentally deranged drunkard, but this is Zimbabwe today. Incidentally, the tractor displayed no licence and had no registration plates.

Mr. Gurure of the DA's office has said "Please bear with us". We cannot do so much longer. When Simukayi is on a drunken rampage life is dangerous.

Sunday 11th. March 2001

For many weeks past, two ARDA tractors have been using Simukayi's Warvet quarters as their base. They deploy each day from here returning to park overnight. Although it has been raining almost continually, each day they still move off somewhere. [The tractors are unlicensed and unregistered but the police know this.] The following information was passed to me:

Dr. Ibbo Mandaza [a wealthy, Mugabe supporter, a newspaper publisher, and spoken of as "The Minister" by the local people] has acquired a farm at Passaford further down the Selby road. On Sunday afternoon Dr. Mandaza, driving his 4x4, drew up at the Stockade store. The "Minister" alighted. There was a big crowd of people drinking at the nearby bar—twenty or thirty I am told. Dr. Mandaza asked where he could find the house of Simukayi. He was directed to the house with the flag and two people went with him to show him. At the house, the wife of Simukayi came out. Then Mandaza asked for Simukayi, but the woman told him that Simukayi had "gone somewhere". As reported to me, the Minister then said to the wife:

"Tell Simukayi that I want him and those tractors off this place." And again: "If I see Simukayi here I will shoot him!"

Ibbo Mandaza then returned to his Toyota 4x4 and drove away. Have the ARDA tractors been poaching in Mandaza's territory?

Tuesday 13th. March

Martin receives a phone call from Mr. Gurure at the DA's office. Mr.Gurure says that Simukayi visited him yesterday. There was a discussion and Simukayi told Gurure he did not know that government policy was to let the farmers be. Martin can't believe his ears. Asks if Simukayi was drunk. Sober, says Gurure. He feels sure that Simukayi will not give us further trouble. How many times have we heard that? Gurure also says that it would be unwise to have him moved. What does that imply? Skulduggery in high places.

In the afternoon, Simukayi is driven up to the factory in a ZRP 2200 Mazda with canopy, Registration No. 112 M. Simukayi is drinking beer from a bottle. The driver is a uniformed policeman. Simukayi leaves the vehicle, walks through the gates, ignores the security guard and enters the factory to speak to somebody—probably Douglas whose woman runs the bar. He is still drinking from the bottle. Simukayi returns to the Mazda and the policeman drives off taking his passenger with him. I understand they drove down to the bar.

Saturday 24th.March

Karissa came to speak with me today at the start of work. It was to tell me that two Warvets had entered his house in the compound at 4 o'clock that morning. They accused him of "ghosting" in the Trianda farm village. I understood this to mean that he crept among the workers houses in the middle of the night knocking at doors and windows in order to frighten the inmates. Needless to say, Karissa denies this, saying it is all lies.

The intruders threw water all about the room in which Karissa was sleeping and smashed up a flowerbed outside. Karissa was told that he must get off the farm.

This sounded like the doings of Simukayi, but in fact it was the Number 2 Warvet, Chauka, who was accompanied by a mujibha [a Party youth]. I asked Karissa if he knew why they had picked on him to give him this trouble and the reply I got was that the Warvets want to take over his house.

Ten months ago, Simukayi forcefully ejected the people occupying a house in our village and took it for his Warvet base. At the present time he lives in this building with his woman. Also in the house are Chauka, the young mujibha, another unknown man and an unknown woman. In addition there are two tractor drivers employed by the government agency, ARDA [Agricultural Rural Development Corporation]; making a total of eight.

The house is obviously crowded and Simukayi is planning to get more accommodation for his purposes. Earlier this month he nearly succeeded in scaring two other farm workers off the farm and out of their houses. He used his familiar terror tactics. By the grace of God, he failed; for I can now plainly see that he would have occupied them. I fear that he will not give up. The deviousness and wickedness of these people knows no bounds.

Karissa says that if the Warvets come again he will kill them. What comment can I make? I can hardly tell him that the correct procedure is to report to the police. Clearly, after the debacle of the 7th. March, the police are the very last people to turn to for help.

We shall just have to wait and see if there are further developments.

12th. April 2001

After an absence of about two weeks, Simukayi returned to the farm. On the evening of the 12th he was drinking beer at the bar. Norman, our farm worker, was also at the bar. There was a quarrel. Simukayi had discovered that Norman had told me that Simukayi had stolen Butternut sqashes from the field [which he had!] A fight ensued. Norman picked up a fallen tree branch and hit Simukayi. The ARDA drivers and a Warvet mujibha surrounded Norman but I understand they did not strike him and the fight ended.

Previously, Simukayi and his mujhiba, armed with knives, had gone to the house of Obert who had also informed me of the theft of the Butternuts. Luckily, Obert was out but the young wife got the fright of her life.

[Simukayi had indeed stolen Butternuts from our field and I was directly concerned with the follow up, which went on for days and resulted in considerable drama. Involved were two loyal farm workers, two disloyal Tredar guards, a rampant Simukayi backed up by the Warvet Ghendi, and the police officer, Assistant Inspector Mupariano, who revealed himself as a double-dealer beyond belief. The affair was such that, when writing it up, I gave it the title: *The Tale of Simukayi and the Butternuts*—a cross between Agatha Christie and Beatrix Potter. Requiring a small book of its own, I decided against including it here!]

All this time Simukayi had been drinking beer and it is said that he collapsed and became incoherent. Leastwise I gather that Douglas and Eugenia at the bar were sufficiently worried to phone her relatives in town. These people came out in their vehicle and carried Simukayi to hospital. Another vehicle arrived later and the driver asked for Simukayi. He was told that Simukayi had been taken to hospital "very sick", sweating and speaking nonsense. Oh that he would pass out forever!

20th. April 2001

Simukayi is back on the farm. Someone has told him that the farm workers worked on Wednesday, Independence Day. As usual, Simukayi has been drinking and in the madness of his brain, he latches on to this to make trouble all round.

At 7.30 am, Simukayi, this time with three others, goes to the factory. He is drinking from a beer can. The factory workers are assembling to begin the working day. Simukayi insists that the factory be closed and he turns the workers away from the gate. Farm workers, who have also assembled, are ordered to go back to their houses because he, Simukayi, is shutting down the farm.

Martin arrives to get work started only to find the workers are prevented from entering the premises. Simukayi strides towards him and bellows: "MISTER WILES, I am shutting the factory." He turns to the Tredar security guard: "You Guard. Lock the entrance doors." Mister Wiles countermands this and tells Simukayi that if the factory closes, the workers will not be paid so he had better explain that to the workers himself.

Simukayi's voice resembles a high volume Tannoy system. I am very much aware of this because I have come to the factory to find out why the farm workers are not in the field. The reason is very clear. Simukayi is bawling out his standard string of invectives and Martin is at the receiving end.

"You are another fucking, white pig. When we take over the factory, you can return to Britain"

Martin coolly retorts that he was born here and has every intention of staying. Then he directs the factory workers to enter the building. Work is eventually started with a loss of approximately one hour's output. This is not before Simukayi tells the factory supervisor, Tichoana: "We in government intend to take all industry from the whites and hand it over to the workers".

Martin tried to telephone the police at Marlborough, but the lines at the police station were out of order. Simukayi then became adamant that Martin should go with Simukayi to State House and brought before the President himself—TODAY. It was very irksome; Simukayi was drunk, dirty and dishevelled. We know too that he is mentally deranged.

Simukayi knows that Martin goes to the town office every morning. Martin was able to divert matters temporarily whilst seeing to business matters. Still shouting his determination to take Martin to State House, Simukayi moved up the road to the farm entrance to await Martin on his journey to town. Other Warvets had collected there.

In the course of the next hour we learnt of certain events on the Selby Road. Some 200 metres from our entry gate a large truck carrying thousands of chickens had overturned onto its side. The accident was blocking the road and any passing vehicles were brought to a near halt at this scene.

We were told that Simukayi, who had been joined by extra Warvets, was waiting for Martin at this point where the road was blocked. It seems that the intention of the Warvet party was to waylay Martin at the breakdown, hijack him and the vehicle, and have him drive them to State House. On a very busy Friday morning, this was something Martin could do without. In the circumstances, we decided it best that he take an alternative, circuitous route to town. I moved to a position, hidden within the trees, where I could observe the accident scene. The Warvets waited for three hours in vain. Then they drifted away carrying a few chickens apiece. Simukayi was still drunk.

Later in the morning Martin called at the Marlborough Police Station. A\Insp. Mupariano expressed concern at the turn of events and promised that either the O.I.C. or he himself would come out to the farm as soon as transport became available.

Tuesday 23rd. April

The following report is based on information supplied by the persons directly concerned including the Tredar security guard stationed at the factory.

At 8.30 a.m., three Warvets came to the factory. They were Chauka, Moffu, and a third one unknown. With them were two young mujibhas. At that time there was a Zesa power failure. The three Warvets had with them a 2 litre Scud of Chibuku beer and were drinking from it. They said they wanted to speak with The Boss. Martin had already left for town so they then spoke to the supervisor, Mr.Tichoana, and told him that no work could start until they had seen The Boss. A radio mssage, insisting that Martin should return to the farm, was put through to the Nola office. Martin, accompanied by John Aird, drove out to the farm.

In the meantime, the Warvets continued to drink and they were also smoking mbanje [marijuana]. I asked the guard how he knew that they were smoking mbanje. He replied: "Because we saw them smoking. They were just outside the fence by the gate." I then asked the guard how he knew that it was mbanje they were smoking. His reply:

"I could tell by the smell." When the Warvets had finished drinking the 2 litre scud, one of the mujibhas was sent to the bar to fetch another.

By the time Martin arrived at the farm, the Warvets were thoroughly intoxicated. At about the same time, 10 am., the electric power came on. Martin ordered the workers to enter the factory. The Warvets became very loud and aggressive, shouting in English and Shona. Martin asked Tichoana to come and interpret what they were saying.

The Warvets had prepared certain demands:

1. Douglas, a factory worker, should not be charged rent for the store and the bar which his wife leases. Furthermore, we must repay all the rent which Douglas and his wife have paid over the past two years or from when they first leased the premises from us.
2. Mr. Wiles must pay increases and bonus payments to the factory workers, backdated for 2 years.
3. Because the farm workers worked on Independence morning, they must be compensated [even though, AT THEIR OWN REQUEST, they were given equivalent time off in order to extend their Easter holiday.

Whilst these demands were being made, the Warvets acted with viciousness and hostility. They suspected Martin and John Aird of carrying pistols and told them to turn out their pockets. Satisfied that neither was armed, they then physically pushed and poked the two men. Chauka held a stick and he prodded them with that. John Aird was told to get outside the security gate. He was prodded with a stick and told to take his hands out of his pockets. The Warvet Chauka attempted to tear off John's glasses but failed.

Martin was then left on his own, standing on the office veranda and here the Warvets again demanded what he was going to do about paying the money. Martin tried to reason with them and managed to temporise with some success because eventually he and John were able to drive away in their vehicle. The factory work was not after all interrupted.

At 5.30pm. Warvets Simukayi, Chauka, Moffu and three others came up to the factory and asked for The Boss. They waited until Martin arrived at 5.45. The guards words to me were: "Mr. Martin greeted the Warvets very politely". I know that this is Martin's habitual manner. As is usual with these people, civility is returned with uncouth rudeness, foul language and viciousness.

The Warvets, who had again been drinking, closely surrounded Martin shouting in his face. The demands of the morning were repeated. Tichoana, the supervisor, came out and was asked by Martin to try to reason with the Warvets in Shona. Tichoana was immediately accused by the Warvets of being on the side of the Whites, a sell-out, to which he replied that he was but an employee and doing his work for which he was being paid. He had no connection with politics.

Simukayi pulled from his pocket a sheet of paper and gave it to Martin to read. It was a doctor's bill for the sum of $11 275. Simukayi rolled up his trouser legs and revealed that he had a large number of nasty sores all about his legs and ankles. He also indicated that he had other sores on his torso. He told Martin that all these sores were the result of the single tooth puncture given him by my dog Moppet on 12th. February last—over 2 months' ago. He wanted cash—not a cheque—for the full amount.

The bite was so minor that Simukayi never bothered to attend a clinic, although, as is his wont, he used threats to extort $5 000 from us at the time and signed an agreement that compensation had been paid in full and that he would make no further demand.

The doctor's bill now presented stated that the treatment was for dog bites. Martin suspected at once that either the account was a forgery or at least the work of a dishonest doctor. [The Warvet leader, Hitler Hunzvi is a doctor trained in the communist East.] Martin said that he could not possibly pay and if necessary the matter would have to go to court. Needless to say this response did not please the Warvets who became more and more hostile.

In view of the harassment to which he was being subjected, Martin entered the factory and told all the workers to stop work and leave because he was closing up. As the workers were leaving, the Warvet party came into the factory. They became even more abusive and threatening, shouting: "We are going to fight you. We are going to kill you. We shall kill your father."

Martin was manhandled by four of the drunken Warvets. He was pulled by the shirt and pushed hard against the wall. Chauka grabbed an iron bar and held it to Martins throat. Once again he threatened to kill him. His head pressed against the wall, Martin yet kept cool. The Warvet's face only inches from his own, he looked into the drug-glazed eyes and smelt the foul breath of his assailant: "Come on you guys. Lets discuss this reasonably." With that, he was able to free himself. It was, however, a tense moment. Any attempt at retaliation could have ended fatally. [All this was witnessed and told to me by our Tredar security guard who, you must remember, has strict instructions not in any way to become involved in "political" matters!]

The factory doors were closed, the workers dispersed, some to feed at the canteen others leaving for their homes. The Warvets continued to crowd in on Martin; not allowing him to reach his pick-up. Martin felt that the only way to calm the Warvets and to resolve the issue of the doctor's bill was to call the police. This he did from his cell phone. After an interval of one hour, he phoned again to be told that the police had no transport. In the circumstances, he decided that Simukayi and he himself should proceed to Marlborough police station.

Somewhat to Martin's surprise, Simukayi agreed to this as did the other

Warvets, but first they wanted to take Martin with them to the local bar to get more to drink. Martin refused; nonetheless giving them $100 to buy the drinks. The Warvets were very suspicious and feared that Martin would drive away but Martin said that he would keep his word and await their return. This he did.

Simukayi returned with Moffu only. Martin, afraid that he might be hijacked, took a Tredar guard with him. The four set out for Marlborough. On the journey, Martin thought to ease tension by talking, but regretted doing so because his overture resulted in further invective and insult.

By this time it was 9pm. There was only a constable manning the charge office. The latter was polite and listened to the story. Martin, of course, claimed that he was the victim of extortion and blackmail; the bill was an obvious fraud and that he and his family had been threatened with death if he didn't hand over the money—in cash. The constable insisted that he was of too junior rank; the matter must be heard by a senior officer in the morning. Martin drove the party back to the farm and arrived back at 10.30 pm.

At 8.30 the next morning, Wednesday 25th. April, Martin once again drove to Marlborough taking with him the same number of people. This time he was able to speak with an Assistant Inspector. There was much discussion revolving around the authenticity of the bill. The policeman thought that the doctor should be traced. However; Martin was given to understand that the responsibility of finding the doctor who wrote up the bill was Martin's. It was NOT that of the police.

Martin had already spent valuable time and money, not to mention fuel, on this matter. The thought of trying to trace an African doctor [who might be non-existent but, if not, is certainly a crook] in a high-density suburb of Harare was appalling. Martin felt that it may be cheaper to submit to the blackmail. However; in offering to do this, he requested that the police prepare and witness an affidavit to the effect that Simukayi would make no further claim on him. The inspector agreed to this and went away to procure an appropriate form.

A tall African man happened to be on the premises. He was either a CIO man or a very senior plainclothes policeman. When he heard of the matter, he came across and overruled the inspector. He said that the police could have nothing to do with the business. Payment must be regarded as an out of court settlement in which the police were not involved.

Martin asked if there was no way to stop Simukayi blackmailing him over and over again. The policeman replied that Martin could take the matter to court, "But you will have to take the consequences of what the Warvets might do to you before the case comes up for hearing," he added.

Martin, bowing to the inevitable, had asked John Aird to come up to the police station with the cash—11 275 dollars. This was handed to Simukayi in the presence of the police inspector. Martin had Simukayi sign a receipt and, in the absence of the plainclothes officer, the inspector was co-operative enough to put a police stamp on the receipt.

By way of a footnote:-

We have been told that the Warvet leader, Chenjerai Hitler Hunzvi, has set up his own clinic specifically for Warvets. However, we cannot say that the fraudulent doctor's bill emanated from there. We suspect Simukayi's sores are syphilitic.

Saturday 5th.May 2001

I have Faxed copies of the recent farm reports to the DA Concession and by telephone requested that he assist us by attempting to restrain the excesses of Simukayi and Chauka. I explained to him that we could not continue our activities in the light of the intolerable strain put upon us. The DA agreed that he should visit the farm.

Yesterday, 4th. May, the DA came to the farm. The following account of the visitation has been compiled after I had questioned the three Tredar security guards and the farm foreman, Johannes.

The DA's party was travelling in three Landrovers. One of these belonged to the Z.R.P. Mazowe. The vehicles drove into the compound at the farm store entrance and proceeded to the house which the Warvets have made into their base. This was at lunch time. They picked up Simukayi and Chauka and took them away with them. The vehicles did not return until 5pm. By this time, an army staff car had arrived with a colonel and his wife; but as they are frequent callers, this may have been coincidence.

From the compound the three Landrovers drove up the Selby road to the main farm entrance. Here one vehicle carried on towards town and the other two drove down to the factory. At the gate, the people alighted and stood around the cars. Chauka came up to the gate and spoke with the guards who were on duty. He came through the gate and told the factory guard to open the factory door because; "We want to see if they are making MDC Tee shirts."

The guard told Chauka that he did not have the keys to the factory. The latter then returned to the DA and the other people, who were still standing outside.

There were 13 people in the party; the DA, one uniformed ZRP constable with a flag emblem on the top sleeve, a ZRP driver out of uniform, Simukayi, Chauka, Takawira, Smart, the Army Colonel, the husband of the storekeeper's sister, who also comes here regularly, and finally 4 others who are habitual Warvet supporters in the district.

I asked the Tredar guards if the DA asked them any questions and they said, no. I then asked if Simukayi was drunk as he usually is. They replied, "Yes he was drunk; but all of them except the DA were drunk".

"What makes you say they were drunk?" I asked. "Because they were shouting and behaving in a drunken manner," the guards explained.

The guards say they heard someone say that they did not want the factory and that it could stay working. It was the land they wanted. Simukayi was reported as saying that he had warned the azungu not to plant any more crops, but we had gone ahead and ploughed and planted the garlic in spite of the fact that the land no longer belonged to us.

From the factory the party moved off to the soya bean field. It was here that Johannes met with them. Johannes confirms that, except for the DA, most of the others appeared to have been drinking heavily and that they were carrying and drinking from beer bottles sometimes mixing the beer with cokes. The colonel was very drunk.

Johannes says he heard one of the Warvets say something like: "They first told us we could take the land and we paid 3000 dollars. If they now tell us we can't have the land, we shall lose our money. If it is like this, we must go to the offices and give them big trouble on Monday and then we shall go back to the farms and make more trouble again on Tuesday and Wednesday."

Johannes says that the DA remained silent during this time. However, he asked Johannes his name and told him to tell me that I could expect a call from him. It was too late to visit me now.

Returning from the forest land at about 5.50pm., I saw the two Landrovers parked on the road at the top gate. From that distance I could hear Simukayi shouting. I supposed the DA may have been asking him about the maize land he took from us or about the potatoes he was seen stealing. They drove away after 10 minutes. It was becoming dark then.

Mention has been made of the Army colonel. We do not know his name. We only know that he drives a smart Peugeot 504 staff car. Whatever his position is, it is apparently one which falls into the President's category of landless peasants and, as such, he must be allocated land taken away from white farmers. He is the person who planted [or more correctly got one of his men to plant] a sugar bean crop in a field near the compound. He "borrowed" a District Development Fund tractor to prepare the field and planted it with a machine planter.

I am told the crop suffered badly because of excessive rain and disease. Nonetheless, he reaped the beans, haulms and all, into bags and transported them into town. I asked if he had used a lorry to carry them. No. He stuffed the bags into his army staff car—in the boot, on the back seat and even on the front passenger seat; some on the roof. He returned time and time again until he had taken them all in; petrol, of course, by courtesy of the army. Being a colonel carries benefits in these hard times.

I am informed also that the colonel frequently gets so drunk at our bar; that his wife has to drive him home—the colonel passed out on the back seat. Being such an influential figure, I expect the bar-keeper, Douglas, gives him free beer. Everything comes free to the colonel; our land included.

We await developments.

29th July 2001

This date looms large in my life. It marks Beth's birthday and also the day of her death. Missing her though I do, I am thankful that her time to leave me came before this time of constant danger and dreadful uncertainty. This day also happens to be Martin's birthday but I doubt if he will turn it into one of gay celebration. The ready laughter is missing and he wears a strained expression.

I see I have not made diary entries for several weeks. I think that this may be fairly put down to exhaustion and mental weariness. The forays of Simukayi, Chauka and other Warvets continue. Sometimes I spot parties of complete strangers driving onto the farm. They treat me as if I didn't exist. If I confront them I could get an angry rush of blood to the head only to end up with that same blood spilt on the ground! I have to keep alert and use avoidance tactics.

It is winter and that means it is cool and dry. Fortunately all these invaders take little interest in my forest so I often drive up there with the two dogs in the early morning having first loaded my truck with containers full of water. The water I dispense to some of my young trees, which I planted in the field only 6 months ago – those of my special children who I know will benefit from a little extra care. Here I can find a few hours of respite in communion with tranquil life forms.

Clearing my post box one day I found a letter from the Commercial Farmers Union or CFU. [The CFU used to be the Rhodesian Farmers Union but the name was changed when Zimbabwe came into being.] As I read it, I could not help but think how bizarre the letter was – how indicative of the present plight of our land.

Agriculture and farming has been the economic mainstay of this country since the earliest days of British settlement. Not surprisingly the Farmers Union grew into a very influential body and its activities expanded to cater for the general and the particular; this because there was a host of agricultural commodities being produced each requiring specialized business inputs. In those flourishing days, a fine set of new buildings was erected in Harare to house these varied departments and to provide a venue for regular farmers meetings. When a farmer came into town, a visit to the CFU would almost certainly be on his list.

The letter I opened was in the form of a notification. Farmers from all across the country were invited to attend a series of meetings at CFU Headquarters over the coming weeks. The subject was: How best to cope with Trauma and Stress. They would be addressed by a panel of experts including a psychologist, and a constitutional lawyer. There would be time for questions and advice. Townsfolk had offered to open their homes to farming families needing a respite and a list of these good people could be obtained at reception.

This then, had become the urgent role of the Farmers Union - to help farmers withstand the stress and to stay on their land. I attended one meeting. The room was packed with farmers and their wives. I looked across at the faces in the rows. I saw here competent, self-reliant people caught up in a swirling gale of anarchy and brutality. They appeared calm and steady yet many described hair-raising experiences. It was quite moving.

Jean confides that she fears Martin is heading for a nervous breakdown. He allows his mind to wander, habitually looks over his shoulder, and is obsessed with locking doors behind him! This is completely out of character. I have encouraged them to attend one of the CFU seminars. They really need to take an away break but the more relentless the pressures are, the more difficult it is to do so.

7th.August 2001

The following report was given by the farm factory supervisor, Tichoana, and the worker's committee chairman, Tendayi.

At 12 30 p.m. on Monday 6th. August, Simukayi passed through the security gates. He told the Tredar security guard to call Tichoana. On the latter's arrival, Simukayi said he was going to address the workers. To this end, he walked into the building and called the workers together.

Simukayi asked the workers why they had not attended the meeting held by the D.A. at the Stockade store and bar on Sunday—which was the previous day. The workers replied that they had gone to their homes over the weekend and had not the money to spend on a fare to attend a meeting out on the farm.

Simukayi said "The Boss" also should have gone to the meeting but failed to do so. If the workers and The Boss had gone to the meeting, they would have heard what was being said. This was to the effect that this farm has now been designated.

Because the farm had been designated, the factory would be closed in one week's time. After this coming week the workers should not come to work here again. If there are any people with long service, they should see that they get their money now.

All the machines and goods within the factory should be removed because; "when we take over the place there may be some looting and we cannot help that". Simukayi also said that he doesn't want to see "Mister Wiles" on the farm here.

Statement from R.F.Wiles: Stockade Farm 25th. July 2001.

Subject: Theft of Soya Beans.
Reference Z.R.P.Marlborough RRB 824174 & Nyabira E 810121.

For those whom it may concern, copies of correspondence with Z.R.P. Marlborough and the DA Concession are attached. They refer to a crop of soyas planted on the farm by ourselves. In addition to the letters, the subject was covered in numerous direct conversations and telephone calls to these authorities.

By way of threats made against my person, the man known as Simukayi has used extortion to obtain the soyas for his own gain.

The Officer-in-Charge, Marlborough had previously explained that although Simukayi had issued threats, whilst the soyas were still in the field they could not be said to have been stolen. This being so, it was only after Simukayi began removing the soya beans from the field and from the farm that I made my charge and statement at Marlborough Police Station on 26th. June.RRB 824174.

On 29th.June, the Tredar guard reported that he had observed 9 or 10 bags of soyas stacked in Simukayi's house. I phoned Z.R.P. Marlborough and requested that they should come immediately to the house. They said they had no transport at that time so could not come but would do so the next day.

On 30th. June, the police arrived on the farm. There were several police personnel and the senior man was A/Inspector Mupariano. When they searched Simukayi's house they found that the soyas had all been removed.

Notwithstanding; I understood from the officer that Simukayi acknowledged taking 4 bags of soya. He claimed that he had been given the soya field by the DA. In no way can this be so and in fact the DA has informed us that Simukayi has been told that he should not interfere with our farming operations. Simukayi was taken to Z.R.P. Marlborough.

Information obtained from observers in the farm village was to the effect that the soya beans had been removed in a white Mazda pick-up the evening before the police arrived.

Simukayi keeps a young man or "mujibha" at his house. He is known as Andrew or Tayenga. This man and Simukayi's wife are the ones who have threshed and carried away the Soya beans from the field. I understand that the man Andrew spoke to farm workers quite openly. He said that the white pick-up belongs to a doctor. The doctor "has money" and pays 100 dollars for a bag of soyas. "The vehicle took nine and a half bags of soyas to town from Simukayi's house."

Another report, which was given to me by a Tredar security guard, was that the beans were taken to a clinic in Harare and that the clinic belongs to a Dr. Ngwenya. [I learnt from a friend, that a Dr. Ngwenya was recently in court charged with importing expired medicines. He was cleared.]

On Tuesday 17th. July, I saw a person walking quickly across a grass paddock making for the farm compound. He had a white sack hoisted onto his shoulder. He was some 200 metres distant and did not heed my call. Luckily a Tredar guard was close by so I directed him to run after the man and to discover what was in the sack which he carried. The guard overtook the man and upon looking in the bag, found it to contain soya beans. The guard took a handful of the beans and returned to me. The person carrying the beans was Simukayi's mujibha, Andrew.

Forthwith I phoned the police in Marlborough and asked them to come out at once because we now had good evidence of theft. The police promised to come as soon as possible; however after two hours, it was apparent that they would not be coming.

I learnt later that it was during this time that the bag of soyas was put into a blue Datsun Sunny salon car. The car is owned by the sister of the mujibha, Andrew. She had come to Simukayi's house, found her brother in the soya field and later in the evening she had driven away to town.

The next day, Tredar base at Nyabira having been notified, the base senior officer arrived with a Z.R.P. member from Nyabira. Of course they did not find the soya beans but the mujibha was taken to Nyabira and questioned there. The RRB number supplied is E 8100121 and the investigating officer is Constable Kohwera.

Since these events, Simukayi returned to the farm. He became very angry and threatening towards the Tredar guards. A copy of their report is attached. According to the report, Simukayi was threatening to kill me. For some reason he also gave verbal abuse to the lady keeping the farm store, accusing her of informing the police that he had taken the soya beans.

Upon the information supplied, it would appear that Simukayi has stolen something like one tonne of soya beans for which he may have been paid two thousand dollars by a receiver in Harare. The true value of one tonne of soya is eighteen thousand dollars.

The main machining floor.

*Entrance to the factory complex from main gate.
Office and guard house on left.*

*Proposed Lodge building under construction.
All work was halted in 2000 when workers were threatened.*

Humba and Moppet on sand heap. Johannes beyond.

Thursday 9th.August 2001

On Wednesday evening Simukayi was seen talking to the Warvet stationed on Trianda Farm and also to the Warvets and the ex-convict who live on Maypark. Simukayi called Johannes to him and said that he had just returned from town. It had been arranged that there was to be a big party here on Saturday morning to celebrate Hero's Day. People would be coming out to the farm in motorcars. From the bar people would go to all the farm houses occupied by the local white farmers and disturb them with noise and threats. They would start at Stockade and go on to Trianda, Raffeen, and Estes Park.

This morning at 8 a.m., Simukayi came up to the factory. Martin was in a meeting with the worker's committee. Two letters were handed in to him. One letter contained ugly threats which were deeply disturbing; it appears to have been printed by the Warvet High Command. The other letter was asking for a contribution for Hero's Day!

Just at this time a Z.R.P. Landrover driven by A\Inspector. Mupariano arrived at the farm. We understand that the officer had come out to the farm to fetch Simukayi into the Marlborough police station for questioning. However; Simukayi was heard by our workers to have refused to go with the policeman, saying that he would go in his own good time. With that, Simukayi walked away.

When Martin noticed the police vehicle at the factory gates, he went out to speak with the Mupariano and handed him the threatening letter which he had just been given by Simukayi. This letter should now be in the hands of the Z.R.P. Marlborough. We shall require a copy of it for our own records.

10th. August 2001

Simukayi came to the factory gates at 4 p.m. yesterday. He spoke to the three Tredar guards and also to Tichuana, the supervisor.

The guards say they were told to pack up and to return to their camp tomorrow. Simukayi said that he had been to his headquarters and and heard that there would be a lot of action here on Saturday. "If you guards are seen, I will declare you to be MDC and you will be beaten up. Go; and don't be *caught in the crossfire*."

Tichuana was once more told by Simukayi that the factory would be closed at the end of this week. Anything found still in the building after that may be looted. Simukayi also said that as soon as Bill Clinton [sic] signed the bill for Zimbabwe, then the whites would be taken out. All this was written in the letter which was given to "Mister Martin"; [Now with the ZRP per A/Insp. Mupariano.]

Tichuana phoned Martin to say that Simukayi was at the factory demanding money for Hero's Day. He feared that unless Simukayi was given it the factory would be forced to close next week. Martin agreed to give one thousand dollars to the farm workers to buy food and drink for themselves. Tichuana arranged this and gave the money to Johannes and the farm workers.

Stockade Sat. 11th.August 2001

Johannes bought beer and food at the store for the farm workers. He invited Simukayi to join them. Simukayi refused and told him to "Fuck off!" He did not want that beer. He said the money was not enough and that he needed money for a party at Maypark—not here. He would see that the factory would be stopped from working on Tuesday.

The Warvets fixed up a party on Maypark and there was beer, food and meat. Simukayi went there. It is said that Simukayi tried to persuade the others to leave the party and to go to Stockade. Once there they should get the farmer to give them money. The sum it is alleged he would demand was fifteen thousand dollars. We are told that the other Warvets refused to go along with Simukayi and said that he was too violent. After some altercation, Simukayi left the scene and did not return to the party. The words used were: "He was chased away."

Wednesday 15th. August

At 8 a.m., Simukayi came up to the factory gate and shouted that he was coming to close the factory down. He then proceeded up the road to where all the farm workers were preparing the land for planting vegetables.

Simukayi was armed with a knife. He brandished this and shouted to the farm workers to leave the field and go to their homes. He told them that the whole field belonged to him. He said that if they didn't obey him he would call other Warvets and they would be beaten. The workers left the field.

Simukayi returned to the factory. The security guard had locked the gate and refused him entry. Simukayi said that the factory must close. The guard replied that the workers could not agree to stop working. Tendai, the workers representative, came to the gate to speak with Simukayi. Simukayi told him that The Boss [Martin] did not give him a donation for Hero's Day. Now he must give 30,000 dollars. He said to Tendai: "You have a phone. Phone The Boss and tell him that he must come with the money; otherwise the factory will close."

Johannes was nearby. Simukayi said to him, "I do not want to see you in the field with the tractor. When the Boss pays me the money you can carry on working. You must speak with the son. The father gives me trouble. I will get him off the farm."

At about 12 o'clock the police from Marlborough came to the farm. The A/Inspector questioned the Tredar guard, Simukayi's wife and the wife of Johannes who had been in the field. By this time Simukayi had gone into Harare. No farm work was done today.

23rd. August 2001

Simukayi came to the factory at 8 a.m. He told the security guard that he wanted to speak with The Boss Martin. Martin sent a message that he was busy and that there could be no good reason for Simukayi to talk with him. Simukayi thereupon entered the factory premises and approached Martin. He reminded Martin that he, Simukayi, was an important person and must be treated with respect for his position. Martin left his work in the factory and led Simukayi to the gate. At the gate, Martin was joined by Tichuana, the factory supervisor.

Simukayi brought up the case of Douglas, the suspended worker and the husband of the bar-keeper. The factory workers accuse Douglas of stealing their money savings, which were kept in a box locked in the factory. Simukayi says that he knows Douglas stole the money.

The case has been involved and has been prolonged over many months. During this time Simukayi has given contradictory evidence to the police. The O.I.C. Nyabira, Inspector Masuka, has said that there are no grounds for the police to prosecute Douglas. As far as they are concerned Douglas may be re-instated in his job. However, Martin and the worker's committee have agreed that the matter must be resolved by the National Employment Council.

Asked what it was he wanted to say further concerning Douglas, Simukayi said that Douglas planned to kill him and his wife. Douglas intended to do this by poisoning their beer. Martin must pay all money due to Douglas and tell him to get out of the store, the bar and his house and, together with his wife Eugenia, to leave the farm for ever.

Martin told Simukayi that if he had a complaint against Douglas and could substantiate his charges, he should report to the police. Simukayi replied that he had no need to go to the police because he would call in other Warvets to sort the matter out. He went on to say that if Douglas was re-employed in the factory, he, Simukayi, and the other Warvets would come and drive all the factory workers out and close the factory down. This was the warning to Martin.

Simukayi then asked Martin to give him money for Hero's Day. He said that 1000 dollars was not enough and that other farmers had given much more; also the money should not have been given to the farm workers but direct to him. [As one of the heroes?]

Martin told Simukayi that because of Warvet activities the farm was now broke and that he certainly had no more money to give away. There the discourse ended. We await developments with the usual apprehension.

Saturday 25th. August 2001

Simukayi came out from town. He had been given a lift and got out at the farm store. He was very drunk and began shouting abuse at Eugenia Mabvurume, the lady store-keeper, and her husband, Douglas. Eugenia's sister, Mrs. Jovita Mombeyarara, who was visiting, was also abused by Simukayi.

A message was sent to Maypark and soon four women Warvets arrived. There were now six women and they attacked Simukayi who fell down. One of the women repeatedly kicked Simukayi in the face and when her shoe fell off she picked it up and continued to beat him with it. Simukayi was blooded about the ears, mouth, nose and eyes.

At some juncture, Simukayi's friend, Dr.Ngwenya, drove up in his white Mazda pick-up. The six women turned their anger upon him. They refused to allow him to go to Simukayi, who was now lying comatose—drunken and beaten. The women also surrounded Dr. Ngwenya's car and wouldn't let him drive away. After some time, the doctor persuaded the women to release him. He explained that he was only going down the road to Trianda Farm to get some meat.

In due course, he returned to the store. It seems that it was his intention to pick up Simukayi, but the women threatened to beat him up if he got out of his car and he drove away.

Later in the day Simukayi stood up and walked towards town.

He was accompanied by his wife and his small children.

The next day, Sunday, a vehicle with a canopy reported to be from the Nyabira police post, came to the farm. The occupants were asking for Simukayi but were told that he was not present. We consider that the Z.R.P. enquiry was probably unconnected with the recent assault but more likely with the matter of the stolen staff funds and Simukayi's evidence given against Douglas. This case was being handled by Z.R.P. Nyabira.

By the following Friday, 31st.August, Simukayi had returned to the farm having recovered from the beating dealt him by the enraged matrons. At about 8.30 a.m. he came up to the field where I had my workers planting and watering the lines of vegetables being grown for market. He angrily told them to stop work and to remove the irrigation pipes. The workers ignored him and Simukayi returned by way of the Selby road.

A vehicle, belonging to a contracting company working on the ZESA power cables, had been parked 400 metres down the road. Within twenty minutes from when Simukayi was seen walking down the road, the driver of the vehicle drove into the farm. He explained that his car window had just been smashed and that the car radio had been stolen. There seemed little doubt as to the culprit. I advised the driver to notify his company and the police at once.

As it happens, there was little chance of Simukayi being found with the car radio because at about 10 a.m. he was driven to town in a white Sunny sedan 622972 S. The car followed close behind me to town. When I allowed the car to overtake me, Simukayi leaned out of the rear, near-side window and in his deep raucous voice, shouted abuses at me. I noted that the car stopped at Greencroft and was letting Simukayi alight. He carried a bag. What might have been in it?

The owner of the car is a stout, middle-aged woman who wears glasses. She frequently drives out on the Selby road and stops at the farm compound. Last season the Warvets allotted her a field on Trianda. They say that her husband has died; nevertheless it is apparent that she has money and influence in this district.

The name of Dr. Ngwenya was brought up when describing the events concerning the beating of Simukayi by the six women. He arrived at the scene in his white Mazda pick-up. Approximately 20 bags of soya beans were stolen by Simukayi and transported off the farm over a period of a few weeks. Informants name Dr. Ngwenya as being the receiver of the beans. I have now been told that the beans were loaded into his pick-up at Simukayi's house.

The police have been fully advised on all these matters. Z.R.P. Marlborough and Nyabira, both of whom originally opened dockets, have forwarded the case to the Central Police Station [CR 276 of 6\2001]. The officer who is investigating is Detective\Con. Chirindo. We look forward to a successful prosecution in the courts.

It should be noted that today is the last day of August and that on this day Simukayi is the only illegal occupier present on the farm. His mujibha has gone to his home village and there are not, nor have there been, any "settlers" dwelling on our property. The Minister has declared that no further "settlement" can be permitted after today.

Saturday 1st.September
During the morning, Simukayi was driven out to the farm in a smart red 4x4 vehicle. The driver was a large coloured man. Also in the car were a second man and three coloured women. The party left the vehicle in the compound and Simukayi conducted them up the farm roads where the farm workers were again planting and irrigating the crops. Upon seeing the workers, Simukayi told them to take the irrigation pipes from the field and to stop work. He loudly acclaimed that the land belonged to him. However he was not as vociferous as yesterday, perhaps because his mind was focussed on a more profitable line of thought.

Simukayi led his visitors through my home arboretum and the private nature sanctuary and then they walked down to the rail line to view the field beyond. We suspect that Simukayi was offering these people, who were obviously affluent, a piece of land in consideration of a handsome down payment.

I have been trying to retrieve the nasty threatening letter which Simukayi handed to Martin shortly before Heroes Day. The letter was handed in to the police and now nobody at the police station can put their hands on it. Following up on this, I phoned the police hoping to speak to the Inspector. He was out, but on my enquiry, Cons. Mukura volunteered the information that Simukayi had come into the station—he didn't say when. Apparently he wanted the police to arrest all those women who assaulted him. I asked the constable if Simukayi was drunk and the reply was:

"Yes. Very drunk!"

Monday 3rd. September 2001

In the morning, at approximately 8 a.m., I went from the fields to the farm factory. At the gates I observed two strange men. One of them greeted me as if he knew me. He was short, stout and wore glasses. He said that he was "the second-in-command", so then I knew that he was a Warvet.

I have been advised never to converse with Warvets so I carried on with my affairs of business. Later I learnt that the Warvet, who spoke to me, is known as Chinjerai Munadzi. I was told that he had been briefly on the farm over a year ago but had left. It seems that the other person was not a Warvet. His role was that of a silent supporter because he never opened his mouth.

At the factory there was a meeting. In attendance were the factory supervisor, Tichuana, Johannes and the three Tredar guards. Johannes left early for a funeral. At the talk, Munadzi spoke and the others listened.

Munadzi said that the plan was to make our farm the headquarters for this area. They would take over the unfinished lodge or residential house that I had been building before the Warvet invasion of the farm in April 2000. Simukayi as the commander would have the first big room and he, Munadzi, would have the second. The other rooms would be divided amongst their supporters.

In other buildings they would keep pigs and chickens. A place would also be needed for tractors and a workshop. They would need electricity to be put in but metres should also be fitted. They would then pay for the electricity. A clinic would be built and they also had plans to build a bank. When the bank was operating the local people would be able to borrow money without problems. With regard to land, they would negotiate amicably with us as to which we could have and which they would have. Munadzi said that he was giving us this warning because tractors and lorries might be coming any day and we should expect them.

The suspension of Douglas from the factory and the theft of the staff savings were brought up. Tichuana said that the matter would take too much time and that he was already needed in the factory.

In the afternoon, Munadzi returned to the factory. This time he was accompanied by Sidney Ruziwa. The subject for discussion was the Douglas case. Tichuana abandoned his work and spoke to them at length about the history of the missing money and procedures that had been and would still be taken to resolve the dispute between Douglas and the other workers.

The Warvets returned to the compound to consider the business further. Munadzi said that he would speak with Mister Martin on Monday next.

Tuesday 4th. September 2001

At about 8 o'clock, a group of people came to the factory. This time Munadzi was not among them. He had returned to town. The party consisted of Sidney Ruziwa, a new man named Chaota, a woman Warvet called Rusike, three young men who I may describe as collaborators, and a young woman. Chaote had a whip or sjambok twisted about his waist, Rusike carried a panga knife at her belt, the collaborators carried knobkerries, sticks and a whip.

The spokesman, Ruziwa, said they wanted to talk in private and without disturbance to the whole workers committee of the factory. Tichuana arranged for the factory office to be opened and the workers committee members and the three principal Warvets trooped in. The collaborators remained at the gate.

The Warvets opened discussion by saying that they wanted to see about the workers getting increments and bonuses and so on. However, it did not take them long to get to the real reason of their visit which was that the workers should drop their charges of theft against Douglas and agree that he could be reinstated. They said that the police had found Douglas innocent and that Mr. Martin Wiles [MW] had no case against him. "It is only you workers who refuse to allow him back. You must allow him back."

The workers wouldn't agree. Douglas had stolen their money, It amounted to $ 18 000. Douglas had admitted it to Simukayi. They had consulted a n'anga and she also confirmed that Douglas was the thief. The Warvets replied: "Simukayi is a madman. We have already chased him away from the farm. He will never return." To this, the workers said that they would not be forced into a decision and they would decide themselves what to do. They would wait for MW's return and proceed by the proper channels. They would not be moved by force.

In the late afternoon, Simukayi came to the factory. He entered the premises and called all the workers to hear him. He told them that he knew positively that Douglas had stolen their money. He only retracted his evidence to the police because Douglas had agreed to pay him to do so. [Probably true! Douglas was a clever worker but we knew he was a crafty, two-timing little rat and even looks like one.]

Simukayi went on to say that Douglas had now called on these other Warvets and was telling them lies. Douglas was saying that he was the only ZANU PF person on the factory staff and that all the others were MDC. Douglas was paying those Warvets to take his part. That is why they had come in the morning.

Earlier I had phoned the DA's office in Concession and spoken to Mr.Gurure. I told him of the threats made by the man Munadzi and the serious implications that it would have on the farm if they were implemented. Mr.Gurure told me frankly that if we were designated then we must be prepared to be resettled.

I reminded him that only last month the Governor, Elliot Manyika, had visited Stockade and addressed a meeting of Warvets and settlers. According to reports, he said that the farms in this area were not for resettlement and that all the persons presently here and needing land would be given land in the north where there was land available for them. Transport would be provided to take them there. The Governor reiterated that the farms here were too small for settlement and he specifically mentioned Trianda and Stockade as being examples.

Mr. Gurure became impatient and abrupt so I assumed things had changed. Nonetheless, I reminded Mr.Gurure that half the farm was a gazetted Protected Forest. Was it intended to take that forest land because, if so, application would have to be made to the Minister of the Environment, Minister Nhema. At a meeting we had had with the Minister, he had been very supportive and encouraging with regard to our work on the forest. That work, of course, should be ongoing.

"Well the arable would be resettled then," was the short reply.

Mr.Gurure went on to say that he could not say whether the farm would be taken, but that we should be mentally prepared for such an eventuality. I asked if the farm could or would be taken without any valuation put on it. He assured me that an evaluation would be carried out beforehand. Valuators were working on this.

My next question, quite obviously, was what happens if people move onto the property before the valuators? Mr.Gurure was quite emphatic and said:

"No. They can't do that."

"And what if they do?"

"Refer them to the DA."

[The sending round of a valuation team, is no more than play-acting. We hear the "valuators" are unqualified youngsters. I suppose they have to come up with a figure for the farm improvements—buildings and so on—difficult with inflation running at 100% and rising. Mugabe won't pay for the land.

There is no money anyway so the whole exercise is a big scam.]

Following upon this, I visited the Marlborough police station. There I spoke to A\Insp. Mupariano. I told him of my phone call to the DA's office. I said it was likely that I would require his assistance if invaders descended on us without the cognisance of the authorities. He replied that the police would definitely react and in doing so would bring in the DA.

As I have previously reported, this policeman is utterly untrustworthy and is in the Warvets pockets. But still, given the desperately disturbed climate of the times, the outcome at the end of the day was about the best I could hope for.

Wednesday 5th. September.

I have had our workers preparing the field by the big water tank. This is where last year I had prepared the field, and planted it when Simukayi, blind drunk and drinking from a bottle, brought up some followers and a DDF tractor. He smashed his way through a locked farm gate and proceeded to destroy my carefully sown crop. He went on to plant a pathetic crop of maize which was inundated with weeds. This episode was written up in several detailed reports and sent to authorities including the DA.

This season I decided that I must retrieve the field for our own production. We are in considerable financial straits and cannot afford the loss of irrigation land. The crop we have planted here is early maize with nandolo bean inter row at 5:1. We are already irrigating the crop.

Simukayi having hijacked the field last year now considered the field to belong to him. Mention has been made of him telling the farm workers to stop work. Today he came up to the field and switched the irrigation pump off. He repeated this when it was restarted and in the afternoon he stayed at the pump house to ensure that it was not restarted.

I phoned the Inspector at Marlborough. He sounded exhausted. He said that he could not come out because he had no transport. He said I should call Nyabira police. This I did. Inspector Masuka [with whom I have always had friendly relations] said that he would come out.

At about 4 p.m., I received a message that the Inspector wished me to see him at my big water reservoir. I drove up there and to my astonishment found him waiting with eight or nine heavily armed men in combat gear—soldiers! [I gathered later that they belonged to the Police Reaction Unit.] Also there was Simukayi, who I have to confess I didn't recognize—did he always have a beard? [Grown perhaps to cover sores?] There was another civilian, tall, upright and fairly young—about thirty or so. The Inspector said this man was the area commander. I supposed he was a Warvet. Since the guerrilla war finished twenty-one years ago, he looks mighty young to have been involved.

I had got out of my truck and stood at the back of it, taking in my situation. The Inspector approached to within three yards of me, Simukayi stood some three yards further off as did the commander. Two or three of the soldiers stood at the side of me, guns cradled before them. Occasionally one would stroll about. The remaining men of the unit patrolled around the police vehicle parked on the farm road. Was I really such a dangerous character? This was a scenario for film fiction. I wanted to laugh.

I greeted the Inspector jocularly but he adopted a hard attitude from the start. He wanted to hear "my side of the story" concerning the field. This I was only too willing to do. I have been outraged by Simukayi often enough. Not a single moral thought ever enters the man's head. At one point when I was putting "my side of the story", Simukayi interrupted and called me a liar. I think it was when, in response to the Inspector's query, I said firmly: "No! The DA never, NEVER allocated this or any other land to Simukayi."

Upon Simukayi's calling me a liar, I shrugged my shoulders, turned away and said weakly, "What's the use?" The Inspector made no comment but merely bade me carry on. I explained that I had been in contact with both the DA and Z.R.P. Marlborough in the last few days and both had indicated that any disputes should be settled by the Governor or even the PA in Bindura.

This appeared to please the Inspector and the commander. Up until then he gave me the impression that he considered Simukayi to be the wronged party and that at best I had been insensitive towards an honest person with deserving needs! He even suggested that I should prepare another piece of land for Simukayi.

In retrospect, I cannot believe that the police inspector was naive and that he did not see through the whole business, which due to circumstances, had to be played out like a serious charade. He too was being watched.

"In the circumstances," he might have said but felt that he couldn't, "you have only yourself to blame; because in these circumstances, it is easier to compromise."

In the end, it was agreed that an urgent appeal to resolve the issue should be made to the DA. The young commander, who had remained quiet throughout, emphasized the need for speed—indeed within the next two days. He added, quite pleasantly I thought:

"And please! Don't go any further." What lies behind that friendly warning?

In the circumstances, the "circumstances" look pretty grim.

Some days later.
I fear that I have lost track of time. Much has been going on but I cannot confine it to dates and days of the week. The Nola factory is closing and mov-

ing off. Here is a resume.

Although the hat and clothing factory on the farm could never have been considered part and parcel of the land issue, which formed the basis of the government's rural revolution, it was nevertheless an integral part of our farm economy. When farm work was brought to a halt by Warvet activity it was revenue derived from the factory which kept the farm afloat. In practice, the Warvets focussed their attention on the factory as much as on the farm work. It became a favourite target for them.

Conditions became so intolerable that the running of the factory became a nightmare for Martin. He made the decision to close it down. Alternative premises were found in Harare and translocation of machinery and equipment was to be effected as soon as possible. Meanwhile, he kept his plans secret until they could be put into quick operation. The Warvets should get no wind it.

Until that time, Martin was subjected to threats and abuse on an almost daily basis. Simukayi and the other Warvets were frequently drunk and in that condition were not only obnoxious but also dangerous. I myself always considered Simukayi to be a psychopath.

Martin and Jean had spent seven years on the farm living in Fig Tree House, which I had built in 1977 on a carefully chosen site. It is a home set in lovely surrounds with a panoramic view over-looking our wooded slopes to distant blue hills. Being outdoor types, Martin and Jean enjoyed walking or jogging along the winding tracks of the forest. As unofficial wardens, they kept a watch on the wildlife. However; the present dark evil spreads like a killing poison and an all-pervading dread permeates the land. Even tranquil natural places sense the hand of death. It was unsafe for Holly and Renee, my granddaughters, to wander the farm and woods alone as they used to do and there was no knowing how constant hearing of Warvet brutality, not only in the country at large but also close to home, might be affecting them. Sadly, Martin, Jean and the two girls left their home on the farm at the same time that the factory was shifted.

The Case of the Missing Savings

In the farm report for 23rd. August, 2001, mention was made of a case concerning the theft of some money belonging to the farm factory workers. Because the matter was prolonged over many weeks and became hopelessly entangled, I must have thought to brush over it. However; having set myself the task of recording all the incidents, which have bedevilled us over these many months, I feel the "history "will not be complete without enlargement on this particular matter.

Not least of the tribulations which affected the factory was what I have termed, with a sense of drama: "The Case of the Missing Savings". Had the money been stolen from Martin or perhaps from the petty cash, the whole affair might have been dealt with in short time and concluded one way or another. But the money was the workers' personal savings, kept in their own box and stolen by one of them themselves. When it comes to such matters, the African won't let up. The Workers' Committee reacted true to form.

The money was stolen on 2nd.May. The dispute and efforts at detection went on for four months. Hours of production time was lost and a total work stoppage was only narrowly avoided. Before the end, the National Employment Council, a Trade Union, the police and three witch-doctors became involved. Even the Warvets split into factions.

The suspect was a stooped, little rat of a man named Douglas. Crime writers use the expression, "a shifty look". Douglas has a shifty look even though his eyes are large and protruding—more like those of a frog [or a Gollam] than a rodent. Albeit, he was clever and had earned himself a position on one of the factory's specialised machines. He was one of three who had access to the key of the workers' savings box.

Most of the factory workers commuted daily to the farm from their homes in the townships. Douglas was different. He had married, or at least co-habited with, the widow who leased the farm store and its associated bar from us. Thus he had a double interest. At weekends [or surreptitiously during working hours] he would be actively involved with the running of the store.

The store, and particularly the bar, had become a regular meeting place for the Warvets and political activists in the district. More affluent town-based ZANU PF supporters would drive out from Harare to meet up with their drinking "shamwaries" there. It clearly paid Douglas to ingratiate himself into that community. Foremost of these was Simukayi, who was a permanent resident on the farm and a consumer without rival. I mentioned elsewhere how Douglas became the self-elected and self-appointed chairman on the farm for the ZANU PF party and thereafter offered himself as the local Commissar for Transport. [So often I liken many of these people as children playing at grownups.]

For an understanding of what comes later, it is necessary to introduce other personalities. We had leased the store/bar to two African ladies, Jovita and Eugenia. [For their long surnames refer to August 25th.] They were sisters. Both were mature women, well-spoken, polite and genteel in manner; in appearance, neatly and modestly dressed.

Eugenia was the one who ran the store, but it was apparent that she had the backing of her more dominant sister Jovita. Jovita was a qualified teacher who taught Biology and English at the Chisipiti High School for Girls; an expensive private school for the children of the rich.

When we first met, Jovita explained that both she and Eugenia had been widowed and that it had fallen to her lot to become the breadwinner for the two families. She was helping her sister start in business. They were confident of success and added laughingly that they were both better off without the drain of men in their lives. Comfortably round in build, if Jovita had a fault, it was that she worked too volubly at saying the right things. All in all, we felt we were fortunate in having two such pleasant and responsible ladies renting the store.

The Warvets and their militant hangers-on began over-running the farms early in 2000. This dramatic turn of events had an immediate and profound effect on human relationships. When there is a breakdown of law and, with it, basic ethical conduct, people are exposed in their true colours. At the store, hard-drinking Warvets provided constant business and, as mentioned, this was augmented by carloads of affluent Party supporters making sorties out into the country in a quest for rich pickings.

The store is situated alongside the public road and in the early days I would get complaints from neighbours, who had to drive past that way, of the parties of drunks they encountered on the road outside the bar. I had to explain that we had completely lost control of the store with its bar. To close it down would invite certain and ugly retribution from the Warvets. I had already spoken with Inspector Masuka about this and indeed it was he who had warned me of the consequences should I be rash enough to do so.

However, the inspector had added that "AS IT WAS OUR PROPERTY", we were fully entitled to receive the rent payments. I had brought the matter of the rent up with him because we had received no rent money for the past six months. The women had told me that they lived in fear of their lives from the Warvets. The latter claimed that the rent money should be paid to them as they were the new owners.

I gave this account to the police inspector and added that I feared it could be so because I was sure the two ladies were honest and spoke truthfully.

Inspector Masuka looked at me briefly under raised eyebrows and then, as if not wanting to waste words on a simpleton, his short dismissal was: "No. They are not!" He said he would have a word with them and the upshot was that within a few days Douglas crept up to me with an offering of half the amount due on the rent and a promise to bring the rest later. It was never forthcoming and more months went by. Martin despatched a letter of demand and shortly afterwards I received a visit from the two sisters.

After so many years in Africa, I thought I had the measure of every storyteller. However, I have to admit that the performances of Jovita and Eugenia were brilliant. They expressed outrage at the terrible events going on in the country; dismay at the persecution of the farmers. With no farmers, who would feed the people? They would all starve, they said, shaking their heads in dismay.

Jovita had learnt of my wildlife conservation efforts and immediately aligned herself with me. At her school, she regarded the teaching of conservation of the utmost importance. She would like to bring out her pupils to see the wonderful work I had done. Would I have any objection?

As for themselves, the difficulties they faced were unimaginable. Their lives were fraught with family disasters on every hand. On top of this, they lived in daily fear of their lives from the Warvets. These people were like dangerous animals. Surely only God could put things aright.

Well; only God—and a little sympathy and understanding from yours truly over the rent arrears was her message. At the end of it all, I could never find it in me to get angry or even to display annoyance. If anything I parted from them with a sense of admiration. I was outclassed in this sort of game and inwardly acknowledged it.

I was not entirely naive. The bland remark, which I had made to Inspector Masuka insinuating the honesty and innocence of the two lady lessees, was put in order to assess his reaction. Bits of information were always coming my way. Both the two poor widows had men in tow. In Jovita's case, her choice of man held sinister implications. Her new husband, it is said, is a member of the C.I.O., an organization which in the prevailing circumstances in Zimbabwe may be fairly likened to the Gestapo or the KGB. He and Jovita are regular week-end visitors to the farm and are likely to be well acquainted with the shenanigans of the Party "chefs" in this district. The other sister, Eugenia, has taken Douglas as her partner and as I have already observed, he has clearly shown his colours.

The accusers in "The Case of the Missing Savings" were the factory workers whose money it was that was stolen. They were represented in the matter by the members of their Workers Committee. The latter were daily commuters and therefore not affected by the intrigues going on at the store or in the farm village. It was plain that they enjoyed the affirmation of the sixty-odd factory workers. I was impressed when I noted that the Committee members conducted their meetings in a very professional way; minutes taken, resolutions recorded. Apart from a report to the police, which was automatic, one of the first resolutions was to consult a n'anga or witch-doctor.

In the meantime, Simukayi was putting his oar in and helping to muddy the water. He volubly took the side of Douglas and, as is his wont, warned that if those accusing Douglas of the theft persevered, they would be in big trouble—beaten up or worse.

Whilst Simukayi could mercilessly dominate all persons living in the farm village, it was not so easy for him to deal with the factory workers. Most of them lived in the townships and could safely ignore his threats. They continued on their determined course. They were sure that Douglas was the culprit, but Douglas was holding on tightly with his denial. The only way they could break him down was by bringing in a witch-doctor.

Representatives of the Committee were despatched to seek the services of a n'anga who lived on Mt. Hampden farm some 9 kilometres distant. This n'anga accepted the brief for the modest fee of $800 paid up front. The members paid this and awaited his arrival and investigation.

They were kept waiting for some days and when he eventually turned up he told them; that due to the intricacies of the case [Simukayi and the Warvets?], he required to call in a second n'anga, one who was resident in Passaford 6 kilometres in the opposite direction. Transport was proving a problem. The second n'anga turned up but without the first. Then there was the matter of a fee for the second man. Time was being wasted and the workers were becoming impatient. It was obvious that the local n'angas were getting cold feet and this was the reason for all the shilly-shally. Powerful forces were abroad and perhaps they felt unsure of themselves in spite of the status they enjoyed in African society.

The committee decided to ditch the two local medicine men. They lost their money on the first and refused to pay the second. So the next step was to go straight to the headquarter offices of Zinatha, the traditional healers association. There they were advised to consult a Mrs. Kazingezi, a woman n'anga of renown based in Harare. The workers readily agreed to this and arrangements were made to meet her.

Most of the story which follows was supplied to me by Tichuana, the supervisor who, because of his maturity and responsible position, became involved with the ongoing case. He told me that, when he and the others visited her, Mrs. Kazingezi had stipulated a fee of $15 575 for her services and when this was paid, she would discover the thief for them. I gathered that the workers agreed to this without dissent.

The n'anga came out to the farm twice, stopping both times at the factory and at the store in order to place her medicine and allow it to work. Then she summoned all the persons implicated, including Douglas, to her own place. When they had been gathered, she made her pronouncement. She said that she had discovered that the stolen money had been used to purchase goods for the trading store. Because Douglas was the only person from the factory with the incentive to do this, it was plain that it was he who had stolen the money. In reparation, he should recover the money he had spent on the goods and return it to the workers.

The party returned from their visit to the n'anga and immediately went into a closed session at the factory. The workers confronted Douglas and demanded that he should abide by the n'anga's ruling. By this time Douglas was in a very nervous state. In the words of Tichuana: "Douglas knew he was cornered up."

'What am I to do?" he is reported to have said, "She says she knows the money was spent on the goods for the store and that I am the one." He seemed to be on the point of confession. Tichuana blames himself for what followed. It had been a long morning. He suggested they adjourned for a lunch break. This was a mistake; they should have kept up the pressure on Douglas. A psychological advantage was lost.

Douglas went to his house for the lunch break and there he must have talked to his wife, Eugenia, and given her an account of the meeting with the n'anga. I can't say if Simukayi was present. He may have been. Whatever; Tichuana says that by the afternoon Douglas was a changed man. He insisted that the n'anga's case against him was a pack of lies.

It transpired that Mrs. Kazingezi had intimated to Tichuana that she wished to speak with the owner of the farm and of the factory. She had dealt with the matter of the worker's stolen savings and had positively identified Douglas as the culprit; however, due to the situation, the owner himself could face repercussions. When told, I thought the matter over and decided there would be nothing lost and possibly something gained if I went along with this. Tichuana arranged for us to meet Mrs. Kazingezi at her home a couple of days hence.

The time of the appointment was 8 am. I had arranged to meet Tichuana in town shortly before this and duly found him waiting at the rendezvous. The house to which we were bound was in Mabelreign. Mabelreign, as the name might suggest, dates well back into Rhodesian days. It is an extensive residential suburb built in the forties and fifties in what was then the outskirts of Salisbury. In those days of racial segregation, it was designed to cater for the pockets of whites in the lower income groups; junior civil servants, artisans, the newly-married and so on.

The interlacing roads are many; the houses are single, neat and unpretentious—what in Britain would be termed bungalows. The plots are small for this part of the world, perhaps half-acre size. However the planners of those days gave consideration to aesthetic values and many of the roads have broad tree-lined sidewalks. The city fathers delighted in planting flowering trees throughout Salisbury and Mabelreign has shared this heritage. Jacaranda trees still abound.

At independence in 1980, there was a mass exodus of whites, especially from those groups mentioned. Inevitably, Mabelreign very soon became a suburb which catered for middle-class blacks. One could call it a population replacement

I have taken the time to give a full description of Mabelreign, because as I drove through its neat streets, I couldn't help thinking how bizarre and anachronistic it seemed for me to be visiting an African witchdoctor who lived in a road named after an English small town in a house with a number on the gate. Not exactly a Ryder Haggard image of dark, mysterious Africa.

Tichuana directed me to the house. The steel security gate was locked and we had some difficulty in attracting the attention of anyone within the premises. A young man eventually heard us, opened the gate for us to enter, closed it and then disappeared.

There were two vehicles parked in the forecourt; a saloon and a big 4x4. I left my car on the driveway and took a look at the front of the house. Drawn curtains over the windows suggested the occupants were still abed. Did lady witch-doctors sleep on mats on the floor or in wide beds with sheets and duvets, I wondered.

Tichuana, who knew the way, led me round the house to the back yard where a barefooted young girl was enthusiastically scrubbing pots and pans under a tap outside the kitchen door. Looking up, she stopped and ran ahead to show us into the larger of two thatched rondavels, which had been constructed some eight yards away from the back of the main house. This was obviously the n'anga's consulting, or should I say divination, room.

We stooped through the doorway and into the dim interior. A plaster-cement bench lined the wall over one third of the rondavel's circumference and Tichuana and I took our seats on this. The building looked fairly new; the cement floor was clean and smooth; the thatch, I guessed, had not been weathered more than a season or two.

Rush mats on the floor indicated where the n'anga would sit. Hand woven baskets and winnowing pans of all sizes adorned the remaining floor space and shelving on the walls supported jars and pots of herbal medicines. It was all clean and neat and very ethnic yet oddly out of place at the back of a typical suburban house with a couple of cars in the forecourt and a TV aerial on the roof.

I felt it deserved a better setting; a tourist attraction in that traditional African village they have at the Victoria Falls maybe. It certainly didn't have the traditional flavour known to myself; the pervasive, pungent smell of stale wood smoke and strong tobacco ineradicably permeated into the blackened thatch; a secondary smell of native beer emanating from some unseen corner of an eerily dark interior; no smoke-black roof poles festooned with soot-stained cob-webs. There were no tatty animal skins, no heap of old rags lying on an earthen floor, no suspicious gourds or devices hanging against a knobly, grimy wall. Not even any chickens.

Within the seclusion of the rondavel, Tichuana and I sat side by side in reverent silence for a time. Finally a shadow temporarily eclipsed the light entering the doorway and in the next moment the n'anga, Mrs. Kazingezi, entered in a quick, business-like manner and sat down on the rush floor mat to face us. The young girl had entered to hand her a few accoutrements and then retired. I noticed that each time the girl entered or left, she respectfully knelt down at the portal.

Mrs. Kazingezi I saw to be a mature woman, forty-something I guessed, comfortably built but not fat. She wore a simple gown which could be called a caftan, I suppose. She appeared not to favour bangles and beads. Watching Tichuana closely out of the corner of my eye, I copied him in making what I hoped to be the appropriate greetings for a female n'anga. She asked if I spoke Shona and I shamefacedly replied that I couldn't. My Malawian Chinyanja was much better, but that wouldn't be very helpful. The meeting thereafter was held in a bit of English and a bit of Shona with Tichuana interpreting for my benefit when required.

I feel sure Mrs. K. is fluent in English and could well have used it throughout. However, if she believed that something of the authenticity of African mystical lore would be lost in doing so, I have no hesitation in agreeing with her. Innocent pretences are both called for and desirable in many instances of social contact. Respect for tradition and culture is the better shown.

Mrs. K. began by assuring me that the true body of African n'angas and herbalists were appalled at the wrongs taking place throughout the country. The ancestral spirits were also disturbed. She said the Shona ancestors had no ill will for the white people, who they regarded as benefactors. They were distressed by the wrongs being perpetrated by these bad people. The Warvets were no more than impostors. The spirits knew this.

I spoke to her of my fears that the Warvets and the couple at the store were getting the upper hand. Was there no way we could be free of them? She explained that a certain woman living in the compound, who she named, was using medicine to counter her own. Nevertheless, the woman's medicine wouldn't be strong enough. She predicted that Douglas and Eugenia would definitely leave the farm. As for the Warvets, she could offer her help in giving me protection from them.

The n'anga then lapsed into Shona and Tichuana translated for me. In order to assist me, offerings were first needed in order to please the ancestral dead. It seems that there were a number of different categories of ancestor and at this distance of time, I cannot recall the differences. However, I gathered that the most important group required a mombe, that is to say a cow or bullock; the next, a sheep; the next, a goat. A gift of these animals would please the spirits and assure the success of the medicine.

I asked Tichuana to explain that this would be very difficult for me to do because I didn't have any of these animals. He translated; then came back to me:

"She says not to worry about that. The spirits will be pleased to accept money in lieu:

$20 000 for the mombe, $2500 for the sheep and $1500 for the goat. A total of $24 000."

I thanked her for her offer of assistance and declared I would give the business careful thought. As we were preparing to leave, Tichuana looked over his shoulder, then turned to me and whispered. A consultation fee was expected, he said, and had I $250?

"A consultation fee? Why yes, of course! A doctor's fee. How silly of me! Here it is. Will you pay it her?"

In the end I didn't give the ancestral spirits the cow, the sheep and the goat they needed if they were to protect me from Simukayi and the Warvets. I would not willingly discourage them but I am a bit hard up.

However; there was another angle to this business. Tichuana has said to me that all has not been lost in this affair."The people we are against are very terrible with very powerful friends. We stood up to them and held them off." I admire that attitude.

There was a fall out. The police said they couldn't prosecute Douglas on the strength of a n'anga's verdict; the workers said they would walk out of the factory if Douglas was reinstated. Simukayi quarrelled with Douglas and changed his story, saying now that he knew Douglas had stolen the money. He lied only because Douglas promised to give him half of it. Simukayi accused Douglas and Eugenia of poisoning his beer and then pushed off.

The rent for the store was now seven months in arrears. In view of the police officer's earlier acknowledgement that I was entitled to regular payments, I sent my men down to remove the roofing sheets. The Warvets in the district made a great hullaballoo. Inspector Masuka phoned me and told me I had better put the roof back on again quick—which I agreed to do. It is hard to score a win.

The real loser in all this was Martin, who was obliged to pay Douglas severance pay, back pay, leave pay and goodness knows what else. By this time, the factory had moved to town.

With money in his pocket, Douglas moved away. I was told that he had been given a piece of land far distant; no doubt on a farm belonging to some poor dispossessed farmer. A few weeks later, Eugenia also moved away; whether to join Douglas or her sister Jovita I never heard. From the grapevine, I learnt that Jovita had resigned her teaching job in order to take up a career in agriculture. Perhaps a farm has landed in her husband's lap.

So the lady n'anga's prediction came about. She would certainly claim the credit if she knew, so it would be churlish of me to deny her this.

Unfortunately another so-called Warvet has appropriated the store for himself; that is to say he has put in a relative to occupy it. He himself has a fulltime job with the Harare municipality. I expect he is thinking of his retirement.

Should I bring in Mrs.Kazingezi to sort him out? With inflation running as it is, the ancestral spirits would be asking for a whole herd of cattle and a flock of sheep. They may despise the goats.

On the night of 20th. September 2001, the electric motor operating the vlei borehole pump was stolen. Exactly one week later, the 7.5 HP motor powering the pump near the Danbury border was also stolen. The thieves had to saw through a heavy padlock and chain securing the motor. The night guard said he saw the motor at 2am but it had gone by 4am. I wonder.

Naturally we summoned the Tredar security people who came out to investigate both times. They always pick up a police constable from the nearby Nyabira police camp. If they didn't the police would take days to respond. The system works quite well. Our people lay on the transport, do the tracking, list the suspects, and provide local knowledge. The policeman's only job is to take statements and write up an official report. Then he is driven back to his station.

The two motors went out through Danbury. A pick-up truck was used. It came down a farm road to a collection point. There were plenty of wheel tracks and footprints around. A pick-up had been observed in the vicinity the same night and its registration number noted. I gather from Tommy Bayley that his people are pretty certain they know who the thieves were. In fact one can say that it is "common knowledge". That goes for the people on our farm as well.

I really thought that there was a good chance of the motors being retrieved. However; there is a big BUT! The suspects are the Warvets and their hangers on—young men placed there by ZANU PF. They live on Danbury; illegally according to law, but legitimately according to government and the law enforcement agency—the police. As a senior member of our security concern put it: "When land squatters and Warvets are involved, the police are reluctant to do their job properly." The weeks have passed and, as far as I can make out, there has been little follow up.

The loss of the motors is a great blow. The two boreholes provided the main water supply for our irrigation. The replacement cost would be 350 000 dollars, a sum we cannot possibly afford and even if we could, we should have to put on a twenty-four hour guard to prevent them from being stolen in like manner. Insurance cover is impossible to get. We are carrying on somehow on half the water supply.

I have referred to squatters, invaders, settlers, occupiers, intruders—call them what you will. The one term that is never used by anyone is trespassers. Funny. I think that even the courts have forgotten that there is a law of trespass.

I understand that in the recent Abuja Accord, brokered in Nigeria, the Zimbabwe government agreed that there would be no further land invasions.

Right now, apart from Simukayi who comes and goes from his ILLEGALLY acquired house in our farm compound, we have no established squatters living or cultivating on the farm. I expect an invasion at any time. Will calling out "Abuja!" be of any use?

In the first week of October there were two disquieting episodes. One concerned the report of an armed man on the farm; the other was to do with further abrasive and threatening behaviour by Simukayi. Letters written to the Member-in-Charge, Marlborough Police dated the 4th.and 5th.October refer to the incidents in detail so I need do no more than attach them.

It is worth noting that over the past two years I have written dozens of letters to the District Administrator, to police officers and to government ministries; on not one single occasion have I ever received a written reply.

On 11th.October, a dilapidated pick-up containing three men and a woman drove up to my house gate. I went to meet them. They introduced themselves as staff of Agritex [Ministry of Agriculture]. They told me that they had been sent to gather information with regard to water supplies, fencing and electric lines on the farm. It was required for the resettlement exercise.

They were a pleasant, quiet bunch, far removed from the arrogant types one is so often confronted with. An air photo map of the farm was produced for me to see. I knew it at once. It formed part of the Conex [Conservation and Extension] plan for the farm back in 1947. The lands were depicted clearly. I wondered if they had unearthed the whole, meticulous assessment and recommendations compiled and drawn up by Conex Planning Branch 54 years ago in Rhodesian days. Perhaps the compilers are dead by now. If so, they will be turning in their graves at what is being done to farm land under the fast-track programme. It is a fast-track to erosion and desertification.

It pleased me to learn that the Agritex men had actually heard that part of the farm was a Declared Protected Forest. I was able to quote them the Statutory Notice number and to depict the area on the map. I was also able to mark in the position of the boreholes etc. They seemed impressed with the idea of a protected forest. No doubt environmental protection formed a noteworthy part of their training and it is not yet forgotten. These little people hinted that they were on my side but dare not say so. We parted friends.

It had been in my mind to have notices made and displayed drawing attention to the Protected Forest. However, it would cost more than we can afford and the future is too uncertain so I have shelved the idea. A person in the Forestry Commission suggested that notices might actually antagonize the Warvets.

This time last year I was planting several hundred indigenous trees in readiness for the rains. I was still optimistic. This year finances and spirits have waned. If the government turns me out, I can relocate somewhere but the trees can only stand and wait to be slaughtered. With them will go all the natural life they shelter. Whatever the darkness, hope springs eternal. Yesterday, daughter Bridget's birthday, I planted an Albizia adianthifolia grown from year 2000 seed. By the grace of God, it may outlive us both and survive beyond 2100!

Stockade Farm 8th.October 2001.
It seems that I have not written a report for some time. This has not been because the period has been free of trials. The reason for the lapse I can properly put down to mental exhaustion!

Since the dispute with Simukayi over a piece of our irrigated land and the coming of the police inspector with his army escort, I was able, after great difficulty, to make telephone contact with the DA in Concession. The inspector had insisted that I should go in person to see the DA and to take Simukayi with me. I had held my own counsel. Nothing in the world would have moved me to travel in the same car as an obvious psychopath, especially one who regularly expresses his intention to kill me! [Martin once gave Simukayi a lift to town and, for his considerate gesture, was subjected to a tirade of foul racial abuse].

I gave the DA a brief run-down of the incident that had arisen and in reply to his query, said that there had been no further interference by Simukayi. I suggested that he come to the farm to gauge the matter for himself. He thought that not necessary.

He said that he was glad that the matter had been resolved; agreed that we should continue as normal and asked me to inform him if there was any further interference. Pleased with this response and assurance, I have continued work in the market garden, plantings being made of cucurbits—gem and butternut squash, cucumber and pumpkin. The garlic has been lifted and the peas are being harvested.

Walking down a farm road, I saw a white pick-up coming towards me so I stood in its path. Driving the truck was a middle-aged, round, coloured man. Beside him was an African woman, who I took to be his wife. There were two African men in the back of the truck; they wore blue overalls and looked like workers. The vehicle stopped and the man put out an arm from his window to shake me by the hand—an immediate friendly gesture. I am ever suspicious these days. I immediately recalled that Simukayi had been seen conducting a stout coloured man about the farm. The previous reports were that the man drove a smart blue twin-cab. Today, if it was the same person, he was driving this pick-up.

I moved forward affably enough and shook the proffered hand.

"Are you looking for something or for somebody?" I asked, "Can I be of any help?"

"No, no," he replied, "we are just taking a look around."

"Is there something you are particularly wishing to see?"

"No…just…looking around."

"We like this place very much," broke in the wife.

"Yes, it's beautiful here," the husband added. "Such peaceful surroundings."

"Oh, I'm glad you think so," I said. "You know, believe it or not, I've had something to do with that. In fact I've spent the past forty years trying to make it as you see it now. I'm fond of the place too."

Up until then, they may have been wondering who I was. Now they knew I was the owner.

"Forty years! You have lived here for forty years?" The couple fell into an uneasy silence. I took this to mean that, face to face with me, the legitimate owner of the property, they felt uncomfortable with whatever it was they were about.

Sign-writing on the door panels of the pick-up indicated that it belonged to a diesel engineering company. If this man was the owner of the blue twin-cab, the chances were that he was also the owner of the truck and of the company. I resumed the conversation.

"If I may say so, you are a long way off the beaten track. Surely somebody must have directed you here. And it seems that you have been here before. Please be frank with me. People come and go, but although I am the farm owner, I'm the only one that doesn't know what's going on."

The man, who gave his name as Rogers, agreed that they had come out to the farm on other occasions. "You see," he said," we are looking for some land for ourselves. We learnt how to set about it. You go to the Ministry of Agriculture and ask them to give you the list of farms that government have designated. After looking around to find a place you'd like, you can go back and fill in an application form. It's quite easy."

"But can anybody put in an application?" I asked.

"Oh yes. Anyone can."

"So there would be nothing to stop me from going to apply?"

Mr. Rogers hesitated briefly and replied with a weak smile:

"No. I suppose you could."

The wife chipped in to say, "We don't want a lot of land. We're not wanting a big place." Perhaps she felt that this would make me feel better.

"About twenty hectares," from the husband.

"That's all," from the wife.

"To plant a few mealies."

"Run some chickens."

"Maybe keep a few pigs."

"Grow our own vegetables."

The couple had the idyllic rural life firmly in their imaginations.

"I fully understand your desires," I said. "I really do. You have your home in the town, of course?" they both nodded, "But you would like a small place in the country to come to at weekends and so on…to relax away from the business…get away from the city life." There was more affirmative nodding.

I continued; "Employ a man to work on the holding—he'll put up his own hut. Then it's not too far to drive out to keep an eye on things." Ready mutterings of assent suggested that I had got it about right.

"What could be better," I said. "I envy you."

The coloured man decided to change the subject. He waved his hand towards my house, which was just visible through the trees.

"Is that the homestead?"

"Yes. It's my house—but it's quite modest. There are two other houses on the farm that may be nicer. I looked at him and smiled. "You can take your pick."

I felt there was no more to be gained in prolonging our chat so explained that I must be moving on. Once more the man thrust out his broad brown arm and took my hand.

"I am sorry for what is happening to you," he said, and his wife leaned across the front seat to express her agreement, "But that's just the way of things isn't it? When an offer comes up, one has to take it." Before driving off, I think they even wished me luck!

The short meeting left much unsaid. With this man a fierce interrogation would have got me nowhere, so I refrained. For his part he was contented to offer bland explanations. I doubt very much if Rogers is his true name. The name of Simukayi was never mentioned.

My information was that the coloured man had been observed with Simukayi on previous occasions. I was soon to be told by one of our guards that the two African men, who I had observed riding in the back of the pick-up, have been seen before in Warvets' vehicles. If the coloured man's story is part way true, then there has to be a tie up between the Ministry of Agriculture and Lands [government] and the Warvets.

We have been aware for a long time that Simukayi is the appointed land agent for Stockade. He has been frequently observed showing strangers over the farm. The strangers usually come out at weekends, are well dressed and drive good cars. This suggests that they are professional persons, civil servants or businessmen; known to farmers as "Pajero peasants"; the Pajero being the top of the range 4x4 and a sure status symbol.

We thought that Simukayi was a self-appointed land agent, but perhaps he has official, if illegal, status. [Official and illegal are synonyms nowadays.] I know for a fact that strange visitors have been told to, "Ask for Simukayi." Who has forwarded them hence and from where? There has to be a racket behind it. It couldn't be anything else if Simukayi is in on it.

The Officer-in-Charge,   Stockade Farm
Z.R.P.Marlborough.   4th. October 2001
Dear Sir,

An armed man has been observed on Stockade. The man was present on the farm on Tuesday 2nd.October. I deem it important that you should be informed of this. By questioning three witnesses and making some pertinent enquiries, I have assembled certain facts.

At approximately 12 30 pm, three men came to the Stockade bar. They ordered beer. One of the men was young, about 18 years, the other two were older, perhaps in the late twenties or thirty.

The dominant member is very easily recognized. He is tall and big, tending to be fat. He has a "punk" hair style—the sides of the head shaved and the hair on the crown grown to stand up like a brush. On the day in question he was wearing short jean trousers and a loose long blue tee shirt. He is a frequent visitor to the bar and well known. It seems that he is flamboyant in character as well as in appearance. Although the bar blares out music 16 hours a day, it is said that this man brings his own records to the bar's radiogram and dances to the tunes. This is the person who carries the gun.

The descriptions of the gun given to me by the three witnesses, who I asked, tallied pretty well. They described it as being about 60 to 70 cms. long; a third of the length being the barrel, the remainder consisting of a breech and stock. The stock was of wood. I asked if they didn't think that the gun was a hand-made toy, but all were adamant that it was a "proper" gun. They said it was the sort of gun to shoot birds. It would appear from this description to be a sawn off shot gun.

Apparently the leader sometimes carries the gun at his back attached to his belt. At the bar he placed it on the ground. Perhaps it got in the way of his dancing—I didn't ask. At about 1 30 pm. the three men left the bar and took the path leading to Danbury. Some three hundred metres off this route are two residential houses, known as Fig Tree House and Bush Cottage. One was occupied by my son and his young family and the other by a widow and her aged mother. Ceaseless harassment, intimidation, extortion and death threats by Warvets maddened with drink or drugs, made life fearful and unsafe for the families living on the farm. They have left for a less stressful environment in the city and the two houses are unoccupied.

Two elderly house servants, Grey Zulu and his wife Jalina, continue in employment and are care-taking at Fig Tree House. The gardener, Maston, is also employed there. Next door at Bush Cottage, an old worker [named "House"] is retained to keep up the grounds.

The three young men, who were making their way to Danbury, left the path and walked across to the house occupied by Grey and his wife. At the quarters, they called for him. Grey spoke with them at his gate and asked them what they wanted. The big man with the hair tuft did the talking. One of the others had taken a position seven metres away leaning against a tree and holding the gun. Grey said he felt the men had no real reason to speak with him. He was given a story about a lost cell phone from which Grey could make little sense. He told the big man that he could not help him. With that, the three turned and sauntered back to the path. It was at that point that Maston the gardener came up and he plainly saw the gun. The three men carried on to Danbury and Maston went hurriedly to report to the Tredar security guards but couldn't find them. My son Martin was given the report when he came out to the farm that evening after work.

I have been informed that the three young men have make-shift dwellings on Danbury. They do not work but always have money.

In the afternoon of the following day, the Warvet, Comrade Simukayi, came in a car to Fig Tree House. He called to Grey and asked him questions such as; "Where is the boss?" He then told Grey that the Warvets would be moving into both the houses.

I consider Simukayi's appearance at Fig Tree House significant and sinister. Following closely as it does on the visitation by the other men, strongly suggests collusion between them. Purposeful and heartless intimidation of our elderly servants is obvious. These good people have all come forward to express their fear and dismay. Jalina crying: "The Devil! It is the Devil! Now he has come to strike us." [Jalina worships in a Christian church.]

We can anticipate further development of one kind or another. Simukayi may demand the keys of the houses from Grey and, having gained admittance, establish control of them by putting in his followers. Alternatively, we can expect a break-in and theft. This is a very real threat. Furniture and valuable fittings remain in the houses. We have already the precedent of the electric motors and fittings being stolen in recent weeks, the prime suspects being these very same people and their friends.

Should any such events occur, I am concerned about the use of a weapon. Please would you institute an investigation into this matter.

Yours sincerely,
R.F. Wiles.

The Officer-in-Charge,   Stockade Farm
Z.R.P. Marlborough.   5th. October 2001

Dear Sir,

I draw your attention to recent activity by the person known as Comrade Simukayi.

On Wednesday 3rd. October at approximately 3 p.m., a car drove into the farm yard. The car was a steel-blue Ford saloon with Registration No.542 823 Q. There were three occupants; a tall man in a black shirt and broad-brimmed hat [the driver], another short African man and Simukayi.

Several of the farm workers, the farm foreman and a security guard were in the close vicinity. Simukayi, as is his wont, ignored the workers and rudely conducted the intruders past my employees. The three men walked over to a farm shed and proceeded to examine it at some length.

I myself arrived just then and saw the group. My staff informed me that it was Simukayi who was showing the strangers around the farm shed. I did not approach them.

You will recall that on several occasions during the past eighteen months, Simukayi has threatened to kill me and indeed further to that effect, you hold in your station a letter written by Simukayi threatening death to myself and my son, Martin. You will also recall that in reports made to yourself and to the D.A. Concession, I have repeatedly expressed my belief that Simukayi is a psychopath. He is given to violence and is dangerous—an opinion since confirmed by information gathered from certain reliable sources.

It is against this background that I have been advised never to involve myself in confrontation with Simukayi. In the circumstances with which I was presented, I decided that I should leave the scene.

Returning after about half an hour, I found the car and the occupants had left the vicinity but only to drive to another part of the farm. Upon my enquiry my staff told me that Simukayi was offering the farm shed to the tall stranger as a place in which he could keep chickens.

Simukayi has as a friend a certain Dr. Ngwenya. This Dr. Ngwenya runs a medical clinic in the city. He also has a residence there. It seemed odd when I learned through police investigation that it was this doctor who received the bags of soya beans stolen from the farm by Simukayi some months ago. There is an explanation.

I learn that Dr. Ngwenya keeps a large number of chickens on Danbury, the next door farm. Without the permission of the owner, he has appropriated buildings belonging to the farm and converted them into chicken houses for his own commercial use. The doctor has the housing virtually for free but the chickens require to be fed. Naturally, the cheaper he can obtain the food, the greater the success of his commercial enterprise. Maize and soya bean growers in the area would be unwittingly, but almost certainly, contributing to the success.

These things were in my mind when I was told that Simukayi had earmarked this farm shed of ours for a chicken house. Perhaps his friend, Dr. Ngwenya, intended to expand.

Upon my questions, my workers told me that the tall man in the black shirt was definitely not Dr. Ngwenya, who, as a frequent visitor to the compound bar, is fairly well known. Nevertheless, the stranger has been seen in the area before and because of Simukayi's close association with Dr. Ngwenya, I suspect there could well be collaboration between the three.

There is no question that the shed in question will not be required by us ourselves. The rainy season is fast approaching. From November onwards produce from the market garden will be coming off the lands and covered areas are needed for shelter, grading and packing. Other shed cover is required for hay bales yet to be taken in from the lands.

Should Simukayi and his confreres exert force or coercion in order to take from us this shed or any other buildings rightfully the property of the farm, we shall require the assistance of the police. My objective in writing to you is to keep you informed. Naturally, I hope that no disturbing situation will arise.

There are further matters concerning Simukayi upon which I would be grateful to obtain an explanation and an understanding. I refer to CR 45\6\2001, a charge of extortion; and CR 276\6\2001, a charge of theft. Both of these cases were handed over to CID Harare Central, Law and Order Div. D\Con. Rudzivo handles the first case and D\Con. Chirindo the second.

On 3rd.July Simukayi was taken to court on the extortion charge. He was ordered to pay 1000 dollars bail and to report every 14 days. I understand that he has not been reporting as ordered by the court. On the theft charge, he has not yet appeared in court because he can never be found.

Both Con. Rudzivo and Con. Chirindo have repeatedly assured me in person and on the phone, that Simukayi will be arrested and court proceedings initiated. They have asked me to notify them when Simukayi is seen on the farm so that the arrest can be made. The same request was made to the farm storekeeper, the plaintiff in the extortion case.

In compliance with this request, I have reported to the two constables in Harare Central, whenever I learn that Simukayi is present on the farm. The storekeeper assures me that he has done likewise. Whenever I relayed the information to the C.I.O. an assurance was always given that the police officers would come out directly. They never did.

On follow up enquiry, I learnt that the problem is transport. It appears that Harare Central police station never has any transport for its investigating officers to carry out their duties. If and when a vehicle is available, then there is no fuel to operate the same.

In view of this chronic state of affairs, I asked how they intended to arrest Simukayi [or for that matter, any other criminal suspects]. Con. Ruzivo said that he would have arrangements made for Z.R.P. Marlborough to pick up Simukayi on behalf of Harare Central. I think that may have been about four weeks ago.

I would be pleased to know if you have received such instructions. Simukayi is frequently seen on the farm and is active in the district.

Recently, we have had two electric motors stolen during the night. Together they were worth 350 000 dollars. By coincidence Simukayi was on the farm the day before each theft and again on the afternoon following. It is known that he has accomplices amongst illegal occupiers on Danbury Farm through which the electric motors were taken by a pick-up truck. [A registration number was provided for the police.]

You will understand that my farm workers and I are thoroughly disconcerted that Simukayi is allowed to evade prosecution time and time again. Please would you contact a senior officer in CID Central to at least get action taken on the two outstanding indictments?

Yours sincerely,
R.F.Wiles.
CFU, Atherstone & Cook, et al.

Week ending 14th. October 2001

On Tuesday I went to Marlborough police station to hand in my letter of the 4th. and 5th. Inspector Mukungunugwa was in. At the sight of the letters he told me to send copies to the DA. I said I would be doing so.

On his desk, the inspector had a number of lists which had been sent to him from the Ministry of Agriculture. One list referred to delisted farms. On this list was Madzugetu but the Inspector thought this only referred to Trianda of Madzugetu. We looked at other lists for Stockade. It turned up as Stockade of Madzugetu in a list of farms awaiting processing.

The inspector, who was in a helpful frame of mind that day, said that Mr. Townsend was somewhere around the station and he could probably advise me on the matter as his farm, Lowdale, had recently been delisted. Mick Townsend was found and came into the office and I had quite a lengthy discussion with him—the inspector, between attending to police business, chipping in from time to time.

Of course I explained that we had gone through all the legal processes open to us by way of objections to designation and had made formal requests for delisting, using the criteria laid down by government itself as proper grounds. The last application had been made six months ago addressed to the Governor at Bindura. Follow up enquiry proved fruitless.

Mick Townsend observed that this was normal and was part of a wearing down process. It was expected that you would give up trying. That could be interpreted as meaning that you had dropped your objections and accepted the designation of your property.

It was essential to persevere.

The inspector agreed, saying that in this business nobody will volunteer to help you. I took the advice to re-apply at once and to send copies of my application to all parties involved along the line.

On Wednesday I called on Mrs.Tsuakwi at the Ministry to get some delisting forms. She remembered me from last April. I explained that I had had no response to my application at that time. She looked through her farm lists and confirmed that I should re-apply and take the fresh forms to the Governor, Elliot Manyika, in Bindura. I asked her if I should attach another lot of back-up material. She replied:

"No. Just write down SINGLE FARM OWNER." This indicated to me, that what the President keeps on saying in public viz; *farmers with only one farm would not have them taken from them*, is to be honoured.

The trip to Bindura is quite long and tiresome, so I thought to phone the Governor's office to ask if the original form and attachments, which I had given the Governor last April, was still in the office awaiting his attention. If this was the case it would save me having to come again. I suggested that my application form may have been "mislaid".

The Governor's secretary, whose name was Helen, if I recall correctly, took this to be an insult to the Governor. "You imply that the Governor does not know how to do his work. I will tell him what you have said. He will not be pleased." I was certainly taken aback. The woman was in no mood to accept reasonable explanations.

"I don't know what you and Mrs.Tsuakwi have been saying together. Be careful!"

With some foreboding, I set off to Bindura on the morrow. On the journey I determined that I would present myself as pleasing and polite as it is possible to be! It didn't help me much. The secretary treated me with the same incivility as on the phone. "You are the one tarnishing the Governor's name—I will tell him. He will hear about you."

This I suppose, she presented as a fearful threat. Well…he has a reputation.

Perhaps the woman was hoping to get me angry. I didn't oblige and remained duly obsequious. In the end she sent me off to the Provincial Administrator's office and told me to give in my form there.

I fared a little better at the PA's but not much. The PA said the application would be put before the Lands Committee in a week's time. I asked if I could have a receipt for my form. This proved to be another mistake. It implied that I didn't trust him. I muttered something about previous experiences, didn't press him further, and hurriedly departed from his office only to find I had left my hat behind and had to go back to retrieve it. I drove back to Harare hot and bothered.

Week ending 21st. October.

At 12 15 on Thursday 18th., a dark grey Isuzu Twincab Reg.No.698 828 V entered the farm. Simukayi was in the vehicle with four other men. The report was that one of the men was an army colonel in uniform. [Johannes was given the name Col. Matarutse by the driver.] Another man was described as being bald and stout. He had a large notebook. This man sat next to Simukayi. They had a 2 litre scud of Chibuku and took turns to drink from it. They had bought the beer at the farm bar.

The twin-cab, travelling fast, took a shortcut through a paddock and in doing so smashed an irrigation pipe. At the farm bwalo, the car stopped. Here Simukayi spoke to the Tredar guard. He asked for Johannes and said that Johannes must leave the farm before Saturday or he would call other Warvets and fix him. Now he was going to show these people the fields. They were away for about twenty-five minutes.

On the return of the party Johannes stopped the vehicle near his house. He demanded to know from Simukayi what was meant by his threat to chase him off the farm. It seems that Frank, one of our ancient workers, had left his job during working hours and gone to the bar to drink beer with Simukayi. When Johannes found Frank lying drunk on the ground, he sent him off the field and said he would get no pay. Frank, the rat, complained to Simukayi, hence the threat.

Such is life with this bully around. Fortunately, both Johannes and the other workers have shown much more courage of late and are prepared to stand up against this vicious devil. Johannes offered to fight Simukayi there and then. Apparently the others in the car were happy to remain passive observers—soldiers or not. The Isuzu drove off the farm with Simukayi in it.

At 7 15 pm. Simukayi came back onto the farm. This time he accompanied two other men in a white Mazda pick-up. The registration number is 539 274 R. They drove to the field immediately below Fig Tree house and parked the vehicle by the hay bale stack. There they got out.

Because it was nearly dark, one of the Tredar guards moved close and overheard the men speaking. According to the guard, Simukayi said: "This is the field I am going to give to you. I will co-operate with you to plant the crop and we should have a good harvest." Then Simukayi asked for money from the men but they replied that they had no money at that time. The three men spent about twenty minutes in the field. During this time, Sinai, the wife of Johannes, also heard the men talking and because Simukayi was very loud, she heard him telling the others that he wanted money for the field. The pick-up then drove back to town.

On Friday afternoon at 4.45 I was speaking to the guard at the factory gate when Simukayi approached from the direction of the guard's quarters. Because I always avoid confrontation with him, I drove off and up to where the field workers were. As I drove away the guard reported that Simukayi picked up a half brick to throw at me saying, "Why does he run away?" Simukayi was accompanied by a short person wearing a red hat. They followed me up the road. On seeing this I climbed into my vehicle and drove away.

At 5 15 pm. on Saturday 20th.the same white pick-up, 539 274 R, came from town. This time there were three men with Simukayi. The vehicle stopped at the factory gate. The irrigation sprinklers were working nearby in the market garden fields. Simukayi told the security guard the irrigation must be switched off and that he didn't want to see anyone working in the fields. The pick-up proceeded to the Fig Tree paddock.

On Sunday at 10 30am. Simukayi came up to the bwalo. The irrigation was switched on and the crop being watered. Simukayi was angry and abusive shouting that he had ordered work to stop. Once again he said he would chase Johannes off the farm. He said that the farm gates must be left open because the road would be needed for the tractors which would be coming. If the new invaders bring in a DDF tractor, will it be used to plough in our freshly planted crop as happened last season?

Stockade Farm Monday 22nd.October 2001

This morning I learnt that a man has been cutting trees in the vicinity of Fig Tree House. My heart sank because I have planted many hundreds of indigenous trees in this area and many of them are ten years of age and grown to a good size. They comprise a great number of species. Upon investigation, I discovered that the trees being cut were in the paddock below the house which Simukayi has "sold" to the people from town. The trees are mostly Acacia seiberiana and polyacantha but also some Brachystegia boehmii. The man cutting the trees told the guard that he had been ordered by Simukayi to cut the trees. The man gave his name as Innocent.

The soil in this place is quite unsuitable for cultivation. The soil is described as sedimentary arenite. It is markedly unstable and because it has a high percentage of fine clay particles, it is readily subject to erosion. If proof is needed, further down the slope, a network of erosion gullies, some up to ten metres deep, can be seen. The terrible damage was done in a very short period of time probably some seventy years ago when soil conservation measures were not practiced. Soil scientists, who have examined the area, consider that sheet erosion removed all the topsoil.

Over the past fifteen years, I have put in a lot of effort and money to halt further erosion in this area. It has been incorporated into the forest reserve; no woodcutting or grazing has been allowed for the past ten years; large quantities of mulch have been carted in. There are signs of slow stabilization and restructuring. The gullies themselves will remain for a thousand years.

The Fig Tree paddock is sloping land immediately above this terrible erosion. Some thirty-five years ago it was very carefully surveyed and contoured by Conex. There followed arable cropping rotated with grass ley. Notwithstanding, I observed deterioration of soil structure and soil erosion taking place even between contours. I therefore determined that the soil would only be safe if protected by permanent pasture using selected grasses and legumes.

It has been my policy with permanent pastures to have Acacia trees spaced throughout. The reasons are:

1. The tree roots, by penetration, work in decomposing the deeper rock formation and thus assist in soil formation.
2. Acacia tree species are members of the leguminosae family and as such they add nitrogen to the soil. Leaf, pod and bark litter also provides nutrients. Where Acacias are grown, improved grass sward results.
3. The extensive root system of the tree improves soil aeration and water penetration.
4. If grazing has been heavy [which it shouldn't be!] and bare soil exposed, the tree canopy effectively breaks the force of raindrops, thus minimizing the dislodgement and carrying away of soil particles. Raindrop action on exposed fine-grained clay soils is a particular erosion hazard.
5. Shade provided by the trees is enjoyed by cattle. Also the shade ensures an equitable microclimate for the vital soil bacteria to function.
6. Above the soil, above the grass, high in the trees, there exists a branched and leafy canopy teeming with natural life.

One may call this biodiversity superbly integrated with practical land usage.
Reference Statutory Instrument 147 of 2001. Forest [Declaration of Private Forest][Stockade Farm] Notice; the following paragraph applies: "The

Minister of Environment and Tourism has declared the non-arable parts of Stockade Farm, situated in the Mazowe District and described in the Schedule, as a protected forest."

The Forestry Commission survey depicting the protected forest actually bisects the land under review. However, as explained, the whole of this area must be considered as unsuitable for cultivation.

I have described the history, the geology, the planning, the experience and other considerations concerning the piece of land on the farm known as the Fig Tree paddock.

This is the very piece of land which Simukayi, in crass ignorance, has given to his town acquaintances to plough up for a plot of mealies. A man, NOT from this farm but resident on another has been called in to start cutting down trees.

This action will result in ecological disaster. Surely, it would be shameful and reprehensible to allow it to proceed. A serious commitment to protect every facet of our environment by persons in responsible positions is called for. In truth, honouring the environment should be the foremost consideration in these times of human stress. All said and done, human happiness is dependent on the healthy, diverse, benevolent natural world on which we are all reliant.

From what I have written, it is plain that the land in my trust and care concerns me intensely. We can discount "designation" and the loss of the property to the State because the President reiterates the promise that government will not take the land from owners with single properties. Because we meet this and the other criteria specified, delisting will inevitably follow when government machinery gets down to it. It is in this light that I see the responsibility of the farm and forest to be still in my hands.

24th.October 2001

My last entry of 22nd., took on an unusual form. This is because, having begun it, I found myself turning it into a compulsive, even impassioned, written argument; this being to persuade the DA to take resolute action to halt Simukayi and his friends from wrecking the Fig Tree paddock. The result was a mixed homily on trees and conservation.

Resolutely, I faxed the whole report off with a covering letter to the DA in Concession. ZESA are the only people operating a fax machine in Concession, so I had to send it through them. I expect their office staff found it an exhilarating change from faxed complaints concerning electricity bills and power cuts.

On the whole, town phones work but rural phones don't; so I took the opportunity to ring and speak with the sergeant in charge of the Nyabira police station. The police were supposed to have come to the farm on Monday but didn't. The sergeant explained that his only vehicle was used to attend a case of theft at Windmill Farm and after that he himself was delayed trying to get a phone call through to the DA at Zimba. I understand he wanted to get a local government directive on my complaint involving, as it did, Warvets and invaders. But why Zimba? It is miles away. The sergeant must be new to the station and does not know where we are.

After lengthy discussion and research the other end, the Nyabira sergeant was told that there was no Stockade Farm in the Zimba DA's district! Of course I was able to confirm with him that we fall within the Concession administrative district. Whilst on the subject, I told the sergeant that he might as well know that the DA in Concession believes Stockade to be in the Marlborough police district and therefore communicates, when needful, with Marlborough. However, when it suits them, Marlborough police insist that we come under Nyabira. [On the map the farm is bisected.] We get the best, or worst, of both worlds.

Well, the sergeant's story seemed genuine enough and fortunately no crisis had arisen. I spoke to him of my contact with the DA in Concession and that should there be a need for urgent response to please liaise with him. The sergeant expressed his willingness to do so. [And if I can't get through to the Nyabira police, I shall call up the police at Marlborough who will tell me that they cannot communicate with Nyabira either and that they have no transport anyway. So you see…?]

From yesterday until now there has been no resumption of tree cutting and no strangers with a tractor invading us. Nevertheless, I am never without anxiety. Apart from the group with obvious intentions on the Fig Tree paddock, there was the army colonel. What was in his mind when he and his confederates drove down to the lands in his smart twin-cab?

[We have much damage done to the leaves of the young cucurbits.

Di Taylor, the entomologist at CFU, has identified Thrips. She was very excited—never seen such an infestation on cucumbers! Why can't Thrips eat Warvets?]

    The Officer-in-Charge,   Stockade Farm
    Z.R.P. Marlborough.   29th October 2001
Dear Sir,

On Stockade we are threatened with imminent land invasions. I have had communication with the DA Concession and I attach hereto letters and reports which I have sent to him.

Simukayi has been allotting fields to unknown persons for monetary gain. I anticipate that the DA will contact you in order to establish who the people are.

The following are clear:
1. The President has stated that farmers with single farms will not have their farms taken.
2. The agreement reached at Abuja, [I gather the accord still stands], specifies that there will be no new land invasions and that there shall be a return to the rule of law.

I request the relevant government authorities to protect this farm from wrongful land invasion and furthermore to recognize and uphold our proper ownership rights.

Yours sincerely,
R.F.Wiles.

[Footnote for personal records made 2 months later: As expected, the police did not respond in any way to my letters of 4th., 5th.and 29th.October.]

The District Administrator,   Stockade Farm
Concession. 23rd.   October 2001
Dear Sir,

The Warvet Simukayi has given a certain piece of land on this farm to a party or parties apparently resident in Harare. We learn that these people intend to bring out a tractor to plough the land in question. The felling of trees has begun.

A copy of my farm report will be faxed to you along with this. It will be self explanatory.

My request is that these people should be immediately restrained from proceeding in this ill-conceived plan.

Please note that there are no occupiers, settlers, squatters, illegal residents—whatever the terminology—presently on Stockade, nor has there ever been. The only exception could be Simukayi who, because he has a monthly income and a home in his own village, could more aptly be termed a political protester.

I understand that at the Ajuba accord, agreement was reached that there would be no further land invasions. Ongoing occupation of our land at this stage must surely be a violation of the accord.

You will understand that authoritative action is called for and I request that you please provide me with the necessary support.

Yours sincerely,
R.F.Wiles.

Additional note dated 26 10 01

This is a confirmation copy of my fax sent to you on the 23rd.by kind cooperation of ZESA.

This letter with attached farm report was delivered by Martin Wiles personally at the D.A.'s office in Concession on 29th. October. A receipt was obtained.

To: The District Administrator, Concession,
Per kind favour ZESA Fax 075 6 2876
From: R.F. Wiles, Stockade Farm, Box EH95 Emerald Hill
Fax 04 303462 28 October 2001
Dear Sir,

I write to you concerning imminent farm invasions. I shall try to reach you by phone, but communication by phone can often be difficult so I am sending you this fax at the earliest opportunity.

On Saturday 27th.October Simukayi instructed his wife and a certain man by the name of Innocent, who is normally resident on Selby Farm, to burn the grass off a field below the railway line. No firebreaks have been prepared there and a fresh wind was blowing. An uncontrolled fire in these conditions could burn out the whole farm. There are 10 000 hay bales at risk. Their value is 380 000 dollars.

I sent the farm workers with water and sprayers to extinguish the fire. The woman left the field but said that she would return in the afternoon and start burning again.

Due to the seriousness of the matter, I tried to phone the DA's office but there was no reply. After a number of phone calls, Constable Nkurora of ZRP Marlborough advised me to call them at once should Simukayi become a danger to persons or property. A reaction group was stationed at Mazowe who would be asked to respond.

A car was seen yesterday with Simukayi and two persons. They viewed the land in question. It is apparent that Simukayi has allocated the land to a third party. My information is that the persons seen in the car are from town. They have not cultivated any plots here before. Because Simukayi sent his wife to burn the field, he is sure to be receiving payment. This aspect of reward was revealed in my report of the 23rd.inst.

On Saturday afternoon at 4pm.yet another car entered the farm, Reg. No.584538 Q. There was a single male driver. He drove down to where Johannes, the foreman, was baling star grass hay in a field beyond the transformer. The man told Johannes that the bales of hay must be removed on Monday because a tractor would be coming to plough all round this land and it was to be burnt off prior to ploughing.

The unknown driver told Johannes that the tractors for the ploughing were to be provided by a very prominent business man.

Notes concerning the behaviour of Warvet Simukayi.

Within the past seven days Simukayi has:

1. Smoked out and destroyed two wild bee swarms one of which was in the nature sanctuary.
2. Doing the above, lighting a fire and leaving it uncontrolled. The fire was doused by a farm worker who chanced to notice it.
3. Attempted to subvert a security guard by asking him to give him iron roof sheets. Later asked for onions from stored farm produce.
4. Poached fish from a small pond constructed for the benefit of wildlife in the private nature reserve and bird sanctuary.
5. Conducted a certain vehicle off a farm road and in so doing driving over and smashing a water pipe used for irrigation.
6. Attempted to undermine the authority of the farm foreman by:

    i.] Taking the side of a farm worker, who was reprimanded and disciplined by the foreman for drinking beer with Simukayi during working time and found lying drunk and incapable by the side of the field. Simukayi demanded that the worker should not have his day's pay docked and that the foreman must get off the farm or he would be "fixed".
    ii.] Ordering that work in the irrigated market garden fields must be stopped and telling others that he would drive the foreman away.

7. Used threatening gestures against myself as related by the farm security guard and shouting verbal abuse at me from a motor car driven past my home gate.

Diary continues.

On the farm next door, Trianda, I was dismayed to learn that they have sixteen illegal squatters dispersed around the farm living in huts. Give me Thrips any day. The human invaders will despoil the surroundings all about them. These people have been placed there by the Party network.

Trianda was delisted months ago and, once delisted, it was said that any squatters would be relocated to vacant land which was available elsewhere. For political reasons connected with the forthcoming election, this will not take place. My attention was drawn to all this when I discovered that a new squatter on Trianda had come into our forest reserve and cut down as many as a hundred trees to build his hut. This was only last week. The trees had just been cut and the hut on the Trianda farm is still being constructed. It is obvious that fresh land encroachment is taking place.

My neighbour to the East, Tommy Bayley of Danbury Park, has fared far worse. When he turned out his tractors to prepare his lands for the forthcoming season, he was told to take his tractors out and to do no more ploughing. The instructions were given verbally by the Officer-in-Charge, Mazowe police who came onto the farm backed by armed members of the Support Unit.

Tommy Bayley asked for the order to be given him in writing. He was told that it was not necessary to do so. The police officer said he had been given his instructions. Tommy insisted that he wanted to see a written order before he would stop land preparation. Unfortunately, and understandably, his tractor drivers were scared to carry on with the work. Here is a case of the Party, the Warvets and the Police working in collusion. It takes nerve to stand up against force such as that.

THIS HAS HAPPENED SINCE ABUJA. So much for diplomatic agreements.

Meanwhile Tommy has Dr. Ngwenya, [the medical doctor and aspiring chicken farmer referred to earlier in these reports] ploughing some twenty hectares of his land with a borrowed tractor. There is no question of the police stopping HIM. But then I was told that Dr. Parirenyenatwa, the deputy Minister of Health, has a personal stake in part of Danbury Park farm. It is understandable that medical men should stand by each other.

Thursday 1st. November 2001 Halloween and Full Moon.
There is a stack of hay bales in the "small dam" field. We were loading a National Food's truck with bales there, when I heard the noise of a heavy diesel vehicle and thought it was another N.F. truck arriving. Not so. It was a large tractor with a harrow and it immediately started harrowing a circuit around the large field above the small dam. Apart from the tractor driver there seemed to be about three or four other men.

There is never any courtesy, no by your leave, with all these people. It seems that anyone rounded up to serve the Warvets, be they old or young, automatically adopt the same insolent, abrasive manner as the Warvets themselves. I asked an old man, standing by the roadside, who he was working for. He replied that he had come with the tractor and they had been told that they were to burn all the grass off the field. The tractor, he said, belonged to Ibbo Mandaza. Ibbo Mandaza has a farm property further down the Selby road. He may be termed a rich, business tycoon well in with the ruling Party.

There are about 1500 hay bales scattered in this field. We are too busy to collect them at this time. Needless to say, I became extremely anxious at what was going on. I phoned the DA but the woman secretary said that the DA would not be in the office until next Monday. I was put through to his number two, Mr. Gurure.

Mr. Gurure went straight into his usual avoidance routine when I told him that the farm was being illegally invaded by persons unknown to me or to people on my staff.

A dangerous fire had been started and it threatened to burn our hay bales within the field.

"And on whose authority had this tractor come to plough my land?" I asked.

"Well we have our people pegging farms all through Mazowe right now," he replied.

I forbore to say this implied that government ministries were completely ignoring the Abuja accord; but went on: "In my last letter to the DA, I wrote that we would be unable to continue our farming business and to employ our workers, unless we had complete freedom to operate on the whole farm without hindrance. Now I have these people intending to plough and plant maize here."

"But these are the settlers you have."

"No, they are not," I replied, "They are persons from Harare. Apart from Warvet Simukayi, who illegally and criminally took over a house in the farm compound last year, we have had no settlers."

"Well, we all know Simukayi. You have had him a long time now. There is no call to make a big issue out of a minor matter." There was little point in continuing. Oddly enough, many months ago, Mr. Gurure himself had agreed that Simukayi was mentally deranged and ought to be removed. He told me that even the Warvet higher command was aware that Simukayi was "wrong in the head".

With some difficulty, I then got onto Insp. Mukungunugwa, who was on his way to Concession. I asked him to please try to sort out the matter of these invading Warvets with the DA. I had already supplied them both with the full background and reason for my complaints.

Shortly after speaking with the police inspector, I went down to the bwalo. The guard on duty came to me to say that a grey 4x4 had driven down the farm road, stopped at the irrigation and four of five African men had got out to look at the crop. Then they climbed back into the vehicle and drove down to the bwalo. Here they spoke to the guard. He was to inform me that I must stop the field work. The guard said that he did not recognize the men but they looked "powerful". So who were this lot?

Friday 2nd. November 2001

At 2.15 pm. a car came through the farm. It swung past me without slackening speed and went down to the lower fields where the burning had taken place. The car was a blue Ford salon Reg. No. 525 239 L. On its return through the farm sheds, I stood in the road and waved it down. The driver got out. He was a tall middle-aged African man, fairly heavily built. He wore a smart broad-brimmed hat, a loose tee-shirt with a flamboyant design, and from a neck-chain was hung a large platinum cross. I looked at the cross and remarked that he must be a Christian. Was he a visiting churchman? If so what denomination did he belonged to? And was he on pastoral business?

This took him back a bit. He muttered that he was Roman Catholic and upon my asking his particular church, he brusquely said: "The R.C. Cathedral." He hadn't greeted me very civilly and didn't mean to be put off his mission. "I am a Warvet," he pronounced.

"Oh, yes," I said, "will you give me your name?" He paused a while considering this; "Joseph," he replied curtly.

During this time, I had noticed that the mujibha, called Innocent, had been in the car and was now standing by it. I expect he had informed the Warvet of our hay bales being in the field they intended to invade.

The Warvet said that I must remove the grass bales from the field because the field was going to be burnt tomorrow, after which they intended to plough it. I replied that the bales were indeed mine, but that he had no right to order me to move them. Our farm workers were busy on other work. The man said that if I did not move the bales, I would have to bear the consequences. I called over the Tredar guard and the Warvet, speaking in Shona, gave the same warning.

Innocent, Simukayi's young acolyte and Warvets' running dog, is potential trouble for as long as he remains here. His home is on Selby farm, but he has been recruited by Simukayi with whom he has stayed for the past three or four weeks. Innocent, who had got out of the car, stood and glowered at me in the accepted manner. I expect Simukayi has been teaching him the rules of aggressive behaviour. It seems that this man with the heavy crucifix pendant has connections with both Simukayi and Ibbo Mandaza. Also in the car were some young females—Warvets molls? They all drove off.

At 5.45 pm. the guards reported that a white Bedford 3 tonne truck, Reg. No. 136 438 B, drove onto the farm. There were four men in it. I learnt later that one of them was George. It was probably him who told the guard that the farmer should not put the irrigation fields under vegetables because the whole field had been given to him.

Nightfall. Makosa has told me he has made a pot of my favourite soup for supper and bid me goodnight. He will padlock the security gate behind him before walking slowly down the winding path to his house in the farm village half a mile away. Outside in the garden the bulbuls have ceased their routine dusk chatter. All is still. Alone in my familiar home and surroundings of 38 years, I should be at peace. I confide that the strains of this life are leaving me weary, while yet the tensions of the mind will not permit rest. The companionship of the dogs and listening to fine music will give me some solace, but tomorrow another day will dawn and the fight will resume; in what form I cannot tell. I feel embattled like a soldier in a lonely outpost and know that there is not a soul who can relieve me. Yet I carry no arms. Nothing, but nothing, would put me into deeper trouble than to be seen bearing a firearm. The war is one of attrition. Sleep, when it comes, is through exhaustion.

Saturday 3rd. November 2001
   I went down to the farm sheds at 6.30 in the morning feeling uneasy. Sure enough, I was told that four mujibhas had passed through with the intention of setting fire to the field.
   One of the youths was carrying a long stick on the end of which was a sack to facilitate burning. Would they dare destroy my hay bales?
   I hastened back to the house and phoned the police at Nyabira. I could get no reply, so I raised Tredar on the Agric-alert and asked the O.C. Timothy Makunya to pass a message on to the police requesting them to send somebody to the farm to restrain the invaders from burning. As I was speaking I saw through my window smoke rising so I reported this. I received a radio message back to say that Insp. Masuka would come over himself.
   Fearing that the fire might not only destroy the bales but also get out of control, I sent our workers to the scene with water and knapsacks. When I arrived there myself I found that our men had doused most of the fire although the mujibha Innocent was still defiantly rekindling. I was thankful to observe that where the burning was, the bales had been lifted and cast on the side of the land.
   To my surprise, I discovered that the arsonists, apart from Innocent, were little more than children. Apparently they had been recruited [no doubt for a small sum] from the next door farm, Trianda. I looked fiercely at them, encouraged my men to complete extinguishing the fire and that was that. The little incendiaries went away. I don't suppose they got paid. At that moment the big National Food truck arrived to pick up another load of bales.
   Later in the morning, Martin came to the farm with a borrowed video camera. He took film footage of a large part of the farm. The objective of this is to show and to record that there are no squatters or settlers present anywhere. It is a certainty that these new invaders will claim that their presence has been longstanding.
   Yet later in the morning, the blue Ford car drove onto the farm and went down to the field. I passed them on a corner and noted that the driver was not the same man as before. Simukayi was in the back talking on a cell phone. He

managed as we passed to interrupt his conversation in order to swear at me through his window.

We got two loads of bales away during the morning—a total of 900. This job has proved vexatious because we have discovered that vandals [for vandals read Warvets, squatters, settlers or whatever] from neighbouring farms have raided the stacks of bales and stolen the wrapping twine. As a result the bales fall apart. We shall have to re-bale hundreds.

A hot wearisome day has ended.

Sunday 4th.November 2001

At 7am. I walked down with the dogs to the sheds. There I spoke to the guards and told them that should there be any further developments, they should come up to my house and call me. At 7.40 I received a message from Johannes to say that Ibbo Mandaza's tractor had arrived with a Rome harrow and had begun to "plough" the top section of the field which had been partly burnt and from which the bales had been taken aside.

This was a setback. I had hoped for more time to induce the DA and the police to put a restraining order on the invaders. This was in line with my letter quoting single farm ownership and, in accord with Abuja, a return to law and order and no further land invasions. The complete lack of response, suggests that the district levels of government and police are getting no directive on the implementation of Abuja at all from higher authority. This is very depressing.

I tried to phone Z.R.P. Nyabira but there was no answer. Earlier in the morning I had picked up the radio message that our close farm neighbour, Maypark, had had irrigation pipes stolen during the night. The Tredar mobile team was investigating. I requested that they call on me at the end of their follow up.

This they duly did and I was able to speak with O.C. Timothy and the B.S.M. I told Timothy that Insp. Masuka never turned up yesterday. However, I learnt from Timothy that Nyabira had entered an official report, [R.B. number] and had transferred the matter to Marlborough who would then handle the business. I should contact Marlborough and inform them of the transfer of the case to them—and to quote Insp. Masuka.

Timothy had not brought a Z.R.P. constable with him on the theft investigation and in the circumstances he felt he couldn't help me in any way with my predicament even as a silent witness. If Tredar become involved in the slightest way with Warvet activities or land matters, they are immediately accused of being MDC supporters. I fully understood. Regrettably, this is how it is.

On the strength of the advice that Z.R.P. Nyabira had officially handed over my complaint to Marlborough, I phoned the station. It must have been shortly after 8 o'clock. I spoke to a Cons. Makora. I told him who I was and asked him who was in charge of the station. He said that A\ Insp. Mupariano was around. From previous experience I knew that this officer would never take action on my behalf. However I had no option and at least I could quote Insp. Masuka. I asked to speak to A\Insp. Mupariano.

My cell phone contact was rather bad, but I gathered from the constable that Mupariano had gone to the toilet. The constable said they would phone me back later.

I knew they wouldn't, so asked when Mupariano was likely to be back and I would ring again then. The constable advised me to try after ten or fifteen minutes.

About twenty minutes later, I rang the station and asked to speak to A\ Insp. Mupariano. The constable said that the inspector was not around.

"Not around? Where is he then?"

"He has gone home."

"But I thought you said he was on duty?"

"It is the weekend."

"But surely crimes take place on weekends. They aren't confined to week days," I said, continuing, "Is your Officer-in Charge in a place where he can be contacted?"

"He is going to Concession."

"On business?"

"He is attending a land committee meeting."

This seemed to me to be the very time and place where Insp.Mukungunugwa could bring up and discuss my complaint. I had not, of course, had a reply to my letter to the DA a copy of which was with the inspector. I requested Cons. Makora to please contact the inspector by police radio or cell phone and ask him to see about my case—adding I was sure it was well known to him.

The constable affirmed that the inspector was certainly familiar with the business. [This suggested that EVERYBODY is.] He said he would contact the inspector accordingly.

I sat at the table. Through the window I could hear the distant roar of Ibbo Mandaza's tractor pounding over my land. My frustration was agonizing. Lying on the table was an old edition of The Daily News and in the top panel, below the broad title, the telephone number was given. What the hell. I would phone them and tell them what was going on. A receptionist told me that the news desk would not be open until 9 o'clock.

Shortly after 9 a.m., I phoned again and spoke to a person on the news desk. He listened to my situation and said they would certainly follow up; a car would shortly be on its way to the farm. Then I received a call to say that the News crew had lost their way. I sensed my precipitate action could end in drama.

The Warvets had been to the field during the morning to watch the tractor ploughing but had left to go to the bar. It was vital that the newsmen came in to get their camera shots whilst the Warvets were away. I was at the entrance when a reporter and a cameraman arrived at 11 am.; so I rushed them down to the field explaining the danger to themselves and their equipment should the Warvets catch up with them. They got the message and sped off to take their shots. I stood concealed with a cell phone watching out for the Warvets and biting my nails. The Daily News men took photos, asked a few questions and soon drove away. Shortly afterwards the Warvets returned.

It was a narrow thing. Phew!

Monday 5th. November 2001

I phoned the DA this morning on a bad line. In reply to my questions, he said that he had asked Inspector Mukungunugwa some while ago to find out which persons were coming onto Stockade. He fell short of saying that they would be stopped. He said he would remind the Inspector about this and I expressed my thanks.

He went on to say that it had been noted that our farm had been the subject of a piece in the Daily News. He asked me to wait and began speaking to somebody in Shona. By the time he was ready to resume, my signal was so poor that I couldn't hear him. However I had learnt that he would be contacting the police inspector.

Martin brought out the copy of the Daily News. There was a picture of the big tractor surging over the land bearing down on the camera in a cloud of dust. The short accompanying article was confined to facts. Although it stated that the tractor belonged to Ibbo Mandaza, it was not contentious and the reader was left to draw his own conclusion of Mandaza's involvement. Mandaza runs a pro ZANU PF newspaper.

Reading ART farm costings, I see that the input cost for maize production last season was about $ 60 000 per hectare. Surely the cost this year will be much higher—$ 100 000 at least. I anticipate the "authorities" telling me that the field is just for Simukayi. Simukayi, who is always scrounging for money in one way or another and who gets his Chibuku beer on credit from the barkeeper.

The Tredar guard from Maypark was here recently to talk with our guards. I asked him some questions. It seems that on Maypark there are eight permanent Warvets—six men and two women. The Parkes family has gone through some distressing, even frightening times, in the past months. The dwelling houses have been besieged and Stewart Parkes, the son, was assaulted by the women Warvets wielding sticks. "They are the worst," said the guard.

It appears that an accommodation has been reached whereby, in exchange for preparing certain lands and providing some inputs, the Warvets have agreed not to interfere with farm work. Notwithstanding, the farm workers are forced to attend regular ZANU PF meetings and indoctrination sessions. Also the two Parkes families have to account for any visitors they have. This I couldn't believe; but the guard assured me that on the arrival of a visitor, the Warvets will not hesitate to knock on the door and demand to know his identity. The guard's words were: "Yes. You may say it is peaceful but everything is done by force." This sounds paradoxical but the meaning is clear.

There is a rule in nature which is applicable here: the parasite will keep its host alive for as long as it can provide nutrient.

Tuesday 6th. November 2001

Activity on my invaded field was confined to two youths moving a few bales off the land. No Warvet vehicles were reported to have come to the scene and the big Renault tractor belonging to Ibbo Mandaza did not come. Albeit, I am by no means complacent. There are some big guns conducting these farm invasions.

I do not forget the swift reconnaissance made by a team led by a Colonel Matarutse; the frequent, purposeful incursions by unknown persons driving out from Harare; the paranormal reluctance of the District Administration and the local police to respond to my complaints; and now the involvement of Ibbo Mandaza, high-powered confidant of the Party and government ministers. One has good reason to believe that what, on the surface, appears to be spontaneous, lawless incursions are in fact well orchestrated.

At the top, there is co-ordination between ZANU PF, the government, the army, the Warvets, the police. That is a formidable array of weaponry to face up to.

If there is a saving grace, it will be because the co-ordination and administration is in all probability chaotic. Unfortunately, these people have a point of ready common agreement. It is basic to their mentality. The best way of getting what you want is to use force and fear.

So today I wait—and wonder.

The District Administrator 3 .12 .01
Concession.
Dear Sir,

New Invasion

I refer to the telephone conversations I had with Mr.Manyame of your office and Insp.Mukungunugwa, Z.R.P.Marlborough, on the morning of Thursday 28th. November.

In these calls I reported that this property had just been invaded by a party consisting of seven men and two women. The gang had entered by foot from the direction of Danbury. Once on Stockade, they had set about axing down trees and constructing a hut.

The information was given to me by the Tredar guard and by my employees. I did not follow up personally for fear of violence. However, my workers say that the people came from Mgutu farm.

When I reported to Mr.Manyame, he asked me to contact Inspector Mukungunugwa and went on to say that a representative from your office would accompany the Inspector to discover who the invaders were.

I was able to reach the Inspector by cell phone and he was at that very time on his way to your office in Concession. I requested him to bring up the matter with you and to please follow it up. Plainly, neither Mr.Manyame nor the Inspector could shed light on who the invaders might be.

On Friday 29th. November, a gang of five men returned to the site of the hut and cut more trees for its construction. Once again they left leaving no presence. It is pertinent to observe that at this point of time, 3rd. December, no attempt of land cultivation has been made whatsoever. In fact we have recent video film of this section of the farm showing that there has been no settlement and no cropping.

I am gravely concerned. This incursion bears the hallmark of being objectively planned. Escalation could follow. This flies in the face of the Abuja Accord and also the President's public assurance concerning the security of single farm ownership.

Of immediate anxiety to me is the threat to the gazetted Protected Forest. As you will know from previous correspondence, half the farm falls into the afforested reserve and indeed we only have 100 hectares of arable land. Much expenditure of work and money has been spent over many years on the protection and upkeep of the forest. Thousands of indigenous trees have been reared and planted. At present levels the cost would be nothing short of $200 per tree.

Last Thursday the gang of invaders cut down 177 trees in the space of a morning.

Please would you endeavour to establish who is behind this latest invasion and restrain them from further wanton destruction of the natural flora and consequential impoverishment of the very land itself.

I look forward to hearing from you.

Yours sincerely,

R.F.Wiles.

cc. Insp.ZRP. Minister of Enviroment; GM Forestry Commission; UNDP et al.

2002

Monday 11th. February 2002

This morning I was told by Johannes of events that took place in the district yesterday.

A ZANU PF meeting was held at Passaford at the farm belonging to Ibbo Mandaza. A verbal message was given to our foreman by a Party youth member. The message was that Johannes and all workers on Stockade should attend the meeting that day. Johannes didn't get the message until 11 a.m.; so didn't arrive until 1 p.m. The meeting began at 10 a.m. and carried on until 5 p.m.

Workers from most of the surrounding area had been summoned; some had come on farm tractors and trailers supplied by the farmers.

The meeting was addressed by Ibbo Mandaza and high-ranking officials of the Party who had come from Bindura and Harare. It was noted that many of the officials came in government registered vehicles.

The people were told that the purpose of this meeting was to establish ZANU PF cells on every farm. A list must be handed in before the close of the meeting giving the names of the persons who had been chosen for the position of chairman, secretary, youth chairman, transport organizer etc.

The people were next told that anyone not registered and who were without IDs. should go to Concession within the next two days. Ibbo Mandaza said that he had given the District Administrator written authority to issue registration certificates. There would be no delay. Mandaza himself would lay on a lorry to get people to Concession. It would leave Trianda Farm at 8 a.m. every morning.

From now on, ZANU PF supportive rallies were to be held in the area each weekend. The newly-appointed Party chairmen were charged with organizing attendance and transport. They were also charged with compiling a list of all the persons living on the farm to which they belonged and to handing this in. In this way anyone not attending the rallies could be identified and dealt with. They would lose their possessions and be "thrown out".

Special mention was made of Stockade Farm and Raffeen Farm neither of which had sent their workers to previously held ZANU PF rallies held at Belgownie. A large fat man addressing the crowd said that those farmers who didn't collaborate would quickly lose their farms. A man dressed in a smart suit and wearing dark glasses spoke. Apparently he was an official from Bindura. He singled out the persons in the crowd from Raffeen Farm saying that he knew Raffeen had held MDC meetings there. "In Bindura we have a VERY thick file on all those living at Raffeen," [here he demonstrated the width of the file]. "I am telling you; we are watching you; you have been warned."

Towards the end of the meeting, a large bale containing ZANU PF Tee-shirts was broken open and the newly appointed chairmen were instructed to hand them out. Douglas claimed confidently that he was the ZANU PF chairman for Stockade and accepted some Tee-shirts for distribution. Ironically Douglas has never been a farm worker and now he is no longer a factory worker. His unwelcome presence on the farm is only due to his marrying Eugenia who rents the farm store. Nothing phases this sort of person. He even volunteered himself as local transport commissar, no doubt with a mind to commandeering my farm vehicles.

The above is the short account of the gathering as related to me by Johannes. Because the meeting lasted for a full SEVEN HOURS, obviously a lot more was said by the conveners. I take it these were salient points as they seemed to him.

In answer to my enquiries, Johannes asked for the day off to go to Concession on Tuesday to get his ID. He also explained that he would be obliged to attend the ZANU PF meetings as would everybody else on the farms around here. They know that ZANU PF threats turn into reality. Only two weeks ago the farm foreman on Danbury, our immediate neighbour, was singled out in front of the workforce and beaten so severely that he was hospitalized.

On Maypark Farm, also adjoining us, a ZANU PF gang descended on the farm compound and assaulted the occupants forcing them to flee their houses. Thereupon the workers' personal possessions were trashed or stolen.

In each case [and countless others beside], the assailants are known and witnesses abound but charges are never laid against them by the police. This is just as well known to the humble farm worker as it is to the farmer who employs him. Faced with the overwhelming power of a state-sponsored terror campaign, I can hardly expect the poor man to face up to pain and loss for the sake of an ideal.

It is interesting to note the government's very sudden decision to fast-track registration of those farm workers without IDs. This is a complete reversal. Only a week ago two of our young workers were told at the DA's office to "come back after the election". There seems to be something behind it, otherwise Ibbo Mandaza would not have gone to the length of laying on his transport to take people to the DA's office at Concession. If this is happening throughout the farming areas, it will be the prelude for something. But what?

Wednesday 13th.February 2002 Stockade.

Yesterday, some two hundred people from farms in the district gathered at Ibbo Mandaza's farm at Passaford in the early morning. These were persons hoping to obtain personal registration certificates. To this end, they had been promised transport to get them to Concession where the District Administration officers would issue the certificates.

Feedback suggests that the whole exercise has been no more than a subterfuge. Mandaza told the crowd that the DA was not ready to handle registrations that day; a few more arrangements had to be made. Meanwhile the transport lorries, which were on hand, would take everybody to Bindura where a ZANU PF rally was being held. Before boarding the lorries, ZANU PF Tee-shirts would be issued and these should be worn.

My informant said that most of the gathered farm workers were disgruntled and headed back to their homes. However all Mandaza's own workers, clad in their Tee-shirts, climbed into the transport and were driven off to Bindura.

It now appears that the promised registration exercise is nothing but a fabrication; a simple ruse to corral farm workers for a ZANU PF rally.

Stockade Farm Report Monday 18th.February 2002.

It will be recalled that at the ZANU PF meeting held at Passaford on 12th. February, the farm workers were told that they must all attend the Party rallies, which would take place every weekend. Threats were made that those who failed to attend would be identified and dealt with severely.

On Sunday morning, the 17th., two Landrover Santanas attached to the Z.R.P. Marlborough, drove out to Trianda Farm, a farm which adjoins Stockade. At least one of the drivers was a police officer of senior rank.

The vehicles had been sent out to take people from the farm village to the ZANU PF rally. Accordingly, the two vehicles "were filled to overload" with men, women and children some wearing the Tee-shirts with which they had been issued the previous week.

The company set off for Passaford at 11.30. When they got there, it was to learn that the venue for the rally was now Bindura, some two hours drive away. The policemen decided to return their passengers to the farm.

Simukayi

Readers of this journal will have long ago acceded that Simukayi stands out as the chief instrument of suffering endured by our little community. Page after page reveals him as a monster. The type of life I have led has not exposed me to monsters and certainly not ones enjoying state funding and protection. My early reaction was one of disbelief. People couldn't behave like this ALL the time. They must show signs of human origin at SOME times. If Simukayi is anything to go by, this is not so. It sets ones mind working on theories such as the influence of Evil in the world.

I thought the following notes, which never formed part of my diary, might be of some interest. I might head them: *One Way to Relieve Frustration*. However, it would be advisable not to repeat the method too often.

In a previous report I told of how Simukayi had come onto the farm and, announcing himself as the Warvet commander of the district, selected one of the worker's houses for his headquarters. The house was shared by two workers and these two unfortunates had their belongings unceremoniously thrown out by Simukayi and two of his thugs.

"The Boss has given this house to me," the workers were told when they returned to find Simukayi installed and their few possessions strewn about outside, "He said you must find somewhere else to live." The men accepted their lot meekly enough. They would have recognized Simukayi as a liar.

It was really quite unnecessary for Simukayi to lie, but then I have learnt that with these people lying is so entrenched into the consciousness that it is an automatic response whatever the circumstance. With brute authority behind him, I stood no chance of removing Simukayi from the house—everybody knew that—he most of all. In short time, one of my gum poles was cut down and erected as a flagpole. From then on I seethed within, each time I looked across at the compound and saw the ZANU PF flag fluttering in the wind.

The house stood by itself on a slight rise. It had been built of bricks on a high foundation. The roof was of corrugated iron and there was a deep front veranda. Access to it was by way of a rough track or by footpaths winding through tall maize plants or rank grass. It being the headquarters of the feared Warvets, most people kept their distance. Simukayi ordered a water tank to be built some thirty metres behind it. Due to the vegetation, the nearest houses were out of direct sight.

There were times when there were three or four Warvets staying at the house together with one or two youths known as their mujibhas and women to cook. Collectively, they were known as "The Comrades".

However, Simukayi was the more permanent and in due course he installed his wife, a fat, heavy woman with a boy of about six and a girl child of about three. She was indoctrinated with the revolutionary hatred against whites, as I was to learn when I had the misfortune to cross her on a few occasions when I found her cutting wood in my nature reserve.

For weeks and weeks we had been subjected to harassment on almost a daily basis. This would be in the form of threats, insults, extortion, stoppages in production, theft and damage to property. At the same time, law enforcement no longer existed, leastwise in respect of the Warvets. For all intent and purposes they enjoyed immunity from prosecution however heinous the crime.

Faced with such abuse of justice and morality and with no hope of redress, can fill one with despair or angry frustration according to one's temperament.

One day I sat at my desk and brooded. How to get back at my chief bane, my tormentor? There could be nothing overt. All white farmers heed the maxim: "Never take the law into your own hands." Whilst the Warvets and Party stalwarts can safely ignore it, woe betide the farmer who does so. The law will descend on him like an avenging demon. No; my revenge had to be subtle and secret—very secret. Witchcraft! It was the only way.

Unfortunately, I had not taken Witchcraft as a school subject and, in later years, had never thought to enrol for such a course in the field of Adult Education. However, over the years I had perforce observed instances of witchcraft in Africa and this, with a slender memory of the opening scene from Macbeth, was the sum of my knowledge.

It must not be forgotten that my fight is for a cause. This is to save all the natural living things, which have their abode on my property, from suffering and death. This is a truth. This is reality. Who better to help me with this spot of business than Nature herself? I set out on a round of the farm to make a suitable collection for my new found calling.

The first to be visited were the three poor trees that had been axed down by Simukayi, George and Mapolisa; the Acacia, the Msasa and the Jacaranda. From each I shaved off some slivers of bark and took tiny chips from the stumps. A skeleton of a dead duiker provided me with a hollow horn; a civet, which had had the misfortune to drown itself in a pond, yielded a tuft of grizzled hair; some delicate bones from a little rodent were poked from an owl's pellet.

I was lucky enough to find suspended by a thread from a small tree branch, a cluster of little narrow twigs glued together so as to resemble a Roman fasca. This, I understand, is the protective sheath for the larva of a certain insect. I thought some thick spider web wouldn't go amiss too.

Then I found a mass of exuding gum from an Acacia tree; legs from a dead stag beetle made a contribution. What should I come across but three tip-wilters having a rare old time sucking the sap from a succulent shoot of a Whitethorn. These are tricky insects to catch as I know from experience when finding them on rose bushes. Apart from being wary, they defend themselves by squirting a noxious, highly-scented juice at you. This day I was dexterous and determined. The three tip-wilters were sacrificed for the cause and in the doing yielded wings and a quantity of turquoise-blue serum. Finally I climbed to a field where antbears dug their holes in powdery, bright-red soil. Some of this I collected in a bag.

The ingredients were locked in a drawer of my desk. Although nobody enters my office, there should be no accidental discovery. I decided to concoct two cunning packages. There was far too much material, but that would make selection easier.

Attention to other matters prevented me from doing anything further in the witchcraft line for a while. Then one day I spread my strange, bizarre collection before me. The duiker horn was stuffed with the red soil; like oxide, it stains blood red! Above this went in bits of this and that; finally it was sealed with hair from the civet and a wodge of tree gum. There was still more to do to make it look authentic. The final package had to look grimy and, if possible, smelly.

A friend many months previously had shown me some cloth, which an African witchdoctor had told her was much feared by people. It was a red cotton material with streaks of black and white. She had given me a piece and I had kept it. It looked pretty innocuous but you never know the strange quirks of man. I dug it out from somewhere and for good measure made it dirty and greasy and then soaked it in blood from the dog's meat. By this time it resembled a piece of stiff oil cloth unwashed in fifty years.

I took up the horn which, I thought with a smile, should be called a witch's hornucopia [after all there was no one around to groan], and rolled it up in the cloth. In turn the cloth was bound up tightly with some thin twine retrieved from the dusty floor of a bagging shed. There was to be a third wrapping. This time it was a small plastic bag I picked from a handy rubbish dump at the side of the road. The idea of all these wrappings was to appeal to the inquisitive side of man's nature.

The second package required greater ingenuity. This time I had to make a sort of hollow cylinder out of the sections of bark from the three trees. I think I managed this by binding them round with bits of thin rusty wire and stuffing gruesome objects in as I went along. I craftily arranged it so that a few thorns protruded through the sides. These were intended to prick the fingers of anyone taking a hold. An extension at one end incorporated a hook so that should the opportunity arise, the sinister looking package could be hung up.

After such a show of keen enthusiasm on my part to become a successful sorcerer, I regret to say that the two magical objects were returned to the desk draw and remained there for many weeks. I cannot now remember when I decided to make a move and at that time I had no intention of incorporating any such matter in my diary notes. I do know that the house of the Warvets was occupied. Simukayi's wife and children were generally there because I saw her frequently fetching in firewood. Half a dozen ducks were kept by her on the veranda. The mujibha, Andrew, stayed at the house more or less continuously but Simukayi himself was often away. He was presumably making somebody else's life hell at these times. Of course we never knew where he went or when he would return.

It may have been in July or August when I started looking for my opportunity.

Let me repeat the purpose of my mission. This was to get back at Simukayi. It was essential that he must be completely taken in by the mysterious appearance at his house of my magical concoction. He would know for sure that the appearance would not come unaccompanied. Inevitably, it would be linked to a magic spell. Of the two, the latter should be the most psychologically effective. It could worry him enough to drive him out.

For my ruse to succeed, absolutely nothing should be allowed to go wrong. I faced a lot of difficulties. Secrecy was vital. On that score, I reasoned quickly that I must not trust anybody; the Tredar guards; or even Johannes. That meant that I must deliver my package to Simukayi's house myself. It was going to be tricky.

The compound is about a mile away from my homestead and ever since the Warvets descended on us and set up their H.Q. there, I have kept well clear. Additionally, it is a well known fact that on every farm, whatever the white boss does or wherever he goes, his movements are always noted by the resident Africans. It follows that I could hardly take a stroll through the compound, let alone enter the dreaded ZANU PF strongpoint, without stimulating instant chatter.

It looked as if my foray would have to be made at dead of night. Even so; when doing so, I dare not be seen approaching or leaving. If I was spotted the game would be up.

One night, I donned some drab, darkish clothing, stuffed the duiker horn magic pack in the pocket of my zip jacket, let myself out of the gate, shooing back the two dogs [wanting to come with me of ALL things!], and set off down the farm road, stumbling somewhat because I dared not use a torch. One of the Tredar guards was supposed to be on patrol and I didn't want him to see me.

I approached the compound by way of a grass paddock. That way I could get to the Warvets house without passing any other houses. I had clambered through a wire fence and had no more than about thirty metres to go when I heard a sound ahead of me. There was a woman drawing water from the water tank between me and Simukayi's house. Why on earth should she be doing this so late? I stood stock-still while she filled her can. The tap stopped running and I heard the woman move away. I was not seen; but it meant that somebody was still awake and the woman could indeed have come from the Warvets' house. I decided to abort the operation, stealthily withdrew, and headed back home.

A few days later I was given another opportunity. I had learnt that Simukayi was away and that the wife had left earlier that morning apparently on her way to go shopping. There was the mujibha, but he too had not been seen recently.

By good luck, a matter relating to the compound was drawn to my attention. I cannot remember what it was, but it gave me the opportunity to put on an act of exasperation and annoyance [emotions of mine with which my staff are familiar] and loudly announce that I would have to look into the matter myself. With that, I set off determinedly down the path to the compound waving aside any offers to accompany me.

Ah, unknown to anybody, I carried something in my pocket which would have interested them! The narrow compound paths wind and twist through grass 7ft. high. I hoped that I wouldn't bump into someone when I turned into the path that led to the Warvets's clearing.

My luck held. At the Warvets house I stopped and looked all about. The tall grass effectively screened it from all other houses. From where I stood there was not a soul to be seen. I mounted the veranda. I tried the house door. It was locked. At one end of the veranda seven ducks were confined in a small, dirty cage—I felt sorry for the poor creatures. Alongside them was an upturned box with an old cloth on the top. I placed the package on the box and covered it with the cloth. Nobody saw me as I left. My mission was accomplished.

There was no possible way of my knowing what Simukayi's reaction was to the "witch's curse". I can relate his and his family's movements only, as I came to learn of them.

The wife departed for her home village almost immediately. She took the children and most of her belongings with her. Some five or six weeks later I was told that the girl child had died. In African society more deaths are put down to witchcraft than to natural causes. If Simukayi DID fall for my hoax, he is certain to believe that the child's death was due to it.

It was about this time that there was a strong rumour in the district, reaching as far as the police, that Simukayi himself was dead. In farm homesteads celebratory parties were held. It had been generally noted that he had been looking progressively sicker and both Martin and Johannes had observed that his body was covered in sores. It was felt that AIDS must have finally got him.

To everybody's dismay, Simukayi resurfaced. I never heard where he had disappeared to. Some said that he had been forced to lie low; it having been discovered that he had hi-jacked a truckload of government fertilizer, sold the fertilizer to the waiting peasant farmers and pocketed the money. Well that story would fit Simukayi alright.

With Simukayi's return from the dead, we lived in trepidation of him re-occupying the Warvet quarters on the farm. In fact he called in at the farm store a couple of times but never went back to living in the house. Naturally enough, I feared that some other Warvets might take up abode there in his place. It required another visit.

A problem arose concerning the farm store; the Tredar guard led me to the compound. I directed him ahead of me and said I would follow. At the Warvet house I stopped; I entered; it was empty. I hung my remaining spooky collection high up near the ceiling. I wasn't seen. The house has remained empty ever since; even the flag pole has fallen down.

21st.March 2002

Alarming and distressing events have been happening on Danbury, the next-door farm belonging to the Bayley family; our kind and neighbourly friends of forty years. I am implicated indirectly, so am inserting an account of these happenings. The Warvets operate under a common command and Simukayi is often seen going to Danbury. Events there could be duplicated here.

It is common knowledge that government is using the country-wide Warvet structure to implement the programme of farm take-overs and the eviction of the farm owners. In turn, the Warvets muster ZANU PF supporters and unemployed youths to forcefully stop all farm work and to threaten and generally harass the farmer and his workers. This has been the pattern on Danbury.

The Warvets assigned to Danbury are one Chengerai and Gendi [or Ghandi]. Chengerai is a cripple. He is driven from place to place; but from his car or wheel-chair he conducts his venomous campaign with extraordinary vigour. Some three weeks ago, accompanied by his gang of thugs, he arrived on the farm to find the workers employed on cultivating a seed-maize field. The farm foreman was in charge of them. The workers were called together at the edge of the field. Thereupon Chengerai ordered his henchmen to single out the foreman and beat him. This they did to such good effect that he was left lying on the ground unable to move. Later he was lifted up and taken to hospital by Tommy Bayley. The police have made no charge of assault against Chengerai or his accomplices.

The other Warvet, Gendi, faces a charge of stock theft. A cow was slaughtered and the meat found in his War-vet headquarters on Danbury. The case is of long standing. So far it has appeared on the court agenda seventeen times. Remarkably, it has been adjourned all seventeen times. Meanwhile Gendi has been enjoying freedom of action out of custody.

In the late afternoon of Friday, 15th.March, Chengerai and Gendi drove into the Danbury building complex in a convoy of vehicles carrying some fifty supporters. The workers employed in the workshop and milling shed were attacked and badly beaten. In the ensuing fracas, the invaders managed to obtain the keys to the sheds. Meal was stolen and diesel fuel was drained from the farm tractors and poured into the vehicles belonging to the War-vet party. Three of the workshop staff ran to the main homestead to seek refuge.

There are three residential houses on Danbury. The old homestead is the home of Tom Bayley senior and his wife Bobs. Some four hundred metres distant and well screened from the first, is the house occupied by Tommy Bayley, the son. He lives with his wife Trish and their baby daughter Diana [2years old]. Further off again and quite out of sight, there is a cottage which is rented by a working couple, Mr. and Mrs. Blair, who commute from town daily.

In what was obviously a prearranged plan, the senior War-vets directed their invasion party to completely surround each of the two houses belonging to the family. Roads and pathways connecting the two or indeed in any other direction, were effectively blocked. Communication was confined to cell phones or the farm radio system—Agric-Alert.

It was now evening and the light fading. However, the invasion force had come prepared for a long stay. They had brought with them bags and bundles containing food and clothing; AND of course, drink! They had also brought African drums or tom-toms. Wood was collected from all about and fires lit at the corners of the houses and at the farm buildings.

The invaders then commenced Tao-taoing, as the Africans call it. To the calling of ZANU PF slogans and the chanting of war-like "chimurenga" songs, the drumming commenced. At regular intervals members of the gang circled the old people's house, banging on the doors and tattooing on the windows.

At their homestead, Tom and Bobs, by then joined by the three fugitives from the workshop, had locked themselves in, securing all doors and windows, closing the curtains. It must have been a bizarre scene touched with pathos.

You see, Tom is ninety years of age. He has recently suffered from a fall and a leg injury. Locomotion can only be effected by support from his walking cage. Bobs is eighty-one. She has been suffering from Parkinson's disease for many years and of course exhibits the unfortunate shaking of this malady. Less obvious but of equal concern, Bobs also suffers from a heart condition, which is only controlled by heavy medication. This then was the little team called upon to withstand the determined efforts of those outside to frighten them to death.

The disturbances went on all night and sleep was out of the question. By good chance, the Africans from the workshop made their escape from the house at first light.

As can be seen, Tommy Bayley had the responsibility of his mother and father, his wife and little daughter on his hands. Experience of the past two years had shown him that attempts to parley with the kind of people presently laying siege to them, was futile and dangerous. Most of the leaders are psychopaths; their followers, easy victims of crowd fever.

The crowd had probably not set out for blood. If drink and drugs were being taken, the best strategy was to keep silent and under cover. Tommy proved himself right. No attempt was made to break into the houses.

The next day, some policemen arrived. The Officer-in-Charge explained that he had not come in his capacity as a policeman but as a member of the district Land Committee. It was necessary for Tommy to "negotiate" with these people. A stalemate was inevitable and the police went away. The invaders remained.

The road into Stockade. My homestead lies beyond the belt of trees.

The homestead.

Saturday night was a repeat.

The innocent renters, Gerry and Cheryl Blair, had been allowed to come and go from their cottage unhindered. This was not to last. Perhaps it had something to do with their surname—the British PM is hated by Mugabe. On Sunday their cottage was broken into and all available food and drink was stolen. This was while they were there!

Police? No action. Incidentally, after the theft, a large picture of Mugabe was pinned to the door. That's one in the eye for Tony.

Monday, Tuesday, Wednesday, Thursday, there was some coming and going of officials, all to no effect. I have been listening out on the radio and spoken briefly on the phone. It seems that there is a determined ploy to drive the whole family off the farm.

Old Tom has lived on the farm since he came out from Danbury, in Essex, as a young assistant seventy years ago. The farm is his life and his pride; highly productive and carefully conserved. Tommy was born on the farm and knows every inch of it like the back of his hand. He is a non-stop worker.

Now the Bayley families face eviction without compensation or damages and certainly without compassion.

In the past months, certain persons have been pegging holdings for themselves on Danbury. They hardly fall into the category of the landless poor. Among them are a business man, a police officer, an army officer, a deputy minister, a woman banker, a medical doctor with ambitious farming and business aspirations [the now familiar Dr. Ngwenya]. Whatever their calling, all may be termed moneyed people; all will be looking to get something for nothing; all will be ZANU PF adherents.

You may be sure; the invading gang will not be making their noise without payment.

The siege has continued. Tommy hasn't seen his old folks, who are only 500 metres away for six days. Neither have any of their friends and neighbours.

Last night the "tao-taoing" reached a crescendo of drumming and noise. Tonight it continues relentlessly. We hear the drumming on Stockade. The Bayley families grimly sit it out in their respective solitudes.

Tomorrow is Friday 22nd.March 2002. The funeral takes place of a murdered farmer—a friend. Tommy and Trish would have wished to attend. It looks as if they will be prevented from doing so.

This is Zimbabwe behind the smoke-screen of lies.

Night of 24th\25th.March 2002

I had a disturbed night. The events taking place on Danbury have been very worrying and on the Sunday I had spent several hours writing up an account from the information gathered from phone calls, radio messages and conversation with some Danbury-based Africans. Of course, the Danbury drama was just an additive to the stress caused by the general crisis in Zimbabwe and one's own problematical future. Thus, when I retired to bed at about 10.30, my mind was in that condition of being restive and exhausted simultaneously.

My dogs, Moppet and Humba, woke me by their barking. I put on the bedside light. My watch said it was 20 minutes to 1 o'clock. I was unable to bestir myself, which was most unusual for me. I felt as if I had been drugged. When the dogs became quiet, I thankfully told myself that they must have been disturbed by the Tredar guard on his night patrol. Then, I must have fallen into a deep sleep.

I was to learn that the dogs had not been disturbed by the guard and that their fury had been directed at other persons who had come up to the security gate in the perimeter fence. The chain of events taking place at this time was related to me by Johannes in the early morning. This is what he told me.

On Sunday, Johannes went to visit his relative, a grandfather, by the name of Gift Jack. This man lives in the single cottage set back in the trees at the juncture of the Selby road and the Maypark turn-off. Johannes left for home quite late, some time after 11 o'clock. The moon is presently full. The walk would take him no more than half an hour.

When Johannes was about fifty metres short of the Stockade farm entrance, he noticed a vehicle approaching from the direction of Passaford. The vehicle moved very slowly and occasionally stopped, switching off its lights. Johannes suspected thieves; irrigation equipment was close by in the field. Also not far away, at the main reservoir, was the irrigation pump with its large electric motor and starter switches.

When the vehicle moved forward again, Johannes slipped into the long grass and under the wire fence on the Maypark side of the road. By chance, the car, a light blue Mazda 323 four-door salon, stopped immediately opposite to where Johannes was hidden.

Three African men got out of the car. In the moonlight, it appeared that they were wearing dark clothing and small caps. One of the men, Johannes described as being tall and burley. He wore a bulky garment which may have been a work-jacket.

Johannes says he heard the men speak in Shona, as follows:
The driver: "Right. Have you taken everything? What about the gun?"
The reply: "Yes I've got everything."
Driver: "What about the cutter?"
The reply: "Yes. We have everything."
Driver: "When the old man comes out, kill him. Just kill him. Don't hang about and don't take anything from the house. Be quick!"

The driver got into the car, started up and switched on his lights. The car moved down the road in the direction of Selby. It then turned round, slowed down and stopped briefly. Then the driver restarted and drove slowly past Johannes in the Passaford direction once more. Meanwhile, the two other men had walked up the road and turned in at the Stockade entrance. This gave Johannes the opportunity to leave his position and cross the road into our land. He still had in his mind that the men might be intending to steal the electric motor, but he saw them walk past the track which leads to the reservoir and carry on down the road to my house.

Johannes had removed his bright yellow Tee-shirt to make himself less conspicuous. However, he still feared to follow directly behind the two strangers. If they turned round they would certainly spot him in the moonlight. He therefore circled right round my security fence, which with its massive thorn hedge is well-nigh impregnable, and through the bush so as to approach my gate from the opposite direction. [In doing so his clothing became matted with "blackjack"seeds!]

Low, leafy shrubs enabled Johannes to creep fairly close to the gate unobserved although he was fearful of the noise he made by treading on twigs and dry leaves. He discovered the men trying to break the lock and chain securing the gate. They appeared to have difficulty because the large padlock was fastened on the inside of the gate and could not be reached and twisted or cut from the outside.

Moppet and Humber had now come to the gate and were barking furiously. This agitated the men. Johannes listened to them talking.

"What are we going to do? Those dogs are too cheeky."

"If we get inside we'll have to face the dogs. They're too cheeky. What do we do?"

"No. There's some meat and muti [poison] at the car. We must get it. This is a mistake."

The two men walked back to the road entrance. When they had gone, Johannes ran diagonally to the maize field where he hoped to find the night watchman, Kariza. He observed that the car on the road had put on its lights and was moving towards the farm entrance. He assumed that the men had contacted the driver. Johannes could not find Kariza so he next went to call the Tredar guard. After some frustration, he eventually found him at the Fig Tree House. Passing his own house, he called out to his wife, Sinai, that he was back and alright but she should remain inside with the children.

Johannes and the Tredar guard, Philip, approached my house once more, remaining out of sight. The two men had returned to the gate and were again trying to break it open. They were talking between themselves. The dogs were barking.

"It's no good. This dog is still too cheeky. What do we do?"

"No, they are fierce. Try another way."

Johannes and the guard were also in a quandary. The guard suggested they blow his whistle. Johannes said, no, they were only two and the men had a gun. They decided to run and call out other men from the farm compound and to arm themselves with weapons of some kind. This they did, but when the reinforcements had been mustered and come to my house, the two men had gone. They heard the car on the Selby road driving away.

My people say that at that point, they tried to summon me by blowing repeatedly on the whistle. I never heard it. Perhaps if they had clanged the ploughshare, which hung by the gate, I would have heard that better. My men left to go home at about 3am.

When I surfaced from sleep in the morning and went out, my workers were there in force to tell me all that had taken place. I have to say that I was taken aback and quite shaken. I couldn't believe that I should have been so utterly comatose whilst all this activity had been going on. Sure enough I saw where an attempt had been made to force open the padlock. However I was even more alarmed when I was shown that handfuls of pork meat and bones had been lobbed over the 8ft. gate and had landed on the driveway inside. It was scattered all about and here were Moppet and Humba sniffing around at my feet as I was examining it.

Poisoning of dogs in order to gain access to premises is now common practice amongst the criminal fraternity. A search around the area turned up a few pieces of grey corrugated paper. My men assure me that a certain unregistered rat poison is sold in such paper. The poison is on sale in the Mbare African market and nowhere else. It is cheap and deadly to rats and everything else. The poison is composed of small black granules—like caviar. The pieces of greasy, half-cooked meat had been freely dressed with it.

Alarm bells! Had Moppet and Humber eaten any? They would have had access to it at any time in the past five hours. They both looked fine, but I could take no chances so I collected the meat in a container and sped off to town with the two dogs.

Charles Waghorn, the vet, knew all about the Mbare poison. He assured me that if the dogs had swallowed any, they would have died in fifteen minutes. The pieces of grey paper were immediately recognised by Charles' African attendant. A lab.test was uncalled for in the obvious circumstances. My clever dogs had refused the poison and escaped. "You are lucky. Go home and look to your security," Charles said.

I record my thanks to Johannes for his loyal courage, to Moppet and Humba for their unswerving defence of the home, and, yet again, to my guardian angel. Had I woken and gone to the gate to investigate I could have been shot.

It was not "luck" that saved me but timely psychic intervention. There are mysteries affecting the sub-conscience which often bear upon our destiny.

This nasty business has meant employing two additional Tredar guards with dogs, which we can ill afford.

It was unfortunate that the money had run out on Johannes' cell phone. Had he been able to contact me by cell phone I could have summoned Tredar base for back up and they might have nabbed the three men. Johannes feels that the big man could well have been George. He also feels that he has seen the Mazda 323 before; stopped at Douglas' bar. Most unfortunately there was no opportunity for him to read the number plate.

It has been reported that George and Simukayi were at Douglas' bar earlier on Sunday evening. Moffu has also been around. After some weeks of absence, it seems that these three Warvets have begun visiting this area again. This is bad news.

Friday 29th. March 2002

With regard to the ongoing troubles at Danbury, I have learnt today that the Warvets and their ZANU PF followers, beat one of the farm workers so viciously that he died. The body, which had been taken to Harare, was brought out again to the farm. The burial took place this morning. The identities of the killers are known.

Isaiah, brother of the deceased had also been beaten at the same time but managed to escape. He has since been in hiding but returned today with his family in order to attend the funeral of his dead brother and to be with the father and other relatives.

When the burial ceremony was over; Isaiah, with his wife and infant child, made their way to the Old Mazowe Road in order to get a lift back to their safe haven in town. However, word had been passed to the Warvets of Isaiah's movements and a gang of men wearing ZANU PF Tee-shirts laid in wait for him on the road. By good luck, Isaiah himself spotted them and had sufficient distance to make an escape. He is lean and strong. He back-tracked through the bush, hurriedly collected his wife with her baby, his father and a younger brother and sought escape in another direction. I was standing in the Stockade farm bwalo at about 6.30 in the evening when they came through. Isaiah explained that he hoped they might get a lift on the Selby road and so avoid their pursuers. There was little chance of a lift at this hour so I bundled them into my car and drove them into town. Tommy's brother-in-law met me and they found sanctuary at his place.

In time, I learnt from Isaiah the circumstances of his brother's death. When the Warvets convoy of vehicles drove down the Danbury approach drive and into the farm building complex, there were six farm men working in the maize milling shed. From the open doorway they saw the number of the invading force and heard the raucous, triumphant shouts as the rabble disgorged from the collection of vehicles. This immediately alerted the Danbury men to their peril and in seconds they scrambled out of the mill shed.

Isaiah padlocked the door behind them and he, with two others, ran to their homes in the farm compound half a mile away. Three others, who were already being challenged, by the Warvets, fled across the lawn of the intervening space which lay between the farm sheds and the homestead where Tom and Bobs were present—not yet aware of the dire fate awaiting them.

The leaders of the raid had more in mind than persecuting and driving out the white families. The farm buildings contained great quantities of stored maize, fertilizers and fuel which was theirs for the taking—the sooner the better. They wanted the keys to all the shed locks. Someone must have known that Isaiah kept the keys and he had been spotted running to the compound. Three of the leading Warvets set off for the compound together with a group of young supporters.

They soon found the house where Isaiah dwelt and they burst in upon him. However a minute before, Isaiah had passed the keys to his brother to hide away. The Warvets demanded the keys from Isaiah who protested that he did not have them with him but had left them at the sheds. The men accused him of lying and hit him with sticks about the face and body.

The brother meantime had sneaked to the doorway but when this was noticed by one of the gang members, he took fright and began to run. Run as he might, the Warvet gang tore after him determined to run him down. When the brother tripped and fell the Warvets gathered round like bestial orcs, beating him with sticks and clubs. As they would do to a stricken animal, they continued beating him until he was dead.

The Warvets collected the bunch of keys and word has already spread that they lost no time in opening up the sheds and looting the valuable stocks.

I have asked Isaiah if those Warvets who killed his brother were known.

"Of course," he replied. "I know them. The police know them. Everyone there knows them."

Monday 1st.April 2002
It being the Easter weekend holiday, I had decided to absent myself from the farm on Saturday and Sunday. Farms had been advised that there was to be a ZANU PF victory celebration to be held on the Saturday at Ibbo Mandaza's farm at Passaford starting at 10.30 am "until late". The printed circular asked for donations. It indicated that the amount contributed would reveal if the farmer gave his support to ZANU PF or not. This party cannot refrain from making threats, direct or implied.

The circular was followed up by a visit to Johannes by two of Mandaza's managers and the army officer, called Charlie, who has staked a piece of land for himself on Spa Farm. The three were driven over in the army Puma truck which the officer uses daily for personal transport. Johannes was asked how much I had given. His reply was that the note had come too late and the boss had already gone off on holiday—a well considered reply.

I was away from the farm from about midday on Saturday until Monday. I phoned Johannes on his cell phone and because he reported everything was quiet, I returned during the late morning. I was glad to be back home and looked forward to a relaxed evening. However, at about 6.30 and it becoming dark, I received a cell call from Johannes. The reception was poor and continuously cutting off. The message I got clearly was:

"Those people who want to kill you; they are in the compound."

I also got the words, "I am leaving."

Contact then broke off until I heard what seemed a different, deeper voice say:" Phone back just now." I did and Johannes said "I have told the guard to speak to you at your gate." At that there was no more contact.

A number of things disturbed me.

1. The killers were on the property.
2. The mystery voice.
3. Johannes saying he was leaving.
4. The phone cutting off completely.

Had Johannes been interrupted when making his call to me? Did the second voice belong to a Warvet? Had Johannes been coerced under threat to make a second call to me? Was I being lured into a trap?

If I went to the gate, instead of finding the guard I could find myself facing a Warvet who, since he had a gun, could shoot me at point-blank range through the wire mesh covering the upper half of the gate. I took a chance and standing well back, about thirty metres from the gate, I waved my torch at arms length to my left side in order to attract the Tredar guard. [I figured that if someone took a shot at the torch there was less chance of him hitting me!] There was no response at all. That looked ominous.

Although the three Tredar guards with their dogs SHOULD be on duty, I had no means of communicating with them. They could be up towards the Selby road entrance. Meanwhile three murderers could be at my gate!

Johannes' brief message to me suggested that he had somehow identified the men who had set out on their bloody mission last week. If I could get a back-up from the Tredar base and the Nyabira police, the men might actually be caught. At that point I thought I should raise Tredar base on Agric-alert. I followed this up with phone calls and after about one hour the Tredar OC arrived with two ZRP men, one in plainclothes and one uniformed man armed with a gun. I explained my concerns to them.

No intruders were seen. The three farm-based Tredar guards with their dogs were on duty—they had indeed been further up the road. Johannes was not found at his house which was locked up. The OC Timothy Makanya and the policemen were reluctant to go to the bar in the compound where the occasional shouts of drinkers could be heard. As things stood, it seemed prudent for me to go into town for the night. I was still very uneasy about Johannes but was now confident enough that the three guards and their dogs would prevent a second attempt to get to my house and poison Moppet and Humber. It was about 8pm. when I securely padlocked my gate and drove to town.

The following morning, Tuesday, I rang Johannes' cell number and to my relief, he answered. Everything was alright. He had just been speaking to Timothy Makanya, who had come out to the farm in good time. He said that he had explained what had transpired the previous evening. It was like this.

At 5.30pm. Johannes asked one of the Tredar guards to change into mufti and accompany him to the vicinity of the bar. People were drinking there and they may pick up some useful information on any nefarious goings on. They reached the road area outside the bar and soon Johannes saw someone he recognised, a broad, pale-skinned man wearing glasses. The man, upon seeing Johannes, appeared to turn away as if he didn't wish to be recognized. It was then that Johannes remembered that it was Chengerai Munatsi.

Chengerai had been one of the Warvets who had plagued us in 2000 along with Simukayi, George and Mapolisa. He called himself an engineer, fancied himself as educated. I was told he had been serving a sentence but had been released from prison in a general amnesty.

Johannes learnt that Chengerai had been out for some hours. He had had food with Eugenia, the storekeeper, and was about to return to town having promised to give a lift to Jovita, Eugene's sister, and her husband both of whom had been staying for the weekend. It is said locally that the husband works for the C.I.O. Before leaving, Chengerai called out to others that he would be coming back. He left with his passengers in his white Mazda pick-up.

[Subsequently, Johannes learnt that Chengerai had been seen on Sunday in the morning. He had driven his truck as far as the compound gate which is permanently locked. He had about eight or nine passengers. They all got out, except for one woman, and the party proceeded to walk up to and past the old factory building. They took a brief look around the buildings in the farm bwalo and returned to the vehicle. After a lengthy absence, it seems that Chengerai is taking a renewed interest in this place.]

Shortly after Chengerai's departure, a big truck belonging to Ibbo Mandaza pulled up to the bar. The driver remained in his cab but his only passenger, a tall, bulky African man, shaven headed and wearing a loose-fitting red shirt, descended. The latter asked the people at the bar if Chengerai was around because he had promised to meet him here. It was explained the Chengerai had just left for town but that he would be back.

At this point, Johannes gave a friend of his a hundred dollar note and asked him to engage the big man in conversation and offer him a drink. This the man accepted and in due course he revealed the reason why he had arranged to meet Chengerai. Chengerai had told him that he had had difficulty cutting through a lock. Ordinary cutters were inadequate. The big man had offered him a gas cutter and he had brought the torch and cylinder to give to Chengerai. Johannes looked into the back of the truck; there indeed was the equipment. Naturally enough, he associated all this with the abortive attempt the previous weekend to break through my security gate. Perhaps another try would be made tonight. And Chengerai and the big man were involved.

The big man seemed to be impatient with waiting. He had the driver start up and they drove towards Selby. Twenty minutes later they returned. He again spoke to the people at the bar but soon decided to leave.

It was as a result of the information he was getting between 5.30 and 6.30pm. that Johannes decided to phone me. He thought that another attempt might be made to get at me later in the night. In case of an unpleasant situation arising, he decided to move his family into quarters in the compound. It was most unfortunate that the cell phone calls that evening were so broken and distorted and finally useless. The mystery voice which I heard, was apparently Johannes himself trying to adjust the volume control. And foolishly, the guard who had accompanied Johannes earlier in the evening, never mentioned a word about the proceedings to his senior officer when the latter arrived with the police.

I have since spoken to Timothy and the advice I have been given is to spend the nights in town and to leave the farm well before sundown in case an ambush was laid for me!

Stockade Thursday 4th.April 2001

There is more. On Tuesday last, our workers were in the irrigation field weeding the lines of nimo beans. A man entered the field and came towards Johannes who was supervising the work. The man wore a ZANU PF Tee-shirt displaying the face of Robert Mugabe.

Upon Johannes' enquiry, the man said that his name was Mavingeri. He added that he was the Warvet base commander for the whole area to the north of here. He stayed on Tavydale farm next door to Belgownie.

Johannes said that this Mavingeri seemed to be unsure of his words, hesitant in his conversation, "beating about the bush". Nevertheless, the words he spoke were in some way connected with the status and size of the farm. He also asked if Warvet Simukayi [our particular bete-noire] had been around. Eventually he asked Johannes to join him at the bar for some beer. Johannes declined. The man then walked away.

Johannes was to learn that Mavingeri was staying with Eugene and Douglas, the bar-keepers. He was not alone but was in the company of a woman [his wife?] and two children of school age. Later in the day, Johannes received another invitation to drink beer with Mavingeri at the bar. Once again he declined.

Today I have been told that Mavingeri and the family have left the barkeepers' house and have gone to Belgownie. Johannes meantime has ascertained that the man seeks to come to Stockade and take up the position of base commander apparently vacated by Simukayi. It all sounds very suspicious.

In the present state of anarchy, chancers and opportunists abound. To claim to be a Warvet, especially a commander, is guaranteed to instil fear into the listener. Although Mavingeri may be a charlatan, it doesn't make him one wit less dangerous. Any move he makes will certainly be for his personal advantage and to my detriment.

As ever it is at the bar and its seedy store where the Warvet blackguards and their abettors meet. We rue the day we leased it to the two widowed sisters—middle-aged matrons—so polite, educated and God-fearing. Too late we learnt that their acquaintances and even their second husbands are associates of the ZANU PF Mafia. If there is a plot brewing, then it will be emanating from that devilish conclave.

Meanwhile at neighbouring Danbury the Bayley families are still under virtual siege. Yesterday a large army truck came to the farm, loaded up with maize from the farm silo and drove away without giving a receipt. At this time, nobody knows where it went.

Monday 8th.April 2002

On Saturday afternoon at around 2.30pm., Chengerai Munatsi came onto the farm in his white Mazda pick-up. He had four men with him. They stopped at the top gates and with bolt cutters severed the chains and removed the padlocks. They then went back to the Selby road, drove through the compound to the lower farm gate and cut and took away the lock there. Golden and a friend from Trianda were witnesses to this. Golden recognized Chengerai as at one time he was a familiar figure here. He also saw the large bolt cutters in the back of the truck.

Tredar were called and 2 IC Moffat has said that he reported the matter to the ZRP. I have today written a letter to the O.I.C. Nyabira relating the latest move made by Chengerai and reviewing the happenings of the past few weeks.

The cutting and removal of the three padlocks: what does it mean? Should

I replace the locks? Or will they just be taken again? At 7000 dollars a time! The suspicion is that it was Chengerai who was behind the plan to kill me on the night of 24th.\25th.March. Does he still have it in his mind to carry out the plan?

Tuesday 9th.April

A report from Kariza, on night watch. At 6.30pm. yesterday he was collecting some wood at the farm entrance. As he was doing so a car slowed down and turned in at the entrance. It stopped. The car was a new model Peugeot 606 [?] The colour was red and the registration number was noted. There was a man and a woman in the car. The man got out to speak with Kariza.

Kariza says that the man wore a uniform of some sort, khaki trousers and tunic. The tunic had a belt and there was a lot of insignia on shoulders and on the breast. Because Kariza would surely recognize a police uniform—even that of a senior officer—my guess is that the man was a senior army officer.

The man asked Kariza a number of questions and he produced a notebook to record the answers. He asked if the farm had any settlers. The reply given was no. Had the farm been pegged? Again, no. Were there any Warvets on the farm? No. The man got back into the car, reversed onto the tarmac and proceeded towards Selby and town.

Questions arise. Who was the man? Why should he choose to visit the farm so late? Why the set of questions put to a simple farm hand? Whatever; in the present evil climate the motif can only be bad. At 2pm. Golden reported to me that Simukayi had come into the compound. He carried a large bag and some cooking pots, and taken a room vacated by one of the factory workers. It looks as if he has come to stay. That's all I need! He is certainly here to give us trouble—the devil has never given us anything else. Does his arrival tie up with last night's visit from the army man?

Fearing that the plan might well be to prevent me from removing any equipment from the farm, I hastily arranged to get a transport onto the farm early tomorrow morning. There is a quantity of valuable house fittings, pipes etc. which I could get away. God knows if we shall have enough time. Tomorrow we shall know.

Wednesday 10th.April

Recent government tactics are to deploy their ZANU PF activists into the farming areas with orders to stop farmers from removing farming equipment. The reports are current and widespread. The government reasoning is at least quite plain; if they have no money to equip the "settlers" to whom they are allocating the land which is being confiscated from the white farmers, the answer is to steal the farmer's machinery and equipment and hand that out as well. And of course, no records need be kept.

With this very much in mind, I started the day full of trepidation. I have seen my workers terrified by Simukayi in the past, and completely under his power. I wondered if they would stand up to him now—especially with the many stories of vicious beatings being dished out to farm workers by the ZANU PF thugs. Would they defy him and load the truck?

I drove onto the farm at about 7.30 to be told that the transport had not arrived but that Simukayi was at the sheds. Oh my! This could be sticky. It was at that point when I heard the 7 tonne truck coming in at the entrance so I rushed up to intercept it. I was in time to stop the driver from taking the road to the sheds and to direct him to my house and into my homestead garden. There he would be out of sight until I learnt what Simukayi was up to. Certain items from my house could be loaded anyway.

Thank God nobody spilt the beans. Soon a message came up from the bwalo that Simukayi had gone back to the compound. With relief I was able to direct the truck to proceed to the main sheds and there loading continued. The whole operation continued without intervention and by midday the load of materials had been offloaded in town. So; all was well ended—although I felt exhausted from hours of anxiety and tension.

Today I was told that Chengerai had spent the afternoon and night on the farm—presumably in the company of Simukayi. He had not come in his pick-up but on foot. He left early in the morning the same way, going towards Danbury. What to do in that murderous hot-spot? Simukayi followed him a couple of hours later.

Another report was that the army Puma truck drove in last evening. It is the vehicle the army must have allocated to one of their personnel who has claimed a plot for himself on Spa Farm. I now have the registration number: 221 GC 75. This army officer and the two managers from Ibbo Mandaza's farm had come again looking for my donation to the President's victory celebration. Johannes once more fobbed them off somehow. Apparently they were not overtly threatening. But they show persistence.

Friday 12th.April

The night spent at Garden Lane as usual. The family is due back from their seaside holiday in Mozambique, arriving home in the afternoon. I made an early start, but what with getting a 25litre can of diesel for the tractor and then hunting down a new cell phone battery for Johannes' cell phone, I didn't arrive at the farm until 10 am.

Johannes came up to the house to report that the men demanding money for the ZANU PF celebrations had come in three more times and were becoming more belligerent. The vehicle they travel in is the same army Puma.

It is parked at the compound store and the men walk across to find Johannes. This time there was the driver of the truck, the foreman from Ibbo Mandaza's Howie farm, and the farm foreman from Brock Park. The latter, J thinks, is a recent recruit to Zanu PF—perhaps pressurized. Of the three, Mandaza's foreman was the most aggressive and threatening. However now they have been joined by Simukayi, who could never be outdone for viciousness.

Johannes was berated for not handing the demand letters to me and accused of lying when he told them that I had not been on the farm. [Which was true!] He was told that he must report to the Warvets main base at Passaford to explain himself and face disciplinary action. In the present climate, that could amount to his life. Meanwhile, Simukayi weighed in with his contribution. This was to tell me that if I didn't come up with the money, he, Simukayi, would fetch the Youth Militias to beat me up.

I learnt that the party had spoken to Johannes only ten minutes earlier and may still be on the farm so I didn't intend to hang about. However, I wrote a letter [as advised by the CFU] to say that a group donation to the celebration party would be forthcoming from the district Farmers Association and that they should contact them. I added that to harass and threaten farm foremen, as they were doing, was unreasonable and ungodly. Since these people appear to be dedicated servants of the Devil, I don't suppose that will cut any ice.

Johannes remains remarkably cool. I warned him to avoid being coerced into going to the Warvet camp.

2002 14th. April Sunday

Since leaving on Friday, I have not been back to the farm. I have had contact with Johannes on his cell phone with the new battery. A lot of interest is being directed towards Bush Cottage. This house has remained untenanted since Mrs. Christianson left some months ago when, due to the disturbances, her sons insisted she should evacuate. Of a sudden Simukayi tells Johannes that he wants to move in there. On Saturday, a tall, strong African came to Johannes' house demanding the keys to Bush Cottage. He claimed to have papers stating that the house had been given to him. He would come again on Monday to get the house keys from me.

In the meantime, Simukayi has again been to Bush Cottage; this time he was accompanied by Chengerai Munatsi. They told the old janitor, who has the confusing name of House; that the cottage was now theirs and nobody else had a right to it. When I think of all the effort I put in to building this delightful place with its two annexes in amongst lovely indigenous trees, I am filled with anguish. Now human brutes are squabbling over it like hyaenas and they have as much sensitivity as those creatures.

So tomorrow brings another day of uncertainty and the almost certain need to take counter measures against the endless tyranny.

Monday 15th. April

I drove out to the farm in the morning. There has been rain over the weekend, 0.72 of an inch. The workers planting potato seed.

I received reports from Johannes and Maston, the garden\keeper at Fig Tree House. Johannes revealed that there had been a large incursion of ZANU PF militants onto Maypark at the weekend. The attacking force included members of the Youth Brigade. I understand from J that this group is quite distinct from the "tame" Warvets who have come to some sort of compromise with the Parkes family.

Johannes also said that there had been a disturbance at Brock Park further down the road. As a result the farmer has decided to move all his cattle off the farm because we have seen truck loads of cattle passing along the Selby road.

Unsavoury visitors continue to want access to the vacant houses. J was given the name of one claimant. It is Reckie Chamunorwa. He travels in a red Nissan diesel pick-up, Reg No.655 966 F.

Maston reported that this man came to the Fig Tree security gate at 12.30 on Friday. He was accompanied by a driver, a tall man with greying hair. Maston described Chamunorwa as a tall, fat man, perhaps about 40 years.

The security gate was locked and Maston was on the inside. He heard the men calling him to the gate. The talk that followed went much as follows:

Chamunorwa: "Open the gate."

Maston: "I can't open the gate."

"Why? I think you are MDC."

"No."

"Is the boss there?"

"No."

"Is there property in the house?"

"Yes."

"If your boss comes, tell him he must move his property. On Monday we want to come here to stay."

The two intruders then left the gate and walked round to the Bush Cottage. This gate was also locked. Chamunorwa called House to him. On being questioned, House told him that there was no furniture and that the house was empty.

"If The Boss comes, he must give us the keys," said Chamunorwa, "We shall start to put in our things". With that, the two men left to find Johannes.

The above episode took place at 12.30 on Friday. At 5.30 in the evening of the SAME DAY, Simukayi and Chengerai come to Fig Tree House. They call Maston to the gate. "Has the Boss taken his things away from his house?" Maston answered no.

"If your Boss comes, tell him he must move his things because we are coming here to stay." The two Warvets then walked to Bush Cottage. I understand they both left for Harare on Saturday.

Tuesday 16th.April
Light rain all morning. Visited the farm at around noon. Spoke to Johannes. I told him that yesterday I had had a telephone conversation with Sgt.Tojha of the ZRP Nyabira. From the sergeant I learnt that the Warvets or other intruders had no right to demand entry into the houses. To my question, could we expect a positive response from the Nyabira police should any persons make a forced entry, he replied, "Yes!" I therefore told Johannes that should he be unable to contact me, he should report to Tredar base and the police should he be confronted with this situation.

I was still at the farmhouse at 1.15 and just about to enjoy a cooked lunch prepared by good old Makosa, when there was clamorous hooting coming from the security gate.

This foreboded trouble. Makosa went to the gate and had the presence of mind to tell the noisemaker that I was not at home. When I learnt that it was Chamunorwa and that he had set off in search of Johannes, I made a dash for my car, threw in some belongings, shouted to Makosa to unlock the gate, and so swept through and off the farm and into town. Goodbye lunch.

Later in the evening I learnt from Martin, that whereas I had escaped a confrontation, Martin had not. The same Reckie Chamunorwa must have been given directions as to how to find the Nola factory [The informant? Probably Douglas.] In any event, he came into the Nola office factory where unfortunately Martin happened to be.

I gathered from Martin the salient points the rude man made. Stockade Farm had been allocated to him, Chamunorwa. His claim is that his ancestors owned the land 100 years ago and had never been paid. If we didn't move off, he would get an eviction order from the Governor, Elliot Manyika tomorrow.

All these people reveal themselves by their boorish behaviour. This one appears to be a lone operator. He doesn't travel with a group of thugs. Is he a chancer? Or does he have the backing of a heavyweight "Chef"? We have been given plenty of attention from the nasties over these past two years, but this one is a complete newcomer. Strange that he should have surfaced only this week and picked on me and Martin to exhibit his racialism.

I chanced to meet Cheryl Blair in town today. She told me that they had been evicted from their cottage on Danbury and moved all their belongings out on Saturday. They have found another farm cottage as a refuge but, by the way things are going, they could easily be evicted again.

Tommy and Trish Bayley helped the Blairs transport their goods and furniture to the new location. When the job had been done, the young Bayleys headed for home only to find on their arrival that a barricade had been erected preventing them reaching their house. Cheryl thought that they are now staying somewhere in town.

This leaves the old Bayley couple, Tom and Bobs, isolated amongst the ZANU PF hooligans. Trish requested the S.P.C.A. to go out to their own home to collect the much loved, family cats. They responded but could only find one of the cats. At this stage I know no more.

Wednesday 17th. April
At lunch time I put through a call to Jenny Taylor, Tom Bayley's daughter. I hoped she would have recent news of what was happening to the family at Danbury. Jenny confirmed what I had heard from Cheryl Blair. Tommy and Trish were staying with her parents in Harare. They had been denied access to their own home on the farm since Saturday. Jenny is able to speak with her mother twice a day on the phone. At least that communication has not been denied.

Winnie, the second daughter, came up from Gweru on Friday last. She came with her husband Richard, to see the old people. They drove out to Danbury with that intention only to be turned away by the Warvet in charge of the blockade. Winnie and Richard drove back to town to request a police escort. After some palaver, this was arranged. They followed the policemen to the house but were alarmed to see the police vehicle driving away again immediately, leaving them alone. Unprotected though they were, they stayed with the old couple for about twenty minutes.

Jenny tells me she will not seek permission to visit her folks. Once there she will be unable to contain her feelings and will vent these on the Warvets. "Three of them are murderers!" Jenny calls out over the phone. Yes; it could be risky. It appears that the police have not arrested and detained the three men who killed Isaiah's brother at Easter.

Meanwhile, the Bayley's third daughter Val, her husband Rob Marshall, together with their three children, were being evicted from their farmhouse at Pearson. They were given peremptory orders to go and the Warvets came into the house in force to chivvy them. The rush was such that their pets were left behind. Once more the S.P.C.A. were called in to rescue the animals. They managed to bring in some tame rabbits along with the dogs. Jenny says that one of the dogs had been savagely beaten and suffered a severely broken leg. I understood that it was still at the Veterinary surgery and may not pull through.

Over the road on Maypark Farm, the Parkes family has experienced a torrid time from Warvets; so much so that at one stage Duncan and Isla took refuge in town. A compromise was reached with the eight Warvets who had descended on them whereby they could return. The arrangement did not last long.

Last Friday, another large group of ZANU PF thugs drove onto the farm and up to the homestead where Duncan was alone. He was given an ultimatum to clear out of the house immediately. The Nyabira police were contacted and they reacted positively. However in the event, their response only amounted to telling the Warvets that the farmer should be given reasonable time to pack and move.

The above information was given to me by Isla, who went out to the farm on the Saturday to help pack their belongings in the house. She found the so-called Warvets [many of them are just hastily conscripted youths], all over the place, wandering from room to room. And who did she discover was the commander of all this lot? None other than Simukayi. Isla noted that he was wearing a brand new and very expensive leather jacket.

[I thought of the contributions farmers had made to the Independence Celebrations.]

The police having gone, Simukayi upped the pressure and told the Parkes' that they must be out by Monday, "because anything left in the house would be thrown out in the grounds and could be looted". On the last day, Isla says Duncan instructed her to draw a large sum of money, bring it to him on the farm and get clear quickly. Isla didn't seem to know what the money was for and she didn't volunteer the amount, however, because Simukayi is a renowned extortionist, it looks as if Duncan was paying some sort of ransom under threat.

The original group of eight Warvets is reportedly furious that a lot of newcomers have usurped their authority over the property. So too are two nefarious businessmen; Chris Pasipameri and Mike Moyo. These men claim that the farm has been allocated to them. It seems that Maypark is being fought for by three gangs of thieves. I have been told by Florian Ferrao, the owner of the PGS farm and market garden at Mt. Hampden, that it is the same Pasipameri and Mike Moyo who were behind the invasion of his farm resulting in its closure.

Saturday 20h. April

I visited the farm this morning, getting there by about 8am. As so often, I had been unable to raise Johannes on his cell so could not be sure what I would run into, if anything, on my arrival. Fancy approaching one's own home keyed up with alertness and suspicion, looking about keenly for any sign of foreign vehicles or groups of dangerous strangers. Such is the tension of life in these times of anarchy. It was a fair, bright April morning. Ordinarily, I would have been out with Humba and Moppet, delighting in the familiar aspects of the bush; keenly observant of sound and movement made by the living creatures in their natural environment. Clouds drifting overhead and a breeze causing a gentle stirring within the tree canopy; these were the things with which I felt in harmony.

Even as I loked anxiously about me, I caught sight of a black-shouldered kite floating lightly and effortlessly high above me. O lovely, lucky creature.

Although events in our neighbourhood have kept me on edge, another day has passed and I have been spared the disaster of a full-blown invasion onto the farm and into my home.

Johannes came up to see me and we discussed the merit of moving one or two items of equipment, which the Warvets would soon steal if they were to descend on us. We could leave a holding gang here. My workers remain remarkably silent and never offer comment on what is taking place although they are aware of the hundreds of farm workers now being laid off work all about. Sometimes I think they must feel themselves to be no more than pawns. They accept an evil fate with resignation.

Johannes was able to add further information with regard to the manoeuvres of our particular "nasties". The man Chamunorwa, who I had last seen leaving my gate on Tuesday, had gone on to see Johannes and demand the keys of the Fig Tree house from him. J told him that he didn't have the keys, so the man ordered his driver to go to the house and find Maston, the garden\keeper.

Apparently, Maston told the man that he had instructions not to open the gate. With that, Chamunorwa returned to Johannes, who had been joined by the Tredar guard. Chamunorwa got out of the car and addressed Johannes.

C. "You foreman. Why did you tell that person at the garden not to open the gate—not to let me in?

J. "Who said that?"

C. "If you are MDC I am going to deal with you. Now! As from today!"

At that point, who should come up to the group but Simukayi. He spoke to Chamunorwa.

S. "Who are you?"

C. "You. Get away! I am the one here now. I have been given this place by Elliot Manyika. [Minister and Provincial Governor.] I have been given Plot 3."

S. "You are a liar. I am the base commander. We here don't know you at all."

Then Simukayi pushed Chamunorwa in the chest.

C. "You Simukayi. Fuck off! Get away! You are nothing. I am a doctor."

S. "You are a nanga. [African medicine man.] You are not a Warvet. I am the one here. If you go into that house, I am going to call others to get rid of you. Nobody can go into that house. If you come again, I am telling this guard here to call me at my house and I will chase you off."

Then Chamunorwa got into the car and left. According to the Tredar guard, he recognised the car as belonging to the ZANU PF youth chairman based on Megutu Farm. The vehicle was a white Isuzu pick-up.

Johannes thinks that it was Chamunorwa who had employed workers from Megutu Farm to construct the hut on Stockade close to the Danbury boundary.

The Warvet George came to the house of Simukayi on Thursday at 7.30am. With him was a young woman. Peugeot 504 Reg..No.401 528.

On Tuesday afternoon, Simukayi went into town but he returned the next day with Chengerai Munatsi in the latter's pick-up. They drove very slowly past the irrigation land and down to the sheds. There they spoke to one of the guards, saying that the man Chamunorwa, who was here, must be chased off.

The Tredar guard noted the registration number of the vehicle that Chamunorwa was in as 684 971 H, purple Mazda DX.

The situation on Danbury has gone from very bad to appalling. I have just spoken to Tommy on the phone. Old Tom has fallen and broken his leg just above the knee. Bobs rang through the message. Being under siege, no help could be given to them until the following day. The family made arrangements for a MARS ambulance to go to the farm and sought police escort to conduct the ambulance through the ZANU PF blockade. The police refused to do this.

The family decided that the two daughters, Jenny and Val, had best accompany the ambulance crew to the farm. They felt that if the men went [Tommy and Rob], this might provoke the enemy garrison into violent behaviour. This way, the old couple were evacuated without mishap and Tom is now in a clinic. Meanwhile Tommy and Trish are banned from their home and the farm.

Yesterday, the District Administrator asked Tommy to attend a meeting to be held with the Warvet chiefs on Danbury. Tommy and Trish went out to their house where the meeting was to be. Then they were told that they couldn't be in on the meeting, but they should just wait apart on the side. This they did and waited for two hours on the garden lawn whilst the DA and the group of Warvets debated their fate.

During their long wait, the youths attached to the Warvets force, arrived and began to torment them. The youths began to kick a football at them. Tommy told Trish to ignore them. Then the youths kicked the ball at the walls of the house trying to break the windows.

The next ruse was to bring up the tom-toms and to the noise of the drums the youths gyrated and sang in front of the couple. They made lewd gestures and remarks to Trish and then called out that Tommy and Trish were going to be strung up like chickens. Eventually the noise annoyed the people in the group, arguing interminably at the meeting taking place further off, and the DA called out to the youths to push off.

The DA came over to Tommy and said that the Warvets were irreconcilable. They accused Tommy of being provoking and of damaging the crops they had planted etc. etc. [I know the format very well. These people are ingrained liars. Provided they can work up enough passion, they come to believe their own lies]. Tommy then said to the DA, that since he had been excluded from the meeting and was therefore unable to refute the accusations, the whole exercise was a waste of time.

Later the DA managed to speak with Tommy on his own and confided that it was impossible to get these Warvets to see any reason. There was nothing further he could do and the matter would have to be referred to the Provincial Administrator.

Tommy says that now, because there is nobody left on the farm, the raiders are stealing fuel, tools, and equipment. They have already stolen all his seed maize and he fears that just now they will begin on his stored fertilizer. The loss will amount to millions. The police will not lift a finger because it is a "political issue"!

Friday 3rd.May 2002

Our good neighbour Tom Bayley died on 1st May. He died a broken man at his daughter's home in Greendale. The funeral took place in the green and open setting of the Agricultural Show grounds. There was a large attendance. Among the mourners were many farmers and their wives who have been forced from their farms.

Tom was a large man with an expansive nature, a well-known "character" in Mazowe. He never lost his Essex accent, was refreshingly outspoken, and had a mischievous sense of humour. Very practical and hard-working, he had for many years been on the Road and Conservation committees of our Rural Council. I shall never forget Tom because he was very helpful to Beth and me in many ways when we began work on Stockade. We always enjoyed his company whenever he looked in for a chat, which was quite often. He invariably had Beth and me in fits of laughter and for that alone I thank him and think of him. What was once a vibrant life has entered the realm of memory.

It had been Tom's wish to have been buried on Danbury. One day he led me to the chosen spot. It was to be alongside the grave of a man who had come up to Rhodesia with the Pioneer Column more than 100 years ago. The man's name was Patterson and he had died of fever. Now that this tranquil farm is in the hands of a vicious, unruly rabble, it is impossible for the family to fulfil old Tom's wish.

Stockade Farm report for Monday 6th. May 2002

I relate the course of events directly as they were given to me by the farm foreman, Johannes, supplemented by the Tredar guard, by Maston the caretaker of Fig Tree House and by others.

At 5.44 p.m., the man, Chamunorwa entered the farm in a vehicle described variously as a grey pick-up with canopy or a twin-cab. He was accompanied by a driver and two other men thought to be his workers. It appears that Chamunorwa does not have a licence to drive because he has never been seen driving himself. The car stopped at the farm sheds and Chamunorwa called Johannes to him and spoke:

"Foreman, I have come to stay here now. I am going to the Bush Cottage and to enter it just now. You Foreman must come there at once with me." Johannes replied; "OK, I am coming." The car then drove off to the Bush Cottage house beyond the railway line and Johannes followed by foot. On the way he heard the car hooting at the house gates. However the old caretaker was not present.

When Johannes arrived he saw that Chamunorwa was cutting through the padlock chain with a hacksaw which he had brought with him. Having cut open the gate, the vehicle entered the grounds. Chamunorwa then went to the kitchen door and with the aid of a tyre lever and a claw hammer he prised open the door at the point of the lock. In so doing the door frame was damaged.

As soon as he entered, Chamunorwa switched on the electricity throughout the house. He then turned to Johannes and said:

"Now, you must tell The Boss that I need him to remove his things from his house next door before Friday." [He referred to Martin and Fig Tree House where Martin and his family were living prior to the breakdown of law.]

Chamunorwa continued; "You tell the young boss that if he is not moving his things by Friday, I am going to break into the house and take all the property out. I am putting other people in there. The young boss must tell his father to remove all his property from his own house and move away before Friday."

At this time Maston, the caretaker for Fig Tree House was present. Chamunorwa repeated the same words. Then he said; "You. I am going to speak to you by yourself." Chamunorwa then dismissed the foreman. [At this point I am sure he put the fear of death into Maston.]

Johannes then left the Bush Cottage. At 8.30 pm. He saw the driver leaving the farm. The driver was alone in the vehicle.

At 11.30 pm. A GUN SHOT was heard at the Bush Cottage.

Stockade Farm Tuesday 7th. May 2002

Early in the morning, the foreman went to the Fig Tree House with the night watchman, Norman, to check on the water tanks. He found the water tanks to be full and set off in the tractor to the borehole pump in order to switch the pump off. When Chamunorwa heard the sound of the tractor, he hurried round from Bush Cottage where he had spent the night. He stopped Johannes and spoke:

"You, Foreman, why are you here? Who have you been speaking with? What are you speaking?"

Johannes replied: "Oh no. I am checking the water in the tanks."

Chamunorwa said: "If you report anything against me I am going to move you together with the old cook who works for the madala boss. Did you hear that gun shot last night?" Johannes agreed that he had. "Yes. That was me. Now come with me. *I will show you the gun."*

The foreman followed Chamunorwa who brought out the gun. It was a long barrelled gun and was contained in a green canvas cover with attached shoulder strap. Chamunorwa unzipped the cover bag to show the gun inside. He then showed Johannes a PISTOL that was held in a pouch at his belt. He spoke again with him:

"That younger boss must not come here at all. He did not speak well with me when I went to his office in town. I was given this place by Elliot Manyika. Come. See here!"

Chamunorwa produced a cell phone and pointed to the dial. "You see. Here is the very number for Elliot Manyika and here is the time that I phoned him." Johannes said that he saw the name and the time was 18.37 and the date 6th.May. Chamunorwa went on to say; "You can tell the boss, or the Police, or the DA, or anybody. At any time. It doesn't matter. They all know that I am here. You, Foreman, may carry on with the farm work but the boss cannot stay here." Meantime the driver had come back with the vehicle and Chamunorwa went away leaving his two workers at Bush Cottage. He returned to the farm at 6pm.

Wednesday 8th. May

In the morning Chamunorwa stopped to speak with Johannes. He said he was going to a big meeting with the DA and other important people. He also said: "I am the one who found all the old graves in the hills. Later on I am going to plough here. I have a lot of things and next week I am going to bring my cattle here. I have lots of cars of all makes."

The Tredar guard said that Chamunorwa had told him that he must not lock the approach gate to my house in the night time. If he did, he would be chased off together with the old cook, Makosa.

Johannes has spoken to one of his friends working at the Old Mazowe Prison Farm. The friend, an officer who has been there for 25 years, says he knows the man Chamunorwa. He has been causing a lot of trouble on farms in the area to the east of us. The foremen on two farms have been beaten up and forced to flee.

Johannes' friend says Chamunorwa uses another name, Thomas Mujuru. He is known for practicing African medicine. Now I recall Simukayi saying during his confrontation with Chamunorwa, "You are a doctor. You are not a Warvet."

Stockade Monday 13th. May 2002
During the morning mechanics from Harare came out to fix the baler. By midday it was working. This, at least was good news as there is plenty of mown grass ready to bale. I had brought out four rolls of baling twine and a can of diesel for the tractor.

It was reported to me that Chamunorwa has been staying at Bush Cottage and was still on the farm. He walks all over the place and enters all the outbuildings.

He makes a point of talking to Johannes and any others who are around the workshop area. He tells them that he is a friend of Elliot Manyika and also of Chenchitengwe, the minister who has just now taken possession of Brock Park farm. He repeated that he had a lot of motor cars. These were the things he was speaking about when he stood by while the mechanics were repairing the baler. Johannes said that whilst Chamunorwa was with them, he brought out his cell phone and began speaking within earshot, apparently to a minister. It went something like this:

"Yes. OK Minister. I am going to visit Elliot Manyika. Then I am going to Guruve to bring my people here." Johannes said he heard no more because Chamunorwa was walking away. This would have been about 10 o'clock.

At 12.30 I was speaking with the mechanics at the baler. Whilst I was there, Chamunorwa walked up from Bush Cottage. I hadn't noticed him but Johannes whispered to me "Here is the man." At his approach, Moppet and Humba gave him a hostile reception but did not bite him. [It is remarkable how dogs will sense an evil presence.] Chamunorwa shouted at the dogs and I called to them and led them off home. These people drip evil from every pore and I will always distance myself from them.

Later, Johannes reported what Chamunorwa said on my departure.

"Is that the boss?"

"Yes."

"What did he say to you?"

"No. He had only come to look at the baler."

"Ah! Tell him I don't want to see him here at all. If I see him, I am going to shoot him straight away! If he keeps coming here I am going to move into his house."

At that, he took his cell phone out and began speaking to someone: "…the dogs wanted to bite me just now…Yes at the sheds…No. I don't want to speak with him at all… I am going to meet Elliot Manyika." He then left in order to get a lift on the Selby Road.

My strong suspicion is that I have been landed with yet another psychopath!

Thursday 16th.May 2002 Stockade

This morning, I visited the farm to ascertain work progress and take in reports concerning unwanted visitors. The Tredar guard, Never, told me that on Tuesday night he heard four gunshots. At the time, he says he was patrolling in the vicinity of my house.

He thought the gunshots were made by Chamunorwa because they came from the vicinity of Bush Cottage. The time was about 7 p.m., and the firing took place over a period of about one hour.

The Tredar guard confirmed that he was too scared to investigate the shooting. Obviously, I suspect Chamunorwa of shooting game. It is utterly sickening. The animals, particularly the duikers, have become so trusting and tame over the years. Late evening is the time when the buck leave the cover of the thick bush to browse in the open. Whenever I drove through at night they would do no more than lift their heads and stare. The poor creatures will be an easy target for this killer.

On Tuesday a number of vehicles came into the farm to visit Chamunorwa. These were a cream Mazda DX 2500 Pick-up, a white Isuzu with a red stripe, and a grey Toyota pick-up carrying two drums. At around 2 pm. a Z.R.P. Santana Landrover drove directly to the Bush Cottage. There were several passengers and one man was wearing police uniform.

The Fig Tree House caretaker, Maston, confirmed this. He said that the police vehicle had the lettering Reserve Police written on the side. He thought there were four or five other passengers—all in civilian clothes.

The vehicle stopped at Fig Tree House and the policeman asked Maston: "Where is your War Veteran?" Maston told him that he would find him next door at Bush Cottage. The visitors went on to Bush Cottage and stayed there for some twenty minutes. Maston says he heard a great deal of laughter coming from the party.

Maston admits that he is very frightened of Chamunorwa. As a result he has opened the Fig Tree House gate on demand and has allowed Chamunorwa to walk inside the property. He has been ordered to keep some chickens for him in the garden.

The Tredar guard is also very scared of Chamunorwa. He has observed the two men, who are Chamunorwa's servants, leave the house every morning carrying axes with them. He says he is too frightened to follow them or to ask them where they are going or what they are doing. The question I ask myself is:

Are they cutting down my trees which the law says should be protected? And then: What if they are? What could I do? There is nothing. Who else cares but me?

Stockade Sunday 20th.May 2002

On Saturday morning I received a cell phone call from Johannes. Early in the morning, Chamunorwa had walked up to my house and called out Makosa, the cook, and Golden, the gardener. He ordered them both to leave the premises forthwith and not return. If he found out that they had returned to work he would chase them off the farm. Under this threat, the two men complied.

Chamunorwa said: "If the boss wants to feed his dogs he will have to come out and feed them himself." This message caused me great anxiety. At least Rosemary, Makosa's daughter, had slipped in and fed the dogs that morning. But how safe are they from this savage fiend? He has a gun. Has he taken the keys from Makosa? Would he loot the house? All these things were going through my mind.

I am obliged to call the police again. Marlborough will not help; so it has to be Nyabira.

Inspector Masuka has left Nyabira on retirement. He was one who had begun his police career in the BSAP and it showed. In a quiet moment one day, he confided to me that he could hardly wait for the day of his retirement to arrive. He was OK. I wish him a happy retirement. For an honest officer of middle rank, it must be unnerving to work under present conditions. Whoever the new man is; he is likely to play an important role in my life!

Martin offered to accompany me to Nyabira so we set off. En route I phoned the police post to tell them we were on our way and would they provide us with a policeman to accompany us to the farm. Whoever answered the phone agreed with the proposal. Yes, we would be able to pick up a constable to go with us.

On arrival at Nyabira, a constable Khowera was in attendance. We learnt that he was the only person on the station that day. There had been two, but the other man had gone to the shops so he was alone. There was no way he could leave the station. Then who was it who had told me fifteen minutes ago that we could pick up a policeman? Con. Khowera could not say.

Anyway, he emphasised that nobody of constable's rank could authorize a mission such as we requested. He would have to get the authority of one of the four senior officers. None of these could be contacted. Agreed, he did try Sgt. Tejha's cell phone number but all he could get was the answering machine which, upon the girl's voice telling you to leave your message, immediately breaks into pop music. I am well acquainted with this pop music because I have had the same response from Sgt. Tejha's phone a dozen times in the past days.

We had to agree with the constable; the best thing we could do was to return to the station on Monday morning.

"What should we do" I asked, "if we go to the farm and find one of our workers severely beaten up?"

"Ah! That's different", he replied. "That's an assault. Certainly we would go there on Monday morning to make a report."

"Or murdered?" I was tempted to go on—but what the hell. Why strain relations.

Martin and I accepted defeat. I would see what response I received on Monday.

Monday 21st. May 2002

The response I get from the police is the familiar one: they say they will come out to the farm—but they never do. I wait in vain.

Meanwhile Johannes phoned to report that Chamunorwa had chased all the workers off the field. This included the farm watchmen. The Tredar guards were told they should return to their base. Johannes added that Chamunorwa had come to him on Sunday evening. He wanted to know if I had been out to the farm.

"If you see the boss go to his house, you must tell me straight away. I will tie him up in chains and deal with him," Johannes quotes Chamunorwa's words to me over the phone,

Oh, my God: another bloody psychopath.! Why do I get them all?

Tuesday 21st.May 2002

Johannes got through to me on his cell phone and warned me not to come out to the farm. Chamunorwa had put his two henchmen at the farm entrance early in the morning. Johannes had heard that the plan was to apprehend me and not release me until I arranged for money to pay off the workers. I understand this is a familiar ruse at this time of anarchy. A whacking big ransom is demanded half of which is paid to the farm workers and half kept by the extortionist.

I stayed in town and sent a fax off to Minister Nhema [Environment & Tourism], with an update of my position and a request to please use his authority to get this impostor Chamunorwa off. [See previous correspondence under MET2 and ZRP.] We shall see. If there is one axiom we have learnt over the past two years, it is; "Never raise your hopes."

A phone call to Johannes in the evening confirmed that the men had been waiting for me all day. My position looks really bad: the farm workers prevented from working, my domestic staff chased out of the homestead, myself under the threat of being kidnapped or murdered if I should go to the farm. I can't know that Chamunorwa will not break his way through the homestead security gate or simply demand the keys at gunpoint.

What of Moppet and Humba? Loving one's animals; leaves one exposed. All Africans know of the white man's attachment to his dogs. A heartless brute like Chamunorwa would not hesitate to kill my two. As long as he had access to them, he could use my weakness to blackmail me or else he might kill them to spite me out of pure racial vindictiveness.

With Martin and Jean, I discussed ways and means of evacuating Moppet and Humba. It may entail summoning the help of Mrs. Harrison of the S.P.C.A. She has been involved with countless rescue operations since the farm invasions began and has had great success. The S.P.C.A. is somehow recognized as equivalent to the International Red Cross. I don't suppose more than one African in ten knows what the initials stand for.

It is a ghastly predicament. At this stage at least it would mean that the dogs would have to be cooped up in kennels. Even when I am not around, I think they must be so much happier in their familiar, spacious surroundings. I decided to give it another twenty-four hours.

Wednesday 22nd. May

During the night, I made up my mind to go out to the farm to assess the position. To do that at minimum risk, it meant arriving there early before Chamunorwa and his men began moving around.

Nobody was about so I motored down to the house and let myself in through the security gate with much welcoming from the two dogs. As I expected, I was unable to find the house backdoor key. Although Johannes must have been fairly close, I could not raise him on my cell phone. Leaving the dogs behind, I proceeded somewhat cautiously down to the bwalo. Still no sign of anyone. Then I was glad to see the girl, Rosemary, approaching from the direction of the compound. She was on her way to get the keys from Johannes. I arranged to meet them back at the homestead.

Johannes said that although most of the workers were still off work, he and Samson had been moving the irrigation pipes regularly and he was keeping the garden watered. This was good news because there are a lot of onion seedlings in the beds. These are intended for the field. Rosemary, the good girl, was sneaking in to feed the dogs.

I learnt that Johannes was still having the Trianda tractor mowing and he hoped to do some more baling.

It was good to see that the dogs were being cared for and that Chamunorwa had made no attempt to break into my grounds. Nevertheless, I had no wish to hang around so, having put together a few of my belongings, I left.

Earlier this month, the new police inpector came to Nyabira. He is Inspector Sengwe. I have made telephone contact with him and he knows of my bitter complaints against Chamunorwa.

From town, I spoke to Insp. Sengwe on the phone. I told him of the recent developments and my contacts with Minister Nhema and, through him, the Governor Manyika. The inspector said he would go to see Chamunorwa today.

In the evening, Johannes phoned me to say that the policeman had called and, having spoken to Chamunorwa, stopped to speak with him. The inspector said that Johannes could tell the farm workers that they could return to work and that Chamunorwa had been advised that the domestic servants should also go back to work.

This sounds like good news. Could it be that Chamunorwa has been told that he has no claim on the farm and must remove himself?

Thursday 23rd.May

I phoned Inspector Sengwe in the morning and the buoyant mood, with which I had begun the day, steadily changed to one of despondency. Although the inspector had persuaded Chamunorwa that he was in the wrong to interfere with the progress of farm work and to threaten me and to prevent my domestic staff from working for me, there had been no question of Chamunorwa being told to leave.

The inspector said that Chamunorwa showed him certain papers which seemed to imply that he had been given some authority to claim land; whether Stockade specifically was not clear. I have been informed by officials in the Ministry of Lands, that an eviction order could only be served by the Ministry itself and by way of a court order. An unknown third party had no authority to evict a farmer. [Of course everyone knows that this is being done all the time, but the authorities keep up the pretence of legality.]

The inspector is well aware of this and he told me that he had spoken with the District Administrator for Concession, Mr.Musaninge. The latter said that Stockade had definitely been designated and that it was only a matter of time before it was pegged and allocated to A1 settlers.

I gathered that Chamunorwa told the inspector that he just wanted to have a quiet discussion with me, without any rancour, in order to come to a mutual understanding. Apparently he told the inspector that when he visited Martin at his town office, Martin had received him curtly and been unresponsive.

The man is a villain and a liar. He is yet another manifestation of the evil which is raging through Zimbabwe.

Who is fooling who? I am faced with the immediate prospect of losing my home of forty years. At the same time, I lose the farm and the forest and with them the pride of my life's achievement. [Let nobody deny that farm and forest will be transfigured into an ecological disaster.] In addition I shall lose all my investment and, like a pauper, be reduced to seeking charity. In the process of being robbed of everything, I am expected to "co-operate". What is the meaning behind that? A private deal? I don't have the money for deals of that sort.

The legislation which the government has put through under the euphemism of land reform, is no more than a blanket cover for a free-for-all land grab. It has turned out to be a sort of gold rush in which the best placed ZANU PF "Chefs" and supporters have the edge on any others for the best claims. One wonders indeed what goes on in the minds of middle level police officers and civil servants. They must know that the election was rigged and now, for their very lives, they must be seen to be supporting the fraudulent government.

In the circumstances, it is hard to read Inspector Sengwe. From his restricted angle, he probably believes that I am on a losing wicket. He told me that the environment lobby would have little influence over the land committees, which are dominated by the hard-line radicals and Warvets. For my part, my need of him is by way of protection against violence and thieving by the invaders. He has assured me that he will respond to any emergency call I make. That is all very well, but the point is he is not on the farm and Chamunorwa is still in situ and well pleased with himself.

He called up my workers after Sengwe had gone and told them that he had magnanimously agreed that they could resume their work but not so Makosa, my old cook. He still accused him of being MDC.

On receipt of this information I rang the inspector this morning. He said he would follow this up with Chamunorwa. Having the inspector on the phone once more, I asked him some questions which I had not previously asked.

Both Minister Nhema and Sgt.Tejha of the ZRP Nyabira, had remarked that Chamunorwa had committed an offence by breaking into and occupying the Bush Cottage house. I therefore asked Insp.Sengwe directly if he agreed that Chamunorwa, by his actions, had committed an offence.

There was a long pause before he replied. Then he explained that in this situation it was necessary to avoid confrontation and to try to resolve issues by discourse. Of course he could not tell me that the police have instructions not to prosecuteZANU PF supporters. Here once more was an instance of unequal application of the law—a complaint heard all over the country. I had intended to ask the inspector if Chamunorwa had firearm licences for his guns, but let it ride.

I went on to tell the inspector that my workers were now thoroughly intimidated by Chamunorwa, my gardener had given notice after many years of service, and my foreman considered that it was only a matter of time before "these people" got him.

[Johannes told me that Chamunorwa and his thugs were the same people who had forced my friends and neighbours Rob and Val Marshall off their farm, Pearson; and on Pearson they had killed the farm foreman in the process.]

Withal; I told the inspector that if I returned to the farm permanently, I was concerned for my own safety. I had already escaped one plot on my life and here was Chamunorwa, known to have two guns, openly proclaiming that he would shoot me. Insp.Sengwe took this lightly. "You know these people only issue threats. He just wants you to move off. If he really wanted to kill you, he wouldn't tell everyone. He would do it secretly."

I said, "I think he is a madman."

"No, I think he is quite sane," the inspector replied, "He talks rationally. He will leave you alone."

"But he does NOT leave me alone and I have no wish to be a corpse on the front page of the newspapers."

The inspector laughed: "No; by being on the farm, you give confidence to your workers."

Friday 24th.May

I went out to the farm in order to assess the situation now that the workers have returned. On my arrival, I was confronted by a large election picture of a belligerent Mugabe tied to my entrance gate. I started to pull it off but thought to avoid repercussions which could fall on the dogs. However this provocation made me seethe. If I could find some like pictures of Idi Amin, Mobuto Sekeseke, Mengistu, Hitler, Milosovic, and a few other bloody dictators, I had the makings of a rogues' gallery.

I learnt that Chamunorwa had put up the pictures the evening before; others having been tied to the factory gate and the Fig Tree gate—Martin's old house. A group of youths had brought them over from Pearson Farm and they had been put in place with appropriate song and dance. Needless to say there was a threat of dire consequences if they were removed.

Just for good measure, I received a warning that if I returned to my house, the youths would be brought over to give me all night attention drumming and toy-toying. Is this but idle threat? Remember Danbury. Where do you stand Inspector Sengwe? For or against?

Sunday 2nd. June 2002

More than a week has passed since my last entry. Far from implying that this signifies a period of quiescence; rather it is the reverse.

On Monday I was lined up for a meeting on the farm at 10 a.m. with the Forestry Commission's man, Wellington Kamuroko. I gathered that he would be coming with some other members of the Provincial Land Committee. I was on the farm by 9 o'clock and waited until 4 o'clock in the afternoon. Nobody turned up. I received no calls on my cell phone and my calls out elicited no information.

At 1 p.m. the police inspector visited the farm alone. He proceeded to the Bush Cottage and spoke with Chamunorwa. On the way back he asked Johannes a few questions. He wanted to know if Makosa, my cook, was back at work. Johannes confirmed that he was but that he was still frightened of Chamunorwa. The Inspector apparently stopped at my gate which I keep locked. I didn't hear him and he drove away. This was as well because I knew Sengwe wanted me to meet face to face with Chamunorwa with the inspector acting as an intermediary. This I would not do. Not only would it be a waste of time but it would also be thoroughly upsetting for me. To talk with a disciple of the devil requires a Christ-like person. I don't qualify.

At some time—was it on Tuesday?—I phoned Mrs. Mandimika at the Min. of Lands. She said that she had had no feedback from the Chief Land Office [Mrs.Makuku], Bindura, in response to her request for an urgent ruling on the delisting application for Stockade. Mrs. Mandimika advised me to contact the Governor or the P.A. direct. I explained that I had gone this route several times and got nowhere. She could only advise me to try once more.

I phoned the Governor's office to be told that Governor was away in Harare. I should phone next Tuesday when next he would be in his office. I then phoned the P.A.'s office and was told that the P.A. was not available as he was in an all-day meeting with the Governor. I could try again next Monday. It all ended as I had anticipated—wasting time, money and patience.

During the week we had been engaged mowing and baling. On Wednesday, Golden came to me and he was considerably perturbed. Coming up from the bwalo, he had been confronted by Chamunorwa, who was on his way to the tar road accompanied by one of his henchmen. Chamunorwa said that he had heard that I had been out to the farm and he demanded of Gordon an explanation as to why he had not gone to him directly to report my presence because these were the instructions he had issued.

Chamunorwa said to Golden: "You Golden. You know my men have killed a person on Danbury. You know too that I have killed a man on Pearson. Look to your life!"

Having given me this information, Golden reminded me that he would be leaving at the end of the week. Later, Johannes confirmed that Chamunorwa had warned all my workers to similar effect.

Pointless though it seemed, I decided that I would phone Inspector Sengwe and at least inform him. The inspector circuited the subject and his advice was for me to speak with the D.A. This would be like starting from the bottom again. I gave up on the D.A. years ago! I am now at ministerial level and still getting nowhere.

The inspector also suggested that the environmental people had little influence when it came to the land issue. He may be right. He probably reflects the views of most Africans. The protection of the environment is something white people have introduced. It has no application for Africans.

One has been subjected to months of uncertainty, never sure from day to day whether one is going to remain afloat or founder. By this time I had plunged down into one of the deepest mental troughs. Tales of merciless evictions of farmers in all quarters of Zimbabwe have been coming through, which is no help to one's morale.

Then on Thursday afternoon, I received a phone call from Wellington Kamuroka, the forest man, asking if we could meet on the farm Friday. Apparently his commission to produce a report still stood. He would bring a representative from the Dept. of Natural Resources. Later the same day, I again phoned Mrs. Mandimika. She had news for me. I gathered that she had been given the task of compiling a dossier on all matters pertaining to Stockade and in particular the Protected Forest. This she was charged to have ready for a meeting of the Command Centre, Harare, next Wednesday, 5th.June. Mrs. Mandimika confessed she had a problem.

It appears that there is general confusion about "Private Forest". Why should a private forest be protected? I explained that the forest came under the surveillance of the state and that the owner could not exploit or alter the character of the forest without state approval. In this case the Forestry Commission would be the controlling authority. I am sure Mrs. Mandimika would obtain a definition from the F.C. and the Ministry for the Environment if she contacted them.

Saturday 8th June 2002

Wellington Kamuroko of Forestry Commission and Jennifer Ngorima, Provincial Officer for the Dept. Natural Resources, Glendale, came out to the farm. At the house we went over the historical background of the forest and my visitors read through various papers relating to the project. After that we toured the whole forest area stopping here and there. I showed them the badly eroded land and explained the steps being made to rehabilitate it.

The visitors left promising to give me support. They both agreed that the forested area was quite unsuited for settlement and indeed, should that occur, would result in ecological disaster. I look forward to receiving a copy of their report.

I learnt that they returned to Stockade on Wednesday, this time with Mrs. Tafire, the provincial F.C. officer. They took her over the ground we had covered. Mrs. Tafire sits on the provincial lands committee. I spoke to her on the phone and she sounded unconfident. She gave me the impression that, although she did not deny the ecological value of the forested area, she felt that she would find it difficult to put this across. Presumably she will know the characters of the other members of the committee.

From her, I gathered the impression that to particularise points such as unstable soils and steep slopes, the necessity to protect the catchment area from run-off, would fall on deaf ears. I think her words were: "They will say; what's different about the conditions on this farm which is any different from any of the other farms in that area? This is a political issue. It has nothing to do with conservation."

Mrs. Tafire asked if I had another farm. I am a single farm owner; I have repeated this ad nauseam. She thought that this may help. I should point this out to the Governor, she said. I told her that the Governor knew full well that I only had one farm because he had received at least four written applications for delisting in addition to a personal interview all of which stressed the fact that I was a single farm owner.

I fear the truth of the matter is that Elliot Manyika so hates whites that he will never countenance a white owner retaining so much as a hectare of land. True to his species, he has picked a plum for himself—a prime farm in Glendale.

Meanwhile, Mrs. Mandimika confirmed that nothing positive came out of the Harare meeting. They have pushed everything back to Bindura, which means Elliot Manyika! She added that a letter was read out from Mujuru alias Chamunorwa. He made typical spurious claims and lying statements. At the meeting he said of me: "He only wants the farm because of his wife's grave and those of his dogs."

I have phoned a certain M.P. who is familiar with my problem. His phone is tapped so the conversation was reduced to the minimum. He told me to contact the Ministry of Home Affairs. The Home Affairs Minister has declared that any person who settled on a farm property after 1st. March this year can be evicted. The police will ignore this.

So? Who do I go to see now?
The Ministry for the Environment and Tourism.
The Ministry of Lands, Agriculture and Rural Resettlement.
The Ministry of Local Government and Rural & Urban Development.
And now:-
The Ministry of Home Affairs, John Nkomo.
Please! Give me a break.

Simukayi has acquired land elsewhere and appears to have relinquished his claim. Chamunorwa only came onto the farm in May, as I reported to the police. Nkomo's ruling should apply to him, but as everyone knows, it is just a joke. All over the country farmers are being evicted in droves regardless of statements, agreements and accords.

There is the other angle. In the present state of anarchy, a "lawful" eviction through the courts could bring retribution from the ZANU PF warlords and one could find oneself in worse trouble.

Wednesday 12th June 2002

The report on the forest produced by Wellington and Jennifer didn't reach me, so on Monday I motored to Glendale to get Jennifer's copy, having explained to her that I needed the report urgently.

With some difficulty I found the Dept. of Natural Resources office on the outskirts of Glendale; a small square building which appears to be rented from the Railways, because to reach it one has to hump over a rail crossing and follow the track along an appalling dirt road which must be a nightmare in the rains. There were no direction signs.

Jennifer apologised for her pokey railway office, which was so far off that even the railways must have found no use for it and were no doubt glad to rent it to government. It was fitted with no more than a phone and a typewriter—no computer, no fax, no E-mail, no copier. "Thus does the government rate the importance of Natural Resources", I said to myself, and commiserated with Jennifer, who is intelligent, well educated and experienced in her field. Later I gathered she commuted daily to Glendale from Harare, a forty mile journey. Today I was glad to give her a lift back to town as she had no car.

On Tuesday morning I photocopied the three-page report and took one copy to the Forestry Commission H.Q. I had an appointment to meet Minister Nhema on Wednesday and I knew he would immediately contact Dr. Shumba, the GM, to discuss the matter. Sure enough, the report had not reached FC HQ., so it was as well that I took it to them. However, I learnt that Dr. Shumba was on leave so there could be a hitch.

In the afternoon, I dropped off the report to the Minister's office together with a covering letter. This would give him time to read up the business before my visit.

My covering letter to the Minister should really be read in conjunction with this, but briefly I stated that in spite of assurances, the Governor had taken no action.

So on Wednesday I met with the Minister. I opened by saying that in the matter of the forest, I had met many people; Forestry, Agritex, Natural Resources, Ministry of Lands—all expressed their understanding and support. However, my impression is that these people themselves fear that when it comes down to it, the politicians will out-gun the conservationists. Also it seems very apparent that the only person who will decide the issue is the Governor, Elliot Manyika.

The Minister repeated what he said at our last meeting; there was no way that the forest status could be changed. He also agreed that the Governor was the ultimate decision maker.

Minister Nhema made the point that the Governor was also a Minister like himself. In the circumstances, it was difficult to intervene directly. Nevertheless, Elliot Manyika did indeed have the matter in mind. The problem was that even he, Manyika, had a political minefield to tread. "The people intruding onto Stockade would be removed." [I interjected to say that there was only one person!] When the time came the police would be given instructions.

I asked Minister Nhema if he had spoken directly to Elliot Manyika and he replied that he had. I assumed that he had contacted E.M. after he had read my letter and the F.C. report. In that case it could only have been that morning.

I then expressed my concern about the forest. It was a certainty that widespread veld fires would be experienced this season. Normally I would be making firebreaks. After two years of harassment, the income from the farm had dried up. There was no money available to spend on firebreaks. Money was needed for cleaning roads and new plantings. Uncontrolled fire would undo all the work I have put in over the years.

The Minister said that he would arrange for the Forestry Commission to do the work. He straight away tried to phone Dr. Shumba who, of course, was away. I said I thought that ministries were always short of money but he replied that funds could be found and that a similar situation had arisen in Wange.

"That sounds marvellous", I said, "If I contact the F.C. who could I speak with?" "You could speak with Bekker", he replied.

Well next week I shall do that. It will be interesting to learn their reaction. All along I have emphasised the need to keep the farm and the forest as a unit. In the event of fire, an effective response can only be made by a farm-based workforce. And then there is the need for continuous policing of the forest. There are no longer any good farming neighbours, who would instantly respond with help when veld fires were seen! A letter to Forestry Commission explains in detail.

Sunday 30th.June 2002

Two weeks since my last entry. I endeavour to push forward with a little farm work. Left much on their own, our motley clutch of farm workers keeps more or less on top of weeding the garlic and the potatoes. The latter have been discovered by a group of bush pigs so the night watchman has been provided with firewood to keep fires burning at each end of the rows. Some rape has been planted and a few lines of carrots and onions. Johannes has been occupied much of the time hay baling. The Trianda tractor has been mowing, especially at weekends. 4650 hay bales have gone off to Agrifoods. By this time there should be about 2500 bales ready for Crest Breeders.

So it can be seen that Chamunorwa, the latest bane which Fate has sent to plague me, has ceased his attempts to stop us from working. [Due acknowledgement given to Insp. Sengwe for this.] That's as far as it goes. He continues to occupy Bush Cottage and now he moves around in a car, which he drives himself. For so long he used to come and go with a driver, I thought he might not have a licence. Well, of course he may well not have a licence, but just drives. He drives a Peugeot 504 No 168 137 T. It is a brownish station-wagon.

Warvet Chenjerai Munatsi came onto the farm at 8 pm.21st.June in Mazda Pick-up 621 019 V. What does he come for? At any time? Let alone at 8 o'clock at night? Was he my would-be assassin? He doesn't seem to be challenging Chamunorwa. Are they, or were they, in league?

Chamunorwa may well be pleased to see us going ahead with the market garden crops and is counting on reaping them for himself. That was Simukayi's method and one blatantly put into practice by government "Chefs" in a really big way; to wit the ex-minister [or his wife] who has just moved in to Brock Park farm down the road from here.

Chamunorwa continues to spew out the ZANU PF line and has endeavoured to enrol Johannes as the local Party Chairman. Johannes says he refused. Good for him! It seems that *orders* to our workers to attend ZANU PF meetings at Passaford have also been ignored.

I only visit the farm for a few hours at a time. I find that the presence of such a wicked man as Chamunorwa on my property too upsetting. At all costs I will avoid him. I will not talk to him. How can I talk with a man who continually threatens me harm to the point of killing me?

What I find so disturbing is that Mugabe has been able to recruit so many henchmen nation-wide, all thoroughly steeped in evil. And, furthermore, that the worst of them are actually quite well educated. Education in Africa seems to be the royal road to greed and dishonesty, with a complete disregard for moral responsibility towards fellow men—let alone other living creatures.

My time off the farm has not been spent idly. For an update of the lengthy Stockade drama, one must really refer to letters and memoranda sent to bodies such as the Minister of Environment, the Forestry Commission, Provincial Land Committee etc. The correspondence is rather one-sided. I usually get a short acknowledgement from Minister Nhema, but otherwise I never receive replies at all.

Goodness knows how the matter of the forest firebreaks will be sorted out, if ever. As for the land question, perhaps the time for the crunch is close. The odds are against me.

Anarchy reigns as ever and the madness of government suggests a collective form of pathological paranoia grips them all.

Close to us, the Millars, friends of ours from long back, have lost their farms. The family has been farming their lands productively for three generations. The local Africans inform me that Chidyasiku, Mugabe's newly appointed Chief Justice, has taken one of the three farms. I suppose it is a sign of equality that a Chief Justice ranks on a par with a "Landless Peasant."

Wednesday 3rd July 2002

The Warvet Simukayi has been around—seen on Saturday and again on Tuesday. He turns up to haunt us like a dreadful spectre. The simile leaps readily to mind, because about a year ago, the rumour of him being dead was so strong that everyone in this district sighed with relief and thanked the Almighty. The good news was toasted in every farmstead. At last we had been freed from the attentions of this depraved specimen of humanity—the drunkenness, the shouting, the bullying, the lying, the thieving; Simukayi the terror-monger, the extortionist. A senior police officer told me that Simukayi had killed six nuns in Mozambique during the "liberation" war. That fits. So we can add murder of innocents to his achievements.

The reason Simukayi disappeared for so long was not because he was dead but because he was wanted for questioning on a matter concerning the misappropriation of some tonnes of fertilizer, the property of the G.M.B. Whatever the truth, it seems that he has talked his way out of his predicament. Perhaps he was given a Presidential pardon. After all, he once told Martin that he was a Lt. Colonel in the Presidential Guard.

On Tuesday morning Simukayi waylaid Johannes at the bwalo. He demanded the store keys from Johannes saying that the farm belonged to him because he was the first Warvet to come here and claim it. If Johannes didn't hand over the store keys, he would call up supporters and they would beat him up and trash all his belongings—they had done this to other people.

This behaviour is all true to form. Fortunately, Johannes recognizes that Simukayi is something of a spent force. He stood up to the man and there was quite an altercation before Simukayi left by foot to Danbury, which, of course, is now solid Warvet territory. However, Johannes has since learnt that the Danbury Warvets have refused to co-operate with Simukayi.

There is another factor which must bear on this business. Simukayi has a rival in Chamunorwa. Both are predators each seeking territory to hunt in. When Simukayi left his territory unguarded, Chamunorwa moved in. From what I hear, it seems that Chamunorwa is the more aggressive. Although Simukayi returns from time to time to sniff around, he seems to be avoiding a face to face encounter. In contrast, when Chamunorwa gets wind that Simukayi has been about, he gets into his motorcar and hastens to catch Simukayi in the compound, issuing threats that when he catches him he will beat him thoroughly. He probably recognizes that Simukayi is being weakened by AIDS or syphilis.

When I learnt that Simukayi had apparently slipped back to his old haunts and was once again upsetting Johannes with threatening behaviour, I decided to phone the Nyabira police. I spoke to A\Insp. Taswa and told him of Simukayi's latest intrusion. I said that from past experience, I feared that Simukayi was planning to steal something. Taswa promised to tell Insp. Sengwe of the matter.

I don't really expect them to do anything, but felt it best to make the report should there be a development. I also told Johannes that should Simukayi return with more blustering threats, to avoid a fight if possible—better to phone Z.R.P. Nyabira first.

Friday 5th.July 2002

It looks as if something momentous is occurring with regard to Stockade. At about 11 a.m. Johannes phoned me to say that a lot of government motor vehicles had come onto the farm. It happened that I was already on my way there.

On my arrival, I learnt that a convoy of ten vehicles had arrived earlier, but that they had all left. Johannes was returning from the distant fields with a load of hay bales when the cars filed past him on the farm road. There were three smart Pajero type 4x4s, two Z.R.P. Landrovers carrying uniformed po-

Fig Tree House showing guest cottage and wild fig trees in the background.

Bush Cottage nearing completion 1993.

lice, there followed an assortment of cars and pick-ups with government number plates—one, inscribed "Rural Council", probably the DA.

None of them stopped so Johannes gained no knowledge of the purpose of the visit. I learnt that nobody called at my house and since there were so few people about, they actually came into the farm unseen. However, I was to learn from Maston, who was at the Fig Tree house, that the whole company went to the Bush Cottage and there they entered the garden and met up with Chamunorwa. It seems that the latter was expecting them. Maston says that in the party were Elliot Manyika and Minister Chombe of Local Govt. & Housing. The company stayed for about thirty minutes and then drove off.

It seems there was no intention to view the forest or the lands because they went straight back across the railway line and thence up to the sheds and the main road. It was then that Johannes encountered them.

Maston said that after the cars had left, Chamunorwa came to him and said that now the farm belonged to him. The women, who stay with Chamunorwa to cook and to tend his sheep and goats, also told Maston that they were very happy because they had been given the farm.

The vitriol aimed at whites by the government in recent days, suggests a collective paranoia. I am hardly likely to escape the sequel to this perverse fixation. I guess my fate will be revealed next week. D-day indeed!

Monday 5th. August 2002

A whole month has passed since my last entry. Chamunorwa remains stubbornly in the Bush Cottage with his two followers. I had a short angry exchange with one of the latter; an adult, bearded man, who spends his day watching five sheep and killing small birds with a catapult. That day he displayed the pathetic little body of a female sunbird. Chamunorwa kraals the sheep in the Fig Tree garden. They have eaten all the vegetables I was growing for the family in town.

During the past weeks we have managed to keep on with hay baling in fits and starts. The garlic is growing but has not started bulbing. Some lines of rape are ready for picking.

Beneath a surface tranquility, there simmers the dreadful uncertainty of my position. Nothing has been resolved on the land issue and no response to my letter and memorandum to the Bindura Land Committee has been forthcoming. I have written another letter to Minister Nhema concerning the matter and have offered the whole property to National Parks; this perhaps being a way to save the forest from destruction. The issue is really a racial one. By removing myself, the white man, from the equation and handing it over to a *responsible and professional* authority like National Parks, the Party hard-liners may be appeased.

A few weeks back, a thief stole 1000 metres of overhead aluminium electric cable feeding power to the borehole in what we call the njange field. When I learnt that thieves were actually lifting up borehole piping and pumps, I arranged for our pump man to lift it up. This he did early this morning. He left the pipes on the ground and brought the submersible pump up to my house. Unfortunately, someone—Maston, it is believed by Johannes—told Chamunorwa.

When I arrived on the farm and driven up to my house, Chamunorwa was at my gate within a few minutes. I received the message that he wanted to speak with me. I went to the gate, which was padlocked and found Chamunorwa and his henchmen waiting.

I had already made up my mind that I would say nothing to him. From the grisly threats I had had passed to me, I was well aware that he was a brutish character and that evil seeped out of him. However I went forward to the gate to see what he looked like close to. Sure enough, he looked the brute I had imagined; fat and thickset with a bull neck. I had already felt my blood-pressure rising and when I got closer I crossed myself twice and brought my palms together in supplication. I felt this quite helpful in steadying me.

Chamunorwa forcefully demanded that I discuss matters with him. I looked at him through the wire mesh at the top of the gate and merely shook my head. Notwithstanding; he angrily accused me of employing a contractor to vandalise the pump, which, considering it belongs to me and not to him, I thought was a bit rich. It would have been absurd to hang around just to listen to a tirade of abuse, so I walked away. This must have vexed him—these people do like to listen to the power of their own invective and are prepared to keep going for an hour or more. Simukayi was just the same.

Chamunorwa vented his anger by loudly sounding his horn. The car was still up against the gate. I went into the house in order to phone the police at Nyabira. When Insp. Sengwe came to the phone, I told him of the situation and of my reason in lifting the borehole pump. He said this was completely acceptable because thieving of borehole equipment was rife all through the district. The ruling was that if there were "settlers" on a property they should be allowed a source of water. Well, Chamunorwa has had free water and electricity ever since he broke in to Bush Cottage.

The inspector said he would come out but his transport would not be returning from Chinhoyi until 3 p.m. I told him that although I would be going back into town soon, I would return to the farm and be here at 3 p.m.

I was not to know that whilst I was speaking to the policeman, Chamunorwa had sent one of his men to the cottage for a padlock and then proceeded to securely chain up and lock my gate from the outside. He then drove away.

Makosa, my old cook, went with me to the gate to see what might be done. The gate had been double-chained at ground level and secured with a heavy padlock. It was impossible to bring the padlock round. The chain would need to be cut on the inside and my hacksaw was at the farm workshop. I was securely stuck inside.

Martin had been due to come out at about 2 o'clock to collect some belongings from Fig Tree house. I phoned him to tell him what was happening and he decided that the best plan was for him to go to Nyabira at 3 o'clock, see the inspector and if necessary pick him up. In the meantime, I would sit it out resignedly.

Fortunately my book shelves still hold plenty of books. I selected one of a philosophical nature.

At 12.30, I handed out some food to the five members of staff trapped with me inside the grounds. However, I was becoming annoyed with my ridiculous position. By luck, a call over the hedge attracted the attention of the two old men, Henry and Daimon, who were just then going off from work to their lunch. We gave them a message for Johannes to come up to the house a.s.a.p.

When Johannes arrived, I was able to pass him a couple of cold chisels and a hammer through the wire. He had hardly started the operation when Chamunorwa's vehicle was seen approaching. Johannes put his chisels out of sight as the car drove up. Chamunorwa alighted and straight away undid the padlock.

Of course the gate was still locked on my side. Makosa came in to the house to say that Chamunorwa had ordered that all the staff should leave and go to the compound. Makosa had our gate key. He asked me what he should do.

Here was a challenge to my authority. My reply was that the gate must remain locked and the staff must stay inside until the police arrived. Makosa took the message out.

The outcome was that Chamunorwa retired without replacing his padlock. I think he felt uncertain of his position vis-a-vis the police should they arrive and question him on this one. [This was born out later when he denied ever having padlocked me in!]

To the staff I said I needed them to protect me, for if they left, Chamunorwa may come back and kill me. The five members of "staff" referred to are:

Makosa, the cook; tall, thin, old, angular; strong in spirit but unsteady in body.

Rosemary, his daughter, doing the garden work after Golden left.

Age 18; a mere slip of a girl; thin, painfully shy, but honest, intelligent and keen to learn.

Febe, a quiet elderly little widow who, mouse-like, scurries in each day from Danbury to help Rosemary sweep, hoe and tidy in the garden.

Maston, gardener for Fig Tree house. However, when Chamunorwa moved his sheep into that garden there was no gardening to do, so I have him here for some hours during each day. He is in mortal fear of Chamunorwa, who has him totally subjected.

Dishon is number 5. Dishon arrived at our gate ten years ago. The poor old man was in such an emaciated state that my wife, in compassion, gave him food, promised him shelter and told him that he could do a little light garden work to earn some money before moving on. Dishon has been doing a little light garden work ever since. You could knock the old man down with a feather.

These then, I declared, were to be my bodyguard to save me from the murderous Chamunorwa. Judging from the blank expressions on their faces, I think these poor little people take me seriously.

The decision by Martin to go to Nyabira proved a wise one, because when he reached there the police vehicle had not returned from Chinhoyi and he was able to ferry the police inspector to Stockade. They arrived at around 3.30 p.m. By that time, Chamunorwa was waiting at the gate and for some nefarious reason he had called together a group of the farm workers. He had told Johannes to come as well, but the latter had refused. It suggests that Chamunorwa wanted to show off his strength in front of an audience.

I didn't go out to join the parley. Martin is fully capable of stating our position. There is nothing to talk about; nothing to negotiate. There is only right or wrong, legality or illegality. However, such distinctions are far from clear in present day Zimbabwe. This results in hours of abortive argument.

After half an hour, Martin came in to tell me what was happening at the gate. Apparently Insp. Sengwe had started off in an authoritative manner taking Chamunorwa to task for not heeding previous warnings and continuing to interfere in the affairs of the farm. He even told him to leave the Bush Cottage, which he was illegally occupying.

Chamunorwa countered this by issuing blatant threats, reminding the inspector of all the influential Party Chefs he knew. After this, Martin noticed that the inspector became more hesitant. He even suggested to Martin that he try to come to some compromise.

Martin politely but adamantly refused. With these people, one must never fall for this ploy.

At the end of the day, the outcome of it all was pretty inconclusive. I phoned the inspector the next day. He told me that he would go personally to Bindura on Wednesday to attend the scheduled Land Committee meeting and discover just what their ruling was for Stockade. Meanwhile he thought it best to leave Chamunorwa be.

Tuesday and Wednesday were relatively uneventful. There was plenty for me to attend to on farm matters, but Chamunorwa made no further move although I did learn that he had gone to Trianda and told them that they should no longer send over their tractor to help me with the grass mowing. Of course I was worrying all the time as to what might come out of the Bindura meeting. Was I at last to know where I stood? Was I to win or lose?

On Thursday I phoned Insp.Sengwe and enquired about the meeting. He confirmed that he had been there, but answered me vaguely. He was inclined to mutter his replies. I strained to catch his words. However, I gathered from him that "perhaps I might sometime" be sent a letter for delisting. It was uncertain.

Friday 9th. August 2002
Tomorrow, 10th.August is the deadline, according to the government, for the hundreds of farmers issued with Section 8 eviction notices to be off their farms and away from their homesteads or face arrest and prosecution. Chamunorwa has been telling my workers that then he will be definitely taking over the farm.

Martin and family having left for their seaside holiday, I am now stationed at their home in Avondale. Here telephone communication is easier. My plans for today entailed driving out to the farm and fetching my farm pick-up truck so that it could be kept off the farm until after the coming long weekend holiday. Monday and Tuesday mark Heroes and Army days when the heroes and the military might throw their weight about and unprotected property will be up for grabs.

I asked a friend to accompany me to the farm so that she might drive the Sunny back whilst I drove the truck. Before leaving, I received a call from Johannes to say that during the night all the MCB electric switches had been stolen from the 2nd. transformer which feeds power to the facilities on the other side of the line. This includes the two houses, Fig Tree and Bush Cottage and the borehole pump which supplies them [and therefore Chamunorwa] with water. On being informed of this, I immediately informed Z.R.P. Nyabira.

When I reached the farm Johannes told me that it was Chamunorwa who reported the removal of the switches. C said it was all my doing. I had arranged for an electrician to take the MCBs off.! He drove off the farm in his car.

Very shortly before my arrival on the farm, Johannes intercepted ZESA electricians who had come to disconnect the first transformer. Johannes remonstrated with them and said the electricity was needed to supply my house and to irrigate the cropping land. The ZESA men said that they had been instructed to disconnect the whole farm by a man called Mujuru who said he was the new owner of the farm. Mujuru had added that the previous owner [that's me!] had stolen all the switches from the second transformer. The ZESA men told Johannes to get me to inform the police of this at once.

Contacted by radio, Tredar agreed to investigate. They would uplift a Z.R.P. police detail to accompany them.

Meanwhile I was pushed for time. I had already loaded a few valuable possessions onto the truck [just in case I was trashed] and my friend had to return to town. I told Johannes to explain everything to the police and Tredar when they arrived and *with their knowledge* take down the remaining overhead aluminium electric cable before that too was stolen.

Later that afternoon I was at last able to get hold of Insp. Sengwe. I told him of what I had learnt and he advised me to phone ZESA area HQ and to tell them that the message they received was from a settler and not the owner of the farm. I tried the ZESA HQ office in Bindura, but could not get a reply from any of their lines. I then tried Concession and was rewarded. Yes, the man who answered said it was their depot which received the instruction from a certain Mujuru. Apparently Mujuru had gone on to the Mazowe police to report the theft of the ZESA and farm switches—adding that I was the chief suspect!

The ZESA clerk added that the police had entered the report and issued an RRB number. That made it official, he said, and ZESA could now install a replacement switch on their side of the transformer. I said, that's all very well for you, but what about my side and my three stolen switches? "Ah! We can't help with that."

Monday 12th. August 2002

Yesterday I managed to speak to Johannes by cell phone. It was a dreadful connection. I gleaned that the police never came out to the farm. I also understood that Chamunorwa had come up to the sheds and called out Johannes and the Tredar guard. Still carrying on about the MCBs and accusing me of thieving them, he then said he would remove the MCB switch from the borehole at the old pig pens and there and then did so. When I heard that, I thought to myself that it showed he was handy with screwdriver and pliers and knew his way around electrical fittings.

I wonder about Chamunorwa -. Rekki Chamunorwa or Thomas Mujuru—even the confusion of names spells duplicity. He speaks English fluently and volubly. He appears to have a fund of general knowledge, which even extends to technical matters. His audacity is mind-boggling. Withal, one can detect an immaturity in his mental make-up; some of his behaviour is positively child-like. It would be very interesting to know his background and what he did before he became a professional charlatan.

My diary entry for the past ten days may be condensed; a continuous chain of troubles sparked off by Chamunorwa and resulting in worry, frustration and exhaustion.

Sunday 18th. August 2002

At the top north-east corner of Stockade, I have a joint boundary with the Prison Farm. On my side the boundary marks one edge of the Protected Forest. On the Prison Farm side there is much woodland; but although they do cultivate a single maize field, generally speaking the area is very quiet—the human population being well under control! Over the years we have had a cordial relationship with the Farm management. A fireguard was maintained on both sides of the boundary fence. On the maize field, it has been their practice to burn off the dry stover annually. In 35 years there were two occasions only when they allowed a fire to escape onto our side of the common boundary. I well remember the last occasion. They had been foolish enough to burn in a strong wind and a spark had leapt the firebreak.

I had a much larger workforce in those days but there was no way they could control the speed and fierceness of the flames, which on occasion reached to the tree tops. My good neighbours from Maypark, Trianda and Danbury mustered all their workers, piling them into trucks and farm trailers whilst others came over by foot. Duncan of Maypark was a brilliant strategist in these conditions and I heard his shouted orders above the noise of the burning veld. Then on my eastern flank I saw a ghost army, figures in off-white prison garb, beating the line of flames. The teams met together in the centre and with shouts of triumph the last flames were extinguished. I recall looking around. It was a memorable sight. There would not have been less than 200 farm workers and 100 prisoners beaming at each other as they took their separate ways through the ashes and dying embers. I never heard that any of the prisoners had taken leave of absence.

A phone call from Johannes on Friday evening informed me that the Prison Farm was burning stubble on the field adjoining us and had allowed the fire to escape. The forest was alight. Johannes said that the prison guards in control and who were operating with a party of prisoners, refused to fight the fire. They said that the prisoners were due back to their quarters to be locked up. There are no longer any neighbours to help. As a result there were only five of our people to fight the fire.

I tried desperately to raise the Prison Farm to give them a piece of my mind and to insist that they should send over a team to fight the fire. Nobody responsible would come to the phone so I hung up.

On Saturday morning Maston pitched up at Martin's house in connection with some keys for the Fig Tree House. I asked him about the fire. He said that the fire had swept right up to the houses and even burnt the hedges and some of the lawn grass. This told me that the whole forest must have been burnt.

This revelation has put me into a state of shock. I am distraught. I really cannot bear the thought of going out to the farm to inspect the charred devastation. This evening Johannes has confirmed that the fire even jumped the railway line and has burnt up to my security fence. However he assured me that it has now been extinguished.

So this weekend my feelings have been those of anger, embitterment, despair, pessimism and depression—more or less in that order. My own scenario is but a miniscule representation of the total scene in Zimbabwe and indeed the whole of Africa. There is absolutely no hope that Africans will succeed in putting together anything worthwhile. They are unable to anticipate. They cannot administer. Responsibility is still a foreign word. Whatever they touch ends in ruin.

For good measure, Johannes tells me that the police inspector never visited the farm as he had promised and Chamunorwa has told my workers that if I am seen on the farm he will shoot me "straight away".

Tomorrow I may learn of the outcome of more than two years of wearing, bitter, and sometimes dangerous struggle. Well, it has to be said, that the land for which I have been fighting, now resembles a blackened battlefield.

Tuesday 20th August 2002

What made me think that a point of finality would be reached?

Things are never like that. The stresses of one day are merely supplanted by the stresses of the next.

On Monday I spent almost the whole day at the house making phone calls to people whose phone numbers were either out of order, unreachable or interminably engaged. If I did get a connection, the person I needed would be out of the office, at a meeting, or just "not around".

In order to learn if the Mashonaland Central Land Committee had come to a resolution for Stockade, the man I needed to talk to was a Mr. Makaza of the Lands office, Bindura. After a few hours, I managed to reach him. I asked him if my case had come up for discussion last Friday and if so what the outcome was. Mr. Makaza replied in a very abrupt manner. Yes, my farm had been discussed. "It seems you are not prepared to share your land with anyone else", he said.

So my lengthy written explanation of 23rd.June had been ignored. As I feared, putting reason before determinedly unreasonable people is a waste of effort. I asked if he had received any communication from the Ministry of Environment. Mr. Makaza's sharp reply was that I must speak with the Governor. "Speak to the Governor. Make an appointment to see him on Wednesday." With impatience, he gave me a telephone number and rung off.

Many months ago, Martin and I went to Bindura to see the Governor on the very same issue. We waited in a cramped and crowded corridor for seven hours and then had seven minutes talk with Elliot Manyika, the Governor. He promised to see to our matter within the coming days and that was the last we heard. I know that if I went all the way to Bindura to see him, it would result in no more than a repeat performance.

Unfortunately, I did not ascertain if the Governor had been at the Friday meeting, but whether he was or not, it is clear that the proposal to have the whole farm taken over by National Parks had not reached the Committee. This was not surprising because Mrs. Sangarwe, of Environment had told me that the copy of the letter sent to Ministry of Lands concerning this issue, had been sent by post to Bindura and this could take a week..

Mrs. Sangarwe said that the original letter was delivered to the Ministry of Lands by hand. She would have to check to see if it had been received. It suggests that hand delivery between ministries is a chancy business.

It seemed to me that Nhema was my best hope for a breakthrough. If only he could put in a word with Elliot Manyika it might be all that is required. Cabinet meets on a Tuesday and the two would meet. I spent all day Tuesday and up to 9am.on Monday, hoping to speak with him on the phone. He never got back to his office. His secretary, Helen, told me that he came in for a few minutes just before the Cabinet meeting. She told him that I had been anxiously wishing to speak with him and I think she would have told him of my concerns. Whether he deduced anything and spoke to Manyika I shall not know. Apparently he will be away for some days; [There is a world environment summit coming off in Johannesburg shortly. Meanwhile Zimbabwe is fast destroying its own environment.]

Tomorrow I shall try to speak with the Permanent Secretary to see if the letter concerning the National Parks occupation cannot be made available to Governor Manyika. I am certainly persevering. Is it against all odds? Mrs. Alice Tafire, the forestry officer in Bindura told me on the phone yesterday: "Whatever you say, these people will just do what they like."

I went to the farm today. Johanes said that Martin has left a radio in the Fig Tree House. It would surely be stolen if left. I told him to bring it up; also any other useful items that might tempt a thief.

On Monday morning Maston came into town and to the house here. He explained that the back door key, which he uses when putting on the lights, was broken. I gave him the spare key also the keys for the side door and the bedroom passage door—these being the doors which the thieves had forced but which Johannes had since fixed. I insisted that the keys should be taken up to my house and given to Makosa after locking up. I fear lest Chamunorwa should get hold of the keys.

Johannes doesn't trust Maston and considers him to be a sell-out or quisling. Maston is a simple man, I know, and he is frightened of Chamunorwa, but he is not mentally retarded. Is his fear so abject that he needs must report all our activities to Chamunorwa like a dog to a new-found master?

On Tuesday morning, 20th.August, Gray, Martin's cook, came to me with a letter. He explained that the letter was from Johannes and had been brought in by his wife, Sinai, who was waiting outside. She was accompanied by Winet, the wife of Makosa. The letter read as follows:

To: Mr. Wiles.

Report from Johannes John.

The story not good to me at the farm. At about 11.47pm.Chamunorwa or Mujuru he send his youth to my house [2 youth] and nock my door. The time I hear a nock I was think it is night watch. May be something wrong. I woke up and I open the door. I see Chamunorwa's youth and I say—Any problem? One say now lets go together to Chamunorwa. He wants you just now. He wants to speak quick and he wants you to go back with us. I went to Bush Cottage. When I reach there he switch off the front lights and he say you do sabotage with your Boss. Now I am going to kill you street away. So he put me in handcuffs at all 2 legs and handcuffs at all 2 hands. He had his gun and told the three youths to close my eyes with a piece of cloth and to put me into his motorcar. Sinai came private and to hear that. One of the youths saw Sinai and reported this to the others. This is very lucky for me and he say, shoot others he didn't know. He switched the car lights off [and shining on] the others from inside the motorcar.

The time they saw Sinai, Chamunorwa get worry and say: take me off all handcrafts and he say to me if I report, he is going to do some thing at me anytime. So Mr. Wiles please if I report to police, police not working proper, he is going to kill me—for sure not play. Monday God still wants me. Luck with Sinai. What I need is to be away for 3 day off from the farm. I want to go to discuss with my sister at Banket. Better help me with $2000 please, please.

Because Maston report to Chamunorwa the day I took the radio for the Boss and other goods, Chamunorwa say why you took those things out. I say what things? And he say Maston reported to him.

Maston a big layer [liar]. When he sees you he talk nice but [then he goes] back to [tell] Chamunorwa.

PLEASE REPLY QUICK TODAY.

Trianda tractor fixed hydraulic. Jack driver is carry on cut grass at Trianda side and womans cut grass with sickles at Port Vally side.

Johannes.

Note: Maston is caretaker for the two vacant houses one of which Chamunorwa has broken into. Certain family belongings still remain in the other but Chamunorwa kraals his sheep in the garden. Johannes brought the radio to me on my instructions.

Having read the letter, I called for Sinai. Sinai spoke of the events of the night. She confirms following Johannes and the two youths when they left the house and proceeded to Bush Cottage where Chamunorwa was. She feared for her husband's life. She says that she stood at some distance from where the people were manacling Johannes and she listened to what they were saying.

She heard Chamunorwa tell Johannes that this was his last day of life. They were going to take him into the bush and kill him. No one would find him. At the car, one of the youths, who had been sent to call Johannes from his house said: "The wife saw us when we went to the house. If you kill this man, she will know we are the ones who have done it."

It seems that it was at this point one of the youths spotted Sinai, who was listening and watching what was happening. They quickly realised that she would be observing them plainly in the lights of the car. It was then that someone switched off the lights and Johannes was released.

Johannes should be eternally grateful to have had the loyalty and bravery of his wife Sinai. As sole witness, she had endangered herself. Fortunately for them both, Chamunorwa hesitated and refrained from committing double murder.

Later:

I was able to meet up personally with Johannes at Greencroft shopping centre on the following Saturday morning. Naturally I was keen to know how he felt and to ask him questions about his abduction. Though out of chronological order, it seems sensible to insert the record here.

On the Monday, Chamunorwa left the farm in his Peugeot station wagon and was away for most of the day, only returning well after dark. Johannes recorded the time when the two youths knocked on his door as 11.47 p.m. Chamunorwa may not have been back at Bush Cottage very long before sending the youths for Johannes.

When Johannes opened the door and spoke with the youths, Sinai came forward from the back. She tried to persuade Johannes not to go with them, but to wait until morning. Johannes replied that he might as well see what it was about.

At the Bush Cottage, Johannes saw 5 people; these were Chamunorwa, 3 youths and one other man. This man was a stranger and must have been brought out that night by Chamunorwa. Johannes said he was unable to see the man clearly in the dark, but he appeared to be stocky and he was wearing a thick [perhaps padded] black jacket.

I asked Johannes about the handcuffs. Were they proper handcuffs as used by the police? "Yes proper handcuffs." When they had handcuffed and blindfolded him, they opened the back of the vehicle to put him inside.

It was at the back of the vehicle that Chamunorwa said to Johannes, "Now I am telling you. My proper name is Mujuru and you may know that now because I am going to kill you."

Johannes added that one of the two youths, who had had come to his house earlier, protested to Mujuru, disclosing that they had been seen by Sinai who would now recognize both of them. Hearing this, Mujuru became very angry and swore at them. "Shit! Dammit! I told you to check that the woman wasn't there. Shit!" It was then that Sinai was spotted standing at a distance. Mujuru swore again and shortly afterwards Johannes was unshackled. However Mujuru warned Johannes to keep silent otherwise he would surely be killed. Mujuru then ordered one of his men to escort Johannes as far as the level crossing.

Johannes believes that the youths may well have seen Sinai in the compound earlier in the night and, in consequence, they may have expected Johannes to be at his house on his own.

It may be remembered that when Mujuru first came to the farm and broke into Bush Cottage, Johannes was shown two guns—a hand gun and a long gun kept in a green canvas bag, which is probably a rifle. It is this rifle that my workers hear Mujuru firing sometimes in the night. I asked Johannes which of the guns Mujuru had that night and he replied that it was the big gun from the green bag.

Next I asked Johannes what role the dark stranger played in this unholy business. Was he an active participant? Johannes said, "No. He was there, but he just watched and said nothing."

I put the question: "Did it appear that Mujuru and his accomplices had been drinking?" Again the answer was no; they hadn't been drinking.

To leave the farm, it is necessary for Mujuru to drive closely past Johannes's house. Johannes and his wife observed him passing very early the next morning and the stranger was with him. One cannot help but speculate upon the role of the mysterious stranger. Why did Mujuru bring him out long after nightfall and then return him at the crack of dawn? If Johannes was to be killed, Mujuru would be wise enough not to use his rifle for the job.

Could it be that the man in black is a seasoned assassin? And one to use silent methods?

There then is a summary of this painful story, which I have put together from the evidence given me by Sinai and by Johannes in his letter and later in his verbal account.

I resume now in sequence. [Now that Chamunorwa has revealed his proper name, henceforth I shall refer to him by this.]

This development really disconcerted me. Johannes is essential to keep things going. Without him there, the remaining staff would wither under the dictates of Mujuru. As it is, he has forbidden the farm workers to irrigate and work the land under vegetables. Garlic, rape, potatoes, carrots, pigeon pea; all are drying up. Without Johannes, who drives the tractor, even hay-baling would cease.

Messages have been passed to me that if I come out to the farm, Mujuru will shoot me. Whilst I think he will stop short of that, he has already chained and locked me into my homestead once and he has shown his contempt for the police time and again. Yet I admit to myself I fear direct confrontation with him. I don't believe he would shoot me out of hand, but there is more than one way to kill a cat—or an elderly white farmer. I think my blood pressure is still pretty good, but I would rather not bank on it.

Should I send out word to the farm that the workers should lay off and just stay in their homes? Of course that would suit Mujuru fine. Like the ogre he is, he could stomp around the farm pillaging and laying waste to the content of his evil heart.

Should I then employ more Tredar guards? A costly business and they too are bidden not to involve themselves in "political" affairs!

Having come to my wit's end, I phoned Hamish Turner. Hamish is our local CFU chairman and a highly productive farmer. He has had much experience dealing with the exhausting troubles that have beset the district. In fact he had just spent three days in police cells in Nyabira. His crime was that he had not moved off his farm by due date in conformity with a Section 8 eviction order. It required a lawyer to explain to the police that he had NEVER been issued with a Section 8 and the farm was not even listed for acquisition. [The farm incidentally is producing high value export crops.]

Hamish is one of those remarkable people, who can accept outrageous iniquity with no more than cynical resignation. He was ready to listen to my difficulties and his advice was to get a lawyer on to the job.

I got an appointment to see Richard Wood of Atherstone and Cook. My appointment was for 3pm. but he was so busy dealing with other farmers that I had to wait for 40 minutes before he could see me. I went through the whole background with him. He was well versed on much of this.

My Section 8 order, he confirmed, had expired and was no longer valid. The government should have issued another one if they still intended to acquire the farm. However, they had not done so. On that score alone, the Court would issue an eviction order on Mujuru.

Nevertheless that was the easy part. He pointed out that the legal costs of obtaining the court order would be in the region of $100 000 and there would also be the bailiff's charges. In all the outlay could be about $150 000.

His considered legal opinion was that, in present circumstances, it is improbable that the law enforcement agencies would carry out the court's order. His advice was to save my money and wait in the hope that there will be some breakthrough which will restore the authority of the courts. His best advice was to persevere with Nhema, which, of course I am doing.

Richard Wood revealed that he was familiar with the Nyabira police station because he had been called there to represent other farmers. Recently he had been kept there for over three hours arguing a case, during which a certain Constable Marimo had threatened to arrest him and then to throw him out of the station. Interestingly this was in front of his superior officer. Angered though he was, Richard kept silent and eventually the atmosphere calmed. He guesses that Const.Marimo is probably a political plant in the station. Oddly enough, I remembered the name and I am sure I have had dealings with the man.

Richard thought that in my case it was unlikely that I would be arrested. He didn't say why. Perhaps he had warned the Nyabira police to check on the validity of the Section 8 orders before making an arrest. Not that I think that would make much difference. It all depends on their racial attitude and if they enjoy baiting us.

Wednesday 21st.August 2002

In the morning, one of my first actions was to phone the Ministry for Environment. It was my intention to speak with Mrs. Sangarwe, the Deputy Secretary tasked to forward the Minister's proposal to have the whole of Stockade Farm placed under the control of National Parks. Although I believed Minister Nhema to be away, at the last moment, I asked for my call to be put through to Helen, the Minister's secretary. This was a bit of luck because Helen told me that all yesterday afternoon [whilst I was at the lawyers], she had been trying to reach me. The Minister had in fact been in and could have spoken with me. More luck; he was again in his office right then. I was put through to him.

To start off, I told the Minister that I was glad that it appeared he had gone along with my offer of the farm to National Parks and I asked him if this was definitely the case. He assented.

I told Minister Nhema as briefly as possible of the intolerable conditions on the farm brought upon by Mujuru. Nhema broke in to express surprise and said: "Is he still there?" I replied, "Very much so," and related briefly the man's recent doings including the kidnapping of my foreman.

I reiterated the need for speed in resolving the issue and Nhema said he would instruct the officer appointed to the business [Mrs.Sangarwe] to move accordingly.

Then I told the Minister that I was getting very negative reactions from the Provincial Land Committee in Bindura, who had obviously no knowledge of our plans. The spokesman for the committee, repeatedly told me to see the Governor. I told Nhema it would be pointless for me to see the Governor if he too knew nothing of the plan.

I am sure Nhema saw my point at once. He said: "What a pity. I was with him yesterday." [Ah, I was aware of that!] However, he promised to contact Elliot Manyika about the matter. I thanked him.

This conversation bucked me up a bit, but there is a positive minefield ahead; the biggest danger, I fear, being Elliot Manyika himself. He is one of the most radical of Mugabe's ministers and it is most unfortunate that he is also the Governor of this province. Just how confident, I wonder, is Francis Nhema in his dealings with him?

Friday 23rd.August 2002
Johannes has stayed on the farm. During the devastating fire that swept the farm, a section of electric cable at our second transformer was burnt. This resulted in Bush Cottage and therefore Mujuru getting no electricity. No skin off his nose, Mujuru finds Johannes and tells him to repair the cable; otherwise he vows to cut off power to the whole farm. He is quite capable of carrying out this threat and this would result in the farm complex and my house getting no light and no water.

The work to repair the cable necessitated splicing in a new section and this, the foreman did. For some reason and in spite of everything, a sort of reconciliation occurred after that. Johannes even went off with the tractor to make some more hay bales.

Whatever; Mujuru erupted again today, Friday. Johannes rang me to say that Mujuru had ordered all farm work to stop. The tractor must not be used; there could be no more baling. Makosa and the garden staff must leave my house. The girl, Rosemary, could feed the dogs in the morning but then must go home.

Hearing this news, I decided to phone the police. Inspector Sengwe was out. I spoke with A\Insp.Taswa and told him of the turn of events and asked him what could be done.

Taswa asked me if I was there on the farm. I said that I wasn't. He said: "If you're not on the farm, how do you know of these matters?"

"Because my foreman has informed me by phone."

"How do you know if it is true?"

"Why shouldn't it be? The foreman is in charge. It is his responsibility to inform me."

"But he is not the complainant. You are the complainant."

"Would it help if my foreman phones you?"

"He is not the owner. You are the owner. Why aren't you on the farm?"

"I am glad you acknowledge that I am the owner. I am not on the farm because this character Mujuru has threatened to kill me if I return."

This statement of mine brought a peal of laughter from A\Insp.Taswa.

"Why do you laugh?" I asked. There was no reply.

"Then you can come to Nyabira," Taswa said after a pause, "We can meet together here."

"I have no intention of meeting this Mujuru."

"Why not?"

"Because even speaking about him over the phone at this very moment is making my heart pound madly." [This was indeed the truth—the condition aggravated by Taswa's attitude.]

There was another pause and finally: "Alright. Someone will go over there some time during the day. But you should come to Nyabira to speak with the Inspector yourself."

Late in the afternoon I again phoned the police. Insp.Sengwe was said to be in town; so too was A\Insp.Taswa. Nobody in the charge office seemed to know anything about going to Stockade Farm, so I asked to speak to the senior man presently on duty. Who was it? I was told it was Sergeant Tezha. This made me a bit uneasy.

Some weeks ago I had received a mysterious call from Sgt.Tezha. He asked me if I was on the farm, because he wished to speak with me. It happened that I was not. When I asked what it was he needed to speak to me about, he replied that it was a personal matter. He wanted a loan. I replied that I was the very last person he could have chosen to ask for money. Due to the Warvet invasions, I was left utterly broke. Whether he was working a subtle protection racket, I shall never know, but he got no money out of me then, and here I was now asking him for police assistance.

Sgt. Tezha came to the phone. He made out that he hardly remembered who I was. In answer to my questions he said he had no knowledge of my phone call to A\Insp.Taswa that morning nor had he been told of any arrangement for a police visit to the farm.

The sergeant asked the question: had I been designated? I replied that the status of Stockade had not been finalised by government. In the meantime I needed to keep on working. The sergeant said that the matter would have to wait for his inspector.

This attitude of the police is all true to form, but I try not to fall into utter despair. In my case the inspector had made a few attempts to control Mujuru, but as the revolutionary movement fast gains momentum, he is standing well back.

Saturday 24th.August 2002

I received an early phone call from Johannes. It was to tell me that he was in town at Greencroft. He had come in because he wanted to buy a part for his TV. Although work had stopped, the watchmen and the guard were functioning and the dogs were alright. I arranged to meet him at the Greencroft shops at 10 o'clock.

Approaching Greencroft I felt slightly apprehensive. It is amazing how the general lawlessness in the country can put one on edge. Could it possibly be that Johannes had been driven in by Mujuru under threat and I was being lured into a trap? I had heard of one farmer who had been tracked down in town and beaten up. I drove into the main parking lot very cautiously, stopping in an open area ready for a quick getaway!

I saw Johannes coming towards me confidently, looking very smart and wearing a wide-brimmed hat and glasses. I hardly recognized him. However he was quite alone so I opened the passenger door for him and he got in. It was clear that he no longer feared being murdered by Mujuru. I asked him if he had handed over the farm keys to him. Johannes said he had refused to do so and he had also refused to leave the borehole pump with Mujuru, who had demanded it. He confirmed that he had employed Kariza as an extra day watchman to be with the Tredar guard on duty at my house. He also said that he himself went with Rosemary in the early morning to feed the dogs.

All in all I felt that things were not so bad. Johannes told me that Mujuru had left the farm that morning but I decided not to go out. The two dogs are my main concern. They must be feeling very lonely without old Makosa and the familiar garden staff around. Right now I have nowhere to keep them in town and I myself will have to find another place to stay when the family returns from holiday in eight day's time. What I need is a house-sitting job; a house with a large garden and no dogs.

I bought some dog meat at the TM store for Johannes to give to Rosemary for feeding Moppet and Humba, and we parted. The rest of the information, which I took from Johannes and concerning his abduction, I have already written up.

Monday 26th.August 2002

I am in a most invidious position. Mujuru has shut down all farm work. Direct confrontation with him will expose me, at the least to a barrage of threats and racial abuse; at worst, physical assault. Neither will do my health any good. Therefore, he is effectively barring me from visiting my farm.

This situation can only be resolved by police intervention. However, as I have already learnt, the police have no intention of reacting to my pleas. More than that, I suspect that their insistence that I present myself in person at the police station, was made with sinister intent. Once there I would be arrested and put in cells on the charge of not complying with the Section 8 government order. Even if I were to meet with them on the farm, I could end up with the same fate. It would not avail me to argue legality. I have just read in the paper that the police have even set up roadblocks to catch farmers.

The only way open to me, if I wish to visit my home, is to creep in clandestinely having first been given the tip off that neither Mujuru nor a policeman is present. I may attempt to do so this week.

Wary though I was, I thought I might speak to Inspector Sengwe, IN PERSON, to ask him if he couldn't get my personal staff back to look after the house. The first time I rang, I was told he had gone to Chinhoyi and the second time I rang the station nobody answered the phone.

Perhaps it was just as well. It may sound strange, but in a way I don't want to draw too much attention to Stockade Farm in certain circles. My counter move through Minister Nhema and National Parks may stand a better chance if the opposition forces are taken unawares—in other words; if Francis Nhema can introduce the plan to Elliot Manyika and win him over before Manyika's hounds have wind of it. Should they sniff it too soon they are sure to start baying.

Of course, this is all pure speculation on my part. I have but a fleeting connection with the few who, I like to believe, are covertly sympathetic to my standpoint. With those who are overtly hostile, I have no connection at all. I cannot read their minds.

This morning I delivered a letter to Nhema. It was reinforcing my concerns. I thought he had gone to the Johannesburg Earth Summit and was surprised to hear that he was still around. I met him at the lifts and told him that I had just dropped off a letter for him. I hope he may have made some pertinent phone calls to key persons this very morning. If so, the rescue of Stockade Farm may have briefly taken precedence over the rescue of the planet. As I have little faith that the latter will be achieved, it makes the first objective pointless, I suppose.

Friday 30th.August 2002.

How is it that I still hold on to a grain of hope? Yesterday I rang Helen, the Minister's secretary, to ask her if Nhema had left any word or written a reply to my letter.

She replied that the Minister was now away at the Johannesburg Earth Summit, but that he had passed the matter on to the Permanent Secretary, Mr. Tavaya. I was put through to the latter's office only to learn that he too was at the Summit. A Mr. Mageza was acting as the Ministry Secretary. I could try phoning him tomorrow—Friday. This I have now done, only to find that he is at the Agricultural Show. His secretary however thinks my matter is being dealt with by Mrs. Sangarwe. And Mrs. Sangarwe? She left for the Summit some days ago.

On Tuesday, having heard from Johannes that Mujuru had gone to town, I went out to the farm. Makosa came up from the compound and helped collect some vegetables and flowers from the garden. Makosa likes to make a vegetable soup for me so I also had cartons of frozen soup to keep me going for a few days.

Moppet and Humba were looking well. They long for me take them walking on the farm.

On Wednesday, Eliot, the Nola driver, took some rations out to the farm for the workers. Food is becoming short and bread is scarce even in the city shops.

We could be lifting garlic now, but our people have been scared off by Mujuru. There are good carrots ready enough to dig up in spite of having had no water for some time. We could also be selling rape.

I phoned Insp. Sengwe to tell him that I was in all kinds of trouble. I said that I knew it was difficult for him to help me with things as they are, but perhaps he could enable us to reap our crops. The inspector was in an amiable mood:

"Help you? Of course I will help you—even if it's every day, I will help you."

He said he was tied up on Friday and there was to be a station inspection on Monday and Tuesday next week. He thought he could meet me on Saturday. I should confirm on Friday afternoon.

I said: "Hearing of all the farmers who have been arrested, how can I be sure you won't arrest me?"

"Ah, we don't arrest old men," he replied.

I thought there would be no harm in telling him that due to my concerns, I had consulted my lawyer, who had assured me that the papers I had first been served with were now invalid and that I was legally quite in the clear.

The inspector then asked me if I could do him a couple of favours. I asked the nature.

"Would you let me have some flowers?"

I thought I had heard incorrectly and asked him to repeat himself. I just couldn't connect a policeman with flowers. But, yes, flowers.

"You mean flowers—flowers from the garden?"

"Yes."

"Willingly," I said. "You may help yourself to as many as you want from the garden when you come." I thought quickly. "Are the flowers for your annual inspection?"

"Yes."

What a beautiful idea. Has anybody, anywhere in the whole world, ever seen a bowl of flowers decorating the counter of a police charge office?

The inspector's further request had to do with a small poultry scheme he was fostering for the women, the wives of his officers.

"I need some iron sheets for roofing the house."

I replied that I could probably assist him with some iron sheets taken from an old building. How many did he want? He said he would have to take some measurements.

In these times of darkness, weak rays of hope are soon extinguished. A moment of light relief is inevitably overtaken and forgotten in the general flow of bad news. I received a phone call from Wellington, the Trianda Farm manager. He handed the call over to Johannes, who had walked over to Trianda to report to me from there. Whilst Johannes was at my house with Rosemary attending to the garden, a man had broken in to his house and stolen several items including his cell phone.

This is a bad blow. A cell phone is prohibitively expensive; at the same time, knowing what is taking place on the farm on a daily basis, and especially in case of an emergency, it is of vital importance. The mere fact of knowing that Johannes could always call me if in trouble, was in itself reassuring. I felt really dashed.

Communications generally are bad enough. The Tredar security base is inaccessible because both the radio and telephone service have been out of order for weeks. Even the local police station is confined to a single line, which is usually engaged.

Another cell phone will have to be found for Johannes. It is an expense the farm can ill afford—but there.

To add to my woes, I also learnt that Mujuru had come up to my house in his car, ordered Rosemary to shut up the dogs, and then proceeded to walk all around. I think this news upset me more than anything else; the arrogant invasion of my home—perhaps even because I was not there—felt like a thrust against my own person. A cared-for garden is a living extension of the personalities of those who have tended it; in my case, Beth was the tender carer.

In every corner, it is imbued with precious memories. This intrusion of an evil presence would foul the very air.

Saturday 31st.August 2002

This morning, after a night of mental turmoil, I phoned Insp. Sengwe to ask if he still intended to visit the farm. The inspector's manner of speech is one of a tired drawl, which sometimes descends to a mutter. I felt that he may have forgotten about the arrangement, but anyway, he said he would come through to me after he had visited his post at Stapleford. This gave me time to drive myself out to the farm.

Crest Breeders were collecting the last of the hay bales when I arrived and I met Johannes at my house where I also found Makosa and Rosemary. Johannes confirmed that Mujuru had driven off the farm earlier in the morning.

At about 11.30 there was a hoot at the gate and Rosemary went to let the police Landrover in. I noted there were only two men in it. It drove up to where I was waiting in front of my garage. Neither of the two men descended so I went up to speak with them.

For some strange reason, I didn't recognize Insp. Sengwe at all. My lack of recognition was such that I really wondered who on earth these policemen were. I even became quite suspicious and wondered briefly if these were strange policemen, who maybe had been given orders to come and arrest me on the strength of my Section 8 order [expired and legally invalid though it is]. My confusion was not helped by the uncommunicative manner of the two men. From their high Landrover seats, they simply gazed fixedly down at me- wordless. I felt remarkably small and vulnerable.

Covering my confusion with some spontaneous rhetoric, I eventually had to ask the driver who he was.

"I am Sengwe," said the driver whose door was closest to me.

"Good heavens!" I declared, "I never recognized you. It must be that you are without your policeman's cap and uniform.

"Well, I am in mufti."

"Yes," I said, now thoroughly embarrassed but scrutinising his features the while. He has a grey patch of hair on his temple.

"But I see you are turning grey like me. It must be all the worries."

The inspector climbed down from the Landrover and we began to discuss my situation. As we conversed, I soon acknowledged to myself that the lazy drawl fading to a mumble, was unmistakably Sengwe's. Yet I had met him face to face at the Nyabira police station and it astonished me that I had lost recognition of his physical features. Once more I felt the need to apologize. He said, "Perhaps it is you haven't got your glasses on." That rescued me.

"Ah, yes!" I exclaimed, "That must be it." and I triumphantly dug my spectacles from my trouser pocket and put them on my nose.

The policemen probably thought that they had come upon an ancient scatterbrain, who had been viewing them through misty, myopic eyes. This was hardly the case. I can only think that when I had met Sengwe previously, I had been so intent on my mission that his face had not registered in my mind or the impression had in some way merged in my memory with the previous incumbent at Nyabira, Inspector Masuka. Or perhaps stress had induced amnesia.

The second man in the vehicle was an assistant inspector. This I noted from his shoulder insignia. I deduced that it was the man with whom I had had so many unresponsive phone conversations—Assistant Inspector Taswa.

"Then you must be A\Insp.Taswa," I called genially looking across at him. "We meet in person at last." Taswa's form of reply was a faint supercilious smile and a nod. He stayed in the Landrover and took no apparent interest in the discussion.

One of the things I did when the inspector arrived was to dispatch Makosa hurriedly to pick the bunches of flowers for the police station. I told Sengwe what was being done.

Oh dear! It seems I had misunderstood. What he wanted was garden plants, not flowers. Dashed was my imaginative vision of a flower-decked police station signifying sweet welcome to the visitor. Makosa was hurriedly recalled.

Insp.Sengwe has the unusual ability to converse whilst rolling a spent matchstick around on his tongue. It is fascinating to watch the match balanced at changing angles on the tongue or the lips yet never falling. Every now and then the matchstick would slide to the corner of his mouth and the inspector would take a draw on the stub of a burning cigarette, which he produced miraculously from his palm in the manner of a conjuring trick.

The discussion strayed rather unproductively on the legal aspect of Section 8's, from which I gathered that whilst it was plain the judiciary and the government held different views, the police were content to follow the government line—the safer side to be on at this stage of the game.

I steered the talk back to Stockade and my immediate problems. I asked Sengwe the proper name of our invader. Was it Chamunorwa or was it Mujuru? He replied that it was Mujuru. Mujuru was the surname. "So his name should be Chamunorwa Mujuru I suppose?" The inspector didn't reply to this question. I sense there is something mysterious about this use of names. Perhaps it has something to do with him being a medicine man.

I made the point that Mujuru, who everyone calls Chamunorwa, did not arrive on the farm until 9th.May this year. Yet John Nkomo, Home Affairs minister, has said that all settlers who had entered farms after 31st.March should be removed. The inspector said that Mujuru claims he cultivated a field on Stockade some time back. I told him that this is a lie. Fortunately Johannes was standing nearby and was able to corroborate that we had never seen the man before May.

Finally the inspector rather reluctantly concluded that he should follow up on Mujuru and told me that he would return to the farm in the evening when the man would probably be back.

Once again I offered Sengwe the iron sheets for the poultry shed. In doing so I wondered if Taswa, his junior, was hearing for the first time, Sengwe's proposal for a poultry scheme in which police officers wives were to participate!

The police Landrover drove away and Johannes was able to tell me more concerning Mujuru's incursion into my garden the previous day. When Johannes heard Mujuru's car driving up to my homestead and entering the grounds, he followed it inside. Mujuru had brought with him another person. Johannes described this person as having long dreadlocks down to his shoulders. He wore a skirt rather than trousers and a white top garment with a blue sash. He had traditional-type sandals made from tyre rubber.

I asked Johannes if he thought the man was educated.

"No," was his reply. "He looked like a Zinatha person or a witchdoctor. His body was dirty and the dreadlocks on his head looked like full of dirt too."

The two Africans walked all around my grounds. Somewhere in the front of the house, the man with the dishevelled dreadlocks stopped and proceeded to hammer a wooden peg into the ground. Johannes was told that this signified that I would never return to the house. The words used in the vernacular would refer to me as "the white man."

This whole issue is a racial one. It is planned and promulgated at the very top and eagerly latched upon by malevolent plunderers.

When I was given this latest report of the dreadlock witchdoctor, I felt that the garden air must be contaminated with evil. One day I shall conduct an exorcism.

Wednesday 4th. September 2002

Things have turned worse rather than better. Insp. Sengwe never put in an appearance on the farm as he had promised. On Monday Mujuru called all the farm workers to a gathering and once more proclaimed himself owner of the farm and that no one must work. The watchmen I employed must leave their posts and even the Tredar guard must return to his base.

The workers should send a message to the Boss to pay them their final money and then they must leave the farm. Notwithstanding, if I was seen returning to the farm, the fact must be reported to him at once and he would personally "chain me up". He cared nothing for the police. He had greater power than they had.

To convey this to my workers took Mujuru the best part of an hour. Like so many of his kind, he loves the sound of his own voice and to feel the power he can exert over his captives—for they are hardly anything more.

I arrived on the farm at around 11 a.m. just when this meeting had ended and my people were dispersing. I found Johannes and when I heard what was going on, I brought him up to my house and out of sight. Mujuru may have got wind of my presence and I had no wish to experience another confrontation with him, so I decided to drive straight to the police station at Nyabira.

On the way to the police I stopped at the Tredar base camp and had a brief word with the duty sergeant. I told him what Mujuru had said about the removal of the Tredar guard from Stockade and that he had better inform his O.C. of the possibility. The sergeant's retort was: "These people are only looking for money. He probably just hopes you will pay him something."

Well yes, I know. The Warvets and the other political thugs are born robbers and naturally they have exploited the opportunities for extortion in a big way. But experience has shown that the extortionist never lets you off the hook. He will take you for everything you've got.

At Z.R.P. Nyabira, there was a meeting taking place, which of course I had learnt about. I had hoped it might have been concluded, but this was not so and when I arrived the whole company was being addressed by a visiting superintendent. I was informed that they might be through by 1 o'clock, which was an hour hence. All I could do was leave a message that I would either return or phone later.

In the event I phoned Sengwe from town shortly after 1.30. He came to the phone and I told him quickly of the latest developments. He said he would ring me back in ten minutes. One hour later, I rang again to learn that he was not around and had gone out "somewhere". He phoned our Avondale number later in the afternoon. I was out at the Ministry of Lands but Martin took the call. The inspector told Martin that he would be speaking with the DA at 10 o'clock next morning, Tuesday, and please to ring him at 11 o'clock. Martin gave me the message when I returned.

At the Ministry of Lands, I had briefly met the Director of Lands, Mr. Tashire, a short, stout man, polite and businesslike. He was about to go to an appointment so suggested I come to meet him the next day. Time? "As early as you can make it. I am in the office from 7 am. Wow! Unusual for a civil servant.

In the event, I reached Mr.Tashire's office well before 8 am. and found that he had already been busy hearing people's petitions. A group of four farmers were emerging from his office when I arrived. They all passed me smiling, which suggested they were happy with the outcome of their meeting.

Mr.Tashire listened to my tale. He appeared to know something of the Protected Forest because he mentioned it before I did. This was refreshing. I explained the need for an urgent decision to be taken and my frustration caused by the Bindura Land Committee, who did not answer my application and letters. Mr. Tashire very quickly saw that I had right and reason on my side.

He skimmed through some of the correspondence I had brought, including letters from his own ministry. When he noted that, by way of a phone message, the Committee had offered me 30 hectares of land, he said in exasperation: "How can you look after a forest without even a house to live in? No. Leave the matter with me. I will deal with it."

I begged him to move as swiftly as possible and told him of the terrible pressures I was experiencing. "Fancy having that at your age," he said. "Who is this man you have on the place?" I gave him the name; Mujuru. "Is he related to the general?" he asked, referring to the retired army general. I replied that I had no idea. This question has been put to me many times, which suggests that the general is feared and still wields political clout.

During the course of the morning, Martin rang to say that a letter had come in from the farm. The letter was from Johannes and in effect it was relaying a message from Mujuru. All my staff had been ordered to stay in the compound and nobody should go to my house. The message for the Boss was a repeat of the previous one. I must bring out money to pay all the workers their terminal pay. After that, the workers must vacate their houses and leave the farm. Now Mujuru had the opportunity to blackmail me. Until such time that I obeyed his instructions and brought out the money, my dogs would not be fed. Naturally he did not care about the dogs.

Here lay the implication. Moppet and Humber were his hostages. Mujuru has two guns. Everyone on the farm knows that and he knows that I know. He has shown himself to be a ruthless and dangerous man—probably a psychopath. Obviously my two dogs were now exposed to mortal danger; either from shooting or by poisoning. Mujuru would not be deterred, because the killing of two dogs would be considered a trivial offence in the law book.

A phone call to the police was answered by Sgt. Muchenagumbo. He informed me that the inspector was at a meeting in Zvimba and would not be returning until evening. I asked the sergeant for advice; did he think I should go to the farm to collect my dogs and at the same time risk an ugly and possibly damaging confrontation with Mujuru? He offered his personal opinion that my situation was safe; things had not reached that stage. This was an enigmatic statement but I think he implied that, on current information available to the police, Mujuru was bluffing. The sergeant promised to tell the inspector of my problem on his return to the station. Filled with anxiety though I was, I felt that the dogs would most likely be safe for another 24 hours, but I would have to muster support on the morrow.

Thursday 5th.September 2002

After forty years of living in one home, my position is a peculiar one. Most white farmers have been ejected from their homes in circumstances, which can be likened to being overrun in a revolutionary war. Their evictions have been rapid, ruthless and final; their homes occupied by one or another of the revolutionaries supporting the Party. Stockade Farm and the Protected Forest thereon and gazetted by government itself, has thrown government officials into confusion.

For the past two years, squabbles have been taking place at local level, but there has been no ruling from the Ministry of Lands, supposedly the final authority. [Mark the word "supposedly", because nothing is clear in this state of anarchy]. Even by the government's own rendering of the law, I am still the rightful owner of my property. This is being challenged by its rabid supporters on the ground, notably Mujuru and, separately, a group of so-called Warvets. The police act as bystanders. My position therefore is indeed unique, because I fall into a category of a semi-displaced person; a legal property owner turned out of his home. As a result, I offer my services as a house-sitter to townies going away on holiday. I advertise myself as an elderly, honest, responsible gentleman, good with pets. I always get on with the pets.

I began my phone calls from my temporary residence; first The Ministry of Lands. I needed to speak with Mr. Tishere concerning my farm status. His secretary said she was sorry, but Mr. Tashire was away and would not return to the office until next Monday.

Whilst with the Min. of Lands, I thought I would take a chance and speak with Mrs. Mandimika, with whom I have had a courteous relationship. What a bit of luck! It was almost as if she expected my call. "I have just been informed by Bindura that your farm is to be delisted," she said. "I shall be writing a letter to this effect and a copy will be sent to you." Naturally, I said I was delighted with the news.

"I will certainly call and collect the letter in person," I told her. "Is it possible to have it today so that I can show it to the police?"

"No, I can't manage that because I shall be out for most of the day," she replied, "but you may collect it tomorrow morning. You can then show it to your police inspector. Have you been in contact with the Ministry for Environment?" she asked. "It is important that they follow up."

"I have been trying to find out what steps they have been taking," I said.

"The trouble is most of the important officers have been away at the Johannesburg Earth Summit. However, they should be back today."

I promised Mrs. Mandimika I would call on her tomorrow during the morning. At this stage, I am unclear as to what steps she expects from the Environment Ministry.

After the Ministry of Lands, I phoned Nyabira police. There I got A\ Insp. Taswa. Today he seemed pleasantly breezy. I spoke of my predicament with regard to Mujuru. "Yes, he is wanting to make trouble," Taswa said. "We will be coming there this afternoon."

I volunteered the information that I had been verbally told that the farm was to be delisted. He merely repeated, "We will come there this afternoon."

My next call was to Wellington on Trianda to ask him to please send a message to Johannes requesting him to go over to Trianda from whence he could speak with me on Wellington's cell phone. I needed to brief Johannes that the police intended to visit the farm and of course, to be kept informed of any developments.

The last call was to Environment and Mrs. Sangarwe. I learnt that she couldn't get on her flight back from Johannesburg and would only be returning tonight.

In the evening, Alan Foot phoned me from his farm Trianda to say that Johannes had been on the Agric Alert radio. He was contacting the Tredar base to tell them that he knew where his stolen cell phone was and who had it. He asked them to come out quickly. A few days ago, I had instructed Johannes how to operate the radio and now he was able to use it to advantage. He had already told me he had a lead on the thief or thieves, who had broken into his house. I shall have to wait until tomorrow to learn if the cell phone and his tapes have been recovered and a party charged.

The day ends. Although there are signs of a breakthrough, the way ahead is fraught with impediments

Friday 6th. September 2002

I spent the whole morning making arrangements to see Mrs. Mandimika of Lands and Mrs. Sangarwe of Environment and in due course meeting them in their respective offices, which are far removed from one another.

Mrs. Mandimika holds a position in the ministry which I imagine is an upper grade, but not as lofty as a Deputy Secretary. It seems she is empowered to write letters per pro the Permanent Secretary. In my dealings with government ministries, I have noted that there are a good number of these women in this category; mature, well-proportioned figures, probably holding degrees.

Mrs. Mandimika has a large office of her own, a large desk and, lining one wall, a suite of heavy easy chairs covered in deep-red plush, indicative of status rather than practicability. I paid my respects and chose a businesslike chair opposite her desk. She greeted me pleasantly and at once handed me my copy of the letter she had just drafted to the Chief Land Officer, Bindura. I read through the letter briefly and we spoke of matters arising from it. What follows is my assessment after I had taken it away and studied it carefully. Below is a section of the letter. I have underlined certain key words.

"The Purpose of this letter is to inform you of the *decision that has been taken* by the Ministry for Environment and Tourism on the issue of Stockade Farm. The Secretary for Environment and Tourism wrote on 8th. August 2002, to our Secretary *recommending* that this farm be given to the Department of National Parks and Wildlife. He is of the *opinion* that this recommendation is in line with the resettlement policy. Your office is therefore *being tasked to inform* the Mashonaland Central Land Committee on the recommendations of the Secretary for Environment and Tourism to our Secretary."

For the introduction, there is a strong commanding theme. Even the word "Purpose" is spelt with a capital P. In civil service parlance, is this a shorthand for: "Take note and obey"?

Unfortunately, this resolute beginning is soon weakened by the use of equivocal words such as "opinion" and "recommendation". However, an authoritative sound returns with the passage: "Your office is being tasked to inform..." etc.

It seems to me that Mrs. Mandimika has introduced some ambiguity into her letter, which the Land Committee may well exploit. They may disagree with the "opinion" and oppose the "recommendation." It will depend on who holds the most power. The much-feared Elliot Manyika is the chairman of the committee.

When I was with her, Mrs. Mandimika expressed confidence that the transfer to Parks would go ahead. At least it is apparent that the two ministries, Lands and Environment are in accord. She went on to say that I should impress on Environment the need to put personnel onto the property as soon as they can, in order to protect the forest and the assets.

Mrs. M added that it was the Lands ministry, who would be responsible for valuations, and these would go ahead as soon as Parks took up the land. She would introduce me to Mr. Moyo, the chief valuator. "They are very fair and you are free to accept or not; but I advise you act whilst there is still some money." To me, such thinking seems premature. As for compensation, I guess this is so much pie in the sky.

From Ngungunyana Building on the Borrowdale road, [How about that for a cultural mix?] I go to Karigamombe Centre in the city centre where the Min. for E and T occupy the 14th. and 15th. floors. I had to wait some time to see Mrs. Sangarwe, who is Deputy Secretary Environment. She had been away at the Summit for ten days or so and was attending to much backlog.

Beyond a short telephone call, I had not had connection with Mrs. Sangarwe, so I was pleased to meet with her in person. She received me very cordially and I proceeded to fill her in with a short history leading up to the current position. I showed her my copy of Mrs. Mandimika's letter to the Committee. Mrs. Sangarwe read it through and noted with professional disapproval, that Mrs. M had not included the Ministry for Environment in the list of copies required for distribution—a very reasonable criticism I thought, since that Ministry is principally involved! I suggested she take my copy and have it photostated then and there, which she did.

I brought up Mrs. Mandimika's point about getting an early presence onto the farm. Once again Mrs. Sangarwe registered disapproval. "Yes, it would be easy to have some National Parks people placed on the farm. But first we must have a written endorsement from Lands that we may proceed." I knew this would be the correct procedure. Much as I wanted action, I acknowledged her point of view. My role was that of a messenger in this frustrating inter-ministerial business.

Mrs. Sangarwe gave me a pleasing impression as she was attentive and sympathetic. She said she would contact Mrs. Mandimika and ask her to *write a formal letter*. I said that if this could be done on Monday next week, I would offer my services as postman.

I had wondered what may have become of my last letter to Minister Nhema, in which I revealed the abduction and fearful ordeal of Johannes by Mujuru and the need for urgent action by Elliot Manyika. My understanding was that he had passed it on to his secretaries. However, Mrs. Sangarwe had not seen it so she thought it may still be with the minister. Perhaps now it will never surface.

Before leaving, I asked for her overall impressions of the Earth Summit. Her criticism was that there were far too many issues to be discussed by too many people. Another comment she made was, that at the end of the day, economics influenced every delegation.

Nothing changes does it?

Late in the afternoon, I drove out to the farm. Martin had suggested that I might have peace of mind if I were to bring the two dogs into town and keep them at the Marlborough house where I am staying. I found the Tredar guard lifting potatoes in the field and then found Johannes at his house. One of his children ran to fetch Makosa from the compound. While we were waiting, I learnt from Johannes that his scheme to catch the thief was a success. The cell phone and his ten tapes had all been recovered at Estes Park. They were now with the police as was the youth who had them. Johannes is sure the real thief is one of Mujuru's men who sold them on. I wonder if the youth will split?

Johannes also told me that Mujuru had been firing shots from his gun around the area of my house. He drives his car about the farm and gunshots are often heard. I said this must mean he is firing at duikers or reedbuck—probably spotting them dazzled in his headlights. Johannes said he had seen a duiker down by the fir trees, which are not far from the Bush Cottage where Mujuru is staked out. The animal was trailing a broken leg.

More news was that Bigg, Kariza and Norman were now too scared of Mujuru to work as watchmen. This means that I only have the Tredar man left. He is presently guarding my house on his own. I called the Tredar base on the radio and asked them to supply an extra guard and dog from tomorrow. We can't afford it.

Thieving is rife. Two more electric switches have been stolen from the transformer. My house still contains my possessions. It would be a target for a thief in the night or in the daytime—especially if Mujuru has chased off my workers leaving the house unattended much of the time. It puts me in a dilemma. Moppet and Humba are a deterrent to a thief, but on the other hand an insensitive brute like Mujuru, who loves the power of his gun, could kill them both.

It was getting dark when I decided to take the two dogs into town with me. What a picnic! Both of them were over excited and Moppet was whimpering and bouncing around all the way in. I was house-sitting for my old friends Frank and Daphne White. On arrival, we were met by their two dogs, softie black Lab, Angie, and slender young Danny. I glanced down at my two. How gross they looked in comparison—nothing but a pair of rough-tough farm dogs. However I knew them to be good-natured and hoping for the best I opened the car door. They fell out like an avalanche.

Bravely, but most unfortunately, Danny decided to object to this rude invasion. As a result Humba and particularly Moppet, were attacking him where he had retreated under my car. In my rush to protect Danny, I fell flat on the ground, half under the car, hanging on like grim death to two collars and yelling furiously at all three dogs and even at poor Martha, the housemaid, who was timidly trying to call Danny to her. Angie had wisely made herself scarce early on. Lying prone, head resting on the driveway, I found myself looking up into three snapping faces. In sheer desperation, I righted myself without losing my grip on Moppet and Humba; then Danny slipped out from under the car unharmed.

I heaved my two back into the car, shut the doors, and worked out some sort of a strategy. There was a netting wire fence around the pool area. It looked substantial, so I led my dogs through the access gate, took off the leads and slipped out. Moppet took only two minutes to get out; Humba a little longer. Moppet I caught and put into the house; Humba I transferred to a wooden garden shed, which seemed solid enough. I was sorry he would have to spend the night there and regretfully turned my back and walked away. Before I reached the house, he was bounding round the garden with Angie and Danny in tow. I went back to look at the shed; it must have had a hole in it. There wasn't a hole. The door was shut. It must have been a magic shed or Humba was a magic dog.

Humba then, seemed to have made friends with Angie and Danny, but I was unsure of Moppet. She is half Staffie. I had her in the house with me. Utterly restless, she moved from window to window, from door to door, whimpering as she went; every now and then coming across to me and jumping up against me with her front paws in the rapid, urgent way she always has.

Driven almost mad by Moppet's restless behaviour, I let her out the door. At least Humba was setting her a good example of togetherness. There was a mad scampering about the garden with all four dogs in company. It seemed like an excited, playful scampering.

I threw myself on the bed exhausted and prayed that I would hear no terrible fighting sounds. In fact my rest was not disturbed by such sounds at all, but by dogs continually coming up to my window to whine and whimper, assuring me that they were all OK—perhaps too, to sniff and assure themselves in turn that I was there. Yes, I was—just all there.

I arose at 4 o'clock resolved that Moppet and Humba should return to the farm. Wonderfully, all four dogs were companionable and unscathed. Notwithstanding the happy outcome, I felt that my two would be happier in their familiar home surroundings. I had now arranged for a 24 hour Tredar guard on my house and I had learnt that Makosa and Johannes had been able to feed the dogs regularly despite Mujuru.

More importantly, I soon figured that in keeping them here in town I would be exchanging one set of fears for another. On my daily business excursions I couldn't take them with me and in their disorientated state of mind, they could panic, find a way out of the grounds and get lost. Perish the thought.

So, after a frenetic twelve hours, I drove back into my farm homestead at exactly 5 am. The guard, I was glad to observe, was present at the gate and would be able to tell Makosa of my change of mind. The guard actually expressed pleasure at seeing the dogs, because from his point of view, they operated as sentinels.

Saturday 7th. September 2002

A day to recoup strength and write up notes. At about 9 am. I phoned Insp. Sengwe and he answered himself. I asked him if, since we last spoke, he had managed to speak with the DA about my situation. I told him that things had not changed on the farm and I myself had tried to get through to the DA, Mr. Mushinigwa, but had been told that he would not be in his office until Monday.

The inspector speaks in a deep, gravelly voice and often I don't catch what he says. This is not because he speaks hurriedly, which is my complaint of many African speakers when talking English, but because his slowly pronounced sentences fade away into a mumble. My advancing age no doubt slows the brain's decoding process. However; I think he said he was to meet the DA at 3 pm. today. My property would be discussed.

By the use of his expression "your property", I believe there is a certain doubt in the minds of the local government officials in Concession, as to the status of Stockade. That uncertainty has been there from the start. I think that the police inspector wouldn't be speaking in those terms if he wasn't getting such feedback from the DA.

In addition to this, Sengwe told me for the first time, that he had actually spoken with the Governor about the person Mujuru, who claims the farm. I expressed interest and interjected:

"You mean Elliot Manyika?" I wanted to be quite certain there was no mistake as to whom he was talking.

The inspector carried on with his mumbled account of the Governor's explanation to him. Here again I didn't catch all of this; albeit, it was plain to me that the Governor's explanation was lengthy and hardly straightforward. However, the inspector used wording in one sentence, which I remember distinctly. When I heard them, it alerted me immediately. His words were:-

"The Governor said he wanted some time to sort the matter out."

"Ah!" I interjected, "I have heard just those words directly accredited to the Governor before; but from quite another source." [I recalled Nhema's account of his phone call with Manyika.] "How did you find Elliot Manyika's attitude?"

Sengwe replied something like: "It was alright."

Well, I have often wondered if Manyika wasn't lying to Nhema when he said he had never heard of Mujuru. Since that time, he has actually driven on to Stockade with his entourage and the cars drove straight to Bush Cottage where Mujuru has installed himself. *Somebody* in Manyika's circle knew Mujuru and where to find him.

Maston reported that Elliot Manyika was in the party. I made a point of asking Maston if he would know Manyika by sight and he replied, yes. He would and did recognize him. Manyika was with the crowd of people, who were laughing and joking there for twenty or thirty minutes before driving away.

Elliot Manyika; Minister of Youth Development, Gender and Employment Creation; ZANU PF Political Commissar; Acting Governor Mashonaland Central, is a person to be reckoned with.

By chance, I spotted the following item in the Daily News of 3rd.September, just four days ago:

Minister Elliot Manyika and 12 war veterans and Zanu PF supporters were last Wednesday implicated in the severe assault of an MDC supporter, Kephas Madzorera in July. The allegation is contained in a chamber application to the Bindura provincial magistrate, Mishrod Guvamombe. Madzorera was represented in court by Obert Chinhamo, a lawyer from the Zimbabwe Human Rights Organization. He is recovering in a private hospital in Harare from injuries he sustained during the assault.

Allegations are that on 3rd.July, in Bindura, Manyika and 12 Zanu PF youths and war veterans and Z.R.P. members, severely assaulted Madzorera for supporting the MDC.

In his founding affidavit to the court, Madzorera said: "They have threatened to assault or kill me together with my family if they see me. They have previously assaulted and stabbed me. They chased me from Bindura."

He said Manyika led youths and war veterans to his house and destroyed his property. He was inside at the time. He said he came out when they threatened to set the house on fire and he was hit on the head with a sharp knife. His doctor had confirmed his various injuries, including a damaged left eye.

He said Gora stabbed him on the right ear with an Okapi knife and injured his eardrum. "I fell unconscious and the assailants ran away thinking I was dead."

He said he had weighty evidence that Manyika and his 12 colleagues actually intended to kill him for his MDC membership.

"On 3rd.July, Manyika hit me using an iron bar and someone else stabbed me with a knife. The 12 actually want to kill me and I don't feel safe at all."

He said there had been no investigations or arrests so far. He needed the protection of the law against Manyika and his party.

End of news item.

Does such a story have a bearing on my own situation? It does. It does, because it identifies and epitomizes the horrifying reality of life today in Zimbabwe. How could I not be affected? Reality for farmers has been devastating, and we are only one group of sufferers as the above story shows.

Hundreds of white farmers have been evicted from their homes and farms in a frenzy of revolutionary zeal. Even as I write this, hundreds more are being evicted; and in the process subjected to harassment and persecution. The term, "ethnic cleansing" is entirely appropriate.

The reason for such a delayed manifestation of racial hatred may be put down to the ruling party's sense of insecurity coupled to psychological factors that lie deep in the African race. The fact is that, willy-nilly, the whites are being drowned in this sudden and unexpected tide.

The only reason why I have not gone down in the general inundation may be put down to the confusion caused by the peculiar status of my Protected Forest—protected by the government itself. The forest may be thought of as a nuisance, even a nonsense, and better off chopped down, by the political big guns who hold sway in the Land Committee but there has always been some last minute hesitation.

My prime concern from the word go, has been the welfare of the fauna and the flora of the forest. My concern now extends to the whole farm; because the forest will not survive without periphery protection and professional administration run from a permanent base. Hence my offer of the property to National Parks.

Fortunately, Minister Francis Nhema has given his ministry's support for this. He probably foresees, as I do, the havoc and degradation of the natural environment, which will inevitably occur on the surrounding farms that have been fast-tracked for small-scale resettlement. Stockade may well become an isolated hospice for endangered wildlife.

As I see it, we are far from being in the clear and the danger lies in Elliot Manyika. In the world of politics, the Environment Ministry is held in the very least regard. I am sure that in this and many other countries, politicians wonder why it should warrant a ministry at all. The environment just is. If it were not linked to Tourism and therefore money, there would be no call for a minister.

Nhema may therefore be termed a lowly minister of little standing let alone influence. He is a Matabele in a predominantly Shona cabinet. Worse, he is quiet and mannerly, aspects of character which can't take him far in the Party.

Elliot Manyika, by comparison is a political firebrand. It is said that his ambitions extend to the Party leadership. A sycophant of Mugabe, he is sure to be a protagonist of ethnic cleansing. Mashonaland Central is his political heartland. Here he has rewarded his powerful supporters with gifts of land. Manyika has shown himself to be cruel, ruthless and devoid of moral scruples. Mujuru has these traits in common with him. Who knows that Manyika has not rewarded his friend and ally Mujuru with the gift of Stockade Farm—even unofficially?

My hope is that Nhema will point out to Manyika that if National Parks take the farm over, the land will no longer be in white hands. [In effect my hands of course.] This may satisfy the ethnic cleansing angle. In turn this might give Manyika the excuse to offer Mujuru a place elsewhere.

It is only a slender hope; I am not at all confident of this. There is some sympathetic understanding for my cause within officialdom, yes, but it could turn out to be vapid in the face of the aggressive people lined up against me. The latter are inflamed by personal power and greed; the last thing they care about is the natural environment. In the revolutionary councils, their voices will dominate.

Mine is a desperate bid to save the trees and the natural haven of my sanctuary. Countless birds and small animals have come to live in quiet harmony here. I am constantly mindful of them. A dreadful fate awaits them if my bid fails. Despoliation and death will follow as certainly as night follows day. It is awesome to contemplate that so much life depends on the efforts of one human being—me. For who else really cares?

Wednesday 11th. September 2002

On Monday Johannes phoned from Trianda to say all the workers had returned to work and were commencing to lift the garlic. He related the bizarre event that led to this change in fortune. Apparently the Warvet Moffu accompanied by some followers, came to the farm on Sunday and confronted Mujuru. There was a noisy argument during which Moffu accused Mujuru of being a usurper, who had no right to the farm. The argument was heated enough for Moffu to tug at Mujuru's shirt.

Moffu also told Mujuru that he did wrong to stop the farm workers. Just how it came about, I don't know, but the long and the short of it was that my workers decided to turn out to work. They must have decided that Moffu had greater authority than Mujuru. That's interesting.

Monday 16th. September 2002

I have learnt that the full name of Moffu is Rusike Moffu. Johannes says that he is a card-carrying Warvet and that he works for the Harare Municipality as a municipal policeman. Moffu managed to get the keys of our old store, which has been closed now for many weeks.

Eugena, the woman who leased the store moved away owing seven months rent money. However, it seems she had left some articles in the store and given the keys to our worker, Norman No.1, who ought to have handed them over to me but didn't. Instead he handed the keys to Moffu on demand. As a result Moffu has installed a son in the store, who is selling a few goods there but mostly Chibuku beer. There is no way I could get him out.

I rue the day I built that store over thirty years ago. For the first four years we ran it ourselves successfully. From the moment we started to lease it our troubles began, culminating in the utter nightmare when the Warvets descended on us and used it as a virtual headquarters and drinking den.

Why should Moffu want our work to continue on our crops? An altruistic reason is the last thing in the world he would have. Either he has the idea of reaping the crop of garlic for himself or he will approach me for protection money. I have told Johannes to move fast. He has all available men and women lifting the crop and putting it in a secure place out of sight until we can run it into town.

Last week I met one Tawanda Gotosa, an ecologist working for National Parks. He has been tasked to draw up a plan on how best to utilize Stockade in the event of Parks taking it over. He asked me to provide him with as much background material as I could and he would work on the proposal right away. I responded immediately and delivered my papers. Tawanda said they would be very useful. He would get the report out in short time.

I also phoned Mrs. Mandimika of Lands. She said she had spoken to Makasa of the Bindura office. He told her that the proposal by Environment to take the farm for National Parks had come too late. The trouble was that: "The owner had said he didn't want to take up their offer and didn't want to live in his house on the farm." Therefore the farm had been allocated to A2 settlers by the Land Committee. The Governor and the PA would now have to be consulted. Here is an example of a mind closed off to reason. More than that; it is a mind that can fantasise excuses to cover its innate wickedness. The deceit is abominable, the lies beneath contempt.

Mrs. Mandimika suggested I should go back to Environment and to the Minister himself. As I have thought all along; the destiny of my land and with it my own future, lies in a balance of wills—those of Manyika and Nhema.

The Director of Lands, Mr. Tashire, remember, had confidently spoken of sorting the matter out for me. I raised him on his cell phone and reminded him of this. His reply was very curt. "You will have to see the Governor," and he switched off his phone.

Tuesday 17th. September 2002

Restless and disturbed of mind, I got out of bed at 4.30 and composed a letter to Minister Nhema. As diplomatically as possible, I wanted to warn him of the people opposed to me—opposed to US really. Once they sense their own greedy scheme may be thwarted, they are sure to think up a counter measure. I suppose Nhema must know his fellow Africans a darn sight better than I do; nevertheless I must trust that, in spite of his alignment with the Party, he is one of the exceptional ones imbued with some integrity.

One has to acknowledge that the forces, which are causing havoc and misery throughout the rural areas, are thoroughly wicked. Whatever it is that motivates a whole section of human society to behave in such a depraved manner falls into the study of mass psychology and social anthropology. I have a nightmare theory.

The fact is the African observes that, with few exceptions, the white man, at least in Africa, is a nature lover. It is the white man who shows such a passionate concern for the conservation of wildlife. I fear that the present wave of hatred against whites, evinced by Mugabe's followers, is not confined to a form of ethnic cleansing. A vicarious revenge is wreaked on those things which the whites hold dearly. That is the reason we see the countryside burnt from end to end; trees wantonly axed down; hundreds and thousands of animals cruelly killed. These are the spiteful actions of a rebellious child made manifest in horrific proportions by adults in the population.

I decided it might be a good thing to speak with Tawanda again about his planning for the farm.There was the clear possibility that Nhema himself might request Parks for a quick statement of their plans for Stockade.

I allow myself to dream—I cannot help it. It is a recurring dream; only the details change. I dream that the whole of my farm is taken by National Parks. My trees may never fear the agony of the axe. They will have limitless time to fulfil their potential to shelter and mother dependant living things. On the hills, the Brachystegia woods will provide for their familiar residents. Where the soils are deeper, I can see great Acacias, with broadly spreading branches shading, softening and sweetening the soil beneath the contiguous canopy. My old arable lands will intergrate with the woodland to make a patchwork of habitats to suit the wants of diverse forms. I know these fields well. In 6 weeks time when the rains come, they will provide a massive swathe of deep-rooted grass. With the grass, a variety of other plants will emerge.

I heard it said within National Parks that my farm could be used to place endangered local animals; those which could never adapt to conditions in the Lowveld game reserves. How I would welcome them; grysbuck, oribi, duiker, reedbuck, kudu, impala; any that could be helped here or were lucky enough to find ther own way here—saved from savage death.

In my dealings with Tawanda, I have laid emphasis on the great potential of the grasslands for antelope species.and the need for National Parks to take the ENTIRE property SOON. I cannot yet discount my dream.

A big Italian-built tractor has been with Mujuru at Bush Cottage for some days. Johannes tells me that the tractor is owned by Galloway Estates, Mvuruwi. The present Tredar guard says he has worked at Galloway Estates. He recognized the truck, which brought the tractor here. The driver is dressed in overalls stencilled Galloway Farm. The tractor is ploughing my grass fields. These are the ones I want for the game animals!

When I heard about this, I had immediately phoned Galloway and had spoken to a lady in the farm office, Bevi Robertson. I asked her why their tractor was ploughing on my property. She seemed puzzled and said she would get Mr. Francis, the farm owner, to contact me. Because he had not done so, I have phoned Galloway again and once more spoken with Bevi Robertson.

She confirmed that she had passed my message to Mr. Francis, who agreed to ring me. I told Bevi that I had received no call and asked for the man's cell number, which she gave me. After many attempts, I managed to get through to Mr. Paul Francis. He appeared to be unaware that I had called his office earlier. [So who's lying?] I spoke to him about the Galloway lorry and the tractor ploughing on my farm.

Paul Francis said that his farm was having big trouble from Warvets. His lorry had gone missing for three days the previous week. However, he said that no tractor was missing. The truck had since returned. He said he would get back to me when he found out more from the driver of the lorry. I was given the impression that conditions on his farm were so chaotic that he had completely lost control. Did he have no idea why his big truck had gone missing for three days and where it had gone to? Was he only now going to ask the driver; a week later and at my prompting? He could offer no suggestion as to whose tractor his vehicle might have been transporting; only saying that none of his tractors had gone missing.

Friday 20th. September 2002

I have learnt from Johannes that the Fiat tractor is still on the farm, but is not operating because of a broken bearing on the harrow. The tractor is parked at the Bush Cottage. Yesterday, I sent a letter per Eliot, the Nola driver, to the police inspector at Nyabira. I explained the suspicious movements of the Galloway truck and the mysterious tractor being used by Mujuru. I suggested the tractor might have been stolen. By putting it on paper, I thought the police might be prompted to investigate. What a fool I can be to believe such a thing!

The starter switch for the dip borehole motor was stolen on Wednesday night. Luckily the motor itself was not taken. I have told Johannes to remove the motor now; also to take off the big irrigation motor at the reservoir. They say that Trianda had two switches stolen and Gwebi, two motors. We can't get electrical equipment insured any more and replacements cost a fortune. There is no alternative but to close down the irrigation.

Johannes reported that the Warvet George came to the farm on Wednesday. George sought out Mujuru and there was an angry confrontation. Johannes moved close to hear what was being said. George accused Mujuru of being an interloper; he wasn't a Warvet; he had no authority to move into the house he was occupying; he had no authority to stop the farm work; he had no permission from the DA to be here. George ordered him to be off the farm by next Monday. George hit Mujuru in the chest.

Well! The last time George was on the farm, which was about 18 months ago, he was giving us hell and acting in exactly the same way as Mujuru. Now he is acting the righteous policeman. What does the turn around mean? It is hard to guess. It suggests a splitting into factions and a jockeying for influence. Are the Warvets fronting for someone else? Is there a change in the wind? Or is it no more than a personal vendetta?

Saturday 28th.September 2002
The foreign tractor remains on the farm and has been deep harrowing my fields. In an attempt to find out where the tractor has come from, I made further enquiries from Galloway Estates and spoke to the lady in the office, Bevi. It turns out that her name is actually Debbie not Bevi, so for the purpose of this retrospective account, she will have to undergo a name change. Debbie told me that Paul Francis was in America attending a meeting of cattle breeders. Charolais I think. [Their trucks show the head of a Charolais bull!] He would be going on to Mexico and would be away three weeks.

Thoughts flashed through my mind. Paul Francis had promised to get back to me when he had questioned his driver about the tractor, which his truck had transported to Stockade. He was hardly likely to do this whilst he was swanning about in the New World. Furthermore, the journey to the U.S.A. didn't sound like the action of a man who was on the point of losing his farm in the fast-track land grab.

I carried on talking. "Because it was a Galloway truck that delivered the tractor, surely it must be possible to find out where the tractor was loaded and who it belongs to," I said to Debbie. She found difficulty in replying, so I went on: "But surely there must be SOMEBODY in charge of the farm; or is there no control over what is happening there?"

"Well, there's William," Debbie said, "but he is hardly ever on the farm. Most of the time he's in town and he's almost impossible to get hold of. But I'll try to do so and tell him what you say."

Debbie was a little reluctant to give me William's cell phone number but decided to do so. William, I deduced, must be Paul's brother, probably the elder of the two because the father, recently deceased, was known as Bill Francis.

True enough, William was indeed difficult to get hold of. I eventually reached him through the Commercial Farmers Union offices. Before doing so, I discovered that the man I sought was not William Francis but William Hughes. A good lady explained to me that William was a step son to Bill Francis. Until recently, he held the post of Director of Regions at the CFU. With that explained to me, I recollect that I once met him. My ageing mind unravels.

Earlier, I have met Johannes at the Greencroft shops and consider it would be a good idea to have him with me when I meet William. Johannes can give him an eye-witness account and description regarding the truck and the tractor. J has said all along that both belong to Galloway. However, when I call William, it appears that he will not be able to meet me until tomorrow at 8 am.

Mujuru speaks with Johannes regularly; he must know that what he tells Johannes is passed on to me. It now seems certain that whenever I speak to Galloway estates on their P.T.C. phone, somebody there notifies Mujuru, because the latter informs Johannes that I have phoned to enquire about the tractor. This has happened twice; once within twenty minutes of my call. I am warned to stop interfering.

I make an arrangement with Johannes to pick him up at Greencroft at 7.30 next morning before going on together to see William. However, I tell him that I will quite understand if he would rather not go through with this. J has every reason to fear Mujuru who it seems has informers within the Galloway camp. Nevertheless, J agreed to meet me saying that nobody would know where or why he was going.

I am afraid Johannes had not thought it all through when I spoke to him. On reaching home, he must have had second thoughts. I waited in vain for him at our rendezvous point and finally left to find the building which houses the ZJRI. This stands for the Zimbabwe Joint Resettlement Initiative; a body set up to have direct communication with government over land issues without recourse to the courts. The people in this body maintained that legal action had proved fruitless, because court rulings were never enforced. More than that, taking the government to court actually inflamed its anger and gave it cause to take vengeful action.

The ZJRI then, is the organization for which William is closely connected. It seeks dialogue and conciliation with government ministries in matters of land acquisition. Cynics would say this is a euphemism for collaboration with the devil. Certainly I have suspected that reconciliation might extend to trade-offs; such as offering to do land preparation for the "settlers" on the farms stolen from other white farmers. This would be in exchange for an assurance to be allowed to cultivate one's own land free from harassment.

As soon as I saw William Hughes I recognized him. Yes we had met before. He is tall, fair, slim, looks deceptively youthful, has a pleasing speaking voice and dresses smartly. As I now remembered, he is mannerly and friendly without being ebullient. Hardly in the mould of the farmer image; I guess he would be a star performer in the corporate field. He carries two cell phones about his person both of which, I am sure, are in constant use.

William told me that he had gone to Galloway the previous evening and had made some enquiries concerning their farm truck. About two weeks ago, it had been used to take a group of mourners to a funeral. It would appear that it had been misappropriated in order to transport the Fiat tractor and the implement. If this was the case, the driver would have to be penalised. He would be looking further into it.

With regard to the tractor, he reiterated what he had said to me on the phone; Galloway had a large fleet of tractors—fifteen or more. But these tractors were huge 140 HP jobs and the harrows were also huge. In no way could they be put on to their farm truck. He felt the tractor must belong to somebody in the communal lands.

With regard to the proof that Mujuru was being informed of my phone calls to Galloway, he freely admitted that he was sure their phone lines were tapped. He gave no hint as to why or by whom. At the end of it all I am still none the wiser as to who is ploughing my land for Mujuru. It is most frustrating. William has said he will get back to me if he finds out more. I can discount that. For some reason, I don't think they want to look into it too deeply.

Meanwhile the tractor stays on Stockade. Yesterday, Friday, I was able to visit the farm for an hour or so. Mujuru had left earlier so there was no chance of my meeting up with him. I took out some oil for our own tractor and some meat for the dogs both of whom looked sleek and well.

The alien tractor is a Fiat-Agri DTS80-66. It has mechanical trouble and is parked at Bush Cottage. Mujuru has told Johannes that he is not worried. "If the tractor cannot be started, I have been promised a much bigger tractor—a 140 HP Fiat with an even bigger implement." I have heard a description of tractors just such as this only the other day!

Mujuru has shown a typed letter to Johannes. It pertained to me and Stockade and the forest. From J's description, it could be a copy of the letter addressed to the Chief Land Officer, Bindura, Mr. Makaza, and written by Mrs. Mandimika. If in fact this was a copy of that letter, then Mujuru has an ally of influence on the Land Committee—probably Makaza himself. Mujuru's remark to Johannes was: "Elliot Manyika will never give this farm to Parks. I shall continue ploughing."

It wouldn't surprise me in the least if Mujuru didn't have spies in the Ministry of Lands offices as well. There is a mixed bunch in there and plenty of them will be political appointees.

There is absolutely no way Mujuru could be expending his own money for this land preparation let alone the ongoing expenses thereafter. He must have the backing of a wealthy Warlord or has discovered a means to siphon off government money—or most likely both. The big guys are the biggest racketeers and Mujuru is a sidekick.

To counter this forbidding prospect, my hopes were raised briefly by some movement from the other side. Mrs. Mandimika has indeed written again to the Province and she has told me that a list of farm names has been sent to them for delisting. Stockade should be among them. [Why did she say "should"?" I wonder?] When she received the reply, she would notify me and let me have a copy of the letter. Mrs. Mandimika has an optimistic, or at least a positive, way of expressing things, which I find disturbing.

Mrs. Mandimika added that a communication had come from Mrs. Sangarwe, Deputy Secretary Environment. It was to say that National Parks people would be deployed on the farm. Sceptic that I am, I phoned Mrs. Sangarwe, whose manner impressed me. Not so, says she. Environment was awaiting a letter of confirmation from Lands before they could take action. Meantime National Parks had been "sensitised"; that is to say that they have been apprised of the situation. I take this to mean that they have been advised to plan for the eventuality should it arise.

Well, I can safely say that I have already "sensitised" the people at Parks. Tawanda Gatosa, their ecologist, has been formulating a plan for Stockade, which I hope he may soon have ready.

Sunday 29th.September 2002

Whilst I was writing up the foregoing notes yesterday, things were happening down on the farm. J informed me that a mechanic had arrived in the morning to fix the Fiat tractor. He spoke with the driver and when doing so he noted the particulars of the vehicle he was driving. It was a white Toyota Landcruiser with some sort of motif on the door; Registration number 529 110 T. The mechanic left and the tractor driver resumed ploughing.

Later in the day, who should arrive on the farm but our old bugbear, Simukayi. He came in a white Nissan Sunny in the company of a man and a woman. They drove straight down to where the tractor was working. Johannes must have hurried after them, because he edged close enough to hear what was going on.

Simukayi shouted angrily at the driver—he is very good at shouting angrily as we know from experience. He told the driver that if he didn't remove himself, the tractor and all his belongings straight away, he, Simukayi, would return and burn his tractor. With that, Simukayi and his companions drove away. I have not yet ascertained where Mujuru was during this fracas.

Simukayi's threats had the desired effect of panicking the driver. He stopped work abruptly and drove off the field. Perhaps he possessed a cell phone; but somehow he contacted a third party requesting immediate help to get the tractor off the farm.

In a comparatively short time, a big Volvo truck arrived on the farm. The truck was fitted with sides to take livestock. The Tredar guard is said to have taken down the registration number, which I hope is true and shows an unusual degree of intelligence. I have asked Johannes to get it for me.

There was some other information I gleaned from Johannes concerning the truck. One of the two Tredar guards says that he remembers it when he was deployed in the Norton district. It could belong to Triple C Pigs, Grassmere Farm, Norton. I only need to get that registration number to establish this one way or another.

More sleuth work. The clues, which first point to skullduggery in Mvurwi, now switch to Norton and completely the opposite end of the map.

What is going on in the Warvet fraternity? Stockade was once a Warvet headquarters and for close on two years we lived with constant interference and intimidation. Then, when most of the surrounding farms had fallen to the invaders and the farming families had been forced from their homes, the local Warvets either withdrew by order or by their own volition. One could say that their Stockade base was deserted and when the ogre Mujuru arrived in May, he found no Warvets stationed here.

This month, on the 8th., 18th., and now the 28th. of September, Warvets Moffu, George and Simukayi, singly, have driven in out of the blue to specifically vilify and challenge Mujuru. None of them have spoken with Johannes or stopped to assert themselves over our workers. I gather that Simukayi, who was our biggest bane, has found a place in Mvurwi. After such a long absence from Stockade, I somehow doubt that he has designs of his own.

Mugabe's self-promoted revolution has resulted in mayhem. Perhaps the first free-for-all land grabbing and looting stage is over and the competition is now for power. Mafia-type organizations are forming and running parallel to government. As with the Mafia, the godfather is not always known.

It is plain that the Warvet faction regards Mujuru as a rival, but not necessarily for possession of the farm. So far Mujuru shows no sign of relinquishing his claim. He surely has patronage. But who is the patron? Is it really Elliot Manyika?

Time will tell.

Wednesday 2nd.October 2002

The General Manager of Triple C Pigs is Dr. Doug Bruce. I have phoned him to tell him of the report given to me that it was one of their trucks which collected the Fiat tractor. He was, naturally enough, astonished at my story and quickly concluded that the tractor would have been stolen. If it was one of their trucks involved last Saturday afternoon, it would have been unauthorized. He would follow it up and get back to me.

If it could be proved that the tractor was stolen, it would suit my books well, because Mujuru would have something to explain. He would never be charged, but at least it might keep the tractor away from the farm and Mujuru out of my hair for a bit.

Z.R.P. Nyabira would appear to have ignored my letter. They have certainly not come to investigate. If I did but know, they would probably regard my letter as a joke. It would be no surprise to learn that there are hundreds of stolen tractors operating all over the country with the full knowledge of the police.

"Tredar" was a security organization set up and paid for by farmers themselves to maintain a sound security network throughout a large farming area. It has employed as many as 600 guards. Over the years, the police have come to rely heavily on Tredar to initiate investigations into crimes committed on the farms and especially to provide transport for their officers to attend and formalize the charges. The ZANU PF hate campaign against white farmers has obviously led to the vilification of Tredar. The Party accuses the African Tredar guards of being sell-outs to the whites and by inference MDC opposition supporters. Oh, the twisted reasoning of warped minds!

Well, the crunch has come. Tredar is closing down. We have had Tredar guards for close on thirty years—that's going back to the Rhodesian years. It was a super outfit; the officers efficient, the guards well trained. To maintain morale in conditions of anarchy is an impossible task. Chinotemba, flamboyant leader of the farm invasions, was given the tip off to undermine the organization and this he did. Our two guards and one from Trianda, together with their dogs, were returned to their base for the last time.

I fear there will be a sickening epilogue to this story. There are 600 dogs spread between the three Tredar depots. Now there is no food and nobody to care for them. A massive extermination of these animals is inevitable. I dread to think how this operation will be handled. The SPCA must surely become involved.

So many farming families, forced to emigrate, have found they cannot find GOOD homes for their pets and have faced the bitter alternative of having them put down. In the midst of all this horridness, I never cease to think of my dear Moppet and Humba.

Sunday 13th. October 2002

During the week I changed my accommodation, moving from the White's house in Marlborough to the Cunliffe's in Avondale. Frank and Daphne White are due back from their overseas holiday soon but Rob and Vivi Cunliffe will be away in Mozambique for some time. This will make my house-sitting job stretch another few weeks. Both households have a pair of dogs and I have made great friends with all four. I feel like the temporary nursemaid, who, having made a loving relationship with the children, has to move on when the parents return from their travels.

I have three houses and two self-contained cottages on the farm but no house elsewhere. In the present dicey circumstances, I am pleased to be house-sitting in town for good friends.

Unlike other poor souls, who have been ordered to move out of their homes lock, stock and barrel, sometimes being given a few hours to do so, I still have most of my belongings in my house and there has been no attempt to storm it by gangs of unruly Party supporters. Mujuru breathes fire every now and then, but the fact that he has not, or possibly cannot, bring in rowdy and ugly reinforcements, suggests that he may be a little uncertain of his ground. Because he is basically such a vicious character, I feel someone somewhere has told him to hold back.

Farm worker, Bigg, seconded to doing night watch duty, apprehended a man stealing two wooden doors. The man was an ex-Tredar guard! Johannes reported it to the police and the man was booked. Now that he has no job, he will join the ranks of Mugabe's landless peasants. The doors would have come in handy when he builds himself a shelter.

After Simukayi's intervention and the rapid removal of the foreign tractor, I hoped Mujuru would have called it a day. Not so. To my disappointment he has procured another tractor and that has commenced harrowing again. It is a New Holland 70-66S with driver canopy. It has Fiatagri written on the bonnet. I went to the farm on Saturday and looked at it

On my diplomatic front I meet with frustration at every turn. In my efforts to keep my problem in the mind of officialdom, I phone up persons to enquire if any progress has been made. In Lands, Mrs. Mandimika was away Thursday and Friday; at National Parks, I learn that Mr. Vitalis Chadenga is in America. At Environment, the Minister's secretary said that the Minister had passed my last letter on to the Permanent Secretary, Mr. Tavaya. She put me through to his office.

Mr. Tavaya spoke to me in a courteous and friendly manner. He regretted that he was not really in the picture as my dealings had previously been confined to the Minister and to Mrs. Sangarwe. However; he did know about the letters which were forwarded to the Lands Office in Mashonaland Central.

He said that the matter at this stage did not belong to Environment, but to Lands. As far as he was concerned a government decision had been made and it was up to Lands to implement that decision. It was their ministry that had to act. I pointed out that the sticking point was the Bindura Committee and Mrs. Mandimika had encouraged me to get Environment to put pressure on them. Mr. Tavaya showed impatience upon hearing this. His words were: "It looks like the tail is wagging the dog." I replied: "That may be so, but I am just the flea on the dog. I am an outsider. The workings of government are beyond my province."

I went on to repeat that my only concern was to save the whole area from destruction. The Committee may relinquish the forest but they wanted the remaining 100 hectares. I said it was stupid for the National Parks to take only the forest without the buildings and infrastructure on the rest of the property. [I should never use the adjective "stupid" I know, but it just slipped out inadvertently.] In the end, Mr. Tavaya said it looked as if some sort of shortcut was needed and he would see what he could do. I thanked him and that's where the matter rests.

Friends, Pam and Alex van Leerhoff, phoned me to say that because they were not allowed to remain on their Karoi farm, they were staying in their flat in Harare. Would I like to join them early on Sunday morning at 6.30? The Harare branch of the Bird Society was going on a field walk at the society's bird sanctuary by Lake Chivero and they would be going along. I thought it would do me good to get away from my introspective thoughts and resuscitate one of my old loves. So I went, and I thoroughly enjoyed the morning spent with fellow birders in lovely natural surroundings. It made me long for more days spent in the bush. Try as I may to avoid negative thoughts, I feel bitter that I cannot enjoy the bird life in my very own sanctuary.

And Pam and Alex? They phoned to say they couldn't come on the outing. They had received a message informing them that their farm workers had been beaten up by local government supporters. They had hurried back to Karoi to find out what had been happening and to try to obtain a police reaction—unlikely but what else?

Monday 14th. October 2002

Today is daughter Bridget's birthday—Martin has reminded me. He didn't say, but I suspect Jean or one of the girls reminded HIM. Women remember birthdays—it must be due to their genes. I have the disturbing notion that Bridget may be 50. She may or may not be disturbed herself with this fact, but as her father, I always think of myself as being sixty-something and this is becoming less and less plausible.

In the afternoon, I phoned Mrs. Mandimika and revealed Mr. Tavaya's assessment of the position. She had again spoken to Makaza, the Bindura Land Officer, who informed her that the Committee had still not made a decision. She went on to imply that it didn't matter what views were held by other ministries, at the end of the day the final say would be that of Manyika, the Governor and Minister.

Mrs. Mandimika has lost her naive optimism. I am again thrown into depression. It is as if my name was Abraham Levi and my only hope of reprieve lay in the hands of Heinrich Himmler.

Wednesday 22nd.October 2002

This morning at 7am.Johannes raised me on his cell. Among other things, it was to give me information on the further doings of Thomas Mujuru.

The invading Fiat tractor [the second one I mean], has continued ploughing our fields since a mechanic in a smart Toyota 4x4 Pick-up came to repair the equipment. Last night, the tractor driver knocked off work at 5pm.leaving the tractor with Mujuru at Bush Cottage. Mujuru's car had broken down, so, nothing lost, he ups on the tractor and drives off with it to visit chums at the Prison Farm. This means driving over a rough road across country and covering a considerable distance.

Mujuru must have been drinking heavily with his friends and returned later that night drunk and driving the tractor at reckless speed. On reaching Bush Cottage, he was unable to slow down. The tractor only stopped when it smashed into one of my precious Acacia trees. The tree was broken in two and so was the tractor. Mujuru having the "luck of the devil", wobbled away unharmed.

In the morning, J was ordered by Mujuru to bring our little MF 135 and pull the big Fiat clear of the tree. The tractor being broken into two, made this impossible. He left it and it was then that he phoned me.

Johannes had a word with the tractor driver when he arrived on the scene to start work. The information is that this tractor has come from Brock Park. Brock Park is the farm which was "acquired" very rapidly and forcefully a couple of months back by the man Chen Chinchengwenge [I shall obtain the correct spelling of that name one day], the ex-ZANU PF Minister of Information and an evildoer of the first degree.

That is not all. J learns that the tractor is on loan to the Minister from Galloway Estates! The driver is employed by Galloway Estates. Pieces of the jigsaw are fitting together. Because Chinchengwenge and Mujuru are close buddies and birds of a feather, they will have teamed up for a racket. Mujuru has no money and although the other may have procured himself a farm for nothing and has doubtless lined his pockets whilst a government minister, I'll bet he has no intention of spending his own money on planting any crops on Stockade. Input costs will come by way of coercion, extortion, theft or corruption. J says there are four drums of diesel fuel at Bush Cottage. I would like to know where that has come from—just for a start.

It seemed a good opportunity to reveal to the public yet another can of worms, so I gave the Daily News the gist of the story. They said they would like to follow it up.

Thursday 24th.October 2002

Two disappointments today. The Daily News reporters must have decided against going to the farm to get a story. I had told them frankly that I couldn't say what they might run into. When on consignments, these brave young people are subjects for violent assault from ZANU PF thuggery. They may have thought that the value of this somewhat minor story didn't warrant the risk of being beaten up and having their equipment smashed.

Then; I had been assured by Vitalis Chadenga, Executive Director, National Parks, that he would travel to the farm with me in the afternoon in order to acquaint himself with the land. I hung about the whole day waiting for his confirming phone call, but it never came. He was tied up with meetings—all concerning the forthcoming CITES conference in Chile. This has to do with the protection of endangered species worldwide.

Chadenga was to fly to Chile this weekend. So little Stockade will receive no attention for the next three weeks and during that time it could well be lost to National Parks. Ironically, the proposal is for Stockade to be used for a safe haven for endangered species; species which will be annihilated in the ongoing fast-track land grab.

Friday 25th.October2002

Johannes phoned at 8 o'clock to tell me that Mujuru had just bidden him to stop all farm work, which now included baling the grass hay. The hay bales in store, now belonged to him, Mujuru. He would turn back any transport sent to collect them.

Mujuru accused Johannes of stealing the electric motor, which operates the borehole pump supplying the Bush Cottage [and thus Mujuru] with water. J fits this motor each morning and as regularly removes it at 5 pm. to avoid it being stolen at night. On Wednesday, a thief stole the motor during the day whilst it was pumping water. When J reported this to me he said that he and several others had searched around the area yet could find no trace of tyre marks. This was odd because the motor was very heavy and difficult to carry by hand. I reported the theft to the police. They will probably never come out. Tredar used to do all the investigative work for them but Tredar are no more.

Mujuru told Johannes to contact me and tell me to remove all my belongings from the farm, at once.

Well, with one thing and another, I reckoned I should ring the Nyabira police. Response from them has been so pathetic that I have been reluctant to communicate with them recently. However, things were becoming impossible. I phoned and was put through to Insp. Sengwe. I described to him the run of events. After listening to my complaints against Mujuru, the inspector asked me to drive to Nyabira to discuss the matter with him there.

Knowing the predilection of police officers to arrest white farmers, I was a bit uneasy about this and said in a jocular manner: "I hope you will not arrest me. You can never tell what will happen these days."

He replied: "Why should I arrest you?"

Anyway, I considered that there had been no change in the position with regard to the farm; I couldn't be put in the wrong. I agreed to meet him in half an hour at Nyabira. Nevertheless, I took the precaution to phone Jean before I left. If put in a cell I would like someone to bring me food and blankets!

Nyabira is a scruffy settlement of a few African stores built on either side of the main Kariba road, a garage, and a line of grass-covered stalls, unused and falling down. The side roads are pot-holed; dusty in the dry season and full of puddles when it rains. The police station is found 500 metres back over the railway line, a long low building built with strict economy and as unprepossessing as the rest of the settlement in spite of the flagpole and a ring of whitewashed rocks. Some old motor tyres let into the ground indicate a car park for three or four cars and here a wild fig tree has somehow survived to provide some blessed shade. There were no cars, but I found this area occupied by a motley group of Africans with blank faces either standing by the tree or sitting on the upturned tyres. I eased my car carefully between them and got out, an object of silent interest to the watchers.

Inspector Sengwe was chatting to others on the veranda when I arrived. We exchanged greetings and I followed him to his office at the end of the block. On the way, he was handed a box of matches. Match sticks, I recalled, were an important element of his life. He sat at his desk and I pulled up a chair opposite.

A youngish African entered after me and the inspector waved him to one of the chairs lined against the wall behind me. I am getting used to African ways of conducting business affairs and it is nothing unusual to find strange, silent persons sitting motionless in the background whilst one is having a discussion with a man of rank. One is never introduced. Sometimes I wonder if they are poor relations.

Before I could launch my list of complaints against Mujuru, the inspector handed me a letter. If it was aimed to take the wind out of my sails then it very effectively did so.

I handed the letter back and at the same time shifted my chair round to the side of the desk, because when looking at the inspector's face, I had the light directly in my eyes. In the process, I noticed that, without a word, he handed the letter to the young man seated by the door. When the latter had finished reading it, I asked to re-read it myself and took the opportunity to copy it out. It was short enough and I took my time to copy the wording exactly.

The following is the letter.

> Department of Lands
> Box 66 Bindura.
> 17th.October 2002
> To: Provincial Police Officer.

Re: Eviction of Farm Owner on Stockade Farm

The farmer was served with Section 8 on April 2002 and expired on 8th. August 2002. However the farmer is still on the farm and making it difficult for the new farmer to proceed with his operations.

May you treat this issue with urgency.

Mr.E. Makaza.

Chief Lands Officer, Mashonaland Central.

Insp. Sengwe obviously had the upper hand. He took up a Section 8 order that lay on his desk and read a relevant paragraph from it. He then read from the letter and said: "This says that you were issued with a Section 8 order in April and that it expired on 8th.August last. On that date you should have ceased all farming operations and should have vacated your house. By defying a government order, you have committed an offence."

The first point I took up was that I had NOT received a Section 8 order in April last.

"This is the first time I have heard of it. No order has been handed to me and I have never signed for one," I said.

Sengwe's reply was that it was not incumbent upon the Lands Officer to hand me an order in person. "He is travelling all over the country. It is sufficient to hand it to someone who is living on your farm. If you want, you can go to Bindura to find out who the order was given to." I looked up at the ceiling. It would be hard to think up a more fatuous remark than that!

"The whole thing is absurd," I said.

I then brought up the status of the protected forest and the claim by Minister Nhema that it could not be allocated. Sengwe replied that all matters concerning land rested with the Provincial Committee. It had nothing to do with the Environment Ministry. If the Committee decided that they did not want a forest then there would be no forest.

In view of the letter, I asked who was considered to be the new owner. He replied that I had no right to ask the question because it was no concern of mine.

The inspector kept returning to the period of time he would allow me to remove all my personal property from the farm. I said that because I had no notion whatever what I would do or where I would go, I would need some weeks. He refused and said he would give me until Thursday. Next I asked about the stolen motor. The inspector said merely, "It will be looked into."

Meanwhile he must have been mulling over my earlier use of the word "absurd" and its place in English Usage. He was silent for a while and then, a little diffidently:

"To make complaints of this nature when you have no right to be on the farm yourself, is absurd." Bright boy! He gets a tick for that answer.

Inspector Sengwe makes me feel uneasy. I find myself looking at him twice. His eyes, which are unusually grey for an African and set wide apart, reflect an unscrupulous nature. He has a slovenly manner and speaks lethargically, out of keeping with a policeman. I have observed that his uniform is decorated with the Zimbabwe flag emblem sewn to the sleeve top. Not all police officers have this insignia and I have asked about it. It indicates one who was an armed revolutionary and who, at independence in 1980, was absorbed into the new Z.R.P. These "terrs", as the Rhodesian forces used to call them, did not undergo the training and discipline, which was imprinted on the members of the old B.S.A.P. It shows up clearly twenty-two years later.

Sengwe reiterated his warning: move my property off by Thursday.

"You have failed to comply with a government order. This is an offence. Many farmers have been arrested for this. Remember—Thursday." His insinuation was that he was being lenient and letting me off lightly.

I again expressed my dismay. "I have absolutely nowhere to go," I said. "I cannot think what I shall do."

"Do you have no friends?" he asked. "Where is your son?"

"I suppose I am expected to transport all my possessions collected over a lifetime and offload them in my son's front garden," I replied.

As I was leaving, the inspector gave me this parting shot:

"Do you remember when they built Kariba? The dam?"

"Yes, of course. That was fifty years ago."

"When the waters rose thousands of people lost their homes and had to find new ones. It's your turn."

There may be a deeper implication behind this. To some Africans perhaps the Kariba Dam is a giant symbol of colonial power; an object of constant resentment. I am certain the displaced tribesmen of that time, unhappy though they may have been, were relocated with due planning and consideration. However, now was not the time to query or quibble.

I walked out of the office and as I did so, noticed the young African still sitting by the door—blank and unmoving. Who was he? A political implant? It was about 11 o'clock on Friday when I left Nyabira. I had six days including a weekend. I hurried back to town and a telephone to make frantic and, often frustrating, calls.

I was lucky to get Mrs. Mandimika, of Lands, in the afternoon. She appeared dismayed at my information concerning the letter from Makaza. She confirmed that he was a member of the Ministry's staff. No such letter had been seen by the Ministry. She would speak with the Director of Lands and would phone me back. She didn't; so I phoned her at 4.30 and she said that they had been trying to call Makaza but had failed. It would have to wait until Monday.

The next people I needed were the lawyers. Richard Wood, the man dealing with farmers' problems, was away in Chegutu, so I was put through to Mr. Franks., who having heard my story, said he would like to consult some of the firm's partners. Later in the afternoon he phoned and put me through to Romaldo, a young African man, recently qualified and working as a junior lawyer. I was told that he had experience in situations such as mine. This must be unusual training and experience for a lawyer I am sure. "How to practice as a lawyer in a country where the rule of law does not exist except when it suits the ruling Party."

Romaldo asked me to give him back-up material and we agreed to meet on Monday.

Sunday 27th.October 2002

At 2 o'clock in the afternoon, Johannes called me to say that at that very moment there was activity going on at the Bush Cottage. A crew had come out to the farm to retrieve the tractor, which Mujuru had managed to break in two. The recovery crew had come with a big lorry and trailer on which was loaded a front-end loader. This was backed up with the familiar Toyota 4 X 4 Landcruiser carrying the mechanic, who has been seen regularly over the previous weeks.

A full description of the lorry was taken down: a Type UD Nissan diesel, light fawn colour; Reg.No.545 383 G. The lorry was fitted with a radio as was the front-end loader. Enamelled on both doors of the lorry were the words, Galloway Estates and the address. Also was the farm's emblem the head of a Charolais [Limosin?] bull. Our people noted that the driver of the front-end loader wore red overalls stencilled, Galloway Estates. The tractor was loaded and the party drove off past Johannes' house at 2.40, the very time I was speaking to him.

When I spoke to Paul Francis and William Hughes weeks ago voicing my concern and suspicion that it was their equipment ploughing my land, both swore that it COULDN'T POSSIBLY be their machinery. They were covering up the fact that they have made a trade-off; freedom to work their own lands provided they do equal work for the ZANU PF mafia chiefs, the ones who have forcefully ejected other unfortunate farmers. It smells. They have a wrecked tractor, which I don't suppose phases them too much because they have twenty others. I would like to tell them: "You may lose money on a tractor; but just remember this; when you make deals with the Devil, you lose your soul."

Wednesday 30th.October 2002

Monday and Tuesday have been hectic days mentally speaking. I am immediately faced with radical changes to my whole life. Decisions have to be made on so many matters, but at the same time, the imponderables remain.

Dealing with government ministries is both exasperating and time consuming. I often feel that there is a general understanding within officialdom at large to frustrate me. I suppose it is not really a conspiracy to frustrate me personally; rather am I a victim of a diseased, malfunctioning system. Within it, there is indeed a hierarchy; rank and station is adhered to and proper obeisance made to seniority; notwithstanding, there is an unspoken acknowledgement amongst all functionaries, high or low, that nobody is expected to make a decision.

Viewed from the outside, it appears that officials are engrossed in endless meetings. These meetings are held amongst themselves and are deemed to be of great importance. I have been repeatedly told that So-and-So cannot be disturbed because he or she is at a meeting. Be it a particular petitioner or the public in general, the one thing all can be sure of is that no decision will be forthcoming from the meeting. The "meeting" is an elaborate and largely symbolic exercise in avoidance. In my dealings with the ministries and even National Parks, I feel I have wasted hours and hours of time in words, spoken and written, in the forlorn hope of getting a response.

On Monday, I called at the lawyers and met Romaldo. He is sensible, straightforward, obviously bright, well educated. [With those advantages and tired or not, why did he have to yawn and stretch so pointedly on first acquaintance—something I have observed before in young African males. Is it a cultural thing—designed to put one at ease?]

I had prepared some notes as he had requested, also copies of letters written to the police, and these I gave to him. He was tied up in court that day, but would attend to my business on Tuesday.

It became apparent to me that an inspection of the records in the Administrative Court was going to be of crucial importance. Richard Wood, a senior partner in the firm, had spoken of this on the phone. Through a strange mix-up both Richard Wood and Romaldo inspected the court records separately and unknown to each other. At least there could be no doubt as to the thoroughness of the inspection.

The result was the following letter addressed to Insp. Sengwe.

> *ATTENTION*: INSPECTOR SENGWE 31st October 2002
> Zimbabwe Republic Police
> *NYABIRA*

Dear Sir

RE: MR R F WILES—STOCKADE FARM

Our client, Mr R F Wiles advises us that you recently warned him that unless he vacated Stockade Farm in the near future, he would be arrested and prosecuted. You referred to a Section 8 Order issued on the 14th.March and served in April.

In order for the section 8 Order to retain its validity, the Minister was required by section 1 [b] of the Land Acquisition Act to apply to the Administrative Court for an Order confirming the section 8 Order.

The writer has carefully checked the Register at the Administrative Court and has ascertained that no application was made by the Minister to confirm the section 8 Order. Therefore the section 8 Order has no validity and there is no legal requirement for Mr Wiles to leave the farm.

Furthermore any attempt to arrest him would constitute an unlawful act. We therefore ask you to protect our client's continued occupation of the farm and instruct members of your force that there is no basis for ordering Mr. Wiles to leave his home.

Yours faithfully

ATHERSTONE & COOK

Obviously the letter had to be delivered by hand—and soon. Romaldo, as a lawyer, was given the task to deliver it. Nyabira is thirty minutes drive from Harare and Romaldo had no transport so arrangements had to be made to get him there.

I volunteered to drive him, but Romaldo was adamant that it would be unwise for me to be seen by the police. Their reaction was unpredictable and I could be arrested under his nose. I was to drop him off at a distance, drive about and wait for him to call me on his cell phone. It was unlikely that the police would have a vehicle to follow us.

In later discussion with Martin, we decided to drop this cloak and dagger exercise. Instead, Martin arranged for the Nola factory driver, Eliot, to be on hand. The result was that we told Romaldo we would call for him at his city office shortly after 8am. This required double parking, hence the need for two of us. As it turned out, this was just as well. I arrived at the office block to be told that the lifts were out of order and that a lift full of office workers was stuck somewhere up above me. As a result I had to ascend fourteen flights of stairs up to the seventh floor and made to realize that I could be fitter.

By dint of motorcar exchanges, I delivered Romaldo to Nola, handed him over to Eliot, who was waiting in the Mazda 323, and bid him farewell and good luck. Eliot would drive him back to town. All this was happening on Wednesday morning. Naturally we were very anxious to learn the outcome of the meeting between Romaldo and Inspector Sengwe. For this, we would have to wait until later in the day.

Martin contacted Romaldo late in the afternoon and was given a rundown of the meeting. Inspector Sengwe was reported to be unwell and was not present. Romaldo therefore handed the letter to A\Inspector Taswa. As related to me, the following points indicate the trend of the meeting.

Taswa said that the letter was of no relevance to him. It was immaterial whether the order was lawful or unlawful. He had been given orders and his duty was to carry them out.

All matters concerning land were political by nature.

If the police don't carry out evictions, the politicians accuse them of accepting bribes from farmers.

Taswa described Mujuru as an idiot. However if an idiot had friends in high places there was nothing a policeman could do about it.

The meeting between Romaldo and Taswa was held with no display of animosity.

From the legal aspect, my lawyers had clearly turned the tables on the police. However, as everyone knows, the police in the rural areas are not there to enforce the law, but to carry out the directives of the revolutionary committees set up by the Party. In this case, the local committee had issued an order without any consultation with the ministry ultimately responsible for land issues.

I had been briefly elated with the contents of Richard Wood's letter, but this had been quickly dashed. Romaldo was not happy with Taswa's negative response. He considered it may be wiser for me to evacuate and carry on the fight away from the farm. Sengwe was the senior officer. When he returned on duty, there was no telling how he would react to the lawyer's letter; better perhaps, thought Romaldo, to leave before any ugly repercussions.

Nasty though my position is; I am still hesitant. In spite of the potential dangers, the saying that possession is nine-tenths of the law could yet have application. If I retreat completely, Mujuru will celebrate with his cronies and consolidate his hold. I think I still have allies in the Ministry of Lands, the Environment Ministry and Parks, weak indecisive and dispersed though they may be. The Party heavies may be prepared to let Stockade go to Parks provided the white man loses his farm. At the moment, Mujuru is no more than a toady, and in their eyes, expendable. I am only guessing I know.

I met Mr. Mageza at the Ministry of Environment. He is the Deputy

Secretary and is now the senior man there as Mr. Tavaya, the Permanent Secretary, is in Chile on CITES. In the absence of the Minister as well, I felt it necessary to keep the most senior person left, properly informed as to what was happening.

I found Mr. Magaza a civil and gracious man to talk to, but of course he had no knowledge of the Stockade story so once again I was called upon to explain the history of the forest and subsequent developments. I had brought in copies of recent correspondence, including my last letter to the Minister, and these he read through.

On completion, his reaction was similar to that of Mr. Tavaya. He said the whole thing was a ministerial matter and that there was no basis for me to be caught up in it at all. He promised that as soon as he found time he would communicate with the Secretary for Lands. His advice for me was to keep calm because the business could plainly be resolved by the ministries. He added that it was a pity the Minister was away or he would see him at once.

Well, I too had hoped to see the Minister. I repeated to Magaza what the lawyer had said: "The whole matter could be resolved by a phone call—Minister to Minister." He agreed saying that Nhema just needed to call Made, [Minister of Lands].

Whilst at the Environment Ministry, I gleaned that Minister Nhema may "look in" to his office on Saturday 2nd.before flying to Chile on Sunday.

Friday 9th.November 2002

A week has passed. The monitor screen on this computer failed to function and I had to put it in for repair. I have started work again, but for some reason unknown to the likes of me, pages 76 to 117 of this document seem to have got lost from my files. As I am fast losing my own wits, I shall not be too hasty in blaming those of the computer. By the grace of God, I had printed all the work up to date so those missing 42 pages are at least on paper even if not in this box in front of me. I can retype them. I have been saved agony and am grateful for mercy shown.

I had remembered that the people in Environment had said that Minister Nhema might come into his office on Saturday morning. There would be no staff present on a Saturday and there would be little chance of meeting with him then. I prepared a brief communication for him, which could be left on his desk on Friday afternoon. A willing friend kindly agreed to process this on her MODERN computer in bold type and in cable style, topped with a bright red "Urgent" sticker. It read:

TO: Minister Francis Nhema: Environment

RE: Your desire for Stockade and Protected Forest to be given to National Parks.

Land Committee refusing to comply. Evildoer Mujuru still on property. Eviction notice given me by Police although proved illegal.

Your intervention by word or note to Governor Elliot Manyika vital and urgent.

Property best secured by immediate "posting" of National Parks personnel.

At finalization I will leave if so required by you.

Richard Wiles.

The Minister's usual secretary, Helen, was off work that week so I gave my petition to Charlene, who was acting. She promised faithfully to put it on Nhema's desk along with some other papers. I noticed that these also had "urgent" stickers attached to them. I pleaded with Charlene to put mine on top!

All along I have been keeping in contact with Johannes by cell phone. The police dead-line had been Thursday. By Saturday everything had remained quiet on the farm. However, repercussions could blow up; either from the police, Mujuru or any other Party activists. If they came, it would be without warning. What to do in an emergency? It would do well to have a plan of sorts.

I spoke to Helen on Monday morning to ask if Minister Nhema had seen my communication. She must have called into the office herself on Saturday, because she said that she saw it on his desk but this morning it had disappeared. Has he taken it with him to Chile? I suppose Ministers of State when on international conferences attend to other business and their flight time is not spent reading the airline's house magazine.

It had been my hope that he may have left a message with Mr. Mageza, but when I spoke with Mageza on the phone, he had heard nothing. However, he confirmed that he would be taking up my matter with Lands. Meanwhile my urgent appeal is either on a flight bound for Peru or lying in a bottom draw of the Minister's desk pushed out of sight.

Anyone who has been reading these pages must have surely noted that my dealings with Minister Nhema have been frank and cordial. The man himself is mannerly, sensible and one is never in doubt of his integrity. He has held the Environment Ministry for many years and all the reports which come my way are favourable. He is approachable, understanding and sympathetic.

How on earth do you reconcile these gracious attributes with being a member of a government hell-bent on destroying all human cultural values? I don't know. To be honest, I don't want to know. I stopped trying to understand human society years ago and have devoted my later years towards saving other, more natural societies on this planet, from it. Perhaps Nhema has the same philosophy. I shall probably never know. If the man is right in his heart with regard to nature, that's O.K.

There is a little thing that has been worrying me. Over the past years, the offices of the Ministry for the Environment and Tourism have become very familiar to me. My letters to the Minister, I have usually delivered in person. Members of staff are now well known to me.

To reach the Minister's office, one first has to enter an outer waiting room and then proceed through another door where his personal secretary is to be found. On four separate occasions, well distanced, I have gone through the door of the outer waiting room to find myself confronted by two men lounging on the easy chairs facing the doorway. I cannot say now if they have been the same men, but they have been the same type of men; youngish, collar and tie, if not wearing, then carrying, a jacket. When I have entered the waiting room, they have stopped me and asked, in good English, who I was looking for. The answer to that being pretty obvious, I was then asked why. It was always casual, no reason given, no polite introduction, no "excuse me". They often wouldn't bother to stand up. They took it as their right to demand to know my business. I was always taken aback, but after the first encounter, I was quick to recognize the oddly familiar situation.

The last time it occurred was quite recently, but I didn't think to note the date. I just remember feeling uncomfortable. I recall putting on my act of behaving like a witless old man [not too difficult for me]; smiling genially at the two men and, pretending to recognize them as members of the Minister's staff, I give them a friendly "Hallo". Without stopping, I proceed past them whilst waving an envelope in the air and cheerily declaiming, "Just on delivery, you know!" and opening the door to the secretary's office where, thank goodness, I found Helen, who gave me a smile of welcome. The door being open, I didn't dare ask her who the two sleuths were outside. It would be nice to ask them directly what their business was, but somehow I think it would be unwise.

There may be nothing sinister in what I have been describing. I have done no more than make a simple observation. In the atmosphere of the present time one finds oneself speculating into realms of the mind which one wouldn't dream of entering in normal times. Alone and in front of this computer, I cannot prevent myself from speculation.

In a den of thieves, the honest man is viewed with suspicion. Honesty itself can breed enmity. If Nhema is honest he will be marked as unreliable. Is the Godfather having him watched?

I have wandered off into conjecture and must abruptly return to reality. It will be recalled that the Police had given me a deadline of 1st.November by which date I was to have removed myself and all my personal possessions from Stockade; not to comply would constitute an offence and make me liable to arrest.

Although the lawyers had intervened on my behalf and warned the Police that should they take such action against me, they themselves would be committing an offence, the police inspector had retaliated that the law was meaningless to him. He would carry out orders given to him.

As may be imagined, it was a stand-off which left me in a highly uncomfortable state of mind. I mentioned earlier that my intuition was to call the policeman's bluff. I would remain defiant. Notwithstanding, harrowing tales were abroad of persecution and eviction of white farmers and their families from their homes—the police acting as bystanders.

The more important and valuable household possessions had already been taken into Martin's house in Harare. Much of the balance would have to go directly to a sale yard. However, if I was to lose my home for ever, I would have to find accommodation for myself, Moppet and Humba. There was no way I could afford to buy a house, so the search had to be something to lease; small, secure and at "reasonable" cost. When all these things are put together, it is surprising how quickly the field of choice is narrowed.

People are very helpful in such circumstances and suggestions and contacts were offered from all sides. I followed up many of these and Martin and Jean helped me at the weekend. Nothing turned up that was suitable; but I have been in such psychological shock that I really didn't know what I wanted. I was faced with certain facts and questions. I posed them to myself:

"You are being forced to leave your home. Notwithstanding that your home has strong emotional attachments and that it is where you have lived contentedly for forty years, you are to be thrown out of it within days.

As with your home, your land is to be taken from you. You will forfeit your farmland and your forest. With the loss of the farm you will lose what wealth you have; with the loss of the forest you will lose the stimulating interests which have become a part of your daily existence.

There has been no war. No foreign armies have overrun the country. As things are, they might just as well have done. You are lucky to still have your life. Everything else will be taken from you and you will be reduced to penury.

Those are the facts. Look at them. Now say what it is you want to do? If you go, where will you go? If you stay what will you do? Are you ready for an old age home? If not, what?"

Here is my answer—for the moment—just for the time being. I wish, yes I wish, I could revert to being a child, preferably a girl child, because I mustn't have any masculine pretensions. Then I would be able to simply stand up and howl!

Tuesday 10th.December 2002

The monitor for this computer went out of order four weeks ago. It has taken all this time added to alarm, distress, gnashing of teeth and monetary outlay to find somebody moderately capable of fixing it. This has been done—after a fashion. Part of the problem seems to be old age. Its reactions have distinctly slowed down since its indisposition.

Over this period, I was hit by a 'flu virus, which kept me groggy for the best part of two weeks. First my computer and now me. In the trough of self-despair I wondered if we were not both bound for the scrap-heap. Yet here we are together again: nil desperandum.

CITES. This stands for Convention for International Trade of Endangered Species. The big thing for Southern Africa and Zimbabwe is elephants and the sale of Ivory.

Needless to say, it does not affect me personally at all. However, it has in so far as the conference in Chile took off all the important people in the Ministry of Environment and in National Parks. They are now back; but for the amount of forward momentum on Stockade is concerned, they might just as well be still in Santiago.

I gather the meeting was a disaster as far as Zimbabwe was concerned. We are now branded as a pariah in international circles. We may not dispose of our ivory any longer because of PROVED corruption at our end. I believe that the bad eggs have long since been removed from office, however it is too late now and our people have to live with the stain. Chadenga told me "It was hard going. Very difficult."

Once again I failed to get Chadenga to come out to inspect the farm and only managed a short chat with him. He obviously still worries about the political aspects of the take-over. He used the expression, "The situation is still very fluid." What he really means is that the situation is anarchy.

For some reason he once again asked me how long I had been living on the farm. I am sure he has asked me before. "Forty years," I told him.

"My God. That's before I was born!"

Whilst at National Parks, I had a word with the chief Ecologist, Mr. Chimuti. It came out that he was familiar with the proceedings of the Mashonaland Land Committee and said that he knew many of them because he lived in Bindura. Bindura is the hotbed of ZANU PF revolutionary politics. Outwardly, I expressed pleasure at the news and said it could be of help. Inwardly, I was thoroughly alarmed. However, he seemed a nice enough fellow, friendly and polite, and, as my ecologist friend Rob Cunliffe pointed out to me later, as a professional man, Chimuti would see at once the unsuitability of Stockade for resettlement. I arranged with Chimuti to meet him on the following Friday morning.

Come Friday, I drove to Parks in my truck and sought out Mr. Chimuti. We greeted affably and he told me that he wouldn't be coming himself but was sending a junior ecologist in his stead. He introduced me to Patience, who gave me a pleasing smile. A slimly-built young lady with rather pale skin and refined African features, I learnt that she had joined National Parks soon after obtaining her university degree in 1999.

Patience, armed with a professional-looking file of papers, took her seat beside me in my old truck and we set off to the farm. All the signs were that it was going to be a very hot day. I chatted with Patience as best I could above the noise of the old truck engine and in a little over half-an-hour I fetched up at my homestead gates.

Absurdly enough Makosa had just that morning dropped the gate key somewhere in the grounds and couldn't find it. So he couldn't let us IN or Rosemary, Dishon or himself OUT. Coincidentally I had left my own gate key behind.

There was nothing for it but to set off on our tour of the farm and forest without the long iced drink I had fondly anticipated. I guessed Makosa would find the key in time.

It only takes someone to show a little interest and knowledge in trees and nature to set me off. Patience only had to examine a few tree species closely and ask a few questions and I was away. I took her all over the place, stopping frequently. I was delighted to find that the trees and undercover had recovered wonderfully from the fire of the previous August. Patience was impressed, as everyone is, with the fine stands of Acacia in the forest glades. Almost everywhere we went, I was able to show her my own plantings. Trees, trees and more trees and the arable fields greening up with star grass ready to accept displaced game animals if only National Parks and Environment get their act together with determination.

We spent more than two hours driving around in the morning and left much unseen. Passing through the bwalo, we found our workers were in great excitement because they had just heard the sound of gunfire coming from Maypark across the road from us. It seems the ongoing feud between rival claimants to Maypark Farm is becoming fierce. But that is another story.

We returned to the homestead to find that the gate key had been found and the gate opened for us. We were given a frenzied welcome by Moppet and Humba, who of course had seen us earlier coming to the gate and then going away again. They joined us later for an afternoon walk in the nearby woodlands and through my beloved arboretum Joy indeed for the dogs after so much dull and scentless living; joy for me to show off my wide collection of trees to a fellow tree-lover.

Makosa managed to scrape up something for us by way of lunch and dur-

Using fire and smoke, the thieves destroyed both bees and the hives. The losses were such that honey production was abandoned.

Beehive shelters under constuction in the forest. Each shelter took 4 or 5 hives. Robbers came at night to steal the honeycombs.

ing this I was able to put a number of questions to Patience with regard to the land resettlement issue. Naturally, her involvement has only arisen when National Parks are brought in to arbitrate or recommend on wildlife matters. However she gave me her general impressions.

The land committees, who are tasked to allocate land taken from white farmers or ranchers, have no knowledge whatsoever of the land which they are disposing of. As far as they are concerned they are just names on a map. It is only after they have allocated the land and the ructions ensue that they discover the problems. Allocations are challenged all the time. It is usually the man who shouts the loudest who comes off best.

Generals and brigadiers are amongst the most successful contestants for land. It has become fashionable amongst this grouping to want land with game animals on it. In fact if they learn that a farm is stocked with game, they will demand to have it although it has already been allocated to a consortium of settlers, who have agreed to divide the game between them.

I asked why these army officers wanted game on the land they took. Patience thought it could only be that they have heard that the white farmers made a lot of money from game. She added this attitude was odd because it also went against African tradition. I asked what she meant by this. "Well in African tradition animals are just for killing and eating."

Once a general, minister or political "chef" has taken up his land, woe betide any lesser settlers. They will not be tolerated anywhere near.

Patience expressed great admiration for her minister Nhema. Her eyes lit up when she spoke of him and she referred to him as Francis. She never would believe that he could be involved in corruption. She would be shattered if it was proved otherwise. Because he had lent his overt support for my scheme, she couldn't see why it shouldn't go through.

I enjoyed talking with a young, educated African and hearing her views. Although she is only three years out of university, Patience was in fact a mother with two children. Her husband is working [odd-jobbing] in the U.K. and is able to send her money for her support. Otherwise, she says, she couldn't cope. She herself is hoping to find a job in her field in one of the neighbouring African countries. In Zimbabwe, salaries never keep abreast of inflation.

For me it proved a very enjoyable day; not least because I was walking abroad for hours on end on my own land and reviving my old interests—the prevailing iniquities I face, temporarily pushed aside.

In these pages, I am sure I must have spoken of the eviction of my neighbours, the Parkes family, from their farm, Maypark. It proved to be a drawn-out, ugly saga. Attempts were made at compromise with various warlike factions of invaders but all to no avail. In the end, a leading ZANU PF activist, Chris Pasipamire took the farm for himself. A bitter battle ensued between the first-comers and the new "owner". According to Johannes, Pasipameri sent out armed youths to patrol the property and keep the Warvet faction out. Shots were heard frequently at night. One Sunday, Lisa, on Trianda, counted 23 shots. Of course the shooting may have been at duikers. Whatever; the shooting which was heard on the Friday morning of November 29th., as mentioned above, was definitely connected to the vendetta.

At the very time that I was viewing the forest with Patience, Chris Pasipameri had sent three tractors and harrows out to prepare the field opposite our entrance. When I drove out in the afternoon, I was able to see where they had begun work. However it seems that the old Warvet faction was not to be put off by youths with guns. They succeeded in turning back the three tractor drivers and their machines. They certainly were not there when I passed.

A week later and Johannes says that Chris [sic] has removed all his workers and there are none left. The fields will be left unplanted. The Warvet faction has no machinery and no money so if there are any crops to be grown at all, they will only be a few plots of hand-planted maize. It is too late now anyway.

The Parkes had an extensive and productive irrigation scheme operating from a dam they built themselves. That has all collapsed and the equipment stolen. Some of the Africans still living there come over to Stockade to draw water.

So much for Chris Pasipamire's acquisition of Maypark. And I believe that is only one farm among many whose owners he has victimized and chased off. Meanwhile, he has taken time off to visit Britain. There is a picture of him in The Daily News, of 9th.Dec. He is sitting in a London restaurant. Apparently he is over there to further his studies and the BRITISH HAVE ISSUED HIM WITH THE NECESSARY VISA TO DO SO.

No! I won't say it!

It is perhaps difficult for someone who has not been "bred to nature", to understand the joy experienced by the enthusiast when he is in the midst of unspoilt indigenous woodland. The diversity of species is so great that delights, surprises and challenges to one's depth of knowledge arise at every turn. Beneath the green expanse of a spreading acacia or wild fig tree may be found a dozen other folk quietly holding their own and waiting their turn to take off into the light though they may have to wait for 50 years. Some, less ambitious, are happily content to remain in the lower storey.

How much more the pleasure, when the woodland is a place of longstanding personal association and where, in surprising enclaves on hillside or valley bottoms, one finds with excitement young trees one has planted with one's own hands. Seeds, which once perhaps were the contents of your trouser pocket, you have transformed into handsome plant life now looking down at you.

I long for a day when I can walk the woods unafraid of ugly molestation by the human species. I think I am dreaming. I must be realistic and realistically evil is abroad in every quarter and in large measure.

My ally of like mind can only be National Parks and they are twiddling their thumbs.

Sunday 15th.December 2002

I have been out to the farm in the truck. On the way I passed two, long queues of motorists. Petrol is a nightmare to obtain and the motorists were queued at a couple of service stations, which must have just taken delivery earlier. If word leaks out of an impending fuel delivery, cars will start to queue even before it arrives. I had about 20 litres of petrol left in the garage on the farm so I was able to put this in my tank. This gives me half a tank, which will keep me going for a bit.

Mujuru is present in the Bush Cottage where he is staying with two old men. After the episode of the broken tractor, I have been anxious to know if he still has intentions of planting on the land he harrowed previously. The star grass is coming through well now and, as I have said earlier, it will be excellent for game animals if these are brought in by National Parks. It is mid December; already too late for maize and only two weeks left to plant soya. Either way it will be a shambles.

However, Mujuru tells Johannes that he is expecting a tractor to arrive any day. He may be lying but there was another piece of information which was disquieting. A Toyota 4x4 Pick-up came to the farm on Thursday. On the side door panels was written the now familiar, Galloway Estates. It delivered 2x200 litre drums of diesel at Bush Cottage. When I heard this my blood-pressure rose immediately and I reached for my cell phone to dial William Hughes' number. By a miracle, he answered my call first time.

It should be recalled that William Hughes is the co-owner of Galloway Estates with his half-brother Paul Francis. I asked William why his truck was delivering diesel to Stockade. It appeared clear to me that it was their intention to follow with one of their tractors and to commence ploughing.

I told William that I had not been evicted from my farm and that the land still belonged to me. I asked him again why he should send his tractors to operate on my farm.

"Well, you know, things are getting…" William began and then trailed off thinking better of trying an explanation. He merely added that he would find out what was going on. He may have no idea what is going on; but he gave no sign of concern, sympathy or apology. I fear he is being led by his new masters. Is he taking a leaf out of their conduct book?

Johannes gives me his understanding of the business. These are his words—not mine. They will, however, reflect common knowledge held by the Africans in the neighbourhood.

"There is a white manager on Galloway, who has made a big friend with this Mujuru. His name is Paul. I have heard Mujuru speak with Paul on his cell phone. He speaks very friendly. When our electric motor was stolen from the borehole pump supplying Bush Cottage, Mujuru asked Paul if he would give him another. Paul agreed straightaway and sent the motor with his driver in a blue pick-up. Mujuru complained that he had no petrol for his car so Paul sent him two cans of petrol at the same time. I saw it myself as the blue truck passed by my house."

Johannes continued: "You see there are some white people who make an arrangement with ZANU PF all very friendly. This Galloway is a BIG company with LOTS of tractors. You will see that they have no trouble from Warvets or people coming onto their farm to settle. They can do what they like on their farm. They have made friends with Elliot Manyika and Chen Chinchengwende and they are ploughing and planting their farms for them now—now as we speak.

This Mujuru is another friend because he and Elliot Manyika and Chen Chinchengwende are all together. That manager at Galloway is lying. Those tractors that come here were all from Galloway. He knows every time."

In the minds of the local African population, this sums up the Galloway connection with complete clarity. The situation reminds me of Vichy France. Then it was collaboration with the Nazis.

I asked Johannes if there had been any developments on the farm over the road, Maypark. He confirmed that Chris Pasipameri's people had all been chased away but the circumstances were not quite as I had first learnt. There had been no running battle between the rival factions.

"One of the first Warvets on Maypark has a brother, who is in the C.I.O. When Chris [sic] sent out the tractors to the farm, the Warvet only had to phone his brother. This one can call out the strong police—not the useless ones from Nyabira or Marlborough, no—but the powerful ones. [J means the Support Unit.] They came with guns, which shoot upwards, and they beat and chased all the youths of Pasipameri off the farm. Now the first Warvets can go where they like and are happy. They have been given some fertilizer and seed."

It's not what you know, it's who you know.

The Warvets George and Moffu, who came to Johannes last week making noisy demands including one to Johannes to prepare some land for them for planting, have not been back. Their relationship with Mujuru was antagonistic. I am unclear if it remains so.

Johannes spoke further of the ineptitude of the local police.

"Every day you can see the police Landrover full of women and children, the relatives, taking them to their fields. The police have their plots on the farms the same as the Warvets. They are all together. When the police say they have no transport, it is because it is used for private."

Johannes told me that the relation of his, who works on the Prison Farm, had walked over to Stockade. He wants to buy my old David Brown tractor. The man says that he is retiring from the Prison Service. All those prison officers who are not ZANU PF are being pensioned off and they are being replaced by recruits from the Border Gezi Youth Brigades [The Green Bombers]. These hold regular ZANU PF meetings at the prison. I would like to ask if the prisoners also get indoctrinated at these meetings. Mind you, in a prison, everyone would have to be a Party supporter if they wanted to come out alive. It is what you would call a captive audience.

Apropos of prisons, Johannes had something to tell me of the Warvet, Gendi, whose name has come up in these pages from time to time. His base, remember, was on Danbury and Tommy Bayley, together with Selby Black of Selby Farm, having found solid evidence of Gendi killing a cow, charged him of stock theft. After about twenty adjourned court cases, during which time Gendi was free on bail, the court eventually sentenced him to seven years jail. J says that after doing a few months, Gendi is back and living on Danbury. The point is not lost on the local population. Everyone knows that Party activists are exonerated and released. Meanwhile, Tommy has lost his father, his farm and now, poor man, his wife Trish in a tragic road accident; he himself crippled. Such is the justice of this world.

Whilst some settlers on the farms in our area are planting small fields here and there; on the whole the arable land, once extensively cropped is lying idle. It has not taken long to reveal this psychological aspect of the African mind. By tradition, land is not looked upon as a place for hard work, productivity and sustainability. It is a personal stake, a piece of territory to fall back upon for bare subsistence if things get tough.

These things, if taken on their own, may appear minor, but when spread nation wide, they present an alarming prospect. Corruption, greed, callousness have penetrated deeply through public life and the ruling elite have added violence to the list. Faced with this, the rural African reacts with abject submissiveness. "We are crying. We shall suffer," or "We shall die", and then there is; "There is nothing we can do." This fatalism in the African psyche has been thoroughly exploited by Mugabe. He knows that those claiming that they are dying of hunger will not be angry. They will just expect to suffer and die. However; he also knows, and probably every one of the sufferers knows, that the U.N. and the F.A.O. will not let them die. Food enough will be brought to them as if by a miracle. Its distribution will be in the benevolent and capable hands of The Party.

Believe it or not, those who thought they faced starvation will clap their hands in traditional manner and bless the name of Mugabe.

Gray and Jelina are the two elderly servants who have underpinned the domestic arrangements of my son's household for the past eighteen years. They provide a quiet and enduring stability to the rush and hurly-burly of modern-day family life and their old-fashioned values are in themselves rare and precious assets.

Jelina is large and maternal, blessed with pacific equanimity based on simple Christian faith. As an elderly appendage to the family, I enjoy Jelina's protective concern for my well-being. She voiced this concern for me one day recently as she stood beside a pile of laundry on her ironing table. I had called in briefly to collect some things before making a somewhat risky visit to the farm. Risky because I had been out of touch with Johannes for some time and was uncertain if I would run across any of my persecutors. These days that even includes the police!

Jelina spoke to me. In a way, she epitomises the African mental attitude I have just referred to. Innocently and meaning well, she plunged me into a further degree of pessimism.

"Master." [Yes I told you she was old-fashioned, bless her.] "You should not be going out to the farm as you do. Why do you worry about your property and your belongings? They are just things. It is your life that is important. What are those things worth if you are dead?

Satan rules Zimbabwe now. I tell you, those people are dangerous. They will kill you, Master, I know. They are the same people who killed my mother in 1978. She was only looking for her cattle and they shot her. Stay away from them. If you have your life, that is good and is enough."

I noted that in her simple, direct way, Jalina can identify the cult of Satanism right back to the War of Liberation and to the start of this regime. "They are the same people".

Hype and myth have ever flourished after wars. For the sake of national pride, a true record of events is purposely erased. Stories of the cowardly and ignoble are confined to the enemy. Such is the manner of our species. Zimbabwe is no exception.

A recent letter to a newspaper reversed the usual trend. The writer was brave and refreshingly open. He appears to write from personal experience and, like Jelina, acknowledges a common truth: the "heroes" presently laying waste to the country, are, and always have been, nothing but bloody despots. And bullies they say are cowards. I reprint it here, because I think it reveals the force we are up against. Unfortunately, it gives me no cheer.

What follows is a transcript of the letter under a newspaper heading.

BLAIR LOATHED FOR NOT TURNING A BLIND EYE TO MUGABE'S EXCESSES

I used to wonder why President Mugabe is so furious about Prime Minister Tony Blair, but now I have the answer.

If we go back to the history of this country from the time the so-called war veterans visited our areas, at that time demanding to be called "vana vedu", or "vanamukoma" [our children or brothers], there was never peace in the minds of our people. The current wave of rape, torture and murder are just an extension of what happened during the "war of liberation".

First of all, these people used to make demands:
1. Free food consisting of sadza and meat [beef or chicken in most cases].
2. Clean blankets, and young girls had to carry these to the "bases" where each girl was forced to select one male "comrade" as a boyfriend every night with whom to sleep.
3. Free clothes, cigarettes and other goodies. In this category, local business persons and workers [e.g. teachers of those schools lucky enough to remain operational] were supposed to contribute.

In exchange, villagers would be beaten or killed each time there was a rumour that one was a "sellout" or a witch or any other weird accusation. Some were burnt alive and in other cases, wives were forced to kill their husbands while the rest at the "pungwes" [all night political rallies] would be forced to sing and ululate.

Moreover, the poor villagers lost all their cattle and goats in order to feed "vanamukoma". Most of these war veterans never shot at an enemy, but at harmless villagers. The "mujibhas" [lookouts] were supposed to spy all over and if they brought any report that Ian Smith's soldiers were coming [especially with a gun called NATO], then vanamukoma would run like madmen never to be seen again until the coast was clear once more.

At independence, there was a Zanu PF office along what is now called Robert Mugabe Road [it was called Manica Road—a good name in my opinion, which should not have been changed]. Its address was usually referred to as 88 Manica Road. At this place, there was continuation of the beatings that were experienced during the war. Each time one was accused of anything from anywhere in the country, one would be dragged to 88 Manica Road and beaten up thoroughly by groups of former "mujibhas" and former "vanamukoma".

It is from this point where I expected the then British government to start applying sanctions against Mugabe. Unfortunately, the then British government even sent soldiers to Nyanga to help train most of the current crop of our soldiers who are now beating up innocent people in the streets.

Moreover, during the Gukurahundi era, the British never punished Mugabe for his actions. Why would Mugabe, as Commander-in-Chief of the Zimbabwe Defence Forces [ZDF], the same force which was in Mozambique on a peacekeeping mission, use different tactics to quell a rebellion?

The rebellion that was in Zimbabwe by then was no different from the rebellion in Mozambique, Somalia and Angola where Zimbabwe soldiers went on a peacekeeping mission and we never heard of these soldiers killing innocent civilians as they did in Midlands and Matabeleland. How does Mugabe as Commander-in-Chief of the ZDF, explain the contradictions on the part of the army?

Moreover, was it not better as the Shona proverb goes, that "muroyi royera kuri kuti vepadyo vakukudze"? [If there is a witch in your community, don't allow them to practice there; they must cast spells further off.] I mean if his soldiers were so bloodthirsty, would it not have been better for them to kill strangers in those countries where they were peacekeepers instead of killing their own people?

But the issue here is that during all this circus, the then British government allowed Mugabe to do what he wanted. As a result he became a spoilt brat. He oversaw corruption, murder and rape and nothing happened to him. Right now he continues doing the same thing but Blair is against it.

He is the first British Prime Minister to tell Mugabe that what he is doing is wrong and that he should behave himself. That's why Mugabe hates Blair so much. He thinks it's his right to send his supporters to kill, rape and steal because he has been doing it before without anyone raising a voice.

So Blair, you are just a victim of history but fortunately the legacy of your predecessors who were moral weaklings.

Comrade Charira

Europe

The letter would appear to have been written by someone whose experiences left a vivid impression on them. He or she may have been a child during the liberation war of the seventies. It is an African viewpoint and, beyond the cynicism directed at the British, it laments the suffering of large numbers of the African population at the present time at the hands of THE SAME PEOPLE, who call themselves war veterans.

My diary is a personal record and my viewpoint, quite obviously, is that of a white farmer, for that is what I am—or was. The letter opens the curtain a little and it shows that the hand of evil is not racially discriminate nor ever was. And incidentally, many a white had a tale to tell of 88 Manica Road.

I return to the everyday.

Thursday 19th.December 2002

On Monday I received a message to say that last Thursday night, our watchman, Norman, had surprised a thief who had broken into the new house. The man was the Warvet Moffu. He had broken off bath handles and was also removing locks and cupboard doors.

This was an awkward one for me. On the face of it, here was a good chance to get a criminal charge against Moffu. However, my unpleasant experience with the police at Nyabira is still in the forefront of my mind. It is true that seven weeks have passed since the threats to evict me and they have taken no action in that time. However they had plainly told my lawyer that the law meant nothing to them. My instinct was to let sleeping dogs lie.

Eventually, I decided to ring them. The main thing was to have a complaint recorded at the charge office. With luck I may only get a duty constable at the desk. I had no wish to speak with either of the inspectors. I put through the call and the phone rang and rang. There was no answer. I then phoned the Marlborough police and to my surprise a man said that as their vehicle was presently at Glenara and not too far from Stockade, he would radio it and tell them to attend to my report.

Needless to say, they never turned up. I learnt this from Johannes when I phoned him on Wednesday. I again rang ZRP Marlborough and gave them my story over again. I was left while those in the charge office went into discussion. A constable came back to say that Stockade fell into the Mabelreign precinct and that I should contact them. I assured the man that in no way did Stockade fall into Mabelreign. The policemen went into conference again. Then:

"We have a sub-station at Mt.Hampden. You can go there."

"But can't you speak with them from where you are?"

"No, but you can pick a constable up from there and take him with you to the farm."

"But I am too short of petrol."

A silence followed and further deliberation was taking place. Then the voice came back in triumph:

"We have been looking at the map. You come under Nyabira.

"Yes, but Nyabira don't answer their phone."

"Don't you have some friends near there, who can go to the police with your message?"

"No. All the friends I had in that area have left their farms. They are not there any more." I paused briefly to sigh and then added: "O Alright. I'll try to think of something."

Monday 23rd. December 2002

The Warvet Moffu and another aggressive character name Machindo came out from Harare where, I am told, they both work for the Municipality. They called a meeting. Using the familiar Section 8 issue, they demanded the keys of my house and told my farm workers that they must leave the farm. They must ask The Boss for their money. It is all very tiresome and time consuming. They will have concocted some unholy scheme for their own advantage. It could be no more than a counter move because Moffu's nephews were caught stealing. It is difficult to know how their minds work.

I must say I am rather disappointed when I learn that my people are so obedient when the Warvets call them together. There was a period when they were prepared to ignore the Warvets commands and quietly drift out of sight. After all there are no resident Warvets nowadays. Their visits are sporadic. I suppose it could be put down to the presence of Moffu's men at the farm's beer outlet.

This whole period of state led anarchy, has shown the African character to consist of two extremes. There is the opportunist element which, when the opening is presented, will manifest itself in ruthless predation on the weak and the exposed. It lies close to the surface. When brought out from the sub-conscious it is acted out in horrifying reality. Greed is the motivation. We have watched it operate at all levels.

On the other hand, there is the faint-hearted characteristic. It cowers before the least show of threat and aggression. The thought of taking a stand against blatant wrongs is just too much for it. It abjectly succumbs.

Tuesday 31st. December 2002

Christmas Day and Boxing Day holidays went by without incident.

However, it was reported that on the Saturday following, a gang composed of ten or twelve ZANU PF youths walked along the railway line below my house. They reached as far as the level crossing and went up to the Fig Tree House where Maston saw them. Mujuru was not at the nearby Bush Cottage at that time.

The youths came from Maypark. As I related previously, Chris Pasipameri employed these youths when he controlled Maypark Farm, which he had plundered earlier from the Parkes family. The youths had been chased off by the Police Support Unit, called in to support the rival claimants to the farm. Now these youths have filtered back onto Maypark. Doubtless they will have no money and no food and so will be living upon what they can steal and scavenge. They pose a real danger.

To further my disquiet, the night watchmen, Kariza and Denis, reported that on Saturday night Moppet and Humba were barking furiously for a long time. However, there had been no sign of an attempted break-in.

Meanwhile, I had agreed with Johannes that it would be a wise move to lift the unused borehole pump at the old pigsties. In the event of a turndown in our fortunes and unstoppable lawless raids, it would be something less that could be looted. J did this after dark, with the help of a friend and borrowed tackle.

Mujuru is keeping a low profile of late and is frequently in town. Nonetheless, on Friday a Galloway Estate white Landrover drove onto the farm to deliver three drums of diesel fuel to Bush Cottage. This means that there are now five drums there or 1000 litres. Mujuru tells Johannes that he is expecting a tractor any day. Whatever he may have intended, it would be the height of madness to plant any crop at this stage of the season although I have to admit that such madness can readily be observed all around the district. A fiasco is in the making.

Galloway Estates: I am determined to keep at them. I couldn't raise William Hughes on his phone. It transpired that he was away on holiday. Paul Francis, the step-brother, I did manage to get hold of. I asked him why his vehicles were delivering fuel to Stockade, a farm of which I am the lawful owner.

Paul Francis gives out the impression that he wallows in such a sea of troubles that he knows next to nothing of what is going on. The control of his extensive operations, he implies, is in the hands of Warvets, illegal settlers, Party supporters and dishonest employees. He was ignorant of the affair of the busted tractor and of his team coming to extract it. He didn't know that his phone was tapped. He knew nothing of his vehicle delivering diesel to Stockade, which is miles away from his Mvurwi farm.

"I hope they aren't stealing our diesel," he said.

"From what you have been telling me," I replied, "you are being ripped off left, right and centre."

"What do you think? Is there any hope of this trouble ever coming to an end?" he asked.

I couldn't suppress a scornful laugh. It seemed so guileless to introduce such a generality in response to my particular and immediate concerns. "Look, I cannot possibly comment over this phone on the future of Zimbabwe. Furthermore, I really don't want to know other people's problems; I have enough of my own. My purpose of ringing is to ask you to please stop your men from coming onto my farm!"

Before we closed the conversation, he asked me the name of the man who was giving me the hard time. I told him it was Mujuru.

"Oh! I have a Mujuru working for me. I wonder if they are related?"

So, I left it at that and muttered to myself: "Bloody collaborator. I hope he gets his deserts."

The presence of those Party youths in the district has been on my mind. They will have the boldness imparted by numbers and one knows who finds work for idle hands. The excursion onto Stockade may have been a recce. Fig Tree House would be a tempting target for a break-in.

Maston is the caretaker, but he is tucked away with his wife and children in his own quarters surrounded by a tall grass fence and a massive hedge, all well outside the Fig Tree security fence. When the Tredar guards were being employed, he could run and call on them for support; since their withdrawal, he is very much on his own. As for his character, I would describe it as definitely timid. If Maston did hear intruders, he may well choose to deny his hearing.

Martin and Jean have left a considerable number of belongings in the Fig Tree House so I felt that it was important that these should be removed. Accordingly, I went out to the farm on Monday, having ascertained that Mujuru was off the farm. With Johannes and Maston, I took note of the all the remaining loose property and told Johannes to put it on the farm trailer as soon as he could do so unobserved, and to take it up to my homestead.

The plan was to have the Fig Tree furniture and the other items taken to Martin's house in town by hired transport. Added to the load would be several items of furniture from my house, which daughter Bridget has expressed a desire to have in her home in SA. My own future being so extremely tenuous, I was quite happy to go along with this and, with Johannes and Makosa in tow, I walked through my house identifying the items to be loaded. An inner voice told me that I should get the stuff away without delay.

Johannes obviously needed time to get the Fig Tree goods and chattles moved in what would have to be a clandestine operation, and as Wednesday would be New Years' Day and a holiday, the earliest I could arrange for a removal truck was Thursday. Before leaving with the family on a short holiday to Kariba, Martin had contacted a transport company owned by a friend. When I knew my time schedule, I phoned them and fixed for the vehicle to be at the farm by 8.30 on the Thursday morning.

At some time on Tuesday morning, New Year's Eve, Johannes phoned me to say that he had successfully loaded and transported the Fig Tree items to my house. He had got his wife and some other women, who he could trust to keep quiet, to help him. The first hurdle had been cleared.

Meanwhile, I was nagged by another worry. Although Martin had left his diesel truck with fuel in it for me to use, this vehicle is vitally important for his company business and I was most reluctant to make use of it. Car theft is so prevalent in these times. Our petrol vehicles however were all dangerously low on petrol. When a friend rang me to say that a petrol queue was forming at one of the filling stations on the town's periphery, I dropped what I was doing and sped to join the queue. My friend and I arrived simultaneously at 2 pm. There were about 100 cars ahead of us and, following some drama when the filling station threatened to close at the official time of 6 pm., we finally got our cars filled at 6.40. We drove away leaving behind a queue that would be kept going until 8 pm. I drove to Martin's house and there left the car with the full tank, swopping it for my farm truck, which was close on empty. I thought to scout for more petrol in the morning.

By the time I got back to my digs, it was 8.30 and my cell phone showed that there had been three missing calls—all from Johannes.

"I have a problem," says Johannes, using his favourite expression. "This afternoon at 3.30, George and Moffu and another one came to the farm and walked up to the sheds. They called all our people from the compound for a meeting—even the wives. The third man is new but he is BIG!—the same like Mujuru. He came with his wife and two children. George, he talk talk—a big noise—just talk talk. Moffu, he talk too, the new one, not. George the most. Moffu had his two sons."

"So what did they say?" I ask.

"They spoke about the Section 8 and how you should not be on the property. They told the workers that they must leave the farm because other people will move into their houses. They must tell the Boss to pay them their money now so that they can go. But they must see that you do not remove anything from the farm until they get the money. The things on the farm, like all the pipes and machines, now all belong to the government and must not be taken away."

"Was that all?" I have in mind the pipes and various fittings, which will be leaving with the furniture lorry.

"No. They said they will be coming again on Thursday and they will be bringing youths and lots of others from Mbare with them—as many as they can carry in their truck. When these people get here they will come to stay and live in the farm sheds. Then they will break into your house and take your things. The workers will be chased away, so before this happens they must get you to pay them their money."

Then Johannes added in a subdued afterthought: "They may just be trying to frighten."

Once again I am faced with a tricky decision to make. The removal vehicle is due early on Thursday morning; the New Year holiday has already begun. To abort my plan would require some pretty hectic action first thing on Thursday—drivers are most often given prior instructions and will leave the transporter's yard before the office opens and phone lines operating.

I am more inclined to go along with Johannes' last remark. So many times I have discovered the Warvets to be blustering bullies whose roaring threats turn out to be empty.

"I reckon we'll go along as planned, Johannes," I tell him. "Contact me tomorrow evening."

What can be the significance of the unknown newcomer? The BIG man? Why the wife and children? From Johannes' description of their clothing, they appeared to be affluent. George carried them out in his own car. Of the two men, who is the master, who the servant?

2003

Saturday 4th January 2003

New Year's Day saw me up at 4.30 in the morning. Before 5 o'clock I was at the same filling station where I had got petrol the previous evening. I was relieved to discover that their bulk tank had not been emptied and that they would resume service at 6 am. This meant an hour's wait but this time I was number six in the queue. The five cars in front of me had been there all night; some of the drivers were still sleeping on the car seats.

There was a slow and somewhat disorganised start, nonetheless I drove up to the pump at 6.30. This time there was a monetary ration, but I received enough to register slightly over three-quarter full. When I left, the queue of cars stretched well up the road. Being the early bird paid off.

Now I had the farm truck with a good tank of petrol. I was glad of this, because it was the vehicle I wanted to take out to the farm on the following morning—just in case I ran into mischief makers.

I made comms with Johannes in the evening. He had already been collecting and preparing the goods for loading next morning. As usual, I asked about the whereabouts of the "nasties". Mujuru had gone to town the previous day and not returned. He is not a part of the Warvet grouping anyway. All in all, it is always good to learn that he is anywhere else but on the farm. The disturbing news was that Moffu had got a lift out from town and was staying at the old store where he has installed his two sons. Was this planned timing? Did he expect Comrade George and Co. to arrive on the morrow?

It was vital that no word should reach Moffu of the arrival of the removal van. Everyone these days seems to possess a cell phone. If the other members of the gang did indeed intend to come to the farm as threatened, I was relying upon them getting there later in the day after we had got away. The last thing I wanted was for Moffu to relay a message to George.

Johannes said he would post someone at the farm entrance gate.

Fortunately the compound houses and the store are half a mile further down the road from the farm entrance and well out of sight. For security reasons we took down the farm signboard years ago. It would be disastrous if the van driver overran the entrance and went to the farm store to ask the way! Johannes was even worried lest he should sound his horn.

It was my intention to reach the farm by 8 am. on Thursday morning. This meant leaving town at about 7.25. When I was about to leave I remembered that I needed to change my cell phone battery. The spare battery had been on charge all night, but for some extraordinary reason and to my dismay, I found the charger to be discharging instead of charging. I would be leaving for the farm with a cell phone that would surely fail on me.

There was no certainty that I might not run into trouble—though God knows who I could turn to if I did; certainly not the police. Whatever; I felt that I could not proceed with this exploit devoid of two-way communication.

I immediately put the one battery onto proper charge and with the last spark in my other battery I called Johannes to say that I would be half an hour late—the time to obtain a full recharge. Shortly before 8 o'clock my charger signalled a full charge. With this I managed to contact the transport company, who confirmed that my removal truck had already left the depot. As I was leaving, I relayed this message to Johannes. I gathered from him that he had put somebody at the road end to wait for it. They had been there since early morning. Nothing like being thorough.

My approach to the farm entrance was a slow and cautious one. I stopped to see if there were any recent tyre tracks on the gravel turning. I saw none so perhaps I was ahead of the removal truck. This turned out to be the case.

All was quiet, not a soul in sight. I drove the Pick-up quietly down to my security gate and on my arrival; it was miraculously swung open for me. Makosa greeted me with a big smile and Moppet and Humba dashed out full of excitement. To them, my farm truck is no less than their heavenly chariot and in no time they had both leapt into the back. Alas, the regular journey around the farm, which was once the exciting pinnacle of their every day, has been suspended. Today I will take them the forty yards from the gate to my house.

Johannes and Makosa had been working hard and nearly all the goods for loading had been collected at the loading point. Johannes had elected to employ a few trusted women for this job. At this time, the hired transport was still on its way.

"Johannes," I said, "You promised you would have someone at the road end to intercept the truck and direct it here. When I came in just now I saw nobody."

"No, there is a girl there. She is hiding in the long grass. If she was seen, anyone passing might ask her questions. When she sees the big van coming she will come out."

"Oh that's good. What about Moffu? Is he still in the compound?

"Yes. I have sent Sinai, my wife, down to buy some sweets at the store. She has come back and says Moffu is sitting outside drinking."

So you see, this exercise is being conducted with military-like preparedness.

Within five minutes we heard the sound of the heavy vehicle and sure enough, in another couple of minutes it was driven into my grounds and the security gate locked behind it. This was good; and even better, the driver had three strong men with him. Loading could move apace. In two hours we had everything loaded; the transport moved out and I followed behind. Hooray!

The next morning, I contacted Johannes. Later that day, the Warvet Moffu had come up to him at the farm sheds to say that he had heard that a motorcar had come onto the farm. Johannes told him: "It was just the boss bringing some food for the dogs."

This seemed to satisfy Moffu; although, if he had been drinking beer from early morning, I expect his head was befuddled.

As for George, his threats turned out to be empty. Or perhaps he simply failed to muster a gang of supporters. One will never know. The one certain thing one knows about the likes of George is that they are all thoroughly evil and it's best to be wary when you are dealing with the minions of the devil.

Thursday 23rd January 2003

The gap in my diary is due to pressure loads bearing on me from all points. With the entry of the New Year, it was clear that a major and rapid decision had to be made concerning my continued involvement with Stockade. Whatever small income I had earned during the winter months from irrigated vegetable crops, had almost literally dried up when electric motors and switches operating the pumps on our several boreholes, were stolen one after another. Hay-baling came to an end at the commencement of the rainy season. In addition to this, Mujuru on the one hand and the Warvets on the other, were continually harrying us with demands that we stop farm operations. We defied them to an extent, but it was a gruelling duel.

There being no productive work, some of our workers were laid off. However, to maintain a modicum of security in the present state of lawlessness, it has been essential to employ watchmen in support of Johannes and also for the protection of my house. We have 13 men on our books; this includes Johannes and Makosa, my cook. Of the number, five are old men who are given special jobs when available.

Wages and ancillary expenses have to be found. The farm income is nil. After three years of attrition, the farm reserves are nil. Only contributions by Martin and withdrawals from personal savings are keeping things going. The financial drain can no longer be borne. I had hoped National Parks would have taken over months ago. They haven't; so now we're up the creek.

Even if, by some miracle, Mujuru and the Warvets were taken off my back for ever, there is no way I could restart where I left off three years ago. Prolongation of this state seems pointless.

As a first step, we agreed that our workers should be paid off and receive their terminal benefits as laid down by government regulation. This will mean a payout of 1.5 million dollars, which needless to say the farm hasn't got. The regulation states that if the farmer does not have sufficient money, the terminal benefits to workers may be paid from the compensation he receives for the farm.

There is a snag; a snag which makes the clause ridiculous. Farmers are not being paid compensation for their farms, nor is it ever likely that they will be. The government is broke. It can only carry on by printing more money. Such matters are hardly in the forefront of the mind of a farm worker—if he thinks of them at all. He is out of a job and the government says he is due a large sum of money from the farmer who has just been forcibly evicted from his farm. Quite naturally the worker's priority will be to look after himself and his family. A failure to pay what the government says is his due, will be strongly resented. The farmer has been caught in a vice.

Martin took the line that somehow we should find the money and pay the workers off regardless of the loophole open to us. We want to be shot of the whole business. I agreed. The last thing I want is to sever relations with my workers with any feeling of acrimony. The money could be raised by selling the Colcom shares, which I obtained over the thirty-six years when I was an active pig producer. Goodbye to those savings.

It was going to take a little time for the money to be released and meanwhile I have had useful discussions with Tony Ndora of the National Employment Council and Tongai of the Agricultural Labour Bureau. I explained our decision to conform with the regulations and to make full and final payment. Both men were helpful with their advice and they agreed to be present when we paid the workers in order to assure them of the correctness of the final package they would be receiving.

Following our decisive decision, my immediate priority was to urge the ministries to come to an equally decisive decision. I phoned Environment and asked to speak with Mr. Tavaya, the Permanent Secretary, who directed the call to Mrs. Sangarwe. I made an appointment with her for the following afternoon.

Mrs. Sangarwe as a Deputy Secretary has a large, remarkably uncluttered office. On one side is a suite of vinyl-leather easy chairs surrounding a low polished table. As on our previous meeting, Mrs. Sangarwe directed me to take one of the chairs and leaving her desk came to join me carrying a file and her note pad. The file was quite thick and I assumed it was the file for Stockade Farm. I hope it was, because during our discussion, I frequently pointed to it with the words: "It's all in there."

I spoke freely and openly, expressing all my fears and frustrations. Mrs. Sangarwe again explained that the Ministry of Lands was responsible for implementing transfer. Parks could not move onto the property without written authority from Lands. And Lands were not replying to the letters written to them by Environment. Well, there was nothing new in this for me. I could only make the comment that it was wrong and disgraceful of them; to which Mrs. Sangarwe agreed with a slight shrug of the shoulder.

Six months had passed, I said, since the Minister had expressed his wish for Parks to take over the farm and thereby protect the forest. Originally, officials in Lands VERBALLY assured me that the matter was quite straightforward. As time went on somebody managed to paralyse them.

I could not understand why there should be this stumbling block. On Stockade, Mujuru had indeed installed himself illegally, claiming he had been given the farm, but he can produce nothing to substantiate this. As for the Warvets, they come and go sporadically and when they do, they also claim the farm. I do not believe their claim is serious. Here, Mrs. Sangarwe commented that the Warvets may be acting as a front for a person of influence. If this is so, then the influential person will be a rival to Mujuru, because there is no love lost between him and the Warvets.

However it may be; I emphasized to Mrs. Sangarwe that we had come to the end of the road. We had been caretaking the assets on the property for all these months with the prospect of a transfer to Parks; one conducted in a professional and amicable manner. No valuation had been undertaken—also a responsibility of Lands. At this rate it could take months to be done; if ever. There was no alternative but to abandon the farm. This would mean abandoning it to looters and vandals. The standing assets would be stripped.

Mrs. Sangarwe told me that Chadenga had said he wished to see the farm himself later in the week. She would go too if possible. It could be Friday. I said this would be brilliant and here our serious discussion ended. At this point I noticed Helen, the Minister's secretary, standing at the open door from the outer office. I have had so much dealing with Helen that we have become good friends. I greeted her affably and she came forward to shake my hand. In the light-hearted banter which followed, I said that if I had my way, I would appoint Mrs. Sangarwe as Minister and Helen as Permanent Secretary. "In that case," they replied, "We will appoint you as President." I hope none of the three worthies are listening. We all might be arrested for treason.

It seems possible that Mrs. Sangarwe had contacted Chadenga prior to her meeting with me and both of them had considered that a visit to the farm was necessary. Whatever, it was a positive move.

On the Wednesday I managed, after the usual difficulties, to get through to Chadenga. I explained that I had heard that he intended to visit Stockade on Friday and to please tell me how best I could fit in with the arrangement. His short reply was given in the tone of the overworked executive: "Come to my office at 10 o'clock on Friday morning." That was all; no confirmation with regard to the farm visit. Despair. I had gone through this before. My mind took a pre-run. I would arrive at the National Parks offices on Friday morning to be told that Mr. Chadenga had been called away to an important conference. "Oh," I would say, "When will he be back?"

"We can't say," would be the answer, "The conference is in Timbuktu."

I was staying with the Cunliffes at the time and on Friday morning, Rob Cunliffe [a man of many skills] was instructing me on how to deal with the whims of this computer. This delayed me a little. Not to worry. Never yet have I gone to an appointment without being kept waiting. I arrived at Parks H.Q. at 10.10. Imagine my astonishment and dismay at finding Chadenga standing on the far side of the car park apparently waiting for me to arrive. He was wearing a sporty, open-necked blue shirt as if prepared for a day's outing. Chadenga is a very big man and has a big personality. He called across to me pointing to his watch—"10 o'clock!" I felt myself to be noticeably smaller than usual.

I was soon comforted when I realized that his reprimand had been made in jest. We were to wait for Sangarwe who had not arrived and transport had still to be sorted out. I suggested that if they had a 4x4 available it may be more suitable for the forest roads. "No no, we are not going into the bush. We are just going to have a quick look around."

Chadenga then disappeared with another man and only returned shortly before Sangarwe arrived from her office wearing, I noted, her city clothes. Naturally I asked them what they particularly wished to look at. To properly do the rounds of the farm and forest could take several hours. Both exclaimed in horror at this suggestion. They couldn't possibly spare the time.

"Well is it the buildings you are interested in seeing? Or is it just the forest and the land?" I asked.

Says Chadenga, "We just want a general look. You've got a homestead; let's go there."

I spoke no more but I was mystified and perplexed. They could not get a "general look" of the farm and forest from the homestead.

They had settled on a small government car with a driver, so I led the way and the others followed. On the drive out I did some thinking. They were pushed for time yet wanted to get a general impression. That would not be obtained from my house, which was only a few hundred metres in from the Selby road. When we arrived at my gate, therefore, I suggested we drive on to the centre of the farm. At least that way they would see some of the farm buildings.

Johannes was at my gate, so I told him to get in the car with me. I wanted to know if Mujuru was around. Fortunately, I learnt that he was away. It had been my plan to take my visitors down to the approximate centre of the farm to a point where the extent of the forest could be seen and also some of the arable lands, now growing good grass. However as I crossed the rail line, I decided that they ought to see Bush Cottage and Fig Tree House, which were close by. We drove up to Martin's old house and Maston came forward to open the gate.

It turned out to be a useful stop for their purpose. We had brought no map and they had very little idea of the extent of the farm. There is a panoramic view from the houses and the green forested hills can be seen stretching well into the distance. Johannes was able to explain that the forest continued round to the land at the back of us. I also heard him tell them that Mujuru had a gun and was shooting game at night.

Chadenga asked me where the "plantation" was that I had planted. Mrs. Sangarwe intervened to say it must be the old gum trees we had passed, growing close by my house. Oh dear! Oh dear! They have no idea of my work. My indigenous trees are planted in hundreds but scattered all over the place. Thank goodness the ecologist showed a proper appreciation. I told them they must come again and spend a few hours.

Chadenga was keen to learn how I made my living on the farm. I said I no longer made a living. But he meant what I had done to earn a living in the past. Of course I was able to tell him that we had kept 1000 pigs, 250 head of cattle and grown our own feedstuffs to feed them all.

"So the farm can feed a good number of animals," he offered by way of a statement.

"Why yes of course," I said. "There is excellent grazing."

I was hoping that he had wildlife and game animals in mind.

Then Chadenga turned to me and said: "What is it you actually want?" I repeated what I have said and written over and over again; I wanted the farm to be taken over by National Parks and gave all the reasons for so doing.

"Yes yes, but what do YOU want."

"Considering that I have no other property and no money to buy any, it would be very acceptable if I were to receive some compensation."

"Well, how much do you want?"

"I have never given the matter serious consideration. No proper valuation has been done."

"You must have an idea. For instance, how much would you value this house?" He pointed to Fig Tree house by which we were standing.

I was taken aback by this form of question. I was told by Mrs. Mandimika that valuation and compensation, if agreed upon, was handled by the Ministry of Lands. What was Chadenga's role if any? What might he know which I didn't? I must be careful with my answers. I muttered that the house was probably worth 40 million.

"But it couldn't possibly be worth that much."

"It would be if it was in town."

"Yes, but this isn't Harare."

"If I am being asked to bargain, then naturally I shall start off as high as possible. But, let's face it, you know perfectly well that in this matter you hold the whip hand," I said rather too honestly.

Mrs. Sangarwe, sensing my embarrassment, intervened to say that it would be a matter of negotiation.

Chadenga then volunteered: "You will be paid compensation."

These government people hold their cards close to the chest. He will not reveal to me how he can say such a thing. Perhaps he is just guessing.

"That would be fine; but I have heard of no others being paid and I thought the government had no money," I said; then added, "If you do take over the farm, would it be possible for me to remain in my house?"

"That might be difficult if the property belonged to Parks."

"If I was paid compensation then I could rent it from you—at least for a while."

We shook hands and the Deputy Secretary Environment and the Deputy Director of National Parks drove away. I was left wondering. It had been a strange visit. It seemed that they had come to do no more than verify for themselves that Stockade existed. There had been loads of reports from their own personnel, apart from Forestry Commission, Natural Resources and independent professionals in the ecological field. Chadenga did the talking yet he did not seem to be appraising Stockade for a National Parks asset at all. I had made it very plain what I had ACTUALLY WANTED. The financial aspect was of low priority to me. In such matters I suppose I am obtuse.

So much for the diplomatic front. On the other front, skirmishes with the Warvets have been continuing. Separately, both Moffu and George have been coming onto the farm and issuing the familiar threats.

At the weekend, Mujuru and the mechanic from Galloway Estates spent an hour at the cattle dip examining the borehole there. The electric motor and the switchgear have long since gone. They could only have been discussing one of two things; either fixing up the mono pump with another motor and switchgear stolen from elsewhere; or considering the prospects of lifting and selling the pump and borehole piping. The latter I would think is the most likely. And by the way, Mujuru is still operating one of Galloway's electric motors for his water supply—courtesy of Mr. Paul Francis.

On Monday 20th. Johannes phoned to say that George had driven onto the farm in his truck. With him was another man. They had stopped at the sheds and George began shouting, cursing and threatening Johannes—and me in my absence. Once more he claimed the property on the farm was his and forthwith drove to where the factory women's dormitory used to be. There they took off two doors and loaded them into the truck before leaving.

I am reluctant to call Nyabira police, preferring to let sleeping dogs lie. Johannes is also reluctant to contact them. He says that, being friends of the Warvets, the police will tell them who made the report and that will only bring him more trouble.

I slept on it and in the morning resolved to phone Nyabira and make my complaint. There was no reply to the phone, which I guess is out of order. The next morning I called in at Marlborough police station. The constable manning the desk was a Constable Gwandu.

I explained that Nyabira was my local station, but my difficulty was contacting them. He said it was in order for him to enter the report in Marlborough. I wrote a statement and it was booked in as OB 524\03 of 21.1.03 time 10 am. I said, "Shouldn't it be RB for Report Book?" "No," was the reply. "We've run out of report books and are using order books instead." Fair enough.

The same evening, Johannes phoned. It was to tell me that George had again driven in with his truck. This time he helped himself to some steel piping, which was lying outside the workshop. This meant a second visit to Marlborough police. This time there was a woman constable on duty. I explained that I wished to follow up the previous day's complaint with yet another.

"Yes, we can take the report, but you know we have to send it to Nyabira?"

"Yes, that's OK. How long will it take?"

"Up to two weeks."

"Good God. Is your O.I.C. in? I'd better speak with him."

I met with Insp. Mandizvidza and gave him the run down of the case; further explaining that petrol shortage prevented me from going to Nyabira in person.

"That's no problem. I'll call them up on the radio."

The inspector walked into the charge office where the radio had been sending out deafening communications interspersed with violent crackles and screeches. He tried repeatedly to call One Four Nyabira. Yes. You've got it. There was no answer. The Nyabira radio was out of order. "Has been for weeks," offered a sergeant laconically as he passed through the area.

Inspector Mandizvidza had a try on the telephone. With the phone to his ear he looked up at me: "It just rings and rings and there's no answer." Yes, I am familiar with the sound. "Do you know if they have a cell number?" he adds, putting down the receiver.

"Give me some time," I replied. "I just might find something."

I delved into my briefcase and pulled out four small notebooks.

I remembered the occasion many months ago when, for some desperate reason, I needed to contact ANYBODY of senior rank at Nyabira. I was given Sgt. Tehja's number. I remembered the occasion particularly, because Sgt. Tehja had the most remarkable cell phone. After a brief introduction by a female voice, the phone broke into pop music.

I paged through the notebooks and even surprised myself by finding the number. I read it out to the inspector with the warning that there was no knowing who or what he might get at the other end. He tapped the number and remarkably Tehja replied at the other end.

The inspector handed the receiver over to me and I told Tehja what had been happening. He handed the call over to Asst.Insp.Taswa. I did my best to treat the latter as an old friend. Did he know the Warvet George? Yes, he did. I spoke of George's raids on my property. Taswa brings up the old bogey. Had there been any change in the Section 8 Order? No, it was as he knew it and as my lawyer had stated. Was George on the farm? No, he comes and goes in his truck. "Alright ", from Taswa

A couple of days earlier, a displaced farmer friend had told me that Inspector Sengwe had left. I put this to the test.

"Have you been made officer-in-charge Nyabira?"

"No, another man is coming. I am going to Norton."

After a few more words, I left it at that. There is no more I can do but wait to see if Taswa makes a follow up. Judging on past performance, he won't. However, he might have been much under the thumb of Sengwe. Who knows? We must hope that the new broom will be an improvement.

When I told the Marlborough O.I.C., Mandizvidza, of the blatant predations of George, his immediate comment was:

"The man should be arrested." Would that his Commissioner had the same attitude.

Saturday 8th.February 2003

Three weeks since my last entry. I have made three moves over the same time; the last to Glen Lorne, northeast of Harare and full of Scottish names. The land is very broken here and the housing has developed on quite steep hillsides well covered with indigenous woodland. Access and building must be expensive and this is reflected in the houses—for the most part, upmarket houses for upmarket people.

The garden of the house where I was staying, sloped from top to bottom, stony but fertile because the vegetation was growing vigorously and trees plentiful. So too was bird life; I heard four different species of cuckoo calling and that means their hosts must have been plentiful as well.

It might be thought that this particular house-sitting stint was in the perfect place for me, but it is not really so. I have been spoilt by over fifty years as master of my own spread. Being used to walk at will over 1000 acres, even a 4 acre garden makes me feel confined. In addition, I was kept extremely busy over the two weeks there. It was necessary for me to go into Harare on most days and the extra distance was irksome; with the petrol shortage, I was constantly examining my fuel gauge.

At the house I spent some sixty hours retyping my notes, which had been irretrievably lost from the computer memory. Somewhere along the line, I must have struck a wrong button! Thank goodness I had printed as I went along, so I was saved utter chagrin, but the punishment for my lapse was this mass of retyping. At last I have everything saved on disc.

So the two weeks soon passed and I was on the move again—the day before the return of the owners from holiday. I said goodbye to Patch, the dog, with whom I had formed a quiet friendship. Patch is brown and white, medium height, light weight, sort of silky-haired. Life was dull for him, I guessed, and he wore a rather sad and lonely expression.

The house was strictly barred to him. The one exciting moment of his day was when Terry, the maidservant, was preparing his evening meal. Then Patch would jump up and down at the open kitchen door and dare to place a foot beyond the threshold. This would trigger the scolding cry of the maid: "Out Patch! Out!" Patch would retreat a foot or two and whine in anticipation. "Out Patch! Out!" In two weeks these were the only words I ever heard Terry, the maid, speak to him.

I gathered that he used to get biscuits in the morning, but these had either run out, were no longer obtainable or were exorbitantly priced. Imagine trying to explain that to your dog when you return home carrying the groceries. I bought a box of buttermilk rusks and shared these with Patch on the quiet.

My next shelter was a small garden flat in Avondale. I had the availability of this for a full week. A good friend, "Tinks" Bezeidenhout, had rented the flat for a short period. She, together with her son Mark and his wife and family, have been kicked off their farm in Darwendale by the nephew of Mugabe. The result is that they are all homeless—they left behind two lovely homes, a tobacco and a rose-growing enterprise and forty thousand chickens.

Tinks rented the flat as a temporary measure for herself; she has a standby qualification and from rearing chickens she has returned to teaching in order to earn a living. She kindly let me move in to her vacant flat whilst she was moving into her school accommodation. Mark, who holds degrees in horticulture and business management, is emigrating to Australia.

I met Mark at his mother's flat at the beginning of the month. He had just returned from visiting his farm to pay the farm workers their severance packages. Whilst there, he had been manhandled by a group of Warvets and their running mates; his pickup truck nearly turned over, the ignition keys stolen, shouted at and threatened. He told me that he had never been so frightened in his life. He was saved by one of those last-minute interventions by a single individual who had kept his reason. Mark had a brief look through his house. An African woman was cooking food at an open fire burning on the kitchen floor.

A friend in need is a friend indeed and this haven was offered just at the time I needed it, for at the end of the week I would be able to move to my next port. It has given me my first experience in life of living in a flat. In no time at all, my relatively few possessions, which I lug around with me, seemed to fill all available space. The computer, files and books monopolised the one and only sizeable table. I left cardboard cartons and zip bags containing a miscellany of items in places around the floor where I hoped I wouldn't trip over them.

Strangely enough, the aspect from the minute little back veranda looking on to a tiny rectangle of garden, was one of enshrouding, peaceful greenery. It was remarkable how many flowering shrubs were growing in this restricted flatland area and in the background, rising to the clouds, above the roofs and security walls, rooted in goodness knows what concrete yard, some quite massive trees. At times the little garden, enclosed as it was, resembled an aviary; there were so many varied little birds busily flying in and out. And of the ubiquitous pied crows that flock the city, not one did I see in this secret corner. I would hate to live in an urban cell like so many poor wretches have to do, but in this cell at least one gets a touch of nature.

No dogs here [Tinks takes Jodi, her 14 year old Chihuahua to school with her]; only cats, a bright ginger scurrying over the little lawn at the back and a very elegant Persian who took a fancy to the interior of my car.

On 28th.January, Martin sent the Nola truck to pick up our farm workers at the farm and to bring them into the N.E.C. offices at Greencroft. We had arranged to pay them their termination of employment money in conformity with the government regulations known as SI 6. Twelve out of our thirteen workers came in, dressed in their Sunday best. They were ushered in to the conference room where they sat in arm chairs around a table circling the room. It was very impressive. I guess they had never had an experience like this in their lives.

Martin and I spoke briefly of the decision to close down the farm. We said that if they had no other place to go, they could stay on in their houses for as long as they liked. By law the farm still belonged to us and the Warvets had no right to chase them away. We just couldn't employ them any longer.

Then the N.E.C. officer, Tony Ndora, explained the package to them and assured them of the correctness of the amounts as applicable to each one. They filed out and then each man came in turn to receive his money and to sign the forms Jean had prepared for them. The old men sign with an X.

It all went off very well and there were happy smiles and waves for us as they drove away. We thanked Tony Ndora for his contribution. I think he was quite moved to see our quaint little band of rustics going away with their last pay; the bewildered old men sitting in the truck with shy, gap-toothed grins. He replied: "It is too shocking that this should be happening at all."

On Thursday 30th., I phoned Vitalis Chadenga to ask him if he had anything positive to tell me following his visit to Stockade with Mrs. Sangarwe. From the tone of his voice, halting and apologetic, I knew he would have liked to avoid the conversation and that the news was bad.

He said that he had been speaking with Lands only the day before.

They told him that the farm had already been allocated. I was keen to know who "they" were.

"Did you speak with the Permanent Secretary?"

"No. I didn't speak to the Secretary."

"Then who was it that told you this?"

"It was officials—officials of the ministry."

I guessed that this had been a phone call and he had spoken to one official. If not the Secretary; Mrs.Thaukwe? Mrs.Mandimika?

"You yourself are keen enough to take over the farm for National Parks aren't you?" I asked. One can never be sure if there are not hidden motives in such moves.

"Yes, yes. The idea is a good one."

I realized, I said, that he himself was not a Ministry man and this was a ministerial matter. Could it be that Mrs. Sangarwe would be in a better position to get a proper answer.

"No," said Chadenga, "Sangarwe will not be able to do anything."

Then he volunteered: "They say the order concerning Stockade has come from the Governor, Elliot Manyika."

The old bogey arises again—the fearful Elliot Manyika. No wonder everyone is in paralysis—struck dumb or at best communicating in a guarded whisper.

"The only person who may be able to do anything is the Minister," say's Chadenga.

"Yes, I know," I mutter in reply. I've been this route before "Anyway… thanks…goodbye." As I put down the phone, I wonder if I shall ever speak with him again.

On Friday January 31st, I am able to speak with Minister Nhema on the phone. I go through matters point by point.

1. My Section 8 Order is invalid and I am advised that Stockade is legally my property.
2. Certain known Warvets are openly removing moveable property in vehicles. Now underground electric cable worth thousands has been stolen. I am powerless to prevent these thefts.
3. I report these matters to the police, but have no response.
4. I asked the Minister, did he remember Mujuru? Yes, he did. Mujuru is on the property but is inactive.
5. Chadenga and Sangarwe have recently visited the farm to acquaint themselves of the place.
6. Chadenga has since spoken to "officials" at Lands, NOT the Secretary, and he has been told that the farm has been allocated to someone else.
7. The information Chadenga was given is that the decision concerning the farm was made by Governor Manyika.
8. The status of the Protected Forest was not mentioned.
9. I have been maintaining the property for months in the anticipation of it being turned over to National Parks. What is there for me to do now?

Minister Nhema said he thought the matter had already been resolved. He agreed that a finalization was called for. He would not be able to do anything before next Tuesday, [Cabinet meeting day]. I should continue making my reports to the police.

One week later, 7th.February, I tried most of the day to speak with the Minister. Helen said he was very busy with people and later was holding a meeting. She had given him the message. I should try phoning just before five. I tried. Silly me! Just before five on a Friday afternoon the receptionists are already on their way home. There was no one to answer my call.

Friday 21st.February 2003

I have had a two week break from writing my diary up. Nothing is lost by that. I have been considering. My record keeping has been going on for the past thirty-three months and basically nothing changes. It is becoming monotonous—even for me. If other readers have reached this distance without flagging, it will be a wonder.

Thieving raids continue to be made by the Warvets George and Moffu. They are so assured of police "avoidance" that they openly drive in and load what they want. My problem is to keep a record of all the things that are being stolen and their value. The losses are running into millions.

The government issued an order that evicted farmers must not remove fixtures; but then I have had no eviction order, no inventory taken, no valuation made. Gull that I was, I thought that National Parks would have taken over and protected those assets months ago. Had I known what was coming, I could have lifted all those stolen items myself.

So far these robbers have not moved into the houses. They are waiting for me to abandon the farm and they will move in like vultures on a carcass.

As a matter of form I notify the police. I follow this with a letter of complaint to the Officer-in-Charge and send it by registered post. I never expect a reply and never expect follow up action. As I say, everything is normal.

Even Simukayi has returned from God knows where to predate on us.

He turned up at the Nola factory in Harare armed with a letter from a Doctor Kandari stating that he was suffering complications from the bite Moppet gave him just over two years ago and that a large sum of money was due to him. True to form, Simukayi threatened to bring in Chinotimba and his roughs to close the town factory down if he was not paid. I expect he had made a deal with the crooked doctor to divide the extortion money.

Martin and I went to the police in both Marlborough and Mabelreign, in case Simukayi arrived in either of these two areas to harass us for the money. We gave the police the full, documented background—familiar to readers of this journal!

It may be remembered that Martin had obtained a signature from Simukayi for a full and final settlement of compensation. This was signed IN the Marlborough police station and authenticated by an official police stamp. It will be recalled that Martin had difficulty in getting this done, because there was an offensive plainclothes policeman present at the time. The duty constable stamped and witnessed the agreement when the other man had left. Perhaps he knew a thing or two of the other's racist attitude.

It came in useful now. The police saw it as a clear case of extortion. If Simukayi were to continue with his demands, we were to call them and they would take him in. We shall see if anything develops, but it is disquieting. Simukayi embodies evil.

As does Mujuru. He is strangely quiescent just now; like a hibernating snake; a deadly poisonous one. It can't be just because his car has broken down. George is making all the running and Mujuru is leaving him unchallenged. What's behind it?

George has brought in four men to live in the compound and Simukayi's second wife, "the thin one who wears a ZANU PF Tee-shirt", has stayed three days at the store. This, of course, is in the hands of Moffu. Chengerai Munatsi is seen from time to time. It seems as if all the old terrorist gang is collecting here again. Because they enjoy immunity from prosecution by the police, it is surely reasonable to assume that there is a political directive behind this development.

Sunday 23rd. February 2003

It was my hope to avoid repetition but it is not possible. If I am to make an accurate record, it has to be more of the same.

On Saturday, George came onto the farm. He put out word that everyone on the farm, including the wives, should assemble for a meeting. When they were gathered he addressed them at length. All those who were living in the farm village must now turn out and work for him in the field which he had chosen for himself. The people refused to accept this, which made George angry. He told them that anyone refusing to work would be thrown out of his house and sent away from the farm. He called for another meeting for early the next morning.

[I was pleased to learn that my little band of rather simple farm workers had spunk enough to stand firm against George's gross intimidation. When it comes to fair dealing, farm workers know exactly where they stand. Should they work for George or any of his like, they are certain to be cheated. Often enough pay-day never comes around at all!]

I learnt of this development on Saturday evening, so at 8am. on Sunday I called Nyabira police. They now have a line through the Darwendale exchange, which is an improvement although not so good for a cell phone. I received an echo of my own voice throughout the conversation.

I managed to speak with an Assistant Inspector who mumbled his name. I supposed it was Taswa again and that he had therefore not been transferred to Norton as yet; however on second thoughts I believe I spoke to a new man whose name sounds similar—perhaps Tasha.

I explained what had been happening and spoke of the threats given to my workers by the Warvets. The policeman commented: "They can't do that."

"You mean they can't turn them out of their homes and they can't force them to work?"

"No, they can't."

"So will you come and tell them that?"

"We have no vehicle."

"You always say that, but your vehicle has been seen driven in this area."

"Who said that?"

"The people here said your Landrover was seen recently at Maypark and Spa.'"

"We had a call from Maypark who sent their own vehicle."

This was becoming tiresome. "Anyway," I said, "for now, I can tell my men to ignore the Warvets threats because they cannot be turned out of their houses—correct?"

"Yes, that's right."

I left it at that for indeed I thought the threats to be a bluff.

As it turned out, it was not exactly so.

On Sunday, George and Moffu returned to the farm and harangued some of our people in their usual bullying style. From Karisa, the watchman, George extracted the information that Johannes had been taking some of our equipment down to Trianda Farm. At about 12 o'clock, George, accompanied by Moffu and the driver of their vehicle, drove up to the house of Johannes. It seems that George particularly demanded my small disc harrow.

George and Moffu were armed with sticks. They pushed and pulled Johannes into the vehicle. When Sinai, his wife, attempted to intervene, she was struck with a stick by Moffu. The vehicle then drove away. It was at this point that Holly, at Martin's house in town, received a phone call from Maston, the caretaker, at Fig Tree House. Johannes had left his cell phone with Sinai, who knew which number to ring. Meanwhile she had called for help from Maston. Fortunately, I happened to be visiting and was not far from the house so I soon got back to Maston. From his broken account, I managed to get the gist of the story.

I phoned Nyabira and a constable answered. There were no officers present and the duty sergeant had gone to the shops to look for food. I could try again in ten minutes. By then Sgt. Matikenya, the shopper, may have returned. I was told that there was no transport at the station.

Maston's excitable account of Johannes's abduction had me worried and I had the feeling that I would never get any action from Nyabira so I tried Marlborough. From where I was it was the nearest police station and if I offered transport, I could drive a policeman out to Stockade fairly quickly. A woman constable who answered my call offered confident, even enthusiastic help. However, this was all dashed as soon it was revealed that Stockade fell into Nyabira territory. Explanations were to no avail. A senior person did at least offer to phone Nyabira on my behalf and said he would call me back after he had spoken with them. Of course he never did.

After about an hour I phoned Nyabira again and a woman constable called the sergeant for me. He had returned from the shops. I began my story and it appeared at once that he was writing up a report because he asked for my full names. [I am usually asked for my age as well, but he dispensed with this.] I gave him the statement, giving the facts as they were related to me.

The sergeant confirmed that their only transport was away in Darwendale. Meanwhile, if Johannes was released and I had a vehicle, could he come to Nyabira to make his statement? Then, rather surprisingly, he continued by saying that because of the alleged thefts that I have been reporting, could my vehicle also be used to make a follow-up into the African township of Kambuzuma? That was interesting. The police must have some information with regard to the stolen goods. I explained that I was the driver of the vehicle. Johannes did not have a driving licence.

"Would you allow your vehicle to be driven by a police driver? was the policeman's next question. [Martin, who had just walked in and learnt what was happening, was making negative signals to me.]

"Hold on...No. My friends here tell me that the petrol tank is nearly empty. To take the vehicle out to Nyabira and run around in the townships is just not on." I don't like telling lies; but really! There are times...

Notwithstanding, the sergeant said that when the police Landrover returned from Darwendale, they would come to the farm. I thought I could discount this. He did go on to say that if there were any developments or Johannes was released, to let him know. This sounded more positive.

In the afternoon, I dialled Johannes' number a few times and got Maston or nothing. Eventually Johannes himself answered. He spoke guardedly in monosyllables and I quickly realized that the Warvets were with him so I told him to ring back as soon as he could and rang off.

A half hour later he contacted me and was able to give me his account. Johannes was driven to Trianda by the Warvets. There an angry altercation took place. A witness to this was Wellington, the Trianda manager. The latter told the Warvets that the equipment was jointly owned. Sometimes it is used on one farm, sometimes on the other—which is largely true. In any event, it was personal moveable property and in no way could it belong to the Warvets. Needless to say, they shouted this down.

Johannes was driven back to his house. Here he was given an ultimatum. He was to move off the farm tonight and take away all his belongings. George would come out on Monday morning bringing with him ZANU PF youths. [This is the Border Gezi Youth Brigade named after Border Gezi a fiery nationalist and the previous Minister of Youth Development, Gender & Employment Creation. He died crashing his car. Elliot Manyika took over the Ministry.]

Johannes was warned: "If you are found on the farm, these youths will beat you thoroughly and your property will be smashed." I asked Johannes if he felt the threat was meaningful. He thought it well could be.

Later, Martin rang me to say that Eliot, the Nola driver, could be used tomorrow morning. He had contacted the police and they agreed that the vehicle should reach them early. Martin said the driver should reach them between 8.30 and 9.00 having picked up Johannes.

I have advised J to move his valued possessions up to my house this evening; to arrange for his wife and children to stay overnight with friends; to lock up his house and make himself scarce. Johannes plans to wait for Eliot in the early morning at the Sigaro turn off, about two kilometres down the road. They would then proceed to Z.R.P. Nyabira.

Johannes phoned me again later to say that he had spoken to the police on his cell phone. He told them that the Warvets' plot was to get him off the farm so that they could break into the buildings and steal whatever they wanted. If questioned afterwards; they would then say that it was he, Johannes, who had stolen the property. [Typical!]

Johannes told the police that the man, Moffu, who works for the Municipality, does not usually leave the farm early on a Monday morning because he is on night shift. If they did not delay when Eliot came to pick them up, they would find Moffu still on the farm. Whoever it was he spoke with, agreed that a good opportunity presented itself and that an early start on the morrow was called for.

Monday 24th. February 2003

At 8.15 I rang Nola and Jed Aird confirmed that Eliot had already left the factory and was on his way to Stockade. I then called Johannes. He was still at his house apparently, because Senai answered and I heard children's voices. When he was handed the phone I asked him if all was well. Yes, it was. But I detected a tone of disquiet in his reply.

"What about last night? Were there any problems?" I wanted to know if he had moved his belongings to my house.

"Last night I was with Samson and Norman. Moffu came with two others and he took away my gate key to the old factory yard."

"How was that?" I thought to myself, here was a situation of three against three.

"The other two men were carrying reggins [catapults]."

"So he took the key by force?"

"Yes."

I reminded Johannes that the police said they would welcome our vehicle early so as to return to the farm in good time. Eliot was already on the road and should be there shortly. J said he was ready to go. It seemed that he was not scared of any interference from George at this stage. I asked him to phone me if he ran into problems at the Nyabira police station.

At about 10 o'clock I phoned J to ask him where he was and how the investigation was going. He was at Nyabira waiting in the charge office and Eliot was waiting in the truck outside. If J had not kept Eliot waiting any length of time, I reckoned that they should have reached Nyabira at about 9 o'clock. An hour had been lost.

I asked Johannes if he was speaking with anyone and who was there.

"There is just one man typing."

"You should really be going quickly to the farm. Perhaps I should speak with someone."

"Hold on." Johannes must have gone outside and handed his phone over to another.

A voice came over:

"Tezha...Yes, Wiles?"

"Hello Tezha." [If he wasn't going to honour me with a "Mister", I wasn't going to honour him with a "Sergeant".] It was most unlucky that he should be the sergeant on duty.

I tried to put across to Tezha the need to act quickly because the offender, Moffu, may leave the farm and a chance missed to interrogate him with regard to the whereabouts of the stolen property. I went on to say that I believed some people knew where this was. [Why else would one of Tezha's fellow police officers have asked previously if our vehicle could be used to make a follow up to Kambuzuma Township?]

"Do you know where this place is?" from Tezha.

"No. I am going on what I have gathered from one of your people. I believe there are others who know."

"I am not asking others, I am asking you. Do you know where this place you speak of is?"

I am tiring of this form of questioning and am becoming impatient with what I suspect to be calculated delaying tactics.

"No. Of course I don't know. How could I? I don't live in an African township."

"If you are going to answer like that, no one will help you. You will get nowhere."

"Well, what I am trying to say is that in this connection a certain African township was spoken of—I cannot remember which—but most probably someone will come up with it. My foreman may have obtained the information. George and Moffu are coming and going all the time. They must go SOMEWHERE. "

[George, Moffu and the other Warvets have been operating in this vicinity vociferously and violently for the past three years. It would be astonishing if the police themselves don't have dockets on them.]

Tehja continued: "Why don't you call them High Density Suburbs?"

I can't think what he means. Was he picking me out for using the term, African Township?

Oh, my God! I feel my blood pressure rising. I am in the midst of yet another crisis on the farm. I am being systematically and openly robbed by known persons. The same persons rough up and threaten Johannes and hit his wife. They treat my few workers as if they were slaves. I ply the police with a deluge of reports, letters, messages and phone calls—all to no avail. Now I have laid on transport and a driver to induce them into taking some action, which is plainly not forthcoming, and what do I get? Needling and rudeness from Sergeant Tehja. As I write this, I am wondering if he is not in league with the criminals.

I am painfully aware that my position is highly disadvantaged. A retreat is called for.

"Anyway," I say, "PLEASE; all I ask is that you remove these people. They are giving us a mountain of trouble."

"It is not our job to remove them. That is for the Ministry of Lands and the DA."

"And if they have been stealing?"

"Then they will be arrested."

The cell phone cut off at that point, which was as well because by then I was feeling emotionally stressed. If Tehja is put on the case himself, he would see to it that no evidence would be found against the Warvets. Worse, in collusion with them, he might trump up a case against Johannes. In this evil world, it is just the sort of thing these types would do.

After another twenty minutes of brooding and pacing, I decided to call Nyabira; but this time to ask to speak directly with the O-I-C, Inspector Majoni. This was my request when I got through. The brief answer I received was: "He's not around".

"What about the Assistant Inspector?" There was a long delay before a second voice asked me who it was I was waiting for.

"The Assistant Inspector? No, he has gone somewhere."

"Has the truck for Stockade left, do you know?" I asked the voice.

"What colour is it?"

"Blue."

"No, it's still there."

"What is causing the delay? It should have gone long since."

"It will be going just now. The right officer has to go with it."

"Tell someone that the truck and driver are only borrowed. It may have to go back to the owner."

"Mr. Wiles, it will be going just now."

So whoever I am talking to knows who I am. By this time I expect every policeman in Nyabira does. For good or for bad? I really don't know.

Later in the day I spoke on the phone to Alan Foot. He was not on Trianda at the time, but since the Warvets had gone there in an attempt to extract my disc harrow from their farmyard, it was important for me to know how they would react. Alan revealed that this was not the first time George had made an angry protest. Wellington had given the explanation that our equipment was jointly owned and was not the property of anyone else. This was good news. They were not going to wilt under threat. Alan went on to say that on Trianda in recent weeks, they had suffered a number of incidents of theft and one of assault. The reaction of the police had been so abysmal that now they didn't bother to contact them. As for transport, it was generally recognized that the police transport was used for personal business, especially transporting relatives and friends—to their fields on erstwhile white-owned farms!

For the remainder of the day, I continued to smart from the verbal clash I had had on the phone with Sgt. Tezha. It seemed that, in my use of words, I had been guilty of a racial slight.

By chance that evening, I met an African lady with whom I am on friendly and cordial terms. She is a well educated, thoroughly emancipated woman with connections in the more affluent section of the community. In the course of our chat, I spoke of my apparent faux pas when speaking with the policeman and being reprimanded for using the term "African Township." Would most Africans be hurt by the use of this term?

"Well, you know nowadays people are very sensitive. It is best to speak of the high-density suburbs, or dormitory locations, or better, refer to it by name. In other words, avoid the label "African", she said.

I thanked her and in future will tread more warily. [For all that, the psychological implication is a sad one.]

Tuesday 25th.February 2003

By providing our transport for the police yesterday we have been rewarded by positive action. In spite of my impatience at the start, the investigating officer, Constable Mariwo, spent the rest of the day until late afternoon on Stockade taking statements and viewing evidence. Johannes was with him.

Moffu was found to be still on the farm and was questioned. I learnt that he was told that he had no right to be on the farm and no right to give any orders to the farm workers or to intimidate them in any way. When it came to the robberies, Moffu disclaimed any involvement and laid the blame firmly on George.

Finally, Cons.Mariwo produced a Stolen Property form and Johannes detailed all the items that had been stolen over the past weeks. [Reported to ZRP but no action taken.] It was a formidable list and on return to Nyabira, the form was given to Eliot, the driver, to be given to me for completion and affirmation together with a valuation figure. I was requested to return it to ZRP Nyabira a.s.a.p. In the event, Jed Aird faxed the form through to Martin that evening and I worked on it this morning.

In order to ascertain replacement values in respect of the materials stolen, I spent an hour phoning various suppliers of the miscellaneous items. To my astonishment the total figure came to 6.8 million dollars. Such has been the effect of inflation and rising costs.

On completion of the Stolen Property form, I drove out to the Nyabira police post at about 11 o'clock. Today black, uniformed policemen were all over the place. In these surroundings, say what you like, a lone white man with wispy grey hair and a long nose, bearing a semblance [he imagines] to Daumier's Don Quixote, looks and feels decidedly incongruous.

Determined to be chivalrous in every way, I fixed my smile and set out across the puddle-pocked grass-gravel yard to the charge office. Upon hearing my business, a helpful constable directed me to an office building to be found beyond the main block. As the path deteriorated and the puddles became more numerous, I looked ahead and saw low houses with women outside them, washing hanging and children playing. Surely this must be the living quarters; I must have gone wrong. But no; another man assured me that the office I wanted was just up there.

Sure enough, what I took to be an ablution cubicle for the married quarters opposite, turned out to be the criminal investigation office and it boasted a notice to that effect nailed above the door. Here I was greeted affably by Constable Mariwo, who obviously knew me from previous encounters. He had been given the Stockade assignment, and it was he who Eliot and Johannes had conducted around the farm yesterday.

I showed Mariwo my Stolen Property form, but explained that I had forgotten to add the angle iron and steel pipes stolen by George. That was alright; I should add it now and also it was necessary for me to write a statement. I was conducted up a couple of steps in order to enter the converted shower room. By leaving the door open, there was just enough room to fit a little table with a chair on each side. I took the chair at the door-opening and a corner of the table was cleared to enable me to write.

Another constable occupied the chair opposite me and Mariwo, who perforce was standing, explained that he had to leave on a job, but the other man would take my statement. That sounded OK as far as it went, but it didn't take us very far, because the next thing I am aware of is two other men climbing the steps at the back of me and easing their way around the desk effectively closing Mariwo in. Don't get me wrong. There was nothing sinister about this. The newcomers were also policemen. They just had something of importance to impart to the other two. I am temporarily ignored and sit silently whilst the four men hold a voluble discussion above me and across me. Then, over my shoulder, I am aware of a fifth man entering the doorway of our narrow space. This man seems to be set on a mission singular to himself. He determinedly squeezes past the others, who do not cease in their talk, and succeeds in replacing the man in the chair—the one who was supposed to be taking my statement.

Meanwhile, Mariwo has eased himself sideways towards the door. Before he leaves I want a word with him. I am keen to learn more from him concerning his investigation on the farm. In order to talk with him, I see I must move outside so I stand up. At this point a little boy, who has been playing with other children across the yard, enters. I elicit from Mariwo that it is his son. There are now seven persons in the shower room. Then, as if at a signal, everyone files out leaving a sole victor occupying the chair.

There is something one has to get used to in African society and that is an oblivious disregard for interruptions. The interrupter demands instant attention. He has a childlike need to disburden himself immediately of that which is foremost in his mind. The interrupted, far from being irritated by this, accepts it with equanimity. His facial expression suggests that he may even find the interruption a pleasurable diversion, a break from single-minded concentration. It is the poor visitor who is the victim. He may have his words cut off in mid-sentence and be left open-mouthed to listen to an animated verbal exchange, which might even carry the other two parties out of the room altogether. By the time he has taken in the wall-charts, admired the picturesque calendar and finally tried to read upside down the correspondence lying on top of the desk, he will have forgotten what it was he was talking about so intensely at the point of the interruption.

I digress. Mariwo told me that he had solid evidence against George. It remained only to find him and charge him. Moffu, with whom he had spoken, disclaimed any involvement in the thefts. However, the two young men he employed could be involved and he had opened dockets for them.

We had walked to the main block and here Mariwo introduced me to the new O.I.C., Inspector Majuni, a stocky man and judging by the flag on the left shoulder of his uniform, an ex-combatant. This is usually a dreaded sign, but I must say he greeted me very civilly. He smiled pleasantly. I suggested we go into his office because I would be glad to give him a general resume of the position on Stockade. He listened to me quietly. I felt that his lack of comment was a positive rather than a negative sign. I left him feeling that here was a distinct improvement on Sengwe.

Mariwo's counterpart ushered me into an adjoining office telling me he would be back to take my statement. I assumed that he had gone to collect a special form. There were two men working at separate desks in the office—this time there was no premium on space—and I sat idly waiting. One of the men, I noted wore the shoulder insignia of an assistant inspector. He must be, I reckoned, the replacement for A\Insp.Taswa. Eventually:

"So, Mr. Richard, who are you waiting for?" Odd that Mr. Richard bit.

"I have been told that I am required to write a statement with regard to the stolen property," I say, still puzzled.

My interlocutor opened a book, tore out a page of thin blue paper and handed it to me.

"I can make it out on this? Alright. Thanks," I said, and then added:

"You must be the new assistant inspector. I must get your name right. On the phone it sounds much like Taswa, but of course he is in Norton now."

"It is Tayger." [phonetically]

"Please would you spell it for me?"

The Assistant Inspector leant across the table and wrote with pencil and paper:

Tezha.

"But that is the same name as the sergeant," I exclaimed.

"Yes, it is the same person too. I have been promoted."

So THIS was the cause of all my confusion. My embarrassment was total. I could have fallen through the floor. And Tezha of all people! It shows that, to me, African policemen all look alike and I rely heavily for recognition on tags and badges rather than features. By way of excuse, I suppose I can say that my dealings with Tezha have been far more frequent on the phone than in person. [Previous entries in this diary refer to a man named Tehja or Tejha. These persons may now be identified with Tezha. I apologize for any confusion caused.]

I wrote out my short statement confirming that the property stolen was mine and then did my best with Tezha to talk myself out of my corner. I found him to be pleasantly communicative—even sympathetic. Far from being an ally of the Warvets, he said the tide was turning for them; [or words to that effect].

Tezha and another man wanted a lift to Westgate, so on the way I was able to chat further. Using somewhat brief sentences, he conveyed to me that "changes were taking place" and that a decision had been taken to "sort out the mess". He went as far as to say, "They want the white farmers back," and even, "You will be able to return to your farm".

Well, as a newly appointed assistant inspector, he is still very low on the ladder and goodness knows there are really bad men at the top. If there is change taking place I cannot imagine who will be directing it. For the present one must leave it as straws in the wind.

Wednesday 5th.March 2003

When the news got out that the police had been to the farm and that Moffu had been questioned and warned, I felt that George would keep clear. However, on Sunday 2nd.he drove out to the farm and twice came to Johannes' house. J was away visiting the prison farm, but the wife, Sinai, was there and George spoke with her.

"What is this of your man calling the police? I will kill him. Just now you will find his dead body lying on the railway line."

When Johannes returned and was told of the threat to kill him, he phoned Cst. Mariwo. The latter said that he couldn't come to the farm because "The

Chefs have taken our transport." J also phoned Martin, who advised him to lie low and Eliot would pick up the police from Nyabira and go to the farm on Monday morning. Martin also spoke with Inspector Majoni, who confirmed that there was no transport available at the station and things would have to wait until Monday.

I think everyone acknowledged that George's threat was an empty one, ugly though it was. One has been exposed to so much of this sort of thing in the past three years. I am thinking that threats and intimidation are an integral part of African culture.

Moffu has been telling the police that his connection with George is a distant one and that he was not involved in the robberies in any way.

For the record, it is worth noting that on the recent occasions when threats and intimidation have been used against Johannes and my farm workers, George has been accompanied by Moffu, who was equally vocal and vicious. On Sunday evening, Sinai was confronted by both of them together. We on the farm know that this relationship goes back nearly three years, when the band of brigands included Simukayi, Mapolisa and Chengerai Munatsi. Johannes is sure that George and Moffu plan to drive him off the farm. If they succeed they will purloin all they can lay their hands on. It seems George couldn't wait.

On Monday 3rd., Eliot, the driver, left the Nola factory and arrived at Nyabira in good time. There he collected two policemen; Const.Muriwa, who today was accompanied by Sergeant Mugauri. Both men equipped themselves with hand guns.

Upon reaching the farm, Eliot drove them to Johannes' house. Here the police heard the evidence of Sinai. It is my understanding that next, Johannes described the items that had been stolen and showed them the evidence such as the missing baths and basins, the doors and cupboard, the sawn off pipes where the gate valves had been removed etc.

The party then drove to the compound store where the two young men were found, Cephas and Tawanda. Apparently these two are not Moffu's sons but what, by anglicising Shona, might be roughly described as "nephews". Needless to say, both denied any knowledge of the robberies and claimed they didn't know where George stayed in town. Because witnesses had given evidence that Tawanda was seen loading George's vehicle, this denial didn't go down too well with the policemen. Although Cephas had not been seen loading the stolen property, he had been seen on previous occasions accompanying George to town.

I learnt from Eliot that the two youths got short shrift from the policemen. They were handcuffed and told that they would be held in cells for "one week, one month or 5 years if necessary" until George came to the police station. It was even suggested that they would be sent to the remand prison, which, I take it, implied the most dire doom. [What did I say about the role of intimidation in African culture?]

Eliot said that the two policemen spent about four and a half hours on the farm conducting their investigation. All in all, the strong line and the recording of so much evidence, suggests the police are determined to prosecute. In turn, this would mean that there is indeed a change in directive. Surely this energetic and positive reaction cannot solely be put down to the fact that we have provided the police with transport. Although I have to ask: what would have happened if we hadn't?

Friday 7th.March 2003

The co-operative attitude of the police had the effect of changing my mood from one of desperate anxiety to one of hopeful buoyancy. On Thursday, I travelled out to the farm with some money for the staff and food for Moppet and Humba. Admittedly, there are aspects of the scene which are not conducive to lifting one out of depression.

There has been almost continuous rain over the past week. I have no right to complain of that. The seasonal rainfall has been well below normal and this addition is welcome indeed. Always I think of the forest and the young trees that I have planted there. The development of an extensive root system is very important to see them through the next dry season. Now, of course, even was I to return to my home on the farm, I have lost the means to nurse them through it. Massive theft of electrical and pumping equipment means that two-thirds of the farm has no water supply. [This, incidentally, includes Fig Tree House and Bush Cottage.]

No; whilst the rain and wet is so welcome for nature, it is a disaster for narrow-width man-made tarmac roads. The Selby Road leading to our farm; is one such. It is maintained by the local rural council. This council is broke. Because the farmers in the district, who were once both councillors and ratepayers, have all been kicked off their farms, there is no reason to believe that the council will not remain broke.

The result of all this is that the road is in a chronic state of disrepair and driving on it becomes a nightmare, especially in the wet. Rain-filled potholes of unknown depth and jagged, precipitous edges to the tar make for a test of nerves and tyres. Here and there, deceptively smooth-looking earth verges invite one to drive on them for a gentler ride; a dangerous choice in the wet with a chance of a slide and final settlement in the water lying in the drain at their base. The road has never been so bad in the forty years I have been using it. This scenario is depressing because it signifies regression. I expect it is the same story in all the rural districts once run by the white farmers.

The halt to all activity on the farm for so many months has given the place a dilapidated, unkempt appearance. I rather wearily acknowledged this to myself as I drove in. The recent rain has done wonders for grass growth, which has grown to waist high on the farm roads and head high elsewhere. A multiple variety of weeds are growing in profusion where last year we had our market crops—I am sure the birds prefer the weeds! Notwithstanding, I tell myself this is nature at work. One day it can be trimmed and tidied, and to be lived with in gentle harmony. Better that my land should look like this than recklessly hacked and despoiled as can be seen elsewhere.

Thus it was that I arrived at the homestead to meet Johannes, Makosa, Rosemary, Moppet and Humba; everyone seemed to be cheerful; the garden taking on more and more the appearance of a wilderness. Since I was last out, J has moved many of his personal possessions up to my house and these are stored either in the garage or, in the case of his hi-fi gadgetry, in the sitting room.

Whilst I was with Johannes, I thought to phone Cst. Mariwo. We wanted to learn if he had made progress on the case and if he had located George. The signal on the cell phone was very bad and his words intermittent; however, I was able to catch the sentence:

"They say the matter is political." My God! My heart sank. That dreadful phrase—the blanket cover for all evil deeds.

I wanted to know who "they" were. I heard the words, War Veterans Association. Before the signal went dead altogether, I think I had the gist of what Mariwo was relating. George and/or Moffu had gone to the Warvet's H.Q. in order to get their support. Someone from there had telephoned Z.R.P. Nyabira to protest at the police action. There was disagreement as to whether the case was criminal or political. The Warvets' leader said he would come out to Nyabira to sort the matter out. I just had time to tell Mariwo that if George was let off it would be a disaster. He would return to give us hell.

That was yesterday. Today is Friday. Both Johannes and I have phoned Mariwo during the day and we haven't had much further information from him. He says he still doesn't know where he can find George and meantime the Warvets have failed to come to Nyabira. He thought they may come over the weekend. Johannes understood from Mariwo that it was George himself who phoned the police and it was he who said he would be coming with the chief Warvet. [Name supplied but forgotten.]

It all sounds typically vague, inept and suspicious. The irony is that George is not a card-carrying Warvet at all; although it is amazing that a type like him didn't find a way to cash in on a free hand-out and a pension for life. There were hundreds of spurious "freedom fighters" that did. Perhaps, because of his incomparable record as a brutal terror-monger, the War Veterans Association has given George honorary membership. On the other hand, it could be that George is bluffing and is attempting to intimidate the police all on his own. We shall learn soon enough.

Johannes is taking no chances. When he phoned me this evening he was in Banket staying with a sister over the weekend. He says he has told Muriwo this and that the latter agreed that it was best. Somebody is staying in the house with Sinai and the children. He learnt that Moffu came to the house and made a lot of noise—"talk, talk, talk," as he put it. George however was not with him.

The Government has re-opened talks with the Commercial Farmers Union after months of cold stand-off. On my way back from the farm, I called in at the C.F.U. offices and spoke with Gerry Davison. I asked him if there had been any signs of the government easing up on its policy of land reform i.e. persecution of the white farmers.

"We have been holding talks, yes, but the situation is worse rather than better," he explained. It would appear that the opening of dialogue is little more than a Public Relations exercise.

Ministers are putting out bland statements for the consumption of the general public and the international community that the fast track exercise is over and there is peace and reconciliation. As they speak, evictions are taking place and yet more farms are being gazetted for appropriation.

All this reminds me of Adolph Hitler's words: "This is my last territorial claim in Europe."

These people are consummate liars. They don't have to be taught their trade; it comes naturally to them. If you tell a lie make it a big one. And if you repeat the lie often enough, people will come to believe it.

Gerry brought Stockade Farm up on his computer. This revealed the date and number of the original gazette notice declaring the government's intent to acquire the property. This was 118 of Sept. 2000. The government had not followed up with the correct legal procedures and consequently the original notice had become obsolete and null and void. To acquire the farm now, they would have to go through the whole procedure all over again. However, he warned that in some cases that is exactly what they are doing, so it would be best not to draw attention to this. When making my complaints to the police, preferably stick to the criminal aspect.

Saturday 8th.March 2003

The rain persists and there is flooding in some parts of the country thus confounding the forecasters. In the face of the rising temperatures foisted on her by us humans, Mother Earth is making her own decisions as to how she will react.

I write this in the shelter of a comfortable modern cottage in the grounds of a larger house. The grounds consist of an immaculately kept subtropical garden; glorious trees, palms, creepers, shrubs and lesser plants in a wealth of variety. Intersecting all is lush lawn; beside the main house a glittering pool and a fountain. The lady owner is devoted to her garden and cares for each and all growing therein. Yes, she is away on a holiday; and yes, I am house-sitting. I have been promoted from the flat with a garden the size of a pocket handkerchief, to this little Eden and I have been here a full month.

The adoption of this house-sitting style of life has proved fortunate for me in my constrained circumstances. "Positions" have come to me through good friends and word of mouth. I earn no money, but am assured of a roof over my head. In exchange, the house owners may proceed on holiday carefree in the knowledge that a mature, trustworthy gentleman of intelligence, integrity and veracity; of sober habits and strict sense of responsibility; will be watching out for the safety of their home and precious possessions. [I am thinking of having a prospectus printed.]

Here in Little Eden, I have become good friends with the animal residents; Abbie, a miniature Dachshund; Pixie, a mini Schipperke; Schmole, a 15 year old miniature Poodle; Oliver, the most tiny, vibrant, adorable Yorkie I have ever met; Oboe, three times the size of any of the others [which isn't saying much], long silky grey hair, huge ears that fan out at right angles, a serious expression, a loveable cartoon dog if ever there was one. Oboe is an octogenarian [age x 7]. There are two grey cats, who sit around and view the dogs with disdain; and five bantams. As a group, the latter make regular garden patrols, but in between will often be seen resting alongside the dogs and the cats. After all, they are all much of a size so no one has the edge over any of the others.

In spite of what I was saying so modestly earlier, the person who really looks after the property and cares for the pets whilst the mistress is away; is the household domestic, Ruth. Ruth has served the family here for over twenty-five years, has become an indispensable part of it, and is, I know, loved and valued. The pride she takes in her position of trust is both old-fashioned and charming. Tall and broadly-built all round, she suffers from a painful knee ailment and moves with the assistance of a single crutch. She is going to have an operation she tells me. Madam has promised to pay for it.

For the most part I cater for myself over in the cottage; however I take a light breakfast each morning in the kitchen nook. Here Ruth prepares me tea and toast and, being something of an age and outlook, we discuss a wide range of subjects ranging from the irresponsibility of the young [anyone under fifty], exorbitant prices in the shops, and the iniquities of the government. I have tried to follow the intricate connections in the lives of Ruth's sons, daughters, sisters, brothers, nephews and nieces. It was a revelation to me that most of the latter seem to be living and working in England or even the United States.

Joan, my absent hostess, mistress of the property and all contained therein, will shortly be returning. I hope she will allow me to stay a little longer. I have another offer of a posting but not until the 26th.of the month. Before then, events on the farm could throw me into turmoil. I have said that many times before I know. It remains a truth nonetheless.

Monday 10th.March 2003

Stockade was designated for acquisition by government in September 2000. An appeal was immediately lodged by the lawyers and since then many other appeals have been made to the authorities concerned. It would be incorrect to say that these appeals have been refused or turned down. The true fact is that they have been completely ignored, which is not exactly the same thing. No correspondence whatever has been received from the government side. At the same time they have not taken legal steps in order to acquire the farm; the legal procedures, which they themselves have initiated and passed into law. As I have noted previously, the original Section 5 and Section 8 notices have become legally obsolete.

The pages of this diary have been a narration of almost non-stop harassment and intrusions by Warvets and sundry blackguards enjoying Party and government protection.

Taking both these matters into consideration, it is remarkable that thirty-one months after the issue of the Section 5 notice, I am still keeping a toehold. From the word go, there seems to have been some uncertainty in official circles with regard to the status of Stockade. I have never received overt support from the police or the DA, let alone anything in writing; nevertheless, in response to my bitter complaints and urgent appeals, the excesses of the Warvets were frequently curbed if only for brief periods.

There has been something else exceptional in my case. In spite of frequent threats to do so, gangs of militia youth and militant Party supporters have never been bussed out to persecute me. I think it could be that such action would require liaison with Party headquarters and this may not have suited the likes of Simukayi, George, Moffu, Chengerai and, more recently, Mujuru. Each in his turn has regarded Stockade as his own for picking and he didn't want interlopers from town muscling in on his patch. Of course some of them may have formed an alliance between themselves.

Unquestionably the aim of each one of these scoundrels has been to drive me off the farm. That has been made plain in the pages of this diary. It is possible, I suppose, that they front for an unknown person wishing my removal. If so, he remains a shadow.

Whatever the truth may be; I was proving stubbornly averse to leaving and certain plotters [at least three] thought of a way to eliminate me. Alive, I had been the principal obstacle preventing them from securing the farm for them themselves. Dead, the way would lie open to them. I believe those who planned to murder me last March had this objective. Although the plot failed, it forced me into making a strategic retreat. Fortunately, the front line position, whilst fluid, has been held, thanks to the resolve and bravery of Johannes and a little band of loyal servants.

[I do not use the word "murder" lightly because, almost literally, I have been within a hair's breadth of being murdered. One night at my homestead a few years back, I was sitting quietly in the lounge with Moppet as my only companion. She was then little more than 9 months old. Without making a sound, she came to me and then moved to each of five windows in turn, sniffing the air. She was telling me that somebody was outside. Loading a shotgun, I let her through the outside door and followed her closely as she traced the scent around the house. A figure appeared from a passage way and I was struck with an iron bar which narrowly missed my head but cut open my shoulder. I saw the iron bar poised to come down at me for a second blow when I shot my assailant who fell at my feet. The man had a long knife in his belt—proof of intent. It was a close thing. Apart from Moppet, I owe my life to my Guardian Angel—but that story doesn't belong here.

I mention the matter because in the African criminal world, there is a callous disregard for life. Elderly whites of either sex are considered to be soft targets with the result that old people are often brutally murdered in the course of a common house robbery. These murders receive a minimum of publicity. I am known as the "madala boss" or the old man, so a would-be killer might regard me as a soft target. Thus; experience added to discretion, bid me make this temporary "strategic retreat".]

Regarding the land, I recognize that my own case seems to be exceptional. Hundreds and hundreds of farmers have been evicted from their homes. Sometimes the government has used its hastily prepared legal format to do this, but often this route has not been followed; the farmer and his family being literally overwhelmed and evacuating in the face of blatant terror tactics. The role of the police, if they appeared at all, was to warn the farmer to get off as quickly as possible. Farms all around this district have been overrun; the owners have moved far afield, their homes occupied by high-ranking ZANU PF officials or leaders of invading gangs.

When I have spoken to farming families, who have experienced eviction in sudden and frightening circumstances, they say that in retrospect it was probably the best way. The immediate impact was traumatic and devastating. However, it came with a realization of finality; there was no hope of redress. They faced the abrupt reality; a new way of earning a living had to be found and it was no good standing around.

I have been impressed by the imperturbable spirit shown by so many good farmers. With long experience in Africa, they hold a cynical philosophy. Anything the African turns his hand to inevitably results in calamity. When a hurricane and a massive flood hits a country, it is certain to cause widespread devastation; when the government embarked on its land reform programme the result could have been predicted with certainty. Let's call it a "natural disaster".

Today I spoke on the phone with Tommy Bayley. He has recovered sufficiently from his physical injuries to operate a small sawmill business just out of town. His mental injuries must be deep, but he shows no outward sign of this. I asked him if he had any information concerning his farm, Danbury, which of course adjoins Stockade.

"Yes, I took a drive down the main road recently to see what was going on," said Tommy. "Also had a word with one of the guys that used to work for me. He filled me in with some information. Jonathan Moyo [Minister of Information in the President's office] has taken the land on one side of the main road. He has erected a boom and put a guard on the entry gate to keep people out."

"Is there anything planted?" I asked.

"Oh, yes. There's quite a nice crop of maize growing…well, so there jolly well should be! I left behind fifty tonnes of ammonium nitrate and fifty tonnes of compound fertilizer in my sheds and it has all gone, together with 20 million dollars worth of crop chemicals."

Tommy went on to tell me that Dr. Parirenyatwa [Minister of Health] has a portion of the farm being run by his brother. It is said that Ignatius Chombe [Minister of Local Government] has also taken a section, but as yet this is unconfirmed. I expect it means that the minister has been observed coming out there and is probably installing a relative.

Ballineety Farm is owned by Cathy Townsend. The farm has been in the family for over ninety years and in 1911 her grandfather introduced pedigree Sussex cattle. The herd which was then established has been bred on into the present time and has the reputation of being one of the finest in Africa.

Last year, Ballineety was designated for African resettlement and Cathy received the full gamut of legal notices. The managers and the farm workers were paid off; as much as possible of the machinery was removed into storage. Half the cattle herd was sold—mostly to the abattoir. However, there is a property adjoining Ballineety, known as The Lily, which Cathy's father had purchased many years ago for additional grazing. It was adequate for this purpose but unsuitable for cropping, the soils being shallow, infertile and prone to water-logging. For this reason very little infrastructure had been put in place.

The government land committee told Cathy they did not want this property and she could keep it. Needs must when the Devil drives; Cathy, emotionally bound to the historic herd bred by her forbears, selected the finest animals and moved them from Ballineety onto The Lily.

I paid Cathy a visit last week at the house she rents in town. I found her in considerable distress. The previous Sunday night, a gang had entered The Lily, rounded up the cows, slaughtered five and loaded the carcasses into a truck. A further five had been maimed, three of them so severely that they had to be shot. The poor animals had been so used to regular gentle handling that they were completely docile. The killers found their task easy.

People surmise that the men and transport came from an army barracks. The police were notified and brought to the scene. If army personnel were the culprits, they would be immune from prosecution, but in any event there have been no arrests.

The day I met her, Cathy had been speaking with people, who might give her advice on how best to dispose of the last of the Ballineety Sussex Herd. The odds stacked against her for saving it are proving too much.

Sunday 16th.March 2003

The days of continuous rain during the week cooled the temperatures down to the extent that I was glad to pull on warm clothing and keep it on for most of the day. Ruth had thoughtfully provided me with an extra blanket for my bed, and made me hot porridge for breakfast. Last night, a nearly full moon shone brightly in a clear, star-studded sky and today the sun has returned to warm and dry and cheer us up.

Johannes phoned through the information from the farm that there had been no untoward developments. Nevertheless, Mujuru remains static in Bush Cottage accompanied by his elderly servant and Moffu came to spend the weekend at the store. The police told me that the young man, Tawanda, is being kept in the remand prison and I suppose he is still there. J went on to tell me that this evening, at around 5 o'clock, George, who the police say they seek but cannot find, came to visit Moffu in the compound. He drove out in a cream-coloured Nissan Pick-up, Reg.No.543 718 X. I had better relay that information to the police tomorrow—for what it's worth! Here I should record the police Crime Report number given me by Cst.Mariwo and relating to George: it is C.D.No.117\02 of 2003.

On Monday 3rd.March, I phoned the Ministry for Environment and spoke with Helen, the Minister's secretary. I asked her to please arrange for me to meet with Francis Nhema as soon as possible. Helen replied that she would do what she could, but there were a lot of people wanting to speak with him and he was very busy. She would put my name on the list and give it to him. She would ring me back.

Straight off I recognized this as a blocking manoeuvre. Nhema would anticipate the questions I would be likely to put to him and I suspect he knows he would struggle to find meaningful answers. Doubtless a state of confusion, conflict and uncertainty, prevails in cabinet today when discussing the affairs of the nation and an economy in free-fall. Not least, in the minds of cabinet ministers, will be concern for personal survival. In situations like this, disunity emerges and factions are formed. In an atmosphere like this I cannot imagine Nhema seeking to have a friendly chat with Elliot Manyika about a delisting for a little farm called Stockade. No, Helen didn't ring me back.

My hostess, Joan, returned from South Africa and, even before getting out of the car, was given a tumultuous welcome from the little dogs, each vying for her attention; 16 year old Schmole making strange undoglike noises. Ruth, the maid and Joan, the mistress, greeted each other with a long, affectionate hug. I was touched.

Joan has quietly resumed control of the household. She rises early and works methodically. On her first day home, all five dogs are bathed, shampooed, dipped, towelled, and blow-dried; Oboe, Schmole and Oliver, being long-haired, get a palm of "Staysoft" worked into their coats; bedding is plunged into a tub for washing. The dogs collect in the washroom and stand about awaiting their turn; they are familiar with this routine. Of course I am not, and stand about uncertain of what is going on. The dogs look up at me questioningly. What am I doing here? I am sure they are viewing me as a clumsy novice. Joan gives me a small canister of Frontline anti-flea spray to administer each dog a single squirt between the shoulder blades. I have something responsible to do and this improves my image. The dogs, I sense, are regarding me with a little more respect.

Next, this delightful garden receives attention. Snipping and cutting, thinning and pruning, the sound of the secateurs may be heard for hours on end. I do not offer to help. I suspect that the plants would be even more resentful than the dogs if handled carelessly by a greenhorn. Meanwhile a man mows the lawns, removes the prunings and sweeps the paths. Fine gardens are a product of labour and love.

Ruth, heavy, crippled and ageing though she is, is a hard worker. Along with many others, she "owns" and cultivates a maize garden in a huge vlei several kilometres away. Vlei soils can be a disaster in a wet season, but the dry conditions in the early part of this year have resulted in a healthy maize crop and Ruth's maize was no exception. There is a critical shortage of food and hundreds of vagrants roam the city, so obviously these fat crops have been targets for theft. On Saturday Ruth, her daughter and a couple of helpers, spent the day reaping the maize although it was far from dry. They worked until after dark and "Mama", as Ruth calls Joan, drove her truck down to the field to collect it all. Here at the house, the cobs will be spread to dry. It was timed just right for the cessation of the rain and the return of the sun.

Knowing that I would be interested, Joan suggested that I ask Ruth to relate stories concerning happenings to members of her family during the "War of Liberation". At our usual breakfast chat, I introduced the subject. Ruth was willing to talk, but as always happens when Africans discuss family, a white person finds exact relationships are sometimes difficult to pin down. I guess it is due to lack of vocabulary; however I think I have it about right.

"The Madam tells me you had an aunt, who was killed during the war in the bush," I said. "Would you tell me what actually happened?"

"No, it wasn't my aunt," answered Ruth, "It was my mother's sister. And she wasn't killed. It was her son who was killed."

"When was this?" I asked, not wishing to quibble on the similarity of relationships.

"My aunt was old and her husband had died long back. At that time she was living on the farm with her family. One night the terrorists came to their house and they beat on the door. They said they must be given clothes and uniforms and gumboots for the bush. Also they wanted money. *How can we give you these things?* her son said. *We are poor people. Even ourselves we have no money,* he continued. *You are lying,* the terrorists said, and they led him away. Then they saw the son nearby and they took him to go with his father."

"So, these two the terrorists took away were your aunt's son and her grandson. We would say your cousin and his son. How old might they have been?" I asked.

"About 56 and 18 or something like that," Ruth replied. Then she went on:

"Some time later, the farmer was patrolling his farm on horseback, and he came to a place and found seven or eight dead bodies lying on the ground. When he saw that, he hurried to the police post at the place called Halfway. The police came and put the bodies on the back of a truck. They stopped the truck at the farms and those persons, who had reported that their relatives had been taken by the terrorists, were asked to identify the bodies. If they recognized their relatives they should take the bodies and bury them as soon as possible.

"My aunt went with her in-laws to the bodies and she saw her son and grandson were there amongst them. It was very terrible. The two bodies were lying one on top of the other. [Here Ruth picked up two objects from the kitchen dresser and laid one on the other.] They were stuck like burnt plastic; so mangled and bloodied that they had trouble to separate them. Terrible!

"The terrorists had sent a message to say that the relatives were not allowed to bury the bodies. They said that the bodies must stay on the ground and be cabbages for cattle. But the police said no, the bodies must be buried and they stood by with guns to see this was done while the mourners came and went quickly. After this, my aunt lost her mind and never recovered."

This was not the only ghastly story Ruth related to me. Yet another "aunt" was involved.

The woman lived in Chiota. In those days it was known as the Chiota Reserve, an area of scattered villages under the control of village headmen. It was in one of these that the aunt dwelt with her husband.

"The terrorists came to her house and they asked her to give them eggs because they wanted to eat some. She said she could not give them any eggs because she had none to give them. The chickens had not laid any eggs. She said she had given them eggs before and would do so again, but how could she do so if the chickens did not lay any?

Some time later, the terrorists called the people in the villages to attend a rally at a certain place. When they reached this place, the terrorists pointed to the woman, my aunt, and she was made to sit in the centre of the circle. Her husband was called to join her. Then one of the terrorists went over to the woman and asked: "Why did you refuse to give us some eggs?" She replied as before; she didn't have any. The terrorists accused her of lying. "Someone has told us that you have a lot of eggs. You do not support us. You are a sellout." With that they began to beat her. The husband intervened and said, "Why are you beating my wife?" So then they beat him also and they beat them both on the head so that their heads were smashed flat with no bone left and all that was inside was spilt out on the ground.

At the rally the relatives were told that they must not take the bodies but must leave them where they were, otherwise they would be killed also. Because of this the bodies stayed on the ground for many months until they rotted away. When the ceasefire came, a search was made for the bodies. They were found and the clothes they were wearing were still good and not eaten by white ants. But the flesh had all disappeared and they were buried like that."

The last of Ruth's stories was an event concerning her father. It was in 1980 and after the ceasefire. At that time, her father was ill. Some members of the Zanu forces took him away from his kraal and led him to a place where they questioned him. "Why do you not attend our rallies?" they demanded. "Which party do you support? Prepare your answers very well old man."

His wife who had accompanied him pleaded with the terrorists: "He is a very sick man—you can see for yourselves—he cannot walk—it is too far for him to walk all the way to the rallies—please, please spare him."

"By good luck they agreed to spare him," said Ruth to me.

To incorporate the reminiscences of an elderly African woman in a current diary may seem to be incongruous. The events occurred twenty-three years ago and more, they are in no way connected to me, and they have almost certainly lost accuracy in the telling. Nonetheless; the events have left a lasting impression, an impression which has now passed to me, personally, this very day. The question arises; is the impression meaningful in relation to present daily life. I believe it definitely is.

Ruth tells a story and the same story is related by all the members of her extended family. For each such story, a thousand others are told through the length and breadth of Zimbabwe. The stories all conform to a generality. They tell of merciless cruelty and killing. With repetition they become an important factor in the communal psyche.

In 1980, the terrorists won control. They remain in control and they continue to terrorize. There is no change. The system perpetuates itself. A whole new generation has grown up to maturity, but the choices open to these young persons are limited; either to join The Party and display enthusiasm for brutalizing your fellow man; or to live in subservience, fear and probable poverty; or to try desperately to escape and to leave all the wretchedness behind.

Just now I spoke of the communal psyche. In Africa fear is a major component of that communal psyche. It constantly shows itself. I can give an example immediately.

When I asked Ruth to tell me of the tragic happenings to the members of her family during the Bush War, I was keen to record, as nearly as possible, her exact words. When I wasn't clear on something, I asked her to repeat or explain it to me again. I would go to my office to write up some notes and perhaps return for further clarification.

It was on such an occasion that found me standing in the kitchen while Ruth, at the sink, was reiterating a part of the tale, when a tall African man walked through the kitchen from the main house. I was taken by surprise but supposed he had some business to perform so I greeted him and this he acknowledged but at the same time, giving me what I thought was a rather cold stare. He stood just outside the kitchen door—perhaps he was having a smoke, I didn't see. Meanwhile Ruth had stopped talking abruptly. She caught my eye and whispered: "Later."

"What's this all about?" I asked myself. I took my leave from the kitchen talking amiably and innocently to dogs, a few of whom are invariably knocking around.

Well, when it came to "later" and the coast was clear. I returned to the kitchen.

"Who was that man, Ruth?"

"He is the electrician Mama calls when there is a fault. He is a good electrician but he is ZANU PF!" This last emphasized as if giving a danger warning. "We mustn't be heard saying anything against them," she added.

"I suppose he must tell people that he is ZANU PF," I said.

"Yes. He says he was fighting as a comrade in the war."

"That must put him over forty—he doesn't look it," I remark.

"Well, I don't know, but that is what he says."

By this time, the questions I was asking about dates, places and persons had put suspicions into Ruth's mind.

"I hope you are not writing what I am saying to you into a book. I don't want that. It will get me into big trouble. Please," says Ruth, "if it gets known I have been telling you these things, they will hang me."

"No Ruth, I am just taking down a few notes. It's really for historical record—I am not writing anything for here in Zimbabwe. They will never hang you," I assure her. "Anyway, hundreds of people all over Zimbabwe have stories to tell like yours".

In the telling of her story, Ruth [who is not Ruth!], reveals the African communal psyche.

My sojourn in these pleasant surroundings will soon be over. Joan has said that her daughter who is coming for a month will not now require the cottage and I am welcome to stay longer. However, my friends the Cunliffes are both away for a few weeks and I offered to house-sit their home over the period. I am in familiar territory there and I know my return will be welcomed by Rosie, the bullterrier and Dodo, the grey parrot.

It had been my intention to house-sit during April for Jenny Reynolds and her brother Dudley at Jenny's home in Meyrick Park. Dudley is a South African resident but being retired, he stays some of the time in Zimbabwe at the home of his sister, a retired teacher.

Last month, Dudley was about to drive his car out through the entrance gate when he was stopped by a man who wrenched open his car door and pulled him from the car. Dudley is an old soldier; although over seventy he fought his attacker and forced him to the ground. The fight came to an end abrupt end when a second man ran in from the road and held a gun to Dudley's temple. There were four members of the Hi-jack gang and he could do no more than watch as the gang drove his car away. It was only then that he became aware that he had been deeply slashed in the leg by a knife. The wound didn't heal and Dudley was two weeks in hospital. His car was never recovered.

The Hi-jacking of cars has become widespread and the thieves shown to be violent. Targeted are the elderly or women driving by themselves, sometimes with small children. The situation has become so serious that a group of private men and women has set up a centre in the Farmers Union buildings. Here a hot-line is manned and efforts made to obtain proper police reaction. Reports of Hi-jacking incidents are given to the non-government press along with warnings and avoidance advice for motorists. They will also help those suffering from post Hi-jack trauma! Typical community spirit is seen here.

Meanwhile, Jenny's son Richard has come in from Marondera. Marondera might well claim to have been one of the most highly developed and the most prosperous farming districts of Rhodesia and later Zimbabwe. There, apart from extensive crops of tobacco and maize, might have been found fine herds of pedigree beef cattle, dairy animals and thoroughbred horse studs; sheep, pigs and even game animals were reared there. The Marondera Agricultural Show was noted for its large livestock entries. Veterinarians were in demand year round. Richard is a vet.

Richard joined a veterinary practice in Marondera three years ago. One by one, the other vets working in Marondera left and moved away. Eventually Richard was the only one left. Now it is his turn to leave. Hundreds of farmers have had to vacate their farms. The cattle have gone, the horses have gone. Each farmhouse surely had its quota of dogs and other pets; they have been dispersed along with the families. The Africans who have moved onto the farms have no use for vets, so Richard is left without work. He is presently trying to sell his equipment and has plans to join a brother in England.

Richard's misfortunes were not confined to Marondera. He had not been long staying at his mother's house in Meyrick Park when thieves broke into the premises and removed the four wheels from his 4X4 vehicle. For good measure they also stole the wheels from a trailer. Last year thieves had found a way to de-activate the burglar alarm and got away with a TV.

It was when I was describing these happenings to my family and announcing that I would be house-sitting at Jenny's house for five weeks, that they hinted strongly that I must be mad. They said that it was obvious that the house was under surveillance by robbers of all description. Far from being a deterrent, my arrival may be viewed as an opportunity for a fresh picking. In these times, I would never be able to replace my car if it was stolen and to replace a set of wheels would cost me $700 000.

I phoned Jenny and, with profuse apologies, explained that I had changed my mind. She was very understanding and went so far as to say that in my position, she would have done the same.

Wednesday 19th March 2003
It may be noticed that my entries for the past few days have taken a rather different format. I have wearied of reporting the ongoing frontline skirmishes fought for the control of the farm. For a change, I directed my thoughts and words along more personal channels. Upon re-reading the pages, I discover that in describing personal encounters with other people, I have unintentionally opened up a broader view of the Zimbabwe scene. Clearly, I am not alone;

the stresses of life are affecting everyone. Well, NEARLY everyone!

Despairing of the destructive behaviour of the human race, I resolved, some years ago, to devote what time was left to me into caring for all the gentler forms of life, which shared with me this little patch on the skin of our planet. If they were to avoid suffering and death, I was the only human on Earth who would help them. My endeavours to save the land for them are recorded in these pages. Needless to say, my adversaries have been fellow humans; self-willed beings, lacking reason, sensitivity, and compassion.

The predators probe relentlessly, testing my resolve, watching for signs of weakening. They know the odds are stacked against me; I can call upon no support. Already I have given too much ground. The attempt to kill me was on 25th March last, and shortly afterwards I accepted the prudent advice that I should sleep away from the farm. I employed a night guard but, under present circumstances and in my isolated position, one African guard is inadequate. I needed more but could not afford them. As a result, each afternoon, I left my home and drove into town.

Months have gone by. The legal battle has bogged down and on the ground the harassment continues inexorably—day after day. House sitting has ensured nights of safe shelter and has, at least, provided the environment for one to find peaceful sleep. To start with, my day time visits to the farm were regular and I spent much of my time there. There was still some produce to come in off the fields and grass was being mown, dried and baled. Later, theft of pumps and equipment made further cropping impossible. It was pointless to consider a resumption of work either in the fields or in the forest and eventually all the staff received their final gratuities. Added to this, I could no longer walk freely over my property for fear of being confronted and abused by one or other of the brutal Warvets. In time, I confined my visits to a few hours at most in order to see and speak with Johannes, the household staff and the two dogs.

Moppet and Humba have been my constant daily companions each and every day. Wherever I went on the farm, they came with me, never without excitement and boundless enthusiasm. We have been a team of which, of course, I have been the recognized leader. I do not forget that I owe them much. Fed and well cared for by Makosa though they are, nevertheless it breaks my heart to confine myself to fleeting visits and to drive away and leave them.

When I was on the farm today some inner voice bade me take the dogs out walking. I took the path to the wooded kopje that lies beyond my house. It is a very special place for me—if not a secret garden then secret woodland. Over the years I have spent hours and hours here. It is packed with old friends in a profusion of variety; hundreds of my own plantings interspersed within, or bordering close to, the forest of old residents. Many are now tall, spreading and elegant with a potential for true magnificence. Here and there, beneath their shade and between their roots, lies dust that remains alive in my memory. I got that unhappy feeling that I was making a farewell to it all. Moppet and Humba, dear creatures, appeared to be immune to such sentiment and may have thought perhaps that the good life had restarted.

The past three years have been a time of continual stress and frustration which can leave one worn out. The struggle will continue—I am not giving up. However; I think I will give up writing this diary. It seems to have become a long recital of hopes progressively whittled away. I will attempt to direct my energy and thoughts away from here.

POSTSCRIPT

On the eastern slope of a thickly wooded hill, there is a little clearing in the forest. Here, as through a window, the overhead sun will throw its light for a passing hour onto the bright green carpet of grass in the clearing. At night, the travelling moon follows the same path; its gentle light silvers the dewy green.

It is a place of perfect peace. No raucous voice is heard here. Until now, the trees have never felt or heard the fatal blow of an axe. They just grew up and up. None of them ever seemed to die.

Last year, for the first time in twenty years, fire was set to sear and scorch their slender frames.

The residents here are unobtrusive but numerous enough. The most noteworthy perhaps being a local party of guineafowl, who come to preen and dust themselves in the midday warmth. At dusk it is the turn of some duikers to stir themselves. They steal quietly up through the wood to the clearing, there to nibble at the fresh shoots of the surrounding shrubs. In the morning one can always find their droppings. It tells you they have lingered long.

In this tranquil, silent place, upon the green turf, an unobtrusive stone marks the spot where my wife lies. When she died I buried her here. Nine years have passed; but here, or here about, and if undisturbed, her gentle spirit may choose to come and go.

As for me:
"The bird of time has but a little way to fly
and Lo! The bird is on the wing."
Until now I never doubted where my grave would be.

A CONTINUATION

Friday 4th April 2003

Hello again. My despondent mood has passed. I have shrugged off green and yellow melancholy. Things have been happening, which cause me to resume the battle. In a strange way the writing up of the diary helps me maintain equilibrium.

The Black Mamba Mujuru, who for weeks has been giving us the impression of dormancy, has become dangerously active and I am the recipient once more of his venom. Far from sleeping, he has been plotting to finally get me ousted from my farm and to consolidate his own position. To effect this, he has elicited the help of another snake; this one with BIG MONEY and no doubt an enthusiastic backer of the ruling ZANU PF party.

In the course of the week a lorry has been coming onto the farm delivering forty or fifty rolls of wire and a quantity of steel fencing standards. With the material have come a total of eleven workers with rations and personal belongings. These workers have been instructed to repair and strengthen all the boundary fencing. The materials alone will be worth several million dollars. Johannes has been told that the plan is to bring 900—1000 head of cattle onto Stockade. If so, this represents a further 20 million.

Mujuru has told the workers not to discuss any matters with Johannes; however the latter has learnt that they are employed by an African woman who owns a farm and several subsidiary businesses. The lorry, operating under the name Olympia Enterprises, Box HG 267 Highlands, apparently belongs to her, and the nearest J can get to her name is Mrs.Chipo.

There is a lot of money involved here. Mujuru wouldn't have enough to buy one animal, and however wealthy this Mrs. Chipo is, I doubt if she would expend her own money on a project like this one. The government has set aside some 30 billion dollars to assist emergent farmers. It goes without saying that most of this money will be siphoned off by ZANU PF chefs and their most active and belligerent supporters. I suspect that some such racket is being worked here.

Faced with this latest threat to farm and forest, I have been driven frantic trying to block it. I say, driven frantic, because to get a positive or even a sympathetic response from ANYONE in authority ANYWHERE, is a maddening experience. For a start, the person you may be recommended to talk to will either be on leave, in a meeting, sick, has a phone that is defunct, or is simply "not around". It took me four days and countless phone calls before I could speak with the DA and it took him just two minutes to refer me to the Provincial Land Committee. Well, by this time we all know about THEM don't we? Meanwhile, the police inspector recommended the Ministry of Lands. I settled for letters to Lands and to Environment. These would be a back-up if I failed to meet with the addressees in person. I will insert them both here because they explain everything.

1 3 2003

Stockade Farm
Box EH 95 Emerald Hill
Harare 011 214406

The Director of Lands
Min. of Lands Agriculture & Rural Development
Ngungunyana Bldg. Borrowdale Road.

Dear Mrs. Tsvakwi,

Statutory Instrument 147 of 2001 Forest Notice

I refer to the above notice whereby the larger part of Stockade Farm was declared a Protected Forest by the Minister for Environment and Tourism in consultation with The Forestry Commission and the Department of Natural Resources. I also refer to correspondence concerning the same.

For the past fifteen years much expenditure has been entailed in the protection, upkeep and development of the forest; thousands of young trees have been established. To secure and to maintain the forest for perpetuity and in the national interest, I suggested to Minister Nhema that, for practical reasons, the whole farm should go to his ministry and that National Parks become the operative authority. [It should be noted less than 100 hectares of the farm is arable and much of this intrudes into forested areas.] The minister saw merit in this move.

National Parks were instructed to make a study of the farm and their ecologists prepared a report. On the 8th. August 2002, the Secretary for Environment wrote to the Secretary of Lands proposing National Parks take over the farm. I had spoken with your Mrs. Mandimika meanwhile, and she indicated that a valuation of the property would be undertaken by the Ministry and fair compensation offered.

The situation seemed satisfactory and only awaited inter-ministerial procedures before a transfer was effected and Parks personnel occupied the farm. Eight months have passed; the Environment Ministry tell me that they are still awaiting a reply from Lands. During that time I have had eight million dollars worth of equipment and fittings stolen from the farm.

On 8th. May 2002, a person known as Mujuru alias Chamunorwa broke into one of the houses on the farm and stayed there. He claimed that the farm had been given to him by Minister Elliot Manyika. Naturally I informed Minister Nhema of this. The latter, in my presence, spoke to Manyika who denied any knowledge of Mujuru or Chamunorwa. He considered he must be a fraud. He had gone on to say that the man would be removed, "it just needed a little time." I spoke to Minister Nhema recently and he was surprised to learn that Mujuru was still on the farm because he thought the matter had been sorted out.

On Friday 29th. March, a lorry belonging to Olympia Enterprises, Reg No. 512598 W, of P.O Box HG 267 Highlands, drove onto the farm with eight workers. They carried their personal belongings and with them were twenty rolls of barbed wire. My farm foreman and the farm guards were told that the men were being deployed to fix up all the fencing because 900 to 1000 head of cattle would be coming onto the farm. A further twenty rolls of wire were brought out on Saturday.

The men had been instructed by Mujuru not to say who they worked for or where they came from. In view of Minister Manyika's remarks concerning the man, the events are perplexing and worrying.

Clearly such a huge influx of cattle will have a detrimental effect on the fragile soils of the forest and many young trees that have been planted at great expense will be killed.

When I asked the O.I.C. Z.R.P. Nyabira to please intervene, he replied that I should appeal to the Ministry of Lands. This being so, I would greatly appreciate it, if you would kindly review this matter urgently.

I regard the Protected Forest as a National Asset. The Minister for the Environment, by declaring it such, must also be concerned at this untoward development. Please would you keep him advised on this and also help to resolve the impasse concerning the take- over of Stockade by National Parks.

Yours sincerely,
R.F.Wiles.
cc Minister for Env. & Tourism.

31st.March 2003

Stockade Farm
Box EH 95 Emerald Hill
Harare. 011 21 44 06

The Hon. F.D. Nhema MP.,
Minister of Environment and Tourism,
Karigamombe Centre, Harare.
Dear Minister,

Please find attached a copy of an urgent letter addressed to the Director of Lands. It is self-explanatory.

I think you will share my utter dismay at this sudden and obvious threat to the Protected Forest and the natural vegetation and wildlife it contains.

This is the work of the person Mujuru, whose dangerous excesses I have referred to on a number of occasions. It is my understanding that you have communicated with Governor Elliot Manyika with regard to having Mujuru removed from Stockade and that failure has only been due to remiss on the Governor's part.

You once told me that there was no way that the status of the Forest could be rescinded. In response, I have done my utmost to maintain my guardianship of it. But, as you know, events beyond my control have led to my financial ruin. The delay caused by the Ministry of Lands in implementing the proposed takeover by National Parks has been a bitter blow.

Notwithstanding, should National Parks finally take possession of the property, the maintenance of roads and firebreaks will be a priority and I may be able to assist by way of machinery and experience.

Meantime I hope you will be able to resist the immediate threat to the Forest and indeed to the property as a whole.

Yours sincerely,
R.F.Wiles.

My first call was to Lands. At the reception desk a receptionist was constantly taking incoming calls. Eventually I managed to get a word in: "Please may I speak with Mrs.Tsvakwi." [I had been practicing the pronunciation of this name for days.] He waved a direction. "Yes. Please take a seat." In the waiting room I was joined by several white farmers who, in response to a Ministry notice in the newspaper had come to discuss certain matters concerning their farms which government had recently acquired.

Some ten minutes later, a ministerial official entered, came up to me and asked me politely enough if he could help me. I assumed that he was an assistant to Mrs.Tsvakwi and had perhaps been deputised to assist me.

"Indeed, I do hope you can help me, but I think the best thing you can do to understand my predicament is to read my letter to Mrs.Tsvakwi," I said, handing the letter to him. I stood quietly aside whilst the gentleman read carefully, first one page and then the second. When he had finished, he paused for a while in thought: "So what you are asking is for a valuation to be done on your farm," he said.

I have learnt to remain cool and polite in trying circumstances.

We went into conference with the receptionist, during which continual interruptions of a demanding nature were being made by persons unknown on the other end of a telephone line. Obviously there had been some misunderstanding; a case of mistaken identity. I was not the person the official was supposed to meet. It was agreed amicably that I should return to my seat and continue to wait for Mrs. Tsvakwi.

At this point John Laurie of Concession came to occupy the seat beside me. We had plenty of time to chat. He had been evicted from his farm and was living in town. So far he had been forcibly prevented from taking away his cattle and moveable assets. He had come into the Ministry to seek assurance that he would be allowed to move them without further hindrance.

In the course of our chat, I learnt that the Lauries had been on their farms for three generations. The father had opened up the first farm in 1926. He had been followed by his sons and grandsons. The farms had been highly productive; the land cared for. Now all is lost. It is a story that can be repeated a thousand times in Zimbabwe.

John was called to an interview and I didn't see him again. I hope in the end he receives a mite of satisfaction in retrieving some valuables from the wreck of his lifelong home. Alone now, I waited until I received a message. It was: "Mrs. Tsvakwi will not be in the office today." I asked her secretary on the phone to please collect the letter from reception. I hope she did. At least I witnessed the receptionist stamping it vigorously with the Ministry stamp.

Next, I proceeded to the Ministry of Environment with my letter to the Minister. Once again I was stopped and quizzed by a man sitting in the Minister's outer office. What are they checking on? It can only be the C.I.O. I should have asked him. How easily we can be put on the defensive and cowed by abrupt officialdom.

Minister Nhema was in his office. Helen, his secretary, agreed to take my letter into him then and there. I waited in the hope that he would invite me to speak with him. However Helen came out to me to say that the minister was referring me to Mrs. Sangarwe. On the way to the latter's office, Helen stopped in the corridor and turned to me.

"The Minister says that this matter has been discussed and decided upon at Ministerial level and it is now at the level of officials for implementation."

That leaves me none the wiser. I think he was fobbing me off because he would have been unable to answer my questions; and of course there was the embarrassing reference in my letter to the words of Elliot Manyika. [I admit I have enjoyed exploiting this one on every possible occasion; covered in the guise of innocent belief that such an august minister as Manyika would never tell a lie!] Howbeit, I took the opportunity to read Nhema's pencilled note to Mrs. Sangarwe on the top of my letter.

How far have we got on this thing? Better speak with Forestry.

As it happened I couldn't see Mrs. Sangarwe, because her secretary explained that she was at a meeting. She was very busy this week and would be away all next week. It would be best to see her when she returned to the office on the 14th.

"That's no good," I said. "Mrs. Sangarwe may be the only person in the country who can stop 900 cattle from entering my farm. I shall ring her later."

This I did and thankfully got through to her. She had not read my letter to Nhema but had seen it on her desk. I gave her a brief resume.

Mrs. Sangarwe didn't sound expectant. She knows that the bullies in this set up always want to get their own way. However, she said she had an appointment with a Mr. Mbiribiri, the Senior Lands Officer, at the end of this week and she would make specific reference to Stockade. I reminded her that my Section 8 and Section 5 were null and void so legally the farm was still my property. This raised her hopes and she told me to ring her early next week.

"Will you be in the office next week?" I asked; a bit surprised.

"Yes. I'll be in," was her answer. What was her secretary up to?

As I write today, it seems to me that a culmination point has been reached. I have been ground down in this three year war of attrition; mental and financial reserves have been exhausted. My enemies are riding high. The Devil is in control and his minions are exultant—of these Mujuru not least of any. In the dark corridors of power, expressions of moral probity and honesty equate to treason; at best a timid voice of reason will be ignored. I fear any representations that Mrs. Sangarwe makes will be brushed aside.

From the outset my struggle has been waged on behalf of the defenceless. I mean the multitude of living creatures and plants, which have found sanctuary within the reserve I have established for them. They have formed a robust commune and are actively improving the erstwhile eroded soils. This mass, composed of living entities, makes the forest. As it stands, it is a unique entity.

The forest is alive. It breathes and it transpires; it drinks and it feeds; it consumes yet it nourishes. It is surely sentient, because it is ever responding to natural change. The parts readily and continually inter-relate. Like cells in a body, they die and replicate. The whole is kept in healthy balance. The forest, indeed, is one giant symbiotic relationship between millions of busy entities. The one thing it cannot do is to defend itself from the rapaciousness and destructiveness of Mankind.

My cause has been slightly different to that observed in the general farming scene, which now shows itself as nothing short of a horrific disaster. Ironically, I thought that the insignificant area of arable land on Stockade and the preponderance of non-arable fragile soils upon which the Protected Forest exists, might help my property escape the despot's monstrous hand and the withering death which must inevitably follow.

It has been a lonely battle for me. Nowhere in the world, let alone in Africa, does the human species recognize the right of any other living species to exist other than for the former's consumption or pleasure. The nature lover, the enthusiastic conservationist, is at best considered something of an irrelevant oddity, at worst a break on progress. In the protracted process of obtaining legal protection for the forest, time and again, even speaking with fellow environmentalists, I was called upon to justify myself in terms of monetary worth. Such is today's world.

Yesterday I was driving along one of the main access roads into Harare. As I drove I was observing with sickening regularity lorries, trucks, big buses, commuter buses, even smart, but ill maintained 4x4's, all belching black exhaust smoke into the air; there to disperse but to stay aloft for evermore. This is progress. Zimbabwe is doing its best to catch up with the developed world.

My mind made no more than a passing note of the atmospheric pollution factor and soon returned to my overriding concern—the appalling prospect for the farm and forest upon an invasion by men and cattle.

I have since been reminded of a warning given by the scientist, James Lovelock. He describes the greatest danger facing the planet as being Man's use of the Three C's. These are cars, cattle and chain saws. Of course he is simplifying, but from these three factors alone carbon emissions continue to rise and so are global temperatures. Climate change has begun. What earthly upheavals may result?

Mujuru's choice of cattle to break my hold on the Protected Forest will be no more than opportunistic. However, I wonder if I shouldn't read some prophetic significance in it; in microcosm, an example of Humanity's blind but determined path towards self-destruction.

I am sorry to have slipped back into pessimistic mood. However, a personal diary is of greater interest if it reveals the author's inner thoughts—or so it is said. The stress and tribulation impinging on us in these times invariably results in ups and downs in one's mood and morale. For me, I think that the only hope for the ongoing life of the Forest lies in the utter downfall of the present evil rulers; but it must be VERY SOON.

Tuesday 1st May 2003

My last entry was for 4th. April. Nearly a month has past. It is now necessary for me to record happenings over that period.

The fencing gang continued to repair and consolidate the boundary fencing. More cattle were brought out. I was returning from a visit to the farm when I came upon a cattle truck stationary on the Selby Road just before the railway crossing on Selby farm. The vehicle had a puncture and the cattle had been offloaded and were being herded along the road on foot.

I stopped and asked the driver what the trouble was and where he was taking the animals. He replied that the cattle were going to Stockade Farm. I was

Water reservoir 1999. Bridget with Moppet. This was one of 5 reservoirs providing water for animals, birds and bees; also to irrigate plantings of young tree seedlings. In 2003 all the piping, fittings, and the pumping equipment was stolen.

writing down the registration number of his truck and the name stencilled on the side of the cab: Olympia Enterprises, Box HG 267 Highlands.

"Whose cattle are they?" I asked. The driver was already guarded.

"They belong to the Warvet Mujuru."

I laughed. "He must be a very rich man to own all these cattle. Where have they come from?"

The driver gave me a surly look and didn't answer so I drove on.

Over succeeding days I was able to get a hired truck out to the farm and with hired hands from town, Johannes was able to load up bricks which were lying in the bwalo ever since building ceased after the first Warvet incursion. The lorry also brought in a 500 gallon galvanised water tank. During this period, I had Johannes dismantle the Kitchen units in the uncompleted lodge. To avoid attention, he did this at night with the help of his wife, Sinai, and they carried the sections by hand through the long grass and gum trees. Some of them were very heavy. It took me two trips in the pick-up to move this off the farm but the sink unit is still in my garage.

Mujuru heard that I had questioned the cattle truck driver and this made him very angry. According to Johannes and my staff, he shouted on and on that I must get my things out of my house because somebody else was going to live there.

Meantime I realized that April would soon come to a close and some important decisions had to be made. Moppet and Humba, the two dogs, would have to be moved. All along they had been of great concern to me. Not only were they vulnerable but they were living a deadly dull life without the constant companionship of myself to whom they had been closely attached for most of their lives. Also Humba had developed lameness in the hind leg.

Martin and family went on holiday for two weeks at the end of April. During that time I felt I must bring the two dogs into town and introduce them to Koala the Bouvier bitch resident at the family home.

Due to unusual circumstances, Humba was examined by three vets. It seemed that his leg ailment would, at best, require long treatment. There was an additional worry for me. Humba's thirst to give and to receive affection was unquenchable; he never seemed to learn that others may not have reciprocal feelings and rebuffs left him terribly hurt. I had no home of my own and foresaw this situation lasting for weeks and even months. I felt it was asking too much to foist Humba's physical and psychological failings onto other people. After much mental anguish, I decided to have him put down.

Moppet is a more intelligent and sensitive dog. After a couple of initial skirmishes with Koala the two of them seem to have come to terms.

Within a few days of my evacuation of the dogs, Mujuru became really nasty. I am sure there was no correlation; it was quite coincidental. Having put random bits of information together it was another event entirely which triggered Mujuru to go on the warpath. I learnt from Johannes that on the 27th. or 28th. April, Mujuru received a visitor—none other than Elliot Manyika.

The following day Mujuru came to my security gate with three of his men. I suspect they found the gate unlocked. In any event they entered my grounds. Makosa was not there and those present were Johannes, Rosemary and the watchmen Norman and Denis.

Mujuru was loud and vociferous. He declared that as he was the owner of the farm everyone must obey his orders. Norman was sent away to join those herding the cattle. Next he demanded young Rosemary to hand over the house keys to him. When she claimed she hadn't got them this made him very angry and he threatened her with dire consequences if she didn't get them.

Seeing an opportunity, Rosemary slipped the bunch of house keys to Patience, a young cousin who had come up to the house with her for company. When Mujuru's threats became more violent, Rosemary fled for her life through the gate. She fell and grazed her knee but quickly righted herself and carried on running.

Mujuru and his men next turned their attention on Johannes. According to the latter, there was some rough stuff and he gave as good as he got. However, he was outnumbered 4 to 1 and he would surely have remembered his previous experience at Mujuru's hands. I guess he took off.

At this stage, I have no idea what, if anything, Denis was doing. Perhaps he was just cowering.

That night, at around 9 o'clock, I received a call from Johannes on his cell phone. He sounded exhausted. Fortunately he had called Martin's house number and I was spending the night at the house keeping my eye on the dogs. My own cell phone had been useless all day.

"What is happening, Johannes?" I asked.

"Mujuru has sent his men out to look for me," he answered, his voice drawn and wearied.

"So where are you?"

"I am hiding here in the "manda", below the compound."

The "manda" is the farm's burial ground in the vicinity of the farm village. I know it well enough. It is situated some six hundred yards down a twisting, overgrown footpath. The graves are untended and the area is a wilderness of tangled bush. All about, thick stands of grass grow seven feet tall. To the best of my recollection, the last burial had been well over a year ago and the body had been that of a child. The mother, a young widow, had not lived on the farm but had walked a long distance with the sick child in order to be with her relatives. The child died on the night of her arrival. Death is common in these times. There was no need for a burial certificate. I could visualize the rampant growth of grass that had taken place about the "manda" since then.

"Are you alone?" was my question to Johannes.

"No, my wife and the two children are with me."

"What about Rosemary?" I then asked him. "Is she at her parent's house?"

"No. She is here with us. She heard the men had gone to the house to look for her so she has come here to the manda."

I had a disturbing vision of Johannes and his little band of innocents spending the dark night couched like fugitive animals in a thicket alongside the graves of the dead. I asked him if he couldn't take them all to find shelter on the next farm.

"No," he replied, "It is late. Better we stay here."

I told him to try to contact the Nyabira police by cell phone and tell them what had happened and to make his way to Nyabira in the morning.

Needless to say I was feeling thoroughly upset by this time. By luck, I managed to get a call through to the police and described the turn of events to the constable on duty. He agreed that Johannes should come to Nyabira in the morning to report.

Well of course this is what transpired. At first light and considering it safe, Johannes sent Sinai with his children to friends in another farm village, whilst he and Rosemary went to Nyabira where both of them gave full statements. It seems that the constable taking the reports was disturbed by the stories and suggested that there was certain to be a follow-up. However, A\Insp.Tezha, in charge of the station, kept Johannes waiting several hours before indicating that he would first have to speak with senior officers.

I too spoke with Tezha on the phone and he told me he could do nothing without the authority of the Ministry of Lands. At the Ministry of Lands I was told I should speak with a Mr. Samuwiro [?] who was away until next week. The format doesn't change.

And by the way, the DA, when I finally contacted him after much difficulty, told me to go and speak with the Bindura Land Committee. That's a good recipe for self-destruction.

By way of an aside, I must draw attention to an apparent anomaly in the ranks of the Z.R.P. at Nyabira. Many weeks ago, I was introduced to the new officer-in-charge, Inspector Majoni. He had come to replace Inspector Sengwe. At the same time A\I Taswa was transferred to Norton and Sgt. Tezha was promoted A\Inspector and remained at Nyabira as second officer.

From that time, I have repeatedly asked to speak with Insp. Majoni but he has never been available. Once I was told that he was on leave. His leave period seems to extend for ever; leastwise Tezha is the effective officer-in-charge and flounders under the responsibility.

[Incidentally, I am told that my persecutor, Inspector Sengwe, ex-guerrilla, inveterate smoker, the one with the glazed grey eyes, is on U.N. peacekeeping duty in Kosova. Would you believe it?]

Information came to me that Mujuru, having chased off all my staff with the exception of Denis, forced open the doors of my house using a mattock. Most of my furniture and belongings remain in the house and as he has installed himself inside, I suppose he is using my effects.

The news that Mujuru had moved into my house, filled me with bitterness. The war of attrition had been going on for three years. In spite of some successful counter moves, I had been steadily losing ground and finally quite worn down by my enemies. Nevertheless; I had kept my house free from assault. In a way, the house represented the fort. Whoever held the fort still controlled the surrounding ground. This was true even when I was absent over periods of time, because I was represented by my loyal staff and Moppet and Humba.

Far from being a fort, of course, Beth and I had created a wide and welcoming homestead surrounded by lawns, trees, rocks and beds always ablaze with colour.We had spent 30 years of our 44 years of married life here and Beth turned a house into a home; clean, fresh, and gay with flowers, but always with the look of being "lived in". After Beth died, Makosa and I did our best, but nothing can replace a woman's touch.

Mujuru is savage and evil. I didn't know such beings could exist. I now know that they do and that he is one of many. I was told that he used a mattock to break into the house. To use such a crude swinging tool, suggests a subliminal primitiveness. It could as well have been a knobkerrie and an assegai. I shudder.

I visited my lawyer Richard Wood of Atherstone and Cook. He prepared three letters, these being for The Ministry of Lands, the O.I.C. Nyabira, and Mr. Thomas Mujuru.

The first I delivered in person and obtained a stamped receipt; the driver Eliot took the second to Z.R.P. but Tezha refused to accept it so I sent it by registered post; the letter to Mujuru, which warned him to vacate my property within seven days or face prosecution, was taken out to the farm by discreet means. He received it.

Before these events had reached culmination, I had obtained information concerning the cattle. The workers who had settled on the farm to look after the cattle stated that they worked for Mr.K.Moyana the ex Governor of the Zimbabwe Reserve Bank—"The one who used to sign all the bank notes," the African workers emphasize knowingly. Well, that makes sense. That's where the wealth came from. Now I understand.

A few more enquiries reveal that Mr.K.Moyana deals in cattle in a big way. He has a farm off the Golden Stairs Road and other farms for holding cattle scattered around the country. At this stage I don't know if he owns Olympia Enterprises or where Mrs.Chipo [if there is such a person] fits in.

After two weeks my lawyer had not received any reply to his letter to the Minister of Lands so I instigated my own enquiries. My phone calls to the relevant ministry officials elicited the same response; Atherstone and Cook's letter had not been seen. I took them a Photostat copy of the receipted copy the next day.

In the course of this affair, I spoke with Mrs. Mandimika. Amongst Ministry officials Mrs. Mandimika is one who inclines to be expansive. This is no doubt a serious fault for a government servant, but it may offer snippets of useful information to the listener.

Mrs. Mandimika told me that my farm, Stockade was due to be discussed at a meeting of the Command Centre. The person who presides over the Command Centre is an army man. She named him as Major Muschakavanhu [I asked her to spell it for me!] She said this major settles disputes over farms and will make on sight visits.

Mrs. Mandimika went on to say that there were two rival claimants to Stockade Farm. To my question; was I one of them? I received a silent response; however she said I could phone her back three days hence. In the event, I didn't phone her until the following week. She said that the major hadn't turned up for the meeting.

I see I began this section of my diary on the 1st.May. The month is close to its end now so I'm afraid I have lost exact sequence and allowed days to go by unrecorded. Well, by this time one knows that it is all one and the same. After such long experience of the intransigence of all arms of government, it could be construed that I have been a fool to waste my time seeking redress. I tell myself that at least, when there is a final reckoning, nobody can say that I failed to take the correct procedures.

The lawyer's letters were dispatched on 2nd.May. After about ten days and it was clear that no response was coming from any quarter, I called upon Richard Wood and asked him to proceed with court action. He pointed out that this would be a costly procedure; however having come so far, I feel I must see it through.

The need for a court order is now pressing for a couple of reasons:
1. The eviction of Mujuru and the withdrawal of the cattle.
2. That I be given unhindered, and if need be, protected access to my property.

Obviously, at least to my way of thinking, such an order would infer that I am the rightful owner of Stockade Farm and that the government is not. Or not unless and until they issued me with a new Section 5; in which case the whole procedure would start all over again and, in that case, I should be given 3 months notice.

I am well aware that if I obtained a favourable court order, the chances of it being enforced are practically nil. However, I would have won a valuable legal point which may be of benefit when the day of reckoning comes.

Thursday 29th.May 2003

Johannes has been in town for a couple of days. He came to do a spot of repair work on the kitchen units, which I managed to extract from the unfinished Lodge and transport to Harare before Mujuru occupied my house. J also came to collect some money, which I am lending him in order to allow his wife Sinai set up a small retail business on one of the farms, Teviotdale, further down the valley. He tells me that where she will operate there is much small-scale gold mining activity and, with it, a growing community. [No doubt playing havoc with the environment—but there you are!]

My garage on the farm is full of Johannes' belongings. They were stored there for protection after threats made by Mujuru. The situation is ironic now that Mujuru has moved into my house. He has broken into all the rooms and, of course, the garage. J has learnt that Mujuru has discovered amongst Johannes' boxes a brand-new radio, which J had bought. Mujuru has taken it for himself and is using it.

On Wednesday morning Winet, Makosa's wife, came in to town to speak with me. The situation was bad for them. Mujuru had issued a warning that unless Makosa, Winet and their three small children were out of their house and off the farm by tonight, he would come there and burn the house down. It is too bad. Our old cook, Makosa, has become decidedly frail and unsteady in body and mind in the last few months.

I phoned Nyabira police and was lucky enough to speak with A\I Tezha. I told him what I had learnt from Winet and the ultimatum Mujuru had given them to get off the farm.

"Why is he doing that?" asks Tezha.

"Don't ask me," I say, "I am just telling you."

"How is it that people can be made homeless? They have a right to their homes. They are all Zimbabweans."

I remained silent. It seemed that Tezha was debating with himself. Finally:

"I will phone Mujuru."

"Thanks Tezha. Please tell him to leave them alone. I will tell the wife that I have spoken with you and that you are going to contact Mujuru."

"I will phone him."

It was impossible for me to gauge how effective Tezha's promise of intervention might be; phone communication in itself is unreliable enough. I gave Winet some money and told her to find her way back from town and tell me if things got bad.

A call from Johannes last night on his cell phone was to inform me that he was speaking from the farm. Here he had learnt that George had come to the farm in his vehicle that day and was looking for Mujuru. The report was that he had gone up to my house and, finding Mujuru absent, had confronted the old man who Mujuru has to stay with him. George was filled with anger and demanded that Mujuru should leave my house and confine himself to the other side of the railway line. It would appear that George considers that my house and all the land above the railway line, belongs to him. It may be remembered that George is out on bail pending the outcome of the charge of theft of MY property. To add insult to injury George is presently coming to the farm to reap the maize which he planted on MY field where I had been planting MY crops.

I might ask what the difference is between stealing angle iron, steel pipes, doors and articles of farm equipment and that of removing maize grown with soil nutrients and water on land owned by me. I have to admit that George's court case has been in abeyance so long that it appears that he will never be sentenced. If freed on the one count, he would be freed on the other.

Talking of property, many months ago I had Johannes take a considerable amount of moveable farm equipment and materials down to Trianda Farm for safekeeping. This was done with the kind co-operation of Alan Foot and his manager, Wellington.

I have learnt that Alan received a letter from Mujuru demanding the return of these things, "which Mr. Wiles has stolen from the farm." Alan ignored the letter; nevertheless the effrontery of these government-sponsored invaders boggles the mind.

At long last it is coming home to the urban dwellers, particularly the Africans, that the chronic shortages of food and the horrific increase in the cost of living, is directly attributable to Mugabe's persecution of the white farmers; the orders he gave to have them evicted and the appropriation of their farms.

I am often dismayed at the general lack of knowledge townspeople have on matters pertaining to sophisticated agricultural production. As for such concerns as soil conservation and proper land usage, these are a closed book to them. For the most part African urban dwellers do indeed have connections with families in the rural areas; but traditional farming in these areas has been of a subsistence nature and natural resources freely exploited. The land under these conditions has been "used up"; impoverished by ill usage and a prodigious increase in human population. The African mind may now be waking up to the fact that more of the same spread over the land "historically" farmed by whites is a recipe for more hunger and suffering.

I doubt if the rural African thinks this way. I wouldn't blame him for wishing to set the clock back 120 years or so. In those days there may have been a short expectancy of life, but while it lasted it was probably conducted at a delightfully idle pace and amongst a positive abundance of natural resources—far preferable to the material cravings and acquisitions of the present. But it doesn't avail one to look backwards.

The revolutionary land redistribution programme should have been preceded by a massive investment in education, training and supporting infrastructure. Such a programme would have required slow and careful implementation and a huge assistance package from the Western World. For political reasons Mugabe spurned that route. I fear damage to the land will be swift and irreparable. The general population will be the sufferers in the long term.

Friday 30th May 2003
Today visited Richard Wood at Atherstone and Cook. The building's lift was out of order again so had to climb the stairs to the seventh floor—147 steps. I made it with a short time off for a rest at the fourth!

The purpose of my visit was to sign the papers necessary to initiate court proceedings in order to establish why I should not be considered the rightful owner of Stockade; and also of course to get Mujuru evicted and for me to be given unhindered access to my property.

Richard Wood had prepared a lengthy document with a great number of annexures. I read it through and it all seemed thorough and pertinent to my affair. The 1st and 2nd. respondents were the Minister of Lands and the Commissioner of Police respectively.

RW said he was uncertain which of two routes to take; the one would be expensive, the other less expensive. I opted for the second! "With luck we may get the police to act without having to go further," was how RW put it.

A Commissioner of Oaths stamp was required to affirm my application to the court. In order to obtain this RW took me through the town centre to the offices of another legal firm. We noted queues of people waiting outside the banks and building society offices. There is a shortage of money in the country and when it is available it is rationed.

"What a patient, subservient people the Shona are," was RW's laconic remark. "People of other nations would raise hell!"

Before I left him, I asked RW how soon I could expect any action. It was possible, he said, that the sheriff could be called in to act in the following week. However, a week long work stay away is being called for next week so that may put things out.

8th June 2003

Sure enough the stay away called for by the M.D.C. did indeed take place and was effective as far as a general stoppage of work was concerned. However; an impressive turn out of army and police units manning road blocks was sufficient to deter any would-be peaceful protest marches. In addition, Mugabe's move was to order the arrest of M.D.C. leaders, raid opposition newspaper offices, and to beat up and thoroughly intimidate any M.D.C. supporters.

Because the supporters make up the great majority of the townships' population, this meant the security forces were given the freedom to bash one and all. As I have remarked before, given a gun and a uniform, there is nothing an ill-trained, uncouth man enjoys more than demonstrating his power on the defenceless.

Saturday 21st June 2003

For this nether side of the globe, today marks the winter solstice and, for latitude of 34 south and an altitude of about 4000ft., it is certainly cold. I suppose the temperatures are dropping at night to just above freezing but I am feeling frozen all the day and am dressed up as if it was an English winter. At night I have been getting up to don more clothing, refill a hot water bottle and to find an odd assortment of articles to supplement my blankets. Perhaps I have lived too many years in the sun—or more probably I am simply aging and the blood is thinning.

I am living in a rented flat on the top floor of a double-storey building. Tall trees surround the house in every direction so I look out of the windows into their branches, which is lovely. However they do cut out the rather weak sunshine, which could have given me a little warmth at this time of year.

Feeling the cold as I do, I cannot but recall the fine log fires I enjoyed in my farm homestead. I suppose Mujuru is having the benefit of this. He has even taken possession of my warm bedding; blankets, quilts and douvets and now has my electric fire as well. Now and then the thought of it makes me exclaim…sh--!

Shoosh! I won't spell it out here; but can you blame me?

Johannes has been talking to persons out that way. He has been told that it would be easy to get rid of Mujuru. It would be necessary for me to speak with a certain army officer named Charlie. Charlie has a part of Spa Farm. I think I remember him. He is the one who uses an army truck to commute to and fro and who, with others, once tried to drum me for a money contribution towards Heroes Day celebrations or something of the sort.

It seems that Major Charlie Whatever has as his wife an all-powerful Warvet—"THE BIGGEST". I take this description to mean, if not in size then in influence. She can arrange anything and has apparently assisted certain farmers in their disputes with undesirables, though who, how and where exactly Johannes was not clear.

You may have to pay some money," said Johannes. "But not too much," he added when I raised my eyebrows.

Well Johannes is an African. He may well know the ways of his fellow Africans, but in the doing will opt for the simplistic solution without an eye for the dangers. In a deal of this nature, probity would have nothing to do with it and I could well imagine finding myself exchanging the frying pan for the fire. Withal, I was sorry to dampen his enthusiasm. I had to explain that having initiated legal procedures, I could mess things up by making some sort of a deal with the Warvet leaders.

George has been on the farm again and ironically I received a message through one of the Nola factory workers, who still has connections with the farm. The message from George was that I must remove all my property from the farm because Johannes is stealing it. To sow the seed of suspicion is a ruse commonly used to disturb "The Boss". Naturally enough, it is usually a senior and trusted employee who is targeted for discredit. I learnt this one many years ago. However, it is a bit odd coming from George, who far from being an envious farm employee, is a brash opportunist given free rein by the State.

There has to be another reason and it is probably tied up in some way to the enmity George has with Mujuru. I have spoken with Johannes about the relationships these two men have with Tezha, who is effectively in charge of the Nyabira police. J considers that Tezha is more afraid of Mujuru than George. In other words, the political faction led by Elliot Manyika [Mujuru's patron] is more to be feared than the Warvet faction with whom George is seemingly aligned. This confirms my own opinion.

Feeling cold, frustrated, and generally fed up, I phoned Tezha to ask him if he couldn't assist me to get some of my belongings out of the house. I thought we could send Eliot, the Nola driver, with instructions to pick up Makosa and Rosemary from the compound and to load specified items. Obviously the party would need an escort.

I was a fool to have harboured such thoughts. Tezha said that I should remove all the household property. To do this I would have to make arrangements with "the present occupier". It was not for the police to do this. I complained that there was no fuel for transport and no place for me to store the furniture and remaining equipment.

"The police cannot do anything," says Tezha. "Why don't you go to Bindura and speak with them there?" Here we go again. Nothing changes. If it does it is for the worse.

"I haven't got enough petrol to get to Bindura and I am sick with the 'flu," I reply, developing a croak in my voice. "Anyway, I am in touch with Lands and will get back to you," I add putting down the receiver.

So this strange stalemate persists. So much has to be left unsaid. I cannot explain that nothing on God's earth would induce me to approach Mujuru to ask his permission to collect my property from my home, which he has forcefully and illegally occupied. To assert himself, he has threatened me and my innocent servants with violence, even death. He may be educated to some degree, but I look upon him not only as brutish and uncivilized, but positively permeated with evil. My judgment is made on his behaviour. My reaction is based on principals.

It is in the holding of principals, that to a large extent the African mind differs from the European. Many times over the past three years the advice given to me by government officials and policemen has been that I should acknowledge the new order and demonstrate my willingness to co-operate with it by meeting and talking with the Warvets and Party revolutionaries. The advice may have been well meaning but given from the African viewpoint. Our experiences in this field have been recorded. Some white farmers tried collaboration. In general a mockery was made of them and withal they were taken for an extremely expensive ride.

Saturday 28th June

Tomorrow I am moving into new premises. For the past 15 months I have had no place to call my own; just moving from pillar to post. This has been wearing. There were times when, should a house-sitting assignment be coming to a close, I became desperately worried because I didn't know where I would find the next roof over my head. Martin and Jean had always offered me a home but I knew they had little spare space. Also; I am an independent type and never wish to be an inconvenience. Now at last Martin and I [but mostly Martin] have managed to put the finance together in order to buy a cluster home and one not very far from here.

Because my own furniture remains trapped in the house on the farm, we agreed to buy some of the furniture from the outgoing owners together with their fridge and some bits and pieces. This was an unforeseen expense but, compelled by circumstances, one I could not avoid.

Until now, my clothing has been kept in and out of suitcases, my books and many of my provisions moved around in cardboard cartons. Some things were kept in odd places in Martin's house and I could never be sure what and where. The new house has three bedrooms and is generously fitted with cupboards so at last I shouldn't have to search for things. Nevertheless, because I am forced to purchase items, which I know I have in my home on the farm, Mujuru is roundly cursed every day of my life.

Monday 7th July

The forming of queues has become a part of life for Zimbabweans. Someone said it is a symptom of economic breakdown. Queues are formed for fuel, basic foodstuffs, even for money from the banks. The latter frequently run out of it. Generally speaking, Africans have accepted queuing as a part of daily life and they may be seen lined up on pavements in silent patience, which is really pathetic to watch.

In order to get transfer of the telephone in my new home, I joined a queue at the local P.T.C. office. It was taking the clerk seven minutes or so to deal with each customer and as I was number five in the line there was plenty of time to chat with my fellow queuers three of whom were white.

In these times in Zimbabwe, it seems inevitable that a friendly chat soon develops into swapping tales of woe. An attractive girl next in line to me was gripping a handbag and a bunch of telephone bills with one hand whilst managing a nine month old infant with the other. The girl's complexion was so fresh and clear that it took me by surprise when she said that she had been farming further down the valley from us. When given the surname, I recognized it at once.

There was an explanation for the rosy complexion. She was English. I gathered that she had met her husband at agricultural college in England and after graduating she had joined him on the family farm in Concession. In addition to providing a third generation for the farm, she clearly hoped to work alongside her man and put her agricultural training to practical use.

Like so many of the rest of us, Mugabe's Warvets and marauders drove the family from their farm. I learnt that she was living in an apartment in town whist her husband is seeking employment in Zambia.

Naturally we swapped experiences and I asked how their eviction occurred. The family challenged through the courts. They obtained three separate court orders: one permitting them to reap their crops, one to allow them to remove their farming equipment, and one to say they could carry on farming! All were ignored.

I spoke of my own case. It will be heard in court later this month. It is apparent that a favourable judgement will be purely academic. My lawyer, Richard Wood, has implied this and has encouraged me to go away on holiday. But at least it can be said; should there be any future redress, we went through the proper procedures.

All of us had become quite chummy in the queue and as each one left by turn, they were given a cheery farewell by the remainder, which considering the trials and tribulations we had been reciting, shows how people will put on a cheerful and resilient face in public.

When I left and entered the car park, an African gentleman who had been ahead of me in the queue, was waiting to speak with me. Hearing the baleful tales exchanged by two white farming people in the queue behind him must have distressed him. As a middle-class African he must have felt some inner compulsion to tell me that a brighter prospect lay ahead.

"I can tell you," he said to me, "that there is going to be a change. Just now there will be a U-turn. You will return to your farm. You see."

We chatted on for a bit; myself expressing the fear that the ruling elite have so much to account for that they will go to any lengths to stay in power. I didn't find out anything about the man. I would like to think that he was privy to some secret knowledge or at least representative of a huge African groundswell. However it may be, I appreciated his desire to communicate his feelings to me. There's a touch of common humanity there.

A letter has reached me from Johannes—delivered by hand in some mysterious way. The gist of it was that he has managed to remove most of his belongings, which were stored in my garage. This was not accomplished without heated exchanges with Mujuru.

"Talk Talk, Noise Noise", is how J describes it in his letter.

Johannes had two others with him and luckily Mujuru was alone so force of numbers counted. The only item he couldn't get away was the old hammer mill I have given him. That doesn't surprise me. It must weigh a tonne. However J complains that Mujuru had broken into his boxes and stolen a number of things. He is going to report this to the Nyabira police.

"If Assistant Tezha not take Action I do something. Thanks. Johannes. P.T.O."

I turned the page over and J continues with a somewhat cryptic message to me.

"Thomas Mujuru is lies to the big office he say he saw a letter in your office write bad words to Mugabe and other Big office saw be careful he is planning to come to the Boss yard with C.I.O. to catch you for questioned keep your paper careful please. I fell to phone you. No card for my phone this words I hear with one of the C.I.O. doing a mine at Tatagura. And this words Thomas Mujuru is planning with Manyika go for you to be in prison and lose your property he want to shear for free."

I think I have the understanding. Mujuru will have fed this to Johannes somehow knowing that it would be passed on to me. It has the typical hallmarks of Shona underhand intimidation. Unfortunately, I sense it worries my family more than it does me.

When evil presents itself to me, I have an instinctive need to expose it for what it is and to fight against it. I learnt that at kindergarten. But of course I wouldn't wish to bring burning coals down on others. Yes; in the white farming community there have been ugly stories to tell up and down the country.

I know. Notwithstanding, I get the impression that the cringers and collaborators have fared no better than the honourable. Besides; what of one's conscience?

I am adapting to town life and overcoming the rebelliousness I first felt upon being forced to jostle in a human throng after forty years of spacious quietude spent on the farm. If I am not exactly anchored in my new abode, I am content with the mooring.

This is a tidy little house, a corner one on the edge of the cluster of ten. There are roads on two sides of my plot, one of them a fairly busy suburban thoroughfare. All around is a high wall. The wall encloses a small garden. I have measured this. It is only 450 square metres—less than a tenth of an acre. It sounds awful doesn't it? Like a prison yard. People say how lucky I am; it is so pretty and quiet. I have learnt to look with a townsman's eyes and I think I know what they mean.

For the pretty garden I bless the previous owners, a Mr. and Mrs. King from Lancashire and returning thence after many years spent here. There is a narrow lawn around two sides; and in beds bordering this there is a prolific variety of trees, shrubs and perennial border plants. All are growing in healthy profusion and delightful confusion.

A banana [with a nice big bunch] grows alongside a palm, both emerging from a mass of under greenery. Another tall palm grows through a healthy Avocado surrounded by sword fern, arums, begonias, amaryllis, blue self-sown forget-me-nots, and a dozen other jolly plants whose names I forget. In pride of place, close to the house wall, are two fine cycads. They are flowering—if you can use that expression for a cycad. Imagine a cone from a pine tree so big that it would be a job to cradle it in your two arms.

Yes! And there are two fountains—one with a charming cherub, whose modest posture does not allow disclosure of sex but I think is a boy. Then there are two birdbaths too. What of the walls? Well of course they support every kind of creeper imaginable here—flowering varieties on the inside, vicious Mauritius thorn on the outside; they meet at the top all of a mix thereby increasing the height. I welcome the walls and the creepers; they guard this plot, securing it from prying eyes and thieving hands; my oasis is secret and confined within their perimeter.

It may be said that the northern suburbs of Harare city consist of hundreds of adjoining oases and mine may be considered just a tiny example. Fine trees abound in nearly all the larger gardens and on many sidewalks. Bird life has adapted strongly to this and bird and man live in happy congruence here. I never cease to be surprised. I am almost sure there was a yellow warbler in this garden yesterday; a bird not often seen in my farm garden.

I need to see things through a townsman's eyes. Whatever the future, I shall do my best whilst here for this garden. My first gesture has already been made; two loads of compost from the racing stables. I feel it has put us on friendly terms already.

Time has moved on. My case against the State was heard in court on Wednesday 16th.June. I did not attend; in fact I was unsure when it was to be heard and only found out the following Monday when I rang Richard Wood. I have since obtained copies of the Court Order.

Viewed from almost any aspect, I believe the Order to be very important. It would be well to copy out the significant parts here and now.

THE HIGH COURT OF ZIMBABWE

In the matter between Stockade Farm [Pvt] Ltd. Applicant
and
Minister of Lands, Agriculture etc. 1st Respondent
The Commissioner of Police 2nd Respondent

Wednesday 16th July 2003
Before the Hon. Mr Justice Kamocha
Ms Takawadiyi for the applicant. Respondents in default.
Whereupon after reading filed documents and hearing council

IT IS ORDERED:
1. That the preliminary notice issued by the 1st.Respondent in terms of section 5 of the Land Acquisition Act in respect of the property STOCKADE OF MADZUGETU held by the Applicant under Deed of transfer 104\93 be and is to be of no force or effect.
2. That the Acquisition order issued by the 1st Respondent in terms of section 8 of the said Act on 14th March 2001 in respect of the said property be and is hereby set aside.
3. That the 2nd.Respondent shall ensure that the Applicant and its directors and its employees and its property are given such protection as is reasonably required against unlawful assaults, kidnapping, unlawful occupation, seizure, vandalism, robbery or theft and that reasonable complaints made by the Applicant through its directors are properly investigated and dealt with in accordance with normal police procedure.
4. That there be no order as to costs.

The status of the farm is now clear. Government has never legally acquired the property and Stockade Farm [Pvt] Ltd. remains the legal owner. In effect, that's me.

Furthermore, the order demands protection for me from the likes of Thomas Mujuru. He has committed ALL the offences specified in the 3rd paragraph of the Court Order and we can prove that.

Having a clear cut court order is one thing. To anticipate how events will unravel in the present state of anarchy is quite another.

The country has been ruined. Mugabe and his fat cat "comrades" are entirely responsible. It is hard to find adequate words with which to label these outrageous persons. I find myself turning to Shakespeare for suitable epithets: villains, knaves, rogues, scoundrels. Shout it from the rooftops! Nobody dare.

Front pages in the newspapers seem to indicate that much diplomatic manoeuvring is taking place. The aim is to get Zimbabwe back on track while at the same time allowing the aforementioned villains, knaves, rogues and scoundrels to escape retribution. On the African continent at least, the protocol is for tyrants to enjoy comfortable retirement. "Back on track" means among other things a return to the rule of law. One can see that it will be a tortuous procedure.

I mention these broad issues because they may have a ripple effect further down the scale. For instance, a court order which would have been ignored by the executive last month may possibly be obeyed next month. We shall see.

Away from the newspaper columns and down on the farms the reports are far from reassuring. In fact the Warvets and the youthful Party supporters are more active than ever on those farms which continued operating.

Teviotdale Farm is further down the valley from Stockade. Johannes is living there with his wife's relative. He tells me that farm work has been stopped because of disruptions. In this case the farm is being run by an African who lives in the main homestead. However, I think he may be backed by Alec Morris-Eyton. J was unclear about this.

A long way back in these pages I wrote an account of the beating given to the Bayley's farm foreman and how Tommy Bayley had to pick him up and take him to hospital. Later, there was the killing of Isiah's brother. The instigator of these beatings was a crippled Warvet, Chengerai by name. Now, two years later, it is this same Chengerai who is making trouble at Teviotdale and demanding the homestead for himself. Proof again that a violent supporter of Mugabe is immune from prosecution. Proof too that one man with a few accomplices set on the loose by the Party can cause havoc.

Articles, supported by distressing pictures, have recently appeared in the press telling of the continuing slaughter of wildlife on farms and ranches. The savagery of the ZANU PF perpetrators receives no rebuke from authority.

These and stories like them do not suggest that the police will give Mujuru a rough ride and he is certain to call up support from bigwigs within the Party—a fellowship of brigands posing as politicians.

Having obtained myself a home where I could park my personal trappings, it had been my intention to turn the key on it and take off on a holiday leaving this jungle behind me for a while. For various reasons I delayed; time slipped by. I was not too fussed at the thought of the impending court hearing. The police wouldn't take any account of it anyway. Well, I have the court order in front of me and now I am not so sure.

The Oracle has spoken and, on the face of it, clearly enough. Withal and true to form, it has left me with a basket of imponderables.

The priority fixed in my mind was to remove my property from the house and store it wherever I could. At present I had no control over it whatever. If left, Mujuru or other robbers would take everything. Better get it all off and sell what I couldn't utilize. One might term it a defeatist attitude.

It was rather in this frame of mind that I called at the Marlborough police station to speak with Inspector Mashamba. His appointment as O-I-C Marlborough is comparatively recent. I was pleased to find him understanding and helpful. When I explained my mission and request for police escort to Stockade, he understood my desire to operate the exercise from Marlborough rather than from Nyabira. He agreed to contact Tezha at Nyabira on the matter.

The next day, Friday, I followed up with a letter to him and attached a copy of the Court Order and my list of possessions which I wished to remove. The Inspector noted that the order didn't specifically say that I could take the property away. I pointed out that the order said a great deal more than that. It clearly implied that the whole property including the movables belonged to me and, that being the case; I could do whatever I wished. The point was that I should not be obstructed from doing so. Mashamba agreed. A transport vehicle was arranged for Tuesday morning the 29th July. My request was for the escort to travel simultaneously. The inspector took telephone numbers and said he would phone me or Martin on Monday.

In my letter I purposefully avoided requesting Mujuru's eviction. How they dealt with him would be up to them. They had the Court Order before them and could read what it implied well enough. I have no doubt that neither Mashamba nor Tezha will act on Mujuru without getting the go-ahead from higher authority. In the meantime let me at least get my stuff off.

On leaving the police station I called upon a dear old friend, a bright little lady of ninety. She lives quite close-by. By chance, her son Dick was there. Dick is\was a farmer, a committee man, he knows just about everybody of importance in Zimbabwe black or white. We were soon speaking of my court hearing and of moving my property from the farm.

"The worst thing you can do," says Dick, "is to take your things off the farm. When a land committee, from whatever authority, comes to look at your farm, they will say you have abandoned it. They will allocate it to someone else. You must leave a presence even if it is just a toehold. Let it be seen that you have the intention of returning [even if you haven't!]."

Dick feels that everything is pointing to a change coming soon, a return to law and order and with it an inflow of development money. When that time arrives the farm will be very valuable. In the meantime there is a lot of hoodwinking going on; people are jostling for position.

He likened it to a poker game. Always keep a few chips on the table. "Once you've thrown them in you've lost. And with that Court Order you've been dealt an ace. How are you going to use it? For instance, have you made it plain that you want Mujuru evicted? The police would welcome it if you do nothing. Later they will be able to say you never requested it."

I told Dick that Moyana had his cattle on Stockade—they had been on for months. "Send him a whacking great bill," says Dick. "He's just another one playing at the table. He will never contest it in court."

Already people have suggested that I sell the farm now. They say there are plenty of wealthy Africans who would buy it—with U.S. dollars too. They add that Mujuru would be out on his ear in five minutes. When it's African on African they are probably right. However, I would never be precipitate in the matter of selling.

Never, never, do I forget the forest and the wild inmates. I will not betray them. If I keep a toehold, it will be for their sake. Maintaining a presence is sure to have its difficulties and money is so tight. I will have to think of ways and means.

All these things occupy my mind ceaselessly. The broad political aspect taken together with my particular situation indicate that a culmination point is about to be reached.

I have been writing this on Sunday afternoon 27th July. The next two days could be very exacting ones—even exciting perhaps. And dangerous?

Thursday 31st July 2003

On Sunday evening and Monday morning I was preoccupied with eve of battle plans. The logistics required co-ordination of forces; the hired transport to be met and directed [the last time we attempted such an exercise the transport truck took a wrong road and spent hours in search of the farm]; Johannes and helpers to rendezvous at the homestead; the police escort to be lifted and deployed into the combat zone before the other units in order to deal with Mujuru should he be present.

"The best laid schemes o'mice an'men gang aft a-gley."

Surely I must have brains no better than those of a mouse to have imagined that the police would go along with my ideas.

On Monday morning at 9.30, I called in to Marlborough to speak with

Insp. Mashamba. At that time he had made no contact with Z.R.P. Nyabira or any other persons concerning our talk of last Friday. I explained to him that although my principal concern was to remove my property, I felt that, in view of the court order, the eviction of Mujuru could hardly be divorced from this.

Inspector Mashamba had had time for reflection since Friday and I sensed that he was uneasy with the role he had volunteered to play. He said that because Stockade was Nyabira's responsibility and it would be their job to follow the case through, he felt uncomfortable about becoming involved in any way. Questions might be asked and there might even be suspicions that he was receiving a back-hander.

In the pertaining circumstances I was sensitive to his point of view. I expressed my appreciation for his spontaneous reaction to help, but could see his difficulties. I promised to take the issue to Tezha at Nyabira and that in so doing I would make no reference to my request to Marlborough. Mashamba handed back the court order which I had left with him.

My next job was to get hold of Tezha—not always easy. The duty constable at the station gave me the familiar answer: "He's not around." An hour or so later I got him on his cell phone.

"Hello, Tezha, I need to speak with you about removing my possessions from the house. I received a message from you asking me to arrange this." [True; some weeks ago.]

"Yes, Mr. Wiles, you can speak with Inspector Majoni."

"Good Heavens! Is he back? I thought he was in Kosova or somewhere." [My mind works grindingly these days especially with names. It was confusing Majoni with Sengwe.] "Is he there now?"

"Yes, you can see him."

I had the image of Sengwe in my mind and he was the last person in the world I wished to meet on this issue before me. It was Sengwe who had given me four days to pack and quit the farm way back last November; it was an order which I successfully resisted, but not without accompanying stress. My parting words to Martin as I left for Nyabira were: "I am going straight into the lion's jaws!"

Perhaps the brain automatically extracts and presents past unpleasant images as a warning—a danger signal: BEWARE! It had the programming wrong this time. On the drive out to Nyabira the old brain sorted it out. Yes, I had met Majoni. Sengwe is Sengwe and Majoni is Majoni. "What's in a name?" Plenty, if you mix up the associated images.

Driving into the open precinct of the police station and parking the Sunny between the familiar upturned motor tyres, I took notice of the man standing on the patch of grass in front of the offices. Yes, I recognized him now. "Surely THAT'S Majoni": not tall, but fairly thickset, a rounded face with a pleasing expression noticeable even from a distance. He was hatless and was wearing a woollen police jersey. No mistake: the two pips of the inspector's insignia and the combatant's flag on the left shoulder.

I went forward confidently. "Hello, Inspector. How are you? It's been such a long time I thought you were gone forever."

We chatted and Majoni explained that he had been away for two months on some sort of training course. There had been a lot of physical training and he proudly declared that he had lost ten kilograms. I replied that I couldn't afford to lose one kilogram let alone ten.

I let him know of my mission and followed him to his office where he took his seat. Selecting a chair from those lined against the wall, I brought it up to the desk and sat opposite to him. From the folder in my case I extracted the court order and handed it across to him without comment.

Majoni read through it carefully. Finally he commented that it was paragraph 3 which applied to him—or at least the police. He was concerned that the order was not stamped and not original. I explained that the final documents were still with the High Court waiting official stamping, but would eventually be made available to those concerned. Meanwhile, I had asked my lawyers for copies of which this was one. Because I had lost control over my property, I was now keen to remove it into safety. I felt that this order would enable the police to assist me.

Inspector Majoni revealed that Stockade had been one of the first problems he had been called upon to attend to following his return to the station about two weeks earlier. He had in fact visited Mujuru and been into my house.

"He is using your things; your refrigerator and your stove," Majoni informed me.

"Then you will appreciate my reason for removing them as soon as possible," I said.

The inspector went on to say that Mujuru showed him a letter purporting to come from Elliot Manyika and stating that the farm would be given to him, Mujuru. I gathered that another document was produced as well. However, Majoni told me that the wording of the letters was vague and headed "To whom it may concern", using such wording as "allocations are under review." Majoni had given Mujuru one week to bring him proper confirmation.

"He hasn't come back to me, but he may come in on Thursday".

My own experiences compel me to believe that Mujuru will have forged such letters or concocted them with fellow conspirators. I didn't say this to Majoni. Regardless of any such claims, spurious or not, I am assured that the only LEGAL authority to acquire and distribute land is the Minister of Lands.

Majoni continued: "Mujuru had plenty to say about Stockade. He says you used to have a factory here and it was used to turn out MDC hats and Tee-shirts."

I raised my eyes to the ceiling. Simukayi and his fellow Warvets tried to foist this absurd charge on us three years ago. They knew full well it was baseless. It was used as an excuse to raid and search our premises, terrorize the workers and threaten us with close down. They hoped for, but didn't get, protection money. Now, for his own evil ends, this Mujuru is keeping the old charge smouldering. The iniquity of these...of these...what can I call them? these?...Really! No word is bad enough. Anyway, their iniquity knows no depths.

I had no inclination to be drawn into history with Majoni. My interjection was brief: "He's a liar!"

Majoni told me that he would have to be careful how he handled Mujuru. "He seems to have influential friends, cabinet ministers, perhaps even the President." A senior Assistant Commissioner [I cannot remember his specific position] had spoken of Stockade to Majoni recently and promised to follow up with more information when it came available. To date he had not done so.

Somewhere along the line, Majoni explained, he had seen a stack of correspondence all in connection with Stockade: "Two big piles; much of it from various ministries such as The Ministry of Environment." [So perhaps, I thought, Environment had done their best.]

Next, Majoni asked me if I had any cattle. I knew what he was getting at and told him of Moyana putting cattle on the farm. To this Majoni said he thought he would have to consult Bindura. He did not say why, but if he does it'll be a poor outlook. No good comes out of that quarter.

The purpose of my visit was to get police co-operation in removing my property from my home. To this end I had attached a list of the larger items. I explained that it would take considerable time to box and pack the smaller things and we must be allowed to work without disturbance.

It goes without saying that the police had no transport of their own to assist in the exercise. The inspector made this clear from the beginning. He even suggested that Mujuru would claim to have no vehicle and could not leave my house. What then?

Whilst we had been talking, Majoni had tried unsuccessfully to raise Mujuru on his cell phone. He said it was necessary for all three of us to meet at the Stockade house. I believe he was trying to raise Mujuru in order to arrange for this.

Policemen are an insensitive lot. I had to explain to him that in no way would I agree to meet Mujuru.

"I am an old man," I said. "You know Mujuru is rude, loud and aggressive. I tell you that even the thought of the man gives me palpitations." Here I held my hands across my chest. "To be abused and shouted at by this man could be quite sufficient to kill me."

"The problem is he has brought some of his own belongings into the house," the inspector said.

"There can't be all that much. Let him put them apart. He has a man there. As for my property, should I find anything missing I shall inform you; but on no account will I stand to be confronted by Mujuru shouting in my face and heaping insults on me."

I explained further that I was very keen not to delay and that a removal transport was on standby. Majoni pointed out that he was very tied up with meetings and court cases in Chinhoyi for the remainder of the week. However perhaps he could get his deputy Tezha to see what could be arranged. I should phone them tomorrow, Tuesday.

Upon leaving Inspector Majoni, I reiterated that whatever his own plans, I myself would be following up on the court order. In so doing, I will expect protection and assistance from the police. My first priority was to remove my property to safety. In the longer term, my plan would include returning to the farm and re-establishing the forest with Forestry Commission and National Parks.

On the following morning I was to phone the Nyabira police station. I waited a while to allow them time to make their own assessments as to how to proceed. I rang at about 10 o'clock.

"Is that Z.R.P. Nyabira?"

"Yes it is," said a voice.

"Could I please speak with Inspector Majoni if he is in?" There was a brief silence. "Or failing him, then Assistant Inspector Tezha?"

"It is him speaking."

"Good gracious Tezha, you didn't say. Good morning."

Tezha acts strangely sometimes; I can't think why. I am certain he would have recognized my voice from the start. He has done so at other times. Tezha remains silent, waiting to hear what I have to say.

"I was speaking with your Inspector Majoni yesterday," I say, in order to get the ball rolling, "He said I should phone you this morning to see what plans you might have formulated in order to get my property off the farm. I had a message from yourself some weeks ago, if you remember, asking me to do just that. Well now I am in a position to do so."

In truth I had had more than one message from Tezha over the past weeks requiring me to remove my things. However, each one had added the rider that he could provide no support without the authority of the Ministry of

Lands or simply "Bindura". Well, now I had been given authority but from neither of the former.

Tezha was gracious enough to say: "You did right to bring us an authority," but then he introduced a stumbling block. "This order, which you have given us, specifies the 2nd Respondent. You should have taken it to him."

"The 2nd Respondent is the Police Commissioner," I say. "I am not a messenger."

"Well, the messenger of court should do so. The order is not for us but for the 2nd Respondent and then the Commissioner will receive it. After that, we shall have to wait for orders from our commanders."

Tezha was making rather heavy-weather over his explanation and I found myself helping him out with it. Finally I summarized for him.

"Okay: the procedure is for the Commissioner to be given the Court Order; he passes it on to his immediate subordinates; they in turn inform you. Meantime you can take no action with regard to Mujuru or the moving of my property. Is that the position?"

"Yes," from Tezha.

"Then obviously there is nothing for me to do until I hear from you," I say in the familiar tone of resignation at being frustrated yet again.

That evening I wrote to Inspector Majoni summarizing the position as I saw it. Next morning I sent it by registered post.

On Thursday and Friday I spent some time seeking suggestions and advice on how best to proceed. I am concerned that the big Chef, Moyana, should be brought to account, if not criminally then financially. His cattle have been fattening on my best grass over four months. He has been using the dip, the fencing, the water troughs and the water supply. His workers and their families have been housed in my buildings; undoubtedly they will have been using my wood for fuel.

I spoke with Weynand Hart at the Justice for Agriculture [JAG] office. He says Moyana is sure to play innocent and hide behind an agreement with Mujuru. Nonetheless, the court order is concrete proof of illegality. Weynand says I must operate through a lawyer. Legal technicalities apart, it is DANGEROUS to deal with any of these people directly. Crude threats and violence are their natural weapons. One must always keep a screen between you and them.

Last thing on Friday I tracked down a copy of The Herald. [The Herald newspaper is no more than the government's propaganda sheet.] On Fridays they publish the latest farm acquisition notices. There were thirty or so. Stockade wasn't on the list.

Ironically, front page Herald headlines in massive type read: "Mugabe Says One Farmer One Farm." We've heard that one before. He's the biggest liar of the lot. But still; one must hand it to Mugabe. He has learnt his business thoroughly. I think it was Goebbles who said that if one tells a lie often enough people will come to believe it.

Coarse, uncultured persons heap iniquities on my head. On Saturday I determined to rid them from my mind and did so by seeping myself in an evening of Mozart: two piano concertos, Nos.20 and 27, the clarinet concerto and some exerts from Magic Flute—unblemished joy. I turned into bed quite late and fell asleep at once.

Too often these days I awaken after an hour or so, doing battle with the horrid spectres that haunt me. To cast them off requires getting out of bed, seeking my glasses, checking the time on my watch, shuffling along to the kitchen, preparing myself a cup of tea, returning to the bedroom with same, swallowing a couple of aspirins, finding my place in my current book and reading a further chapter before turning off the lamp. The beasts of the night usually evaporate with this procedure.

I awoke on this Sunday morning to the singing voice of a Kurrichane thrush. It was so loud and clear that the bird must have chosen the top of one of the garden trees as his rostrum. Hearing him reminded me that it had been my intention to fly over to my sister Jane in early June. One of the delights of visiting Jane is her lovely Suffolk garden. Three years ago, a song thrush would sing outside my bedroom window. The notes of the song thrush are rich and mellow. In comparison this Kurrichane is something of an amateur; he should have gone for voice training. Nevertheless, he has the gift of the genus and does passably well with phrasing and variations. I enjoyed his effort to please some unseen lady.

On Sunday I prepared a letter to my lawyer, Richard Wood. The advice, which I had been receiving from others, urged me to keep up the action. Charge! Keep the enemy on the defensive. The easiest way for me will be to insert the letter and attachments; boring, but I tell myself this is a diary of serious record.

Sorry. When assembling my papers I find I cannot lay my hands on the letter to Atherstone and Cook. Briefly I instructed them to proceed with the following action:

1. To secure an eviction order on Thomas Mujuru.
2. To initiate charges against Mujuru for the underwritten offences:
    - Unlawful assault
    - Unlawful occupation
    - Seizure
    - Vandalism
    - Robbery
    - Theft
    - Kidnapping
3. To order the police to protect me and to assist me to remove my property from the farm.

4. Should the police fail to comply, then to charge them for contempt of court.
   5. To send a demand to Mr.K.Moyana, ex Reserve Bank Governor, for payment in respect of unlawful grazing of cattle, use of farm facilities, and damages. An amount was calculated and quoted after appropriate consultation.

I do not know the legal distinction between robbery and theft but I guess I could pin both on Mujuru.

Alone at the desk, the imagination can conjure up a brave crusading spirit. Incensed by outrageous dealings, I allowed myself to be carried away into a fanciful wonderland—a land of honesty and stern justice. I tilt at windmills.

On Monday morning, Martin offers to drive me into the city. On the way he tells me that over the weekend he met a farmer who is in a similar position to mine. An African, claiming the farm had been given to him, moved into the farmer's homestead; furniture and possessions being still in the house. The police told the farmer that he should make his own arrangements with the new occupier to retrieve his belongings.

Martin's acquaintance must have a phlegmatic temperament quite beyond the norm. He has visited his farm on several occasions and spoken with the usurper of his home in order to persuade the latter to release the personal belongings. In the beginning the farmer had to face the familiar racial gibes, but thereafter what might almost be called a rapport developed. The farmer was invited into the house, to sit on his own chairs and to take tea from his own cups. All this has got him absolutely nowhere, the friend told Martin. He cannot get anything out.

This story is not exactly encouraging for me when I leave Martin double-parked and go up in the lift to the Atherstone and Cook offices with my challenging letter. The secretary takes my letter and asks me to wait. Richard Wood is in his office so he calls me in. He has been reading my letter and he wears a long face.

He asks me questions and I fill him in on my contacts with the Nyabira police in greater detail. "What sort of a person is this Majoni?" Richard asks me. "He seems alright," I tell him. "He is an ex-combatant but he treated me in a civil and friendly manner. I think Majoni's concern is not to fall foul of higher authority."

Richard's worry concerns my request to get Mujuru evicted. It seems that I have been under a misapprehension concerning this. My understanding of the Court Order was, I thought, quite straightforward.

To paraphrase: the police shall ensure that I, my employees and my property are given such protection as is reasonably required against unlawful occupation, seizure, vandalism, robbery or theft, kidnapping and unlawful assaults.

As I indicated earlier, the police could prosecute Mujuru on all these counts. In fact the court was guided to this wording by submissions given it by my lawyers and not contested by the Respondents. For a start: is he or isn't he guilty of unlawful occupation?

When I first read the order, my first question to Richard was:

"What happens if the police take no action?"

"Well, then we charge them for contempt of court," he had replied.

As usual, nothing is as it seems. Richard now tells me that we would have to apply to the court specifically for an eviction order against Mujuru. This would take time and Richard is worried about the expense to me. "Like everything else," he says, "our charges are going up."

He quotes a farmer in Marondera who has tasked the lawyers to obtain eviction orders on thirty-three different individuals.

"Imagine the cost involved? It will be astronomical," he says. "The man has lots of money and can afford it," he continues, "but I know you can't."

How right! I was grateful for Richard's concern for me on that score. However, I can see that I am beginning to lose ground. I sigh audibly. I must confine myself to lesser goals

We discuss the practicality of removing my possessions. Of course I have covered this ground before. I restate the problems.

"Such an exercise must be undertaken quickly. Mujuru now knows about the order. If he thinks he could be evicted, he will start pilfering my belongings as fast as he can."

"Of course he will," says Richard in agreement.

"Secondly; the Nyabira police, as I now understand their position, will not assist me in this exercise any more than in evicting Mujuru, until they are given the directive from their senior officers."

Thirdly; under no circumstances will I have personal confrontation with Mujuru."

Richard lifts his eyes to me. I repeat to him what I told Majoni.

"I am an old man. The very thought of this monster gives me palpitations and to be face to face with him and to endure shouted abuse, lies and insults could be enough to kill me." [I am inclined to dramatize this line for effect, but there is some truth in it which I have no wish to test.]

"Couldn't you take Marty with you?" suggests Richard, not for the first time. Richard may be termed elderly—like me. I think he views tall, strong men, thirty years his junior as he would legendary Greek heroes. Personally I am all in favour of slaying dragons and slicing the heads off Hydras and Gorgons. Undoubtedly the ancient world was a better place freed of such monsters. Times have changed and with them methods.

"I have discussed this many times with Martin," I tell Richard. "Martin has already had a confrontation with Mujuru himself and before that with a score of Warvets. One cannot communicate with them. To our understanding they are not normal human beings. It is not that Martin is afraid to go to the farm; he knows that it would be a complete waste of time and end in yet further aggravation for me. I agree with him." I then added, "I think the family may feel that it would be easier to accept the loss of the farm; to write everything off as if to natural disaster."

Richard took up this clue. "As things are you could never go back. What value do you place on the things you have at the house?" Was he prepared to follow this train of thought and abandon attempts at recovery?

"It must amount to several millions. The glass for the new house must be worth 2 million and equipment and fittings another million and so on. Yes; I could usefully sell many belongings to keep myself going. Then there are personal things, books and records I would like to bring out."

I briefly mentioned Moyana and the fattening of his cattle at my expense, but Richard didn't respond. Perhaps he had already seen that any chance of redress was slim. I didn't press him. He seemed to be at a loss as to how best to proceed without committing me to great expense. At this stage I would like him to act on my behalf with the policemen at Nyabira. What is their position and have they received instructions? If they've a mind, they can too easily fob me off. They might be more forthcoming with a lawyer.

There was no more to say and Martin would still be waiting for me in his car.

"Well," said Richard, waving a paper, "this court order did achieve what we set out to do. That was to establish that the farm does belong to you."

AND Atherstone and Cook's legal fees have yet to be paid, my morale has taken a plunge from promise to despair, I stand to lose my private, personal possessions and a bestial creature desecrates my home and vandalises my land… but it has been established that the farm does belong to me. A Pyrrhic victory indeed. [Try spelling that word first time.]

Makosa, our faithful family cook for many years, and Rosemary his daughter have appeared in these pages. Makosa has sired fourteen children from two wives. His son, Samson, shares tenth and eleventh position with Rosemary—they are twins, now 18 years of age. Following upon the closure of the farm and my enforced departure from home, Martin found work for two of Makosa's sons, Norman and Samson, both of whom have proved loyal throughout these troubled years. Norman has been given a job in the relocated factory and Samson works at Martin's and Jean's home as a gardener-cum-groundsman. This arrangement, apart from giving the two young men employment, allows us to maintain communication with Makosa who still lives with his wife and the younger children in their house in the Stockade farm village. The stress of recent events has had a marked effect on Makosa and the old man has had what I can only describe as a mental breakdown which in turn has affected his physical movements. He has become unsteady and uncoordinated.

In addition to Makosa, several other old men still live in the farm village. They are mostly single and have nowhere else to go. Samson visited his parents on the farm at the weekend. On his return he told me that one of these old farm workers, Dishon, had died the previous Friday.

Dishon landed up on Stockade about 11 or 12 years ago like a piece of driftwood. I found him sitting on the side of the road not far from our entrance gate. He made a sad spectacle, weak and emaciated as he was. I asked him some questions; where he was going, where he had come from, was he going to relatives, and so on. He answered me in a thin, old man's voice.

No, he had no relatives. He had been walking the farming districts looking for work but had found none. It had been a year of drought and the farms had little call for casual workers. One look told me that he would be incapable of doing any farm work anyway. I directed him down the road to the homestead and preceded him to the house at my own brisk pace.

I called Beth and told her of my finding a worn and frail bundle of humanity on the road and that it was following behind me. I turned and, sure enough, we saw Dishon plodding round the corner to the gate.

Beth quickly decided that Dishon was suffering from starvation, and exhaustion. She gave him food and drink and arranged for a place where he could rest. If he wished, he could return in the morning, and so that he could earn some money before continuing on his way, she said she would give him a little light work in the garden for a few days until he regained strength.

For an African, Dishon had rather pointed, elf-like features, his eyes, pale with age, slightly slanted. He wore a battered hat that never left his head. His speech was soft and slow. If asked a question or given an instruction, it always took him several seconds to register and sort it in his mind before he could reply. His slow plodding walk never changed whatever the emergency.

In the event, Dishon continued doing a little light garden work for the next ten years. His output was painfully little but it would have been impossible to turn him out on the road. Beth's kindness saved him from sinking towards death and in the event he outlived her by many years. I had kept him on in the garden when all else was collapsing around me, but of course that came to an end when Mujuru took over my house. Mujuru immediately kicked him out along with Makosa and Rosemary.

Dishon lived alone in a hut in the compound. I suspect he caught the winter 'flu which turned to pneumonia. He was not strong and it would have taken him quickly. I was concerned lest he should have been short of food.

"Did he still have money from the gratuity we had given him?" I asked Samson. "Yes, there was $20 000 in his pockets," was the reply.

Fellow Malawians dug his grave and buried him in the farm burial ground of which mention has been made before. Apparently another old Malawi man, Daimon, took the money. At least Dishon will be beyond caring. He drifted into our space, found a safe if lonely shelter and has now drifted out of mind to all.

August 2003

I fear that yet another old man is approaching the end—Makosa. I have always said that Makosa should have been born fifty years earlier. He was a devotee of the white man. Loyalty towards the mzungu he served and a desire to please each and every white person who came to his boss's home was his raison d'etre. He loved to be appreciated and in turn he was appreciated most warmly. Our visitors always exchanged a friendly word with him. Makosa was meant to live in Rhodesia never Zimbabwe.

Makosa was a super farmhouse cook and a great worker in every way, tackling jobs with gusto. To my surprise, I discovered that Makosa was adept at flower arrangement. Beth had always cut and done the garden flowers for the house herself. When she died, Makosa, with touching consideration and of his own accord, continued the routine and regularly placed a small vase beside her photograph.

Makosa had a fault. This was to beat his wife from time to time. Some of his previous employers found this too much and it was the result of such a circumstance that he came to us from good friends and neighbours at Spa Farm. In all other respects they had nothing but praise for him. [It was probably Colleen Millar who encouraged him in flower arrangement.] We experienced one or two noisy and stressful incidents involving his marital life but in time these scenes came to an end.

I honestly believe that the terrible events of the past three years turned his mind. Latterly he lost flesh and looked positively cadaverous. He began showing signs of mental confusion and a lack of co-ordination; the invasion of my house by Mujuru, who ordered him to get out and to leave the farm, was the last straw. I persuaded the police to intervene and the result was that Makosa and his family have been allowed to remain in their house in the farm compound. It is shelter for the body, but not for the mind. The life given in honest service is shattered for ever.

Winet and Rosemary, Makosa's wife and daughter, pitched up at Martin's house in order to tell me that Makosa was very sick and couldn't walk. They asked for money to take him to Concession hospital. They had greater hope of obtaining help and treatment at the rural hospital at Concession than in any of the Harare government hospitals, which now have a terrible reputation amongst the poorer Africans. I gave the women money and they set off for home.

Two days later they were back again. They had taken Makosa to the hospital, but to do so they had been obliged to spend all the money on getting a lift for him and themselves in a truck belonging to some church body and then it took them only part way. They finished up pushing Makosa in a borrowed wheelbarrow. At Concession hospital they were told there was no treatment they could give Makosa. He was given some aspirins and the women were told to take him away. He couldn't walk, there was no ambulance, no food, and they had no more money.

There was no way I could go to Concession myself, so I gave Winet more money—hopefully enough this time. I learnt that they succeeded in getting Makosa home. With the near complete breakdown in the health services it would be pointless to try to get attention or treatment for Makosa elsewhere so I told them they must just do the best they could for him at home.

When it became clear that all operations on the farm would have to be abandoned and that it would be impossible for me to return to live in my house safely, Makosa and the Africans who were still working for me were signed off and given a final gratuity. The amount was difficult to find and of course I no longer have an income. With inflation at 500%, I know their money is devaluing madly. It makes a wretched outlook.

For Makosa and a few others, who have not found work, I have arranged for monthly food packs from an organization to assist destitute farm workers run by the Rev. Tim Nield. This man is something else—one of few true Christians left in the local Anglican priesthood it would seem.

Sunday 14th September 2003

The last six weeks have been hectic ones for me. Good resolutions to keep up the diary were soon abandoned and the more I fell behind the less inclined I became to pick up the threads. For any reader of these lines it is perhaps just as well, because much of what I have been going through has been little more than variations on a familiar theme, which by this time must be coming a bit tedious. This being the case, I have refrained from including a sheaf of letters addressed to the police in the person of Inspector Majoni. They are on file elsewhere.

After a copy of the court order had come to my hand and I was demanding [politely] to be given police protection in order to recover my property on the farm, it may be remembered that I felt Majoni and Tezha were trying to block me on technical grounds. It was claimed that the order was addressed to The Commissioner only and they had to await his instructions passed through appropriate channels.

On 30th July, I went to Nyabira to deliver my letter of that date to the police. I have to say that it was Inspector Majoni himself who suggested that I enquire at the Legal Section at Police H.Q., 7th Street and ask them if they had received the order. He could have done that himself. Perhaps he thought I wouldn't bother. Who knows?

Anyway, I did go to Police H.Q. the very next day and there I was directed to Room 61 Legal Section. I was impressed. I didn't believe such an office could exist in the spare, spartan surroundings of a police building. It had the old-fashioned eloquence of a lawyer's office. It wouldn't surprise me to learn that Room 61 has remained basically unchanged for the past fifty years or so, dating back to the colonial days of the B.S.A.P.

The office was manned by a plump, ironed and polished police sergeant. There were two men in mufti also, who I took to be the legal boffins. One of these looked up and across at me. He may have assessed me to be of great age and prone to falling if kept standing, because he hurriedly directed me to a seat. From there I explained my business and produced my copy of the court order.

The tall senior man read it through. He talked briefly with his colleague. I gathered that this order had not yet come to their office, but it seemed that this was of no consequence.

The tall man came across to me with the order in his hand.

"We have no quarrel with this order," he said. "Section 3 is the only section that affects us and that involves straightforward police procedure."

I brought up the wording of the order. "The second respondent is identified as The Commissioner of Police. What does that mean in practice?"

"The word Commissioner means the Z.R.P. Every member of the police force is bound by the order."

The tall man must have thought for a bit, because of his own accord he went on to say: "If you want to evict this guy you must get your lawyer to apply for an eviction order."

In retrospect this seems odd, because I don't recall mentioning Mujuru and my particular problem. However, he is an experienced man and perhaps he was just reading between the lines. In these times my situation is a commonplace.

I thanked the company for their kind help and prepared to leave. At this one of them said: "There should be no need for you to come here yourself you know. Your lawyer knows all this perfectly well. Make him work for his money!"

I could have parried, "And your police inspectors seem to be ignorant of the law," but I didn't.

On the strength of this information, I quickly contacted Majoni again and this time I finalized arrangements to pick him up and go with him to Stockade on Friday 8th August. Transport and workers also had to be organized and co-ordinated.

I don't mind admitting, I dreaded the thought of coming face to face with Mujuru. I steeled myself for the ordeal and was determined not to allow myself to be provoked.

My transport planning knitted our units together on time. This was something of a miracle. When we arrived Mujuru was taken by surprise, which was probably a good thing. However he soon took the initiative. He refused to accept the court order proffered by the inspector because it was not signed and stamped. The second page of the document was missing. I had to take the inspector back to Nyabira to get it. This lost time. It told me too that the inspector was going to take an accommodating stance in this business. However, I had to let him make the running.

This was the first time I had been able to observe and study Mujuru coolly. Physically he is tall, heavy and bloated with good feeding. To counterbalance a great paunch, his stance is to lean slightly back and he strides widely rather than walks. He is one of those African types who have short, thick necks with rings of fat on the hind neck at the base of the cranium. His ears are small and inconspicuous, his mouth big, so the overall impression is one of a giant toad. Yet his ears and his eyes miss nothing.

Mujuru has a personality which is extraordinary. It is geared solely for domination of all about him. This goes with a rapid, inventive mind and an ability to talk forcibly non-stop. Add to all this, his educated tongue and his close but somewhat dubious connection with African medicine and you have the word DANGER spelt out in giant letters.

Soon after our second arrival Mujuru tried to provoke me into confrontation and argument. One of his threats was: "I have read the insulting remarks you made about our President to Jane. The paper has been handed in to the President's Office for action and you will be hearing from them."

Of course Mujuru has been reading all my papers. I thought I had removed anything personal before I left. I can only think that I must have begun a letter to sister Jane at some time, never finished it, and it got left behind. I am not concerned. Issuing threats is part of the Shona stock-in-trade. Half the African population loathes Mugabe and some at least are not afraid to say so.

In the course of the morning, the inspector came over to ask me if I had left any sheep on the farm. I hadn't. Mujuru had slaughtered a big sheep that morning and the carcass was hanging at the back of the house. I can just imagine Mujuru bloody-handed on the job. Later I knew why it was that all my good kitchen knives were missing.

In many respects Mujuru conforms closely to type. One trait of these people is to create an impression of wealth and so does Mujuru. If the audience is large enough, he likes to produce a wallet and ostentatiously pull out a thick bundle of notes for all eyes to goggle at. I was standing by to load a big wooden chest in which we kept the folding veranda chairs and cushions when he approached me:

"I will buy that chest and any other things you want to sell—for CASH! Name your price," said as if the price was immaterial to him. There was craft in this. He hoped I would be tempted by the notes and lower myself to negotiate with him. I wouldn't fall for that one and merely waved him away. However, I must admit that he had the last laugh. When I got home and in due course opened the chest, I found the chest was empty.

Johannes says that Mujuru offered Majoni money and the inspector borrowed some "to be paid back later". I was not aware of this transaction myself, but I don't believe Johannes would make it up; it was given as an aside. In African society to lend money is an acceptable way to demonstrate friendliness. For a police officer to borrow the money would be only polite. Mujuru could explain this to you much better than I can.

An alarming sight was when, in error, a basket containing an adze and six newly carved knobkerries turned up amongst my things. Mujuru withdrew them from the pile. He explained that the knobkerries were being made for "traditional purposes". I had my own uncomfortable thoughts on that one, which included a vision of split skulls.

Having taken a close look at Mujuru, I wonder that The Party hasn't made better use of him. He is just the kind of material they choose for the Zimbabwe Diplomatic Corps. How he can talk!

I was seeing him waddling around wearing a loose floral shirt outside his pants, traditional tyre-soled sandals, and emitting a whiff of slaughtered sheep. Put him in dark suit, collar and tie and send him overseas—he would run rings round Western diplomats and come home as rich as Croesus.

Removal and packing began but it was a most unsatisfactory business. The inspector had two constables with him and for one of these, Makamba, I had provided a list. He was ticking items off as they were loaded. So too was Samson. It was fine as far as large items of furniture went but the packing and loading of countless smaller items was a complete shambles. It was a miracle that so much of the breakables got through to the other end unbroken.

During the process, I had moved cautiously into the kitchen in the hope that I might point out my belongings to the packers who after all had no knowledge of my possessions at all, they being strangers to the house. I stood dumb with bewilderment. Here was bedlam. A group was struggling to move out the refrigerator; someone was tying up a random collection of kitchen utensils in a table cloth; Norman No.1 was piling our china dinner service into a cardboard carton; and, in the midst of all this, an old African grey-beard wearing a hat was standing unconcernedly at my stove cooking Mujuru's midday meal. Naturally enough, it was sadza and nyama—fresh mutton I suppose. The aged man had all 4 plates on high and sadza was streaming down the sides of the pots onto the red-hot plates. This resulted in the atmosphere in the kitchen being heated and thickened by a mixture of smoke and steam. [I tried to see if the pots being used were mine, but they were so black it was impossible to say.]

At that point Mujuru saw me and came across to accost me "Why have you entered my house without asking my permission to do so?" he demanded. "You will get out and stay outside by the truck unless I choose to invite you in," he added in fluent English.

Fulfilling the promise to myself, I silently slid away. Naturally this gave Mujuru the chance to control affairs to his advantage. No one would be any the wiser if he claimed some of my possessions as his. If the policemen would not be more assertive, there was no way that I could challenge Mujuru without creating an ugly scene. As it was, Mujuru had aggressively banned Johannes, the one person familiar with my possessions, from entering the house.

Mujuru was difficult and interfering all the while. He tried to hurry us and get us away. He would say that he must lock up and go because he was due to attend an important meeting at the President's Office. Then, that he had just been called to join a petrol queue and that it was his only chance to obtain some. Such lies as these he used in order to get us off. Fortunately, the inspector remained silent and unmoved by these ruses.

Mujuru watched me like a hawk. On no account would he let me anywhere near to identify my own things. Occasionally I would have a word with either the workers or the policemen. Mujuru would notice this and come forward immediately to find out what I had been saying. However, trying though the process had been, much had come out of the house and by late afternoon the truck was packed and ready to move out with a full load.

Our small MF 135 Tractor was parked beside the garage and Johannes came to me persistently with whispered reminders to get this away. Mujuru had been using the tractor and would assuredly try to keep it. Johannes said that if we didn't move it there and then, we would lose it. I spoke with Majoni and after an argument Mujuru reluctantly handed over the keys and gave us the battery, which had been stowed in the garage. Thank goodness the tractor started readily and Johannes was able to drive it away with brisk satisfaction.

The truck moved off to my quarters in town; Johannes drove the tractor out to take it to Hamish Turner's yard; I took the inspector and the two constables back to Nyabira, then returned to uplift Johannes and so back to my place to offload in the fading light. It had been quite a day.

There was still much to be recovered and it was agreed that we would carry out another operation on the following Friday, the 15th. Meanwhile my task was to set about checking, sorting, and cleaning the mountain of belongings which filled a double garage to the brim.

Our dear old stove, which Makosa used to keep spotless, was in a disgusting state, thick with grease, switches loose or broken. We cleaned it as best we could, but I could never use it again. It was one of the first items dispatched to the sale yard. I had heard from my men that Mujuru and his people had been sleeping on the beds and mattresses. The thought of that was enough for me. They were contaminated. I hated the idea of even keeping them in the garage. These too were rapidly taken away.

I personally washed everything that was being transferred into my new kitchen. In doing so, I thought of how thorough and exacting Beth would have been in these circumstances. All the linen and blankets were washed whether I thought they had been used or not. The washing machine worked non-stop for days.

There had been foodstuffs left in the pantry. One of my helpers advised me to throw away anything unsealed, warning that Mujuru may have doctored it with his African medicine. I was quite prepared to take his word for this.

Whilst all this was going on, I was also arranging for the next assault, which was to take place on the 15th. This time Inspector Majoni said he would be unable to come. Constable Makamba and Marufu were delegated for the job. The absence of the inspector proved unfortunate.

My carefully made plans experienced a few hiccups with the result that we arrived at Stockade later than I had hoped and short-handed. Johannes was not with me either. It soon became clear to me that the young constables were no match for Mujuru who quickly dominated proceedings. Most of the household furniture had gone the week before, so this day we were to load what one might describe as "bricks and miscellaneous".

Mujuru had no quarrel concerning the bricks. He knew that these were scheduled to be taken. However he disputed and argued with the policemen over many items which I dearly wished to take away. He would claim that they were fittings or had been fittings. This applied even to the house curtains.

The court order rules that all the property is mine whether it is moveable or immovable. To describe and quibble over the term "fittings" is an irrelevance. I have made the point ad nauseam. Of course it is useless to tell this to Mujuru who insists that the farm has been given to him and with it all the fixed assets. He will only acknowledge [with bad grace] that the order allows me to remove my personal property.

Policemen should have a better understanding. I was therefore thoroughly narked when they took up the same line of argument as Mujuru. "You should not worry. You will be paid compensation, you know," one of them told me in all seriousness. The remark was silly on all counts. Who tells them this rubbish? Furthermore; it seems to me that nobody believes that the court order means what it says. Well, why not say so straight out?

It must be born in mind that the purpose of my mission was to extract whatever I could and avoid confrontation. I remembered the inspector's own words to me: "These people are dangerous. They can attack me even in uniform." At all costs I had to curb my tongue and show a dispassionate front. My fortune lay with the two young constables and I watched them being manipulated by Mujuru like a couple of schoolboys. I even suffered his arrogance when he turned me out of the garden precincts and locked the gate on me. This so that he could lead the policemen down to the farm buildings for some obscure purpose. I wondered if they too were being offered a money "loan".

These two trips to the farm to rescue my possessions might be described as salvage operations from a wreck; the wreck being presided over by a bloody pirate. On the 8th there had been all the household property to extract. Observing and noting what was coming out and looking to the packing in the pantechnicon kept my attention away from the enormity of the situation.

A week later on the 15th salvage was slower and largely confined to the bricks and the contents of the outbuildings. On this day too, in the absence of the inspector, Mujuru was more aggressive and obstructive. The circumstances were such that I was forced to take a submissive role. I wandered away a short distance whilst Mujuru, controlling the workers I was employing, decided which items of my property he would allow me to have and which he would not.

Standing back as I was, I silently surveyed the scene before me. The house: I had planned and built it myself, fired the bricks for its walls, clambered all over its roof, laid its floors on my knees, glazed and painted its windows. Here my very dear and clever wife, sewed and knitted, cooked and cleaned, doctored and patched, painted, brailled her books for the blind, accounted and gardened, smiled and spoke—so gently and clearly. Here our children grew up, played and left us. Here was our home for over thirty years—in sickness and in health—a peaceful haven where we lived on with dogs, flowers and trees to care for and aged servants to provide for. Of course, I didn't see all these things as I have written them; they flooded into my mind as a composite vision.

At the back of where I stood, three beautiful, shade-trees, had grown upon a green lawn; a Ficus benjaminii, a Ficus retusa and a Celtis africana. I had kept up a personal relationship with these three trees since the day I planted them as little seedlings about thirty-five years ago. They had been felled to the ground; their butchered remains thrown in an untidy heap to the side. The lawn had been dug up and a patch of rape was growing in its stead.

Mujuru was using my hosepipes to water it.

Elsewhere, where once garden beds ever blazed with colour from flowering shrubs and annuals, all was dead. Potted plants, dependant on the kindness of human hands, had withered and died in the dry dust of their containers.

I did not dare walk further afield or up on the kopje where a close association with all the living trees there had once given me spiritual uplift. I visited them daily and got to know them all. I am powerless to protect them; they are exposed to the axes of brutish men. I am sick at heart.

My helpers told me that Mujuru has built a traditional native hut on the front lawn. This is used to perform rites and sorcery. There are no lengths to which he will not go to extend his power over others.

However, Johannes has tried to explain to me that Mujuru is not, what he can only describe in inadequate English, a "full witchdoctor". Hints from policemen have supported this. Johannes says "he is like an agent". When custom calls for it, wealthy Africans will pay him to organize traditional parties, bringing together the necessary participants; the n'anga, the beer-makers, the cooks, the drummers and the dancers. The celebration goes on and on until everyone is blotto and exhausted. The ancestor's spirit is appeased and the living participants lie about blissfully content.

Nevertheless, Mujuru prescribes traditional medicines and antidotes. In a country where no malady or death is put down to "natural causes", this gives him great psychological power over others, an advantage he will exploit to the utmost.

The second salvage operation had taken place on Friday 15th August. It had been of limited success and much had been left behind. On the 20th I delivered a letter to Majoni and with it attached a list and valuations of the items which remained to be recovered. The items on the list I considered to have been stolen by Mujuru. Majoni said that the list would be shown to Mujuru and he would be warned to have them all in place if he was to avoid charges.

Accompanied by Johannes, I again met with Majoni at Nyabira on 2nd September and handed him my letter of that date. I told him of my misgivings and complained of the lack of authority and inexperience shown by the two young constables. In his amicable manner, Majoni agreed with my assessment of the situation. The next time he would have to go to Stockade himself.

I explained that the best day of the week for me to obtain transport and drivers was a Saturday; would next Saturday be suitable for the police? Majoni looked at his desk calendar. He could not make that day but he agreed for Saturday the 13th and made note. He went on to say that a Constable Mawere had been put on to investigate the case. Meanwhile Mujuru had been given one week to collect my property together. The inspector felt that Mujuru may well have dispersed some of it.

I was thoroughly fed up that there was to be further delay. There was a lot to keep me busy sorting the belongings that had come in from the farm, taking some to the sale yards and even having a few good pieces, which had been damaged in the chaotic move, repaired.

D-Day was to be Saturday the 13th and of course I was co-ordinating the task force in preparation. Driver Elliot in the Nola truck, with Johannes, Samson and Norman One aboard, to proceed to Nyabira to embark the police; the Truck Services pantechnicon and hired hands to drive to the Stockade store where it would wait and rendezvous with the police before the final assault.

On the morning of the 13th I was personally shepherding all parties my end to their points of departure and issuing last minute instructions. The Nola truck had a delay of about 40 minutes but in the end I left it at the Lomagundi roundabout heading for Nyabira.

I regret to say that withal my meticulous planning, I had failed to take into account one vital factor. That was the ineptitude of the police. Later in the morning, Elliot rang from the police station to say that the inspector was not there and that nobody present knew anything about going to Stockade. He was asked: "Why are you coming on a Saturday? You should come again on Monday."

This message threw me into a fury. The whole thing had to be a calculated ploy to aggravate and frustrate me. How could a senior officer not remember my lengthy visit; not act on his own memo; not inform any member of his staff of the plan? The whole operation had to be abandoned. Elliot drove to the farm to inform the transport driver of the situation and all returned to Harare—a wasted effort made at no small expense.

When my party returned, I was still angry. I questioned them as to the behaviour of the police. Did they think the police were giving me the runaround? Surely it had to be that.

No, they didn't think I was correct in my assessment. The few policemen, who they found on the station, seemed genuinely puzzled. There had only been a "miss-take". The inspector must have "just forgotten." Elliot, Samson and Johannes lapsed into silence and eyed me with blank faces. I could read their thoughts:

"OK. The inspector forgot—quite a natural and normal thing to do—we all do that sometimes—why the big fuss?" I feel their eyes are summing me up: "It's just his way. It's because he is White. They are different from us. They do go on so!"

Of course I phoned Inspector Majoni on the Monday. I didn't exactly get an apology, but then apologies have never formed a part of African culture. He said he had been sick for several days and had been in town seeking medical attention.

Here I will try to shorten the account. I phoned around, got in touch with the inspector again, and Thursday 18th was the next date agreed upon. This in turn was aborted at the last minute because the police said that Mujuru was away in Bindura taking part in some traditional ceremonies and would be away for the rest of the week. [That's a fishy story if you like.] At least the police made an effort to contact me in sufficient time to cancel the arrangements I had made.

Offering profuse apologies for the repeated alteration in plan to the management of Nola and Truck Services, who are supplying me with the transport, I procured their co-operation to lay on their vehicles for Tuesday, 23rd. As soon as this was fixed, I advised the Nyabira inspector. He concurred with this date. I added that I would like to visit him on Monday to chat over certain details beforehand. Would he be there early morning? Yes, he would be there. And Tezha? Will he be there? "Yes, he will be here too."

I then phoned Wellington at Trianda. We have a quantity of material and equipment stored in their farm yard. Trianda has recently been listed by government. I consider that Mujuru may well be spurred by this to pressure them into releasing my goods into his hands. He has attempted this before. Alan has been very ill and Wellington could do without added worries. All in all it must be best to move our stuff away.

Sunday 21st September 2003

The next date set for the reclamation of my property is the day after tomorrow, Tuesday. Tomorrow, Monday, I will travel to Nyabira with Johannes. There I will discuss plans for the morrow. I think Tezha will be the one to be heading the escort. Neither Johannes nor I are sure where we are with Tezha. Majoni seems to be stepping back.

Monday 22nd September 2003

I reached Nyabira at about 8.20 in the morning. Johannes accompanied me. In the charge office Sergeant Matakeniya was taking a call. He greeted me from the phone and asked if Johannes was with me. He needed to speak with him. I called Johannes over and then went along the veranda to find Tezha. I had been told that Insp. Mujoni was not in.

Tezha has a small office which he shares with others. At the head end of his table a woman constable was searching through documents and beyond her, at a separate small table, a policeman in uniform was ruling lines on a piece of white cardboard.

Tezha and I exchanged greetings and shook hands. I have come to remember the Shona handshake, which is a sort of prolonged holding of hands. One mustn't grip and let go, but I often forget. In our handshake language, I would describe Tezha's as being "weak" and assess his character accordingly; however this could be inaccurate in the African context.

Tezha is tall and slim, his movements and speech quiet and slow. I don't always catch what he says. He will make extraordinary statements with no hint of emotion or emphasis and pass on to something else.

"Are you ready to go out to the farm?" asks Tezha. "Mujuru has phoned to say that the arrangement is for this morning. Can't you make it this morning?"

"Absolutely impossible. All the arrangements have been made for tomorrow, Tuesday. I confirmed all this with Inspector Majoni." This statement I embellished with a description of the work needed to mount the exercise at all.

It should be remembered that I have come here today to deliver my memoranda of 18th and 22nd September, [q.v.] and to seek the police officers' reaction to all the points which I have raised. I have only Tezha to speak to, but I am determined that he should give answers to my concerns. My concerns are very real and I am prepared to voice them forcibly.

Now I should explain that such a resolution is not easily maintained in a public office anywhere in Zimbabwe—perhaps the whole of Africa. A policeman's office is no exception. Whilst I am energetically putting my points and my questions and Tezha is parrying them rather ineffectually, there is a constant stream of people entering to interfere with his discourse with me. They may be asking for a ruling from him, relaying a message, requiring a signature, or, once, it was to ask for a bunch of keys, which, not being found, involved a prolonged search. There is no, "by your leave"; it is ever so informal and democratic.

It is probably due to the ageing factor; my problem is that when I am stopped in midstream, I find it difficult to regain momentum. Words that were flowing from my tongue, when cut short get strangely lost. I am told that I am a demonstrative speaker; thus I might be observed dead silent, hand statuesquely frozen in the air, whilst I am trying to remember what I was saying before the unexpected interruption.

The disturbances were not confined solely to visitors. The woman constable was sitting close to my right. It seems that she was dissatisfied with some document she was copying. At the same time that I was expounding on my legal rights, she decided to crumple it up [the document I mean] and throw it away. It proved to be a very stiff, noisy paper to crumple and it resented being crumpled. This made her more irritated with it. She stood up determined to be rid of it. Then she couldn't find the wastepaper basket. From my position I could see it plainly. It was under the table close to Tezha's legs. By this time my concise exposition was reduced to a stuttering murmur. Poised as the lady was with the crumpled paper in her hand, I broke off and called out directions to her, guiding her towards Tezha's legs. She bent under the table [she was rather large] and flung away the offending paper. I received no thanks and incidentally, she left the wastepaper basket where it was. It was at about this point that Tezha said; "I had better try to phone Mujuru," and, with no further word, he left the office.

After a while, I tire of watching the woman turning the pages of a grubby, dog-eared report book; and of the expressionless constable measuring his lines; and of reading the duty roster hanging on the wall alongside the list of winners for the "Policeman of the Month" award and the framed Reminder to the office inmates inviting them to maintain good relations with the public at all times. I leave and stroll out onto the veranda.

Tezha is in the next-door office, the only one with a phone. He signals to me through the open doorway. He has been trying unsuccessfully to call Mujuru. At last he manages. There is a conversation in Shona and Tezha calls to me that Mujuru cannot be present on Tuesday. He is going to a funeral. His brother has died.

I voice my scepticism. "He is just making things difficult for me", I say. "Why does he have to be there anyway? He has his own people. We only want what is on the list. At this rate he will put me off for weeks—months. He always calls the tune. Yet he is an illegal occupier and I am the sufferer." Through the open doorway I see the constable ruling the lines smirking; the first bit of animation he has shown.

"No, no," says Tezha, "He is going to a funeral. It will be only one day."

"Oh, alright. Let's make it Wednesday. I will try to rearrange the transport for then."

Tezha speaks again to Mujuru, then puts down the phone and turns to me. "Mujuru agrees to Wednesday. We must be there at 9 o'clock." Another command from Mujuru.

I tell Tezha that I will not be coming, but to please ensure that Johannes is given free access to find all my property.

"You should be there yourself," says Tezha.

"No. If I come I shall only get angry and that will do no good. Johannes knows everything that is mine."

"But he is not the owner of the property—you are."

"The court order says that the police must assist my employees and Johannes is my employee."

"Never mind then," says Tezha. "We will go tomorrow."

I had brought my letter of the 18th. I had gone to much trouble with this; capitals, highlights, enumerated points, short. I had wanted to have the inspectors' reactions to this before the exercise began. Mujoni was absent so it had to be Tezha.

The letter was still on the desk so I pointed to it.

"Do you agree that what I have written is a true reflection of the meaning of the Court Order?" I ask.

"I can't say," replies Tezha, "because I haven't read the Order."

I tell myself to let it ride.

I leave his office only to be called into another further along where Johannes has been closeted with Sgt. Matakeniya. The latter has been taking a statement from J with regard to the items that were stolen from the farm by George. Matakeniya wants me to put a value on the property.

George! Along with Simukayi he was the bane of my life. Until Mujuru came along, I used to think that they must be the most horrid creatures on earth. Simukayi is dead—I think the rumour may be true this time. George apparently is still breathing, which makes him dangerous. I note George's second name—Chipagara. It may be remembered that he was challenging Mujuru for Stockade but seems to have failed because he left our screen.

"George!" I say to the sergeant, "Where is he? It was ages ago that he stole that property. And now you ask me to value it! I can't remember what it was he took."

"He's on remand. Has been since about January. We gave an overall value on the stolen things, but the court need the valuations on each individual item."

We seem to have got George on stealing goods worth 6 million. Witnesses have given evidence. George was seen handling some items; other expensive items were stolen at the very same time that George was seen operating in his truck on the farm. Reports were made to the police. Matakeniya reads out the list and I make guesses as to the values. He produces a calculator and the addition total is now 8.5 million.

"Well, so what," I say. "Prices have increased 500% since last January. By the looks of things, they will go up another 600% by next January."

We had been a full hour at Nyabira. As I drove away, I thought that the misgivings I had were by no means allayed. I felt that I had done just about everything I could. Anything could happen and I could only hope for the best.

On Tuesday, I had diverted the Truck Services vehicle to Trianda. Here, of course, the police were not needed and Johannes and Samson accompanied the truck. Wellington gave help for loading the timber and roofing and the vehicle got back to the storage yard in such good time, that it was decided to return to Trianda to load some farm equipment.

Wednesday 24th September 2003

Another restless night. It is becoming a habit to wake at 1 am, swallow a couple of aspirins, make myself a milk drink and take in another chapter of the current book. This formula usually works. I nod off and sleep until dawn. This morning I must get moving early. I am at Martin's house shortly after 7.

I find Johannes and Samson and give them extra property lists [the police will have probably lost the ones I have given them] and final instructions. I tell J to phone me if he is in trouble. I will speak with Tezha on the phone and come out if need be. The Nola, blue Mazda pick-up has been parked here overnight and little Elliot the driver arrives dapper and polished. The three of them leave for Nyabira at around 7.30.

Orders have been given for the Truck Services vehicle to await me at the corner of King George and Aberdeen roads between 7.30 and 8, so I drive to the corner and wait for it. By 8.10 it hasn't arrived. I return to the house to phone the depot. Communication is difficult, but then a man named Bernard tells me that the truck for Mazowe has left. That usually means that it is just about to leave, the driver having been told to get a move on.

I allow sufficient time for the truck to get from its depot to our rendezvous corner and go there to meet it. I wait 20 minutes and decide that the driver has not received my instructions and has driven directly out to the farm. I pull out from the curb and am driving off when I spot the familiar coloured vehicle in my rear-view mirror. The driver is pulling in to the corner and I am able to stop and reverse back to meet him. Lucky I'd say.

I have asked for four casual workers and the elderly driver has them squashed into the cab alongside of him. I tell them all to get out onto the pavement. They scramble down from the cab and I look them up and down. I tell one of them to take his hands out of his pockets when I am talking. I am in that sort of mood. They are all short, thin, young and scruffy. Mujuru will have them for breakfast.

The driver and one of the men have already been to the farm and I ask them to describe Mujuru to the others. They oblige—vividly. "Eee! He is a giant—a powerful one."

I cast an eye on them and remind them that they are working for ME and not Mujuru.

"The Police are going there to help me take away MY property. You must ignore any orders Mujuru may give you and only take orders from the police. Whatever things the police tell you to load you must do so without fearing Mujuru."

The pathetic little group climb back into the cab and the truck moves out from the curb. I am left standing and shaking my head from side to side as it drives away.

I keep my cell phone handy in case Johannes calls with a message; otherwise I can but wait for the outcome.

In the event, Johannes never did try to phone me although the operation turned out an absurd shambles. What follows is the account I received from Johannes, Samson and Elliot after their return in the afternoon. I wrote it all down at once.

The Nola pick-up arrived at the Nyabira police station at 8 a.m. The morning assembly parade was being held. At the break-up of the assembly, Johannes went forward to find Tezha at his office. Tezha greeted him cordially and said: "O.K. Wait. I will come soon. Wait a while."

Elliot came from his vehicle to hand Tezha a letter of mine. [I think this must have been the letter which was supposed to have been delivered on the 18th but the change of plans prevented it.] While Johannes was waiting, Inspector Mujoni approached and greeted him. They shook hands. "O.K. Johannes, you have come to take your goods from the farm. No problem. Tezha is preparing to go now."

Just then, a big police chef arrived in a Defender Landrover. Mujoni took this officer into his office. Tezha then called Johannes to the other office. "Johannes, I am giving you some of the guys to go with you. You can go." [Elliot's account was a little different. He reports Tezha as saying: "An officer is here so you will have another constable to go with you."]

Johannes said that when he went outside he found only one constable ready to go; a young man of perhaps 26 years. He was in uniform and carried a small bag. J knew him well by sight but did not get his name. He had not been to the farm on the previous occasions. Johannes was unhappy to see only one policeman. He asked if there were not to be others. He was given the reply:

"No problem. Let's go."

The party reached the farm store at about 9 o'clock, met with the Truck Services truck and they proceeded to the homestead together. The homestead security gate was locked. Mujuru saw the vehicles and came to open it. He spoke to the policeman and then called to Elliot. "You! Come in by yourself with the policeman."

Then he spoke to Johannes. "You Johannes, I have told you before. I don't want to see you here. I have phoned you and warned you not to come here."

THE POLICEMAN DID NOT PROTEST. HE REMAINED SILENT.

Johannes and Samson stayed in the Nola truck whilst Mujuru conducted the policeman and Elliot to the house. Meanwhile the removal truck was parked outside.

Mujuru, the policeman and Elliot were away for about half an hour. Elliot reported: Mujuru told the policeman that Johannes had lots of the property belonging to the Boss at his own house. "We should go there and make a search." Mujuru said.

The three men returned to the gate and the policeman says: "Johannes, let's go to where you are staying. Mujuru says some of the things are at your house." Being accused, Johannes says: "O.K., Let's go."

Elliot drives the policeman, Johannes, Samson AND MUJURU to Tatagura Farm where J has his house. It is a long way off and the journey takes half an hour. At the house J opens the doors and invites the policeman to search anywhere he wants. The policeman AND MUJURU enter the house. The policeman agrees there is nothing to be found. They return to Stockade. They have been away for one and a half hours. During this time the Truck Services vehicle has been idle and the workers have been lying in the sun.

[I am paying for both vehicles and the workers by the hour; and petrol for the Nola truck is expensive and short.]

On returning to Stockade, Mujuru allows the T.S. truck inside the gate. Elliot with his Nola pick-up is told by Mujuru to stay outside. Johannes is prohibited from entering.

Johannes speaks to the policeman: "You have seen the letter. I am the one who is to check all the things for the Boss. How can I?

The policeman answers. He says: "Ah! This man he don't want you. I can't say anything."

Samson was allowed in by Mujuru. The workers first loaded the boat and trailer. Then they loaded the long iron bars for the trampoline brought up from Fig Tree House, the terrazzo table [this got broken subsequently in the move], the garage workbench. Thereafter, Mujuru specified what could be taken, allowing a few items from the kitchen and pantry, which had been left previously.

Samson spotted the two artist's easels, which had belonged to my wife. Mujuru allowed him to take them; also a number of paintings of hers which were in a bedroom cupboard. He also said they could take a small white table from the lounge.

Then Mujuru declared: "That's enough! We go." Elliot was called to load the small items into his truck. [Many of the small items had never been recorded on my lists because I had not remembered them. However the policeman and Samson ticked off on the lists those things which did appear.] From the outside sheds and the garage, certain items were given up but others refused. Mujuru allowed the hammer mill and hopper to be loaded. He had refused to release these last time.

Johannes went into the yard and spoke to the policeman.

"Check on your list for the box with the New Holland baler spares."

Mujuru spotted him talking to the policeman and came across.

"Ah! You come again. You are MDC." He pushed Johannes on the shoulder and shouted, "Get out! Get out!" But Samson went into the garage and found the box and took it out.

Then Mujuru said: "Let's go to the sheds." At the sheds a few items were selected for loading. However most of the equipment left there was too big or too heavy to move at this time. Mujuru said that the cattle scale and my grinding mill were farm fixtures and could not be taken.

Whilst at the farm sheds Mujuru said to Johannes: "I know you and your Boss. You are trying to do something for land reform with your Boss but you cannot win." He went on, "You must change your list because some of the things you took already. You are trying to threaten me." The policeman meanwhile was silent.

Finally Mujuru said: "The Boss here has stolen government property. Some curtains and blankets have been stolen from the hospital. You cannot take these because I am going to open a case.

The policeman rejoined: "This is not our business. Why don't you take the matter to the Ministry of Health?"

The two vehicles left the farm and the Nola truck returned the policeman to Nyabira.

Once back at Nyabira, Tezha said to Johannes: "You must tell your Boss he must record all the things that he has found and write another list of all the things that have still not been found. Then, if Mujuru keeps refusing he will be charged."

I had been to the yard and taken note of the things offloaded from the Truck Services truck. I then followed Elliot to the house and sorted and noted the items which had come in with his Nola pick-up. I had a copy of the lists and it was a simple and straightforward matter to tick off the retrieved items.

Saturday 27th September

By chance today I met with one of the casual workers who had come with the Truck Services vehicle. His name is Lazarus. I spoke with him and asked him a few questions. In the situations in which he was involved, he corroborated the account given me by the others. He said he didn't think Mujuru was a Warvet [which he isn't!] and acted "like he was mad."

In this matter of the Court Order and the recovery of my property, the police, in the persons of Inspector Mujoni and A\I Tezha and their subordinates, have been ineffectual. It is now clear that they will not enforce the order in the terms of which, Mujuru has occupied my home illegally and has committed all the offences spelt out in the order. In consequence, Mujuru has been consistently obstructive and defiant.

It is true that some of the effects have been recovered, most of these being items of household furniture withdrawn on 8th August when Mujoni himself was present. I prepared several lists of goods outstanding SUBSEQUENT to this. Efforts were made to reclaim these listed belongings on 15th August and 24th Sept.

These efforts were made at large financial cost. They were fraught with a succession of hindrances and delays. My repeated requests for an orderly, unobstructed removal of ALL my goods and equipment have been ignored. The visits to the farm on 15th August and 24th Sept. may best be described as farcical. I had sincerely hoped that aid from the police would relieve me from overwhelming anxieties—not so. It might be said, that in this matter, police protection as provided, has been a contributory factor to greater mental stress—an expectation denied. On the other hand; had I gone out with the truck personally as Tezha said I should, I would now be on a charge of assault—both on Mujuru and the policeman!

On several occasions Tezha has said to me that the proper way was to call in the Messenger of Court. He has been implying, I believe, that I should apply for an eviction order. He doesn't want to be quoted. I was given a bigger hint, you will remember, by the officer in the Legal Section.

An impasse has been reached. Looking back on my notes, I feared this situation would arise. We had put the cart before the horse. I believe an eviction order is the only option open to me if I am to retrieve the rest of my property. The future beyond that is completely unpredictable. Anything might happen. At least I would put the law to the test.

One can charge the police with contempt of court. Will their bungled and timorous actions be enough to get them off the hook?

Property that belongs to me has been either denied to me or made inaccessible to me or stolen from me by Mujuru. I have compiled a revised list of the same and must charge Mujuru of stealing it all. He broke into and occupied my premises on 10th May 2003. I understand that action itself was a punishable offence. On that date he effectively robbed me of my possessions. That the police have enabled me to recover some of the property is by the way.

This month, Mujuru went to the offices of Atherstone and Cook and showed a letter to Richard Wood. The letter was signed by Minister Made. [pronounced Mar-day.] It stated that Stockade had been allocated to Mujuru and was dated some time in April last.

On 8th August 2003 when I visited the farm with Inspector Mujoni with the court order, Mujuru challenged the order on the grounds that he could not see a signature. [The second page with the registrar's signature had been inadvertently left behind at the police station. I drove the inspector back to Nyabira to collect it.] At that time, Mujuru did not show us any letter from Minister Made accrediting the farm to him. I do not believe it existed. It has materialised since then.

Furthermore, I visited Inspector Mujoni on 29th July and spoke with him at length concerning the court order and matters relating to it. A section of my diary for that date is pertinent. I quote:

Inspector Mujoni revealed that Stockade had been one of the first problems he had been called upon to attend to following his return to the station about two week's earlier. He had in fact, visited Mujuru and been in my house.

"He is using your things; your refrigerator and your stove," Majoni informed me.

The inspector went on to say that Mujuru showed him a letter purporting to come from Elliot Manyika and stating that the farm would be given to him, Mujuru. I gathered that another document was produced as well. However, Majoni told me that the wording of the letters was vague and headed "to whom it may concern", using such wording as "allocations are under review." Majoni has given Mujuru one week to bring him proper confirmation.

"He hasn't come back to me, but he may come on Thursday."

End diary quote.

The week given by Majoni had passed. It is apparent to me that Mujuru did not have this letter from Made on 29th July or on 8th August. Had he possessed it, it is inconceivable that he would not have produced it. Yet Richard Wood noted that it was dated in April.

There is more. On one of my visits to Inspector Mujoni at Nyabira, he told me that the Ministry of Lands had written him. I expressed surprise because I didn't think that Ministry communicated with anybody outside their own closed circuit. The spokesperson told Mujoni that Mujuru had NOT been allocated Stockade. He was going to be given a place at Bindura. Others may be allocated Stockade; it had not yet been decided.

"That means," said Mujoni, "that Mujuru will eventually be evicted. But these things take time." The Lands Ministry is Minister Made's ministry. What bearing does that have on the mysterious letter Mujuru holds? It is all highly suspicious.

I distrust everybody and everything I hear. However, one story seems to persist. There are rival claimants to Stockade.

On the one hand there are George and Chengerai Munyatsi. These two may be acting together. They are backed by the Warvet faction. Chengerai is a confederate of Chinotimba who, with Hitler Hunzvi, led the invasions of the white-owned farms in 2000. George, although not a Warvet, aligned himself with them from the start. Next to Simukayi, George has been my biggest bugbear for years. His name has cropped up continually in these pages.

On the other hand there is Mujuru, who is backed by Elliot Manyika, the Party chefs in Bindura and Chan Chinchengwende [an ex-minister who invaded Brock Park and incidentally grabbed all their irrigation and farm equipment. Brock Park is a short distance from Stockade. My people say the wife visits Mujuru regularly.] The Ministry of Lands, it seems, sits in the middle confused and indecisive. God knows if anyone thinks of the Protected Forest. It is most unlikely. The Ministry for Environment, whose responsibility it is to ensure its conservation, will have forgotten it exists.

Withal, the court declares that the farm Stockade is legally mine.

Mention was made of the police needing "an easy way out". They may well do this by making formal charges of theft against Mujuru. Only some inconvenience is incurred. There will be no question of arrest, sentence and imprisonment. Both the police and Mujuru know this. There are ways and means to protract cases indefinitely.

In spite of solid evidence against him, George, as I noted in these pages on 22nd September, has been out on remand for at least nine months. His active support of The Party during the Land Reform exercise will exonerate him from actual punishment. Mujuru can expect no less.

Next door on Danbury, the Warvet, Ghendi, was convicted of stock theft, sentenced to 7 years and was back on the farm within a week. This, after a prolonged period of remand out of custody and 17 adjourned court hearings. Tommy Bayley told me this week that Ghendi has since been demolishing and selling fixed farm assets. The value is to the tune of millions. Ghendi's near neighbour on Danbury is the minister, Jonathan Moyo. Need more be said.

True the police may well lay charges of theft against Mujuru if I am persistent. Precedents show that the case will drag on for months and may even be overtaken by events. The threat to Mujuru is only nominal. In the areas of power, there is probably a general understanding in such matters. The police will appear to fulfil their legal obligations and the politicians will declare that law and order is being maintained. The lawbreakers remain unruffled.

Tuesday 30thSeptember

I phoned Inspector Majoni this morning. I asked him for the name of the constable who went with my truck to Stockade last Wednesday, and whether he had had a report from him. The constable's name is Chenyawo.

"It seems that a lot of the property is still missing," the inspector said by way of reply.

"It certainly is," I said. "I have now compiled another list, which I will give to you. Many of the larger items we have seen on the farm, but Mujuru's obstruction makes it impossible for me to retrieve them."

I went on to express my displeasure and disappointment at the outcome and complained bitterly about the conduct of the constable.

Majoni repeated that Mujuru would certainly face charges.

He said: "Once that was done, the way should be straightforward."

"Alright, then I will get this list to you as a soon as I can. If you are not on the station, I will leave it for you. I should tell you," I added, "that, for personal reasons, it is likely that I shall ask my solicitor to handle this matter for me. I just wanted to have this direct chat with you today to let you know how I saw things." My plans to get an eviction order on Mujuru and to charge the Police for contempt of Court, were best kept to myself.

At the close of our conversation, Inspector Majoni spoke of the difficulties the police are now having with land disputes. He was expected at meetings in Banket and in Harare during the next few days to discuss the situation. In his district of Nyabira alone, controversy had arisen between claimants on 19 farms. So there is a falling out among thieves.

Earlier in this story I spoke of Makosa being very sick. One day a message came in from the farm to say that he was dying and Samson went out to visit him. Sure enough he died that weekend. I am sorry indeed that he should have gone from life in such stressful circumstances.

Friends from amongst the Malawian and Mozambique farm workers dug his grave and we learnt that there was a big crowd at the burial ground. He had been in the district a long time and was well-known. Martin sent out some money with Samson.

Makosa was a devoted and honest servant. I cannot say that his passing marked the end of an era. That era had passed twenty-three years ago and Makosa was an anachronism.

I have instructed the lawyers to procure an eviction order to remove Mujuru and to charge the Police for contempt of Court. Richard is on leave, so Sheila White has taken on his work. Sheila is madly overworked but found some moments to speak with me. She is concerned for me on two counts; firstly the cost.

"Could you afford around 500 thousand dollars?"

"No, not really. I am living on the sale of things taken off the farm."

Sheila's second concern is the backlash that may recoil on me personally. She spoke of a farming woman who stuck up for her rights with determination. The woman was followed and hijacked twice in a short space of time. It looked very suspicious. If the location of a farmer's town abode is known, there is a fair likelihood of it being broken into should he have been "uncooperative".

I am reminded of Wynand Hart's warning when speaking of the Party Chefs who have occupied the white farms: "These people are dangerous."

Once more I am set back on my heels.

In a free, civilized country where, for the most part, the population acknowledges and abides by the law, one doesn't have to be particularly brave to expose and condemn the merest sign of official coercion. In Zimbabwe the machinery of government works on intimidation, basic freedoms have gone and violent reprisals are taken against dissenters. The country can hardly be called civilized. In these circumstances it takes courage to make a stand for human rights and justice. Many Africans have done this at bloody cost.

In old age, I have come to view the conduct of human affairs with cynicism. Beyond desiring to live out my days in a reasonably civilized society, no political creed would induce me to become a martyr; still less would I wish to jeopardize the safety of my family. So what the hell am I doing? I ask myself this question over and over. Thousands of farmers have been thrown off their farms with no redress, never to return. Why should I be an exception?

Should I accept the material loss and the loss to the soul as ill fate? Close the book and walk away? No, I cannot do that just yet.

Today I happened to drive out of town as far as the Westgate roundabout. From thence the Old Mazowe Road leads out to Selby and to my farm. It is the road I have travelled on to home a thousand times. Now I could not take that road. As I circled past the turning I felt a pang in my heart. This was not because of sentimental reflections of the past. The ache was for the present.

I was acutely aware that at that very moment on my land out yonder, the host of wild things, the natural life to which I had given years of loving attention, much of it intensely individual, were without my protection. I was the only person in the world, who would care for them; and here I was turning away whilst knowing them to be at the mercy of insensitive savages. My mind turned to all those young trees I had raised from seed; seed which I had sought far and wide to find. I had watched the seeds pushing up through the soil, sometimes assisting in a difficult birth! Thereafter the seedlings were tended to daily, finally to be bedded out in the forest, mulched and watered—I looked upon each and every one as a dependant child. Now all had been deprived of my guardianship. God knows how many survivors there are. I wish I could explain my apparent dereliction to THEM. The curse fallen upon them is none of my doing.

Monday 27th October

I met with Johannes. Our hay-baler is the last remaining piece of equipment left on Trianda. Alan has been issued with a Section 8. I have been told that Party chefs have already been out there sniffing around. Although Alan should theoretically have three months to leave, that won't stop anyone with political influence from moving in straight away. We should obviously get the baler away to safety.

I ran Johannes to Mount Hampden Farm where Eric Turner and his son, Hamish, have been keeping our MF 35 tractor for us out of harm's way. Johannes then drove the tractor to Trianda, where he would stay overnight. Next morning he would tow the baler to Harare for storage. Whilst at Mount Hampden, Hamish told me that the Warvets had taken all their arable fields from them. Stress had caused Eric to leave the farm but, for the time being, Hamish had been allowed to stay in his home and continue with 4acres of export roses. He saw that enterprise folding up soon.

Besides being one of the country's largest potato growers, the Turners grew fantastic crops of maize, soya and wheat in rotation. I know, because our route to town took us regularly through their farm lands. Production was non-stop. Now the fields are covered with weeds and, looking across the land, I saw the huge irrigation pivot standing idle. It has been so for 2 years.

Eric and I are of an age. As a young man, during the Second World War, Eric worked on his family farm in Amberley in Sussex. As a young boy, I visited Amberley. It gave me a lasting impression because I remember thinking: "I could never leave England and surely this must be one of the most perfect places in England to live."

Yet Eric and I end up almost alongside one another in Rhodesia. In our separate ways, we were both drawn to a country where hard work and personal initiative was rewarded. Now we are both displaced persons.

The weeks have passed and I have practically lost all connecting threads with Stockade. Samson tells me that his mother, Winet, gets messages from Mujuru saying that because Makosa is now dead she must get off the farm. However, it seems that Winet has learnt to ignore him and she continues to occupy her house in the compound, sharing this with Rosemary and the younger children. I have so far managed to get a food pack to them once a month. I expect the three older children help in various ways when they can.

Samson says that twelve cattle have died of thirst on Stockade. The cattle it will be remembered belong to the ex-Governor of the Reserve Bank, K.Moyana. Apparently the pump supplying water to the animals burnt out and Mujuru failed to replace it. Well; that's the African way.

Our Warvets were heard to say that Mujuru should be reported to the SPCA.That's a laugh. As if they cared about the suffering of the cattle!

This week I met and had a long and earnest discussion with Simon Hale. Simon and his brother Warwick own [and still LEGALLY own] Bramfield Farm. Bramfield is about 7 kilometres southwest of Stockade on the road to Nyabira. I have known Simon and Warwick for many years. They have been leading farmers and have taken an active role in community affairs. I personally have cause to be grateful to them for this.

When writing my diary, I have repeatedly used the word "evil" when describing the Warvets; and to those who have aligned themselves with them; and those who have spawned, instructed and empowered them. I could describe it as a cult of evil—a collective depravity. I am concerned lest it be thought that I have exaggerated or over-dramatized. The story which Simon told me of the build up of his family farm, culminating with its loss in the most horrendous manner, was so moving and astonishing that I feel I must record it in these pages. It puts into perspective, my own confined struggles with the Warvets, policemen, and state officials.

Bramfield has been a highly productive farm mainly because of a large irrigation set-up. The water for this comes from a big dam, with a capacity of 1 800 million litres, built on the Gwebi River. I have spent many hours bird watching on its shores. In season, migrant waders from Europe found it ideal for a short stopover. [My prize sighting was a Terek Sandpiper.]

I asked Simon about the history of the dam and how the farm got its name. Simon's father, Ian, who I well remember, came to Rhodesia in 1947 after the end of the Second World War. He had been dairy-farming near Godalming in Surrey. Those post-war years were grim ones in Britain and Ian decided to sell up and move to a "free" country where initiative was rewarded. He even encouraged friends and employees to go with him. In the first few years, due to an ill-matched business partnership, he lost most of his savings but in 1952 he raised enough money to procure the present farm. He renamed it Bramfield after the small village where he lived in England.

The next twenty years were ones of hard grind. Capital was short; African farm labour in those days was unskilled in nearly every department; on top of that U.D.I. was declared and worldwide sanctions, led by Britain, were imposed on Rhodesia. Warwick returned from studies in England to help his father but, because of the escalation of the guerrilla war, Simon, who held a temporary commission, spent most of his time in the Rhodesian Army.

The vagaries of the weather make farming a risky business. Ian Hale had long seen the need for irrigation to overcome this uncertainty. The Gwebi River flowed through the farm and he eyed this with a view to selecting a promising dam site. In 1976 he had a professional survey done and followed this with a costing. It would be far more than he could afford on his own.

Windmill Fertilizers operated an experimental farm adjacent to Bramfield. He approached them and also the Belinskys on Arden Farm to see if they would come in with him on financing the project. They agreed and the division was roughly 40:45:15.

In 1977 work on the dam was put in hand.

The contractors ran into difficulties constructing the core of the dam wall. As a result the money estimated for the whole job ran out at the half-way stage. It was imperative that the construction should be completed before the rains. In desperation, Ian had to borrow heavily from the bank; his partners did likewise. Work continued and the dam completed in the nick of time. This outpouring of money and effort went on despite the ongoing bush war waged against the "Terrs" [a Rhodesian abbreviation for terrorists] and the unpredictable political outcome. To me, this reveals a single-minded ONE-

NESS of a man married to his land.

A peace was patched up at Lancaster House in 1980; Rhodesia became Zimbabwe; Simon was released from warring and returned to full time farming. There was plenty to do.

In 1990 Windmill Fertilizers decided to wind up their experimental work and to sell their farm known as St.Marnocks. By that time the Hales had reaped the rewards given by the irrigation scheme and were able to purchase St.Marnocks and the 45% share of the water that went with it. Crops of maize, soyas and winter wheat were more than doubled.

Ian died in 1993. I attended the funeral service at his home. It was held in the serenity of a spacious garden of soft lawns and shady trees. The guests, mainly farming folk, came from far and wide. We sat on hay bales brought up from the cattle pens. It could be said that Ian timed his death well. The fruits of his endeavours could be seen all around him in the green landscapes; two capable sons with growing families were firmly ensconced; the farm was prospering. At his death he could have had no idea of the coming plunder that would bring ruination.

The first trouble came in 2001. A Warvet named Thomas Nyaguru arrived claiming that the bones of his ancestors were interred on Bramfield and therefore the land belonged to him and his tribe. [This ploy is an exact replica of the lie that I was given by Thomas Mujuru.] From that time onward this Nyaguru, accompanied by a group of similarly indoctrinated comrades, caused constant interruption of work. This they do by terrorizing the workforce.

The format is so universal, it is certain that these Warvets have been trained in communist subversive tactics. A few trained activists will play havoc out of proportion to their numbers and Mugabe has used them to destroy white farming.

Later in the year, Nyaguru was ousted and replaced by two other Warvets. These two were in fact the top men in the movement known as the Zimbabwe War Veterans Association. Pat Nyarawata is the Acting Chairman. He took over the leadership from the fiery agitator Hitler Hunzvi, the doctor trained in communist Poland. He became an M.P. and subsequently died of AIDS. [Mentioned earlier in relation to Simukayi.]

Endy Mhlanga is the Secretary General of the Warvets. Under the communist system I believe this position makes him the most powerful man in the movement.

If Nyaguru was bad these two men were horrible. The molestation, intimidation and interference became intolerable.

From the strictly legal angle, the Hales should have had no fear of losing their farm. The only legal notice they had received was a preliminary Section 5 and this had since been declared null and void in the courts. Appeals to the police for protection on these grounds proved to be useless.

One day Mhlanga and Nyarawata arrived on Bramfield accompanied by the police and Government officials. They had brought a letter signed by Made [Mar-day], Minister of Agriculture and Lands. The letter stated that Bramfield Farm had been leased to Mhlanga and Nyarawata for a period of 99 years. The Hales must vacate the farm at once. It was apparent the Minister was ignoring his own government's laws.

However the Warvets offered a compromise. They themselves would take over Bramfield but the complete underground irrigation layout must remain for them. The land preparation had already been done. Meanwhile they would allow the Hales to continue farming on the St.Marnocks section free from molestation. In exchange for this protection, Mhlanga and Nyarawata demanded a cash payment of $6 million, paid to each of them. It would be termed "rent".

By this time Warwick, who had suffered a serious heart attack, had pulled out; further stress being positively dangerous for him. The decision, whether to accept the terms, was left to Simon and his son Marcus, who had not long graduated from Cirencester Agricultural College in England. They faced an appalling dilemma. The choice must be immediate; to lose all at a word or to compromise with these two blackguards and gain time to think. They opted for the latter. Seed, fertilizer, machinery and a giant irrigation centre-pivot were all on hand for a big soya bean crop on St.Marnocks. The return would pay off debts and cover the "rent". They only needed five months; beyond that, the future was totally unpredictable.

At this time, Simon and his family were still living on Bramfield; Marcus occupied the old homestead. Mhlanga and Nyarawata came and went but never stayed long. As leaders of the Warvets, they were organizing farm invasions nation-wide. The compromise reached with the Warvets, albeit under duress, did at least give the Hales some time to think and to consider their moves. One of these moves was to remove unutilised farm machinery and to sell off some cattle and other livestock.

The soya beans were planted on St.Marnocks, but only in the most trying circumstances. The $12 million protection "guarantee" given by the Warvets proved to be something of an illusion. Lesser predators were always looking for pickings. Simon was frequently confronted by unknown squatters claiming or actually pegging sections of land in the middle of his big irrigation fields. These situations called for police intervention and resulted in delays.

For the next few months the Hale families were allowed to stay in their homes and to grow their last crop on St.Marnocks. That it was to be the last; became perfectly clear. As soon as the soyas came off the land, government tractors, which had been working for the Warvets, moved onto St.Marnocks to plough. Simon couldn't say who were to be the beneficiaries of this aid. He did note that some squatters were building their huts immediately beneath his centre-pivot, a development which he found intriguing.

The Hales had still not been issued with an acquisition order. When it comes to the confiscation of white farms, it seems government no longer bothers to follow its own legal procedures. The writing was on the wall.

The harvesting of the soya crop being completed, Simon and Marcus turned their attention to moving property off the farm. This time they knew that they must move all they could because it represented the only material wealth left to them. However, aware of the rapacious and violent nature of the Warvets, this action could be dangerous and called for considerable ingenuity and daring.

Tractors, equipment and sundry loose stocks were driven or hauled to an industrial yard at Stapleford for safekeeping. So far so good, but drama was to come.

Simon and Marcus considered the main irrigation pump unit on the dam was detachable equipment and therefore a moveable asset. In any circumstances it was their legal property and they had the right to remove it. So they unbolted it and removed it. This became known to Mhlanga and Nyarawata. Falling into a rage, they picked up a gang of followers and set out for Bramfield. There they sought and found Marcus.

Rekindling their anger, as only these people can, they cursed and shouted at Marcus. Uttering racial abuse, they accused him of stealing their property for which he would be made to suffer the penalty.

Thereupon Marcus was kidnapped and taken to the main homestead—the home built by his grandfather, Ian. Once there they told him that they were going to kill him. Should he have any doubts as to their threats, several men in the gang were ordered outside to dig his grave in the garden. They had come prepared with picks and shovels. Marcus was made to watch while his grave grew deeper and deeper.

Eventually a phone call was put through to his parents, Sally and Simon. "You have stolen our property. We have your son here and we are going to kill him unless the pump is returned immediately. His grave is ready." Marcus was brought to the phone and told to confirm this with his parents. Naturally they complied; the unit was returned, Marcus released and the Warvet party departed.

[I was not told if Marcus filled in his grave. Had it been me, I think I would have filled it with compost and planted a tree—representing life over death!]

It had been an unnerving experience. From then on Simon and Marcus acted more cautiously. However, they still faced a lot of work and plenty of problems. There was a big workforce and many of the farm workers had been on Bramfield for years. A closedown would entail an exacting and costly exercise.

Then one day a telephone message was received from the police at Nyabira. It was to say that the Warvets, Nyarawata and Mhlanga had been into the police station and told the police that the Hales should take their cattle off the Bramfield farm at once. Assistant Inspector TASWA advised Simon it would be best to comply.

In the afternoon of that day Simon and Marcus drove the Land Cruiser to the bwalo. There was nobody in sight. It was decided that Marcus should take some of the staff to round up the cattle. He would then drive them across the Gwebi River\ and walk them to St.Marnocks. Meanwhile Simon would drive around in search of the senior Warvets and tell them that he was moving the cattle in accordance with their message. He failed to find them; but on one of the farm roads he came upon a big party of "Green Bombers", the ZANU PF Youth League. He reckons there were about twenty or more.

The youths halted the car, pulled Simon from the seat and pushed him about between them. They took away his car keys and one from the party started up the Land Cruiser and drove off with it. Simon gathered that the intention was to find Marcus who, with two of his cattle men, was herding the cattle to St. Marnocks.

Simon extricated himself from the remaining youths and set off down to the Gwebi vlei by foot in the hope of catching up with Marcus. He had not covered much distance when he became aware that a pick-up was following him over the grass and rapidly overtaking him. As he turned towards the vehicle, a man got out. Simon recognized the man as being Paratayi—Mhlanga's sidekick as Simon put it.

The man came roaring towards Simon uttering obscenities. He had with him a sjambok and with this he lashed Simon continuously across all parts of the body. Finally, when tired, he ordered Simon to climb into the back of the truck. He then joined an accomplice sitting in the front and they drove back to the farm buildings.

While this had been happening to Simon, another big party of Warvets had located Marcus driving the cattle to St.Marnocks. This party included Mhlanga, He was the very person Simon had been looking for since receiving the message from the Nyabira police. Now Marcus was suddenly surrounded by this gang of thugs led by Mhlanga who had appeared apparently from nowhere. Abuse was hurled at him and he was accused of stealing the cattle. In a fury Mhlanga struck Marcus across the face with a heavy knob- stick. The blow cut open the flesh. In this blooded condition, Marcus was escorted to the stolen Land Cruiser and driven to the farm buildings.

At the farm bwalo, all the farm workers, under orders to assemble, had collected and were sitting in a silent circle. Elsewhere there was a mixed crowd of Warvets, the ZANU PF Green Bombers, and various hangers-on. By now Nyarawata had appeared. Simon and Marcus were hauled forward. They were both bloodstained. It was announced that the two white men had been caught stealing cattle and were to be given a public flogging.

To accuse Simon of stealing his own cattle was absurd. They were in fact branded. His own farm workers would know this. Simon had had years of experience fighting the terrorists and was familiar with their methods—public floggings and executions being one. The charge was a lame excuse, based on a lie, to put on a demonstration aimed to impress the onlookers of the Warvet's frightening power.

The chain of events, starting with the police message, indicated to Simon that he and Marcus were victims of a frame-up to which the police were a party—quite possible since senior police officers and Warvets came from the same stable. A trap had been prepared for Simon and he had fallen into it. The best he could hope for was that he and Marcus would get away with their lives.

Marcus was first. He was taken by many hands and flung to the ground. The man who administered the beating was a farm worker by the name of Oil. He had been employed at Bramfield for many years. Simon told me that he beat Marcus with ruthless force with a heavy stick measuring about two inches in diameter. The blows were struck randomly all over the back of the body; shoulders, back, buttocks, thighs and, most worryingly, in the region of the kidneys.

When it came to Simon's turn, Marcus, who could hardly stand, gallantly demanded to take his father's flogging. He was ignored by the Warvets and Simon stepped forward to be thrown to the ground by the excited helpers. Simon received his beating from one of the Warvets. It was in the course of this that the cell phone he was carrying fell from his clothing. Witnesses told Simon afterwards that Mhlanga had picked it up and put it in his pocket. The performance over, Mhlangha and Nyarawata departed. Simon and Marcus dragged themselves to their home.

The following morning, the Warvets and the Green Bombers were either still on the farm or had returned to it. Now carloads of government officials converged on Bramfield. Top Brass from the Police, the C.I.O., the Administration and the President's Office came out from Harare. There could have been as many as fifty officials, Simon said. Bruised, lacerated and shaken, Simon and Marcus were called out to face them all.

They were volubly harangued, reprimanded, warned and cautioned by one and all. Finally they were given three hours to remove themselves and their moveable property from the farm. With that parting shot the cavalcade returned to Harare. Begging for more time, the Hales obtained a limited extension. Nevertheless; the days ahead promised to be a hectic, non-stop evacuation exercise.

Machinery and equipment collected over fifty years for a large scale farming operation, stocks and stores, cattle, furniture from four roomy farm houses, all this and more had to be moved. To where? Simon's wife, Sally, had a breeding stud and she needed immediate stabling for fifty horses.

St.Marnocks could be used to hold their cattle for no more than a short while because security there was becoming a nightmare. Willing help came from many quarters and by making rapid decisions, the Hales completed the evacuation and even got the cattle away—all except ten, Simon told me.

I asked Simon if either he or Marcus had sustained any permanent injury from their beatings.

"No, we are both pretty wirey and tough. We were lucky,"said Simon."If you had seen what these terrs used to do to their victims, it would make you sick. Marcus and I are still alive—and whole what's more—nothing cut off!" he added with a wry smile

There was another question which I put to Simon and which was exercising my mind. It concerned the farm worker Oil who had thrashed Marcus so mercilessly. He had worked many years at Bramfield. What sort of character had he?"

Simon replied: "I can say I had absolutely nothing against the guy at all. As far as I am concerned, I always looked upon him as just one of the steady hands in the workforce."

This poses other questions. Why did Mhlanga select a farm worker, Oil, to do the beating instead of one of the many Warvets and Green Bombers who were around? This reverts to a method Mhlanga would have used before in order to instill fear into the onlookers and to demonstrate his ruthlessness and power. Mlanga will have threatened Oil. Should he show any mercy towards the white man; Oil himself himself would be thrashed and killed. Coercion of this kind was the way of the trained terrorist in the sixties and seventies and old habits die hard.

The Hales had lost everything apart from those portable possessions which they had managed to put into storage and for which there was no sale value at this time anyway. Warwick's family has left the country as have Simon's two daughters. Simon and Sally have an abode elsewhere the exact location of which they prefer not to disclose. The reason is plain enough. Simon said the last time he saw Mhlanga and Nyarawata they were sitting in his lounge drinking brandy and coke.

I enquired particularly after Marcus. I had reason to be personally grateful to him on one occasion. Peter Horsman had the farm adjoining Bramfield. It was Peter's custom to hold a pre-Christmas party at his homestead, and to invite all members of the local farming community to it. I accepted one year—it could have been 1997 or 1998, certainly before the land grab in which the Horsmans lost their farm along with the rest of us.

Not one to stay late at a party, I bade my farewells and left early. I had driven about a mile or so when my pick-up stopped. I had run out of petrol. Fool! I must have left home with a near empty tank. There was nothing else for it but to trek back along the dark farm road to the lights and Christmas gaiety of the Horsmans home. I crept in, feeling thoroughly embarrassed and foolish.

Looking about me, it was Simon's eye I caught. I knew Simon to be one of those who fits the expression, "a friend in need is a friend indeed". I shyly told him of my predicament. A young man was nearby. It was Marcus. I assumed that he was on holiday from college. There was a brief discussion between father and son; mainly concerning gate keys and fuel tank keys and jerry cans. Marcus was given the keys for the 4x4 in which they had come. "Not to worry. Go with Marcus. He'll get you going," Simon told me.

Well, of course Marcus did. I read in his actions self-confidence and competence. But most of all I remembered his open and cheerful manner. There was not the slightest sign of resentment that this careless old geyser had pulled him away from a happy party.

In reply to my enquiry, Simon sadly confided that since the traumatic events, Marcus seems to have lost his spontaneous cheerfulness.

Simon gave me this account of the last three years in laconic directness. He showed no emotion, vented no anger in the relating. It was as if he presented a clinical report on his experiences; the report merely confirming the depraved behaviour patterns and moral degeneration of certain human types. Presently these types were at large throughout the country and enjoying direct Presidential support and encouragement.

Simon had not lost his own wry sense of humour because, before closing our chat he said: "Now I can bring you up to date and tell you something really amusing."

With the two senior Warvets entrenched and in occupation, the story of Bramfield was over. However the position on St.Marnocks was different. It was different due to quarrelling for possession. First some Warvets took possession. Then these were ousted by a ZANU PF business tycoon, the managing director of the Bokha Trading Company. [The dramatic rise and fall of that company and the rather sudden demise of its founder is another story.] Finally a power greater than all, declared that the farm should be given to the Anglican Bishop of Harare.

Bishop Kanonga had ingratiated himself with Mugabe, publicly supporting him. Further, he did not bother to hide his own racial prejudice He deserved a reward and the reward was St.Marnocks. A delighted bishop soon drove out to the farm to take up his new-found profession of farming.

Simon's farm workers, having nowhere else to live, had remained in the farm compound. Some of these Simon had kept on salary in order to keep a watch on the buildings and the centre-pivot as these legally belonged to him. When the bishop came to the farm he gathered the workers together and told them that he was the new owner and they must get off. If they failed to do so he would call in the Green Bombers to evict them.

Before the workers left, he said, somebody must contact the Hales and tell them that he, the Bishop, was taking the farm and that they should remove all their property except that they must leave all the irrigation pipes. When he was told that the portable pipes had already been removed he was much put out. The meeting ended and the Bishop left.

Simon did not learn from his workers about this matter immediately and in the meantime he had been approached by The Seed Company. The country was desperately short of seed maize this year and, because experienced seed maize growers had been evicted from their farms, there would be even less next year unless growers could be induced back again. The Seed Company had been instructed by government to find growers at all cost. The season was directly at hand.

The Hales had the land, the irrigation and the know-how. It was put to them; if the Seed Company could square it with government; would they grow a seed maize crop at no financial risk to themselves? The Hales said they would consider it. Legally the farm still belonged to them. All illegal occupiers would first have to be moved off.

A week later the Bishop again arrived at St.Marnocks. He must have got wind of the seed maize proposition. He announced that the Seed Company was going to grow a seed crop for HIM. The neighbouring small holders were informed that they must not plant any maize on their lands. [He had been told about isolation requirements for seed maize production.] Even the adjoining Gwebi Agricultural College, which had been growing maize crops for the past sixty years were told by the Bishop not to plant any maize.

Simon had really very little idea of what was going on but when irrigation companies contacted him to ask permission to resuscitate his equipment his reply was brief: "If you touch my centre-pivot or the auxiliary equipment I will sue you."

"The future on St. Marnocks looks as if it will be fun," says Simon.

In order to round off the picture I wish to present, it would be well if I briefly mention happenings which were taking place more or less at the same time when the two chief Warvets were investing and finally securing Bramfield for themselves.

Sigaro Farm borders on Bramfield and some of its lands reach down to the waters of the Hale Dam. It is perhaps one of the most productive farms in the whole district. Sigaro is the headquarters farm for a large seed processing and export business built up over many years by the owner, Jo Kennedy and managed by his son Lance.

Sigaro has had its share of turbulence and threat of closure. Sabrina, Mugabe's sister, once led a party to peg land there and later, in a dramatic incident, Warvets shot at Lance's car, kidnapped him and took him as a "criminal" to State House. However, Lance was eventually left alone and when last I met him he was his affable self and back in full control of his business.

Jo Kennedy had built a magnificent home on Sigaro. [I had visited it only once in order to ask his wife permission to go bird watching on a part of their property.] Near to the house there is an airstrip and a hanger for Jo Kennedy's plane. The hanger was cleverly built into the hillside of the hill upon which the house stood. It is said to have a lift access.

Upon meeting with Johannes, he told me of what was then the talk of the district. The President's wife, Grace Mugabe, arrived on Sigaro with her entourage of officials, police officers and bodyguards. According to the African talk, security men rushed ahead to the airstrip to ensure that nobody in a plane took off! Then the President's wife toured the house, the grounds and the buildings.

It was probably the house and the idea of a handy, getaway airstrip which persuaded Grace. She announced that she would take the property and drove off with her cavalcade. Later, this episode was confirmed to me, if less colourfully, by a policeman. Grace has given part of Sigaro to one of her relations. I am informed he is a wealthy business man who owns a cross-border transport company. Again it was the policeman, to whom I was giving a lift, who told me that the man had "lots of money".

I have no desire to set myself the task of matching dates and it would be of little consequence if I did, but I think it probable that the move the Warvets made against Bramfield coincided with Grace's coup at Sigaro.

Confined as I am to Harare, I am meeting fellow farmers who are in a similar position to me. One such is Chris Ashton of Raffeen Farm. It may be remembered that Raffeen Farm, along with Stockade, had been upbraided by ZANU PF for not sending their workers to Party meetings. Not only was Chris farming; he had also developed a successful furniture-making business on the farm. This employed skilled carpenters and subsidary workers. Chris is transferring his skills to Zambia.

I spoke to Chris of my attempt to get an eviction order through the courts and thereby to get Mujuru out of my house. Chris was very sceptical.

"Yes, you may get a court order, but who will you get to enforce it? Do you know who is going into my house and taking my farm?"

I looked blank and Chris resumed.

"THE BLOODY ASSISTANT COMMISSIONER OF POLICE! That's who!

Meeting my fellow farmers and listening to their stories has been something of a shock to me. For weeks and months, I have been pinned down fighting my own lonely battle. So engrossed have I been, that I knew nothing of the desperate rearguard actions that farming friends were taking in my close vicinity. The conditions were such that we did not leave our outposts; it could even have proved dangerous to attempt making a social call. The government controlled the radio, the TV, and the Herald newspaper. The opposition Daily News was forcefully closed down. Thus nothing of the turmoil on the farms appeared in the media. What news one got was by word of mouth through family or friends or friends of friends.

Now that I have taken full account of my enemies, I realize how blind I was; how ingenuous, to imagine that I could save Stockade and my forest from being overun by them. They have taken up positions all around me; 2 cabinet ministers, the President's wife, 2 Warvet chiefs, the Chief Jusitice, a Police Commissioner, a Bishop, and the Registrar General [who won the election for ZANU PF single-handed]. An ex Reserve Bank Governor has actually turned out his cattle herds on my land.

Sunday 14th December 2003

I thought it time for me to hang a date up. Day to day confrontation with officialdom and police, which has involved me for more than three years, effectively ceased about ten weeks ago. The lawyers have dampened the last spark of enthusiasm I had to continue the struggle. Sheila, out of personal concern, has written to police H.Q. and she suggests that they may help me to get some of my remaining property off. She admits it will cost me money and stress—well not using those words exactly. I don't think she understands the situation fully or is aware of what I have already been through. Unless the police arrest Mujuru for theft and evict him from my home, it would be a pointless exercise. This they will never, never do.

On 31st October, the government relisted Stockade. That is to say it appeared in a government notice inserted in the Government Gazette and in the Herald newspaper. What is termed a Section 5 order is supposed to have been handed to me at the same time. It wasn't but that won't worry anyone. Ironically, they may have delivered it to my house and handed it to Mujuru, which will give him further unrighteous satisfaction. The Section 5 order is a preliminary notice stating the government's intention to acquire, and it is valid for 2 years. This means that the legal advantage I had [for what it was worth] has now been lost.

My lawyers have automatically lodged an objection. I suppose they gave the same reasons as in 2001—it was a bulky document and in it I had included letters of support from highly qualified persons in environmental sciences. I don't suppose it was ever looked at. What do they know? What do they care?

During all our farming years, my wife and I looked upon the city as the place where we went to draw supplies and which we left as soon as possible to return to home and quietude. The occasions when we might venture there for entertainment were rare indeed. If Beth knew the city better than I did, it was because she had spent her schooldays and some of her nursing years there. Salisbury she remembered in a personal way; an unhurried, quiet place peopled by unpretentious men and women often of character. It was small enough to feel that everyone "belonged". When I returned with her in 1963, things, outwardly at least, had not much changed. However; at heart we were both rural beings and the city was never to draw us.

Forty years have passed and I am an occupier of a suburban garden flat. Naturally I spend most of my time in the city and during the past weeks I have come to look at Harare more objectively. It is a degenerating city. Crime and litter increase; upkeep and service standards decrease.

Should necessity require entering the city centre, the journey is an ordeal. I park and lock my little blue car in some impersonal concrete or metalled niche. Before striding away to be lost amongst the moving crowds on pavements and crossings, I give it a last tender glance. Dear car—faithful friend for over thirteen years—I pray you will still be here when I return. Holding my briefcase tightly, I concentrate on the way ahead, looking for gaps through which I may walk without losing momentum. I move at a speed rather faster than those going in my direction; in so doing I hope to outwit lurking predators. I am a strange fish, a conspicuous fish amongst the streaming shoals of dark fish. My single objective is to fulfil my mission and to swim back the way I came until I reach safe waters. Central Harare is no place for idle window-shopping.

Withal, the more affluent householders of the Northern suburbs have on the whole maintained standards and their gardens flourish in this sunny climate. This is to the extent that here bird life is more prolific than on many open, barren areas beyond the city fringe.

There is one aspect of the city which, for a brief period at least, vastly outweighs the discernible crumbling amenities; that aspect is the flowering trees seen, blazing with colour, in wide avenues and private gardens alike. In October the Jacarandas and in November the Flamboyants compete with each other for utter beauty and brilliance. Unlike human contesters vying for beauty honours, it is the very oldest trees that are invariably the winners. For this annual glorious spectacle we must bless the names of the councillors and residents of Salisbury of fifty and more years ago.

Residents of the garden suburbs never, if they can help it, enter the man-made jungle where millions of Africans live in low-cost housing and shanties of sheet iron and plastic. These areas have the appellation—high density. The term tells it all. There is no room for nature here.

The ugly spreading growth is no new phenomenon; the pattern seems to be the same all over the world and so too the cause—rapid population explosion and drift towards the cities. In Third World countries the increase is exponential. The proliferating human race demands more and more material wealth from the planet which, at the same time, it is constantly abusing.

In thinking of these things, my mind has turned back to the dismal prediction I made in my introduction to this diary many months ago. Whither Man?

Friday 19th December 2003

Johannes has phoned me this evening. He has just come into Harare from Banket where he is negotiating for a plot on which to live. Since leaving Stockade he and his wife, Sinai, have been staying at Tatagura Farm. Sinai's relative, Zambira, has been managing the farm in some arrangement with Alec Morris-Eyton. However; constant interference by Warvets has stopped all crop production and all the farm equipment has been collected and stored in the farm sheds.

There was a compensation for the farm workers. Gold has been found in the past on Tatagura in near-surface seams and the old workings were opened up with pick and shovel. Gold turned up in exciting amounts and one or two lucky men have made a fortune.

Johannes was able to obtain a section. Being a strong worker, he extracted something like 8 tonnes of ore. He hired transport and after many delays got his ore to a stamp mill. The result has been that he has made himself a useful sum of money. It is probably this money that has enabled him to negotiate for a plot of land in Banket. I am very glad for him.

Johannes has just been telling me that whilst he was in Banket he received a phone message from Sinai saying the crippled Warvet, Chengerai, had returned to Tatagura with others and had chased Zambira from the farmhouse. Naturally this meant that she, Johannes and their small family no longer had his protection. Johannes was going there tomorrow to move the family to safety. He hoped to find a house on Netherfield as a temporary measure.

In answer to my questions, he said that it meant the end of gold digging for him and the others. Apart from Chengerai, Army officers and C.I.O. men had come onto the farm with ZANU PF youths. They were beating people up and the unemployed farm workers had been told to stop all digging. In the future they will have to work for Chengerai and the new occupiers if they want to stay.

In the forest glade 29th July.

2004

January 2004

When I began this diary, it was my intention to confine my writing to a straightforward recording of local happenings and personal encounters. These became so frequent and unpleasant that they effectively overwhelmed me and I found myself on an emotional knife-edge. In quick time I discovered that, in order to maintain reasonable mental equilibrium, it became impossible for me to refrain from making colourful asides, or spontaneous counter comment.

I was finally driven off my land and now I am confined to a reasonably safe haven in the outskirts of the city. Ostensibly, the fight for my rights remains in the hands of the lawyers but I know there is nothing they can do; the result is a foregone conclusion. The change in my personal position has resulted in a change in the format of this diary and to relating the experiences of fellow white farmers in my immediate neighbourhood. I have drawn attention to the unbalanced and evil mindset of our persecutors, which amounts to a universal paranoia.

An insight into the characteristics and behaviour patterns of a people can be obtained if one has knowledge of their past. There was, of course, no recorded history in Central Africa before the coming of the whites; therefore the very earliest written records pertaining to this particular part of the continent are invaluable to an understanding of these aspects. What follows was written in 1885 before the coming of the British Pioneer Column and before the Boer War. Readers may make what they wish of it.

"The greatest part of the Matabele country is healthy and well irrigated; it is fit for irrigating and for breeding cattle; the population is small in comparison to the extent of the country.

The best part of the country in every respect is, in my opinion, the Mashona land. The country is very healthy in the mountainous regions; there are rivers running everywhere and all the year round. The grass never dies up; the ground is extremely rich and everything can grow there"

The above is an extract from a report written in May 1885 by the Viscount E de la Panoux, ex officer of the French Navy, ex aide-de-camp of the Marechal de Macmahon. A chance enquiry led me to see documents concerning this adventurous person. His report went on: "*....I went north-east in the moun-*

tains and in the basin of the Mazowe river. I saw there the most beautiful country as regards the salubrity, the land and the mineral richness."

In 1885 the whole country was considered to be under the sovereignty of the Matabele king, Moselikatse and the native population was about 400 000.

"The King Moselikase made the conquest of the Mashona country, and his son Lo Bengula is still the real King; but the (Mashona) inhabitants do not acknowledge him; they have got several Chiefs and they often fight between themselves. "Lo Bengula every three years sends an army to take their cattle, and they are such cowards that they generally run away as soon as they see the Matabele, leaving behind their cattle and their provisions, though they live on the top of hills formed by the accumulation of big rocks of granite full of caves where they conceal their cattle and provisions. In some kraals they have got springs and would be able to hold those positions against the strongest army if they would only show fight.

"They never help one another; when the inhabitants of a kraal see another taken by the Matabele they rejoice, forgetting that their turn will come afterwards.

"An extraordinary thing is, that when they are taken prisoners by the Matabele, they never come back to their country, though they are left perfectly free, or if they come back it is with the armies in order to fight against their own countrymen."

The Vicomte de la Panoux's description of the Mazowe valley paints it as one big Garden of Eden. In 1885 he could only have seen it as a visionary and perhaps his vision was that of God's Garden being turned into Man's Garden. A garden can only thrive if given tender loving care and when land and nature receive sympathy and understanding—every gardener knows that.

Strenuous years spent battling to make a living on my own little corner of the Mazowe district, contending with variable seasons and marginal soil types, convinced me that the greater half of my land should be returned to its natural state. Even so, land reclamation, re-establishment of trees and continuous protection would be necessary—such has been the impact of the human species. Before being expelled, I had gone some distance along the way and my land was reverting to a natural Eden.

1885, when viewed from the present, would seem to fade into the mist of a distant time. It is a false conception. It is brought about by the furious pace of Man's proliferation and inventiveness. Bloody wars waged between men since then, have not hindered the pace—quite the reverse. It depends upon where you are standing.

When Beth and I came to Stockade in 1963, our neighbour, Tom, took us to visit an old lady in her farmhouse. She was well into her nineties. Her husband had been one of the outriders in the Pioneer Column of 1890 and she had trekked north to follow him soon after. She told us something of her experiences. As a young girl, the year 1885 was still sharp in her memory. When her man died she lived on in the farmhouse with her son. I remember looking about me and at the simple trappings, much worn with age. Here time had stood still and she lived more or less in a time capsule.

It is nearly forty years on since I met the old lady and it seems like yesterday. In the minds of two people, we have made 1885 seem like the day before yesterday. My woman has died and my farmhouse taken from me. It looks as if I shall have to leave—but it won't be by horseback or ox-wagon.

White men and women began settling and WORKING as farmers in 1890. Those who have followed in their footsteps are now being evicted as being undesirable aliens. Yet in that SHORT period the African population has expanded to twelve million—a twenty-fold increase. Should four thousand white farmers be condemned for that?

It is said that one in three of that population have HIV or AIDS. Are the farmers responsible for that too?

United Nations agencies and international relief organizations are presently shipping in tonnes of free foodstuffs into Zimbabwe by sea, rail and road in a giant Food Aid operation. It means well-paid "jobs for the boys" to organize it; rake-offs for smiling Party stalwarts who will distribute it; and claps and votes for Mugabe from the recipients of it. It will be a great success and can be repeated next year—and the next—and the next. The general consensus seems to be that the farmers, who could have grown the food, can go hang.

As for the land, whether it be arable or that protected for natural life, make no mistake; it is doomed. Erosion and desertification starts now. The conserving farmers, the caring guardians, have been driven off. For God's sake, who else in this world cares?

I have said that I am confined to a reasonably safe place within the city. However pleasant my particular cell may appear to be, I cannot remain encapsulated within it for ever and keep my sanity when outside its four walls violence towards man and nature gets progressively worse. My own lost land with its lost dreams lies far too close. It is there, just over the horizon, yet I am denied access to it and cannot come to its aid. Its countless dependants relied on my personal protection and now, as they suffer, I am powerless to help them. I feel as if I were chained.

The events of the past three years have ruined me financially so I am drained anyway. With the loss of my land, I have lost my capital and income. Whatever small amounts I could salvage, each day become more worthless due to devaluation. Inflation is 500%. It will be impossible to live.

As unemployment escalates, there is bound to be more crime—much of it violent. I have seen my share. In Zimbabwe, one lives uneasily in an atmosphere of evil oppression and in this there can be no change. It is because the oppressors have the full backing of powerful and influential allies in Africa who have one eye on their own backyards and, should their power bases be threatened, will take the very same steps as Mugabe has taken to stifle opposition. This is the reality of Africa.

I lost my three-year battle against the State, a record of which has filled these pages, and I must acknowledge defeat. I hope a reader will have come to a clearer understanding of the odds stacked against me and agree that, above all, my cause was just.

My home? I shall never see it again. Even my dearest memories will be for ever clouded with a vision of the brigand Mujuru strutting and bellowing where once my gentle Beth trod. In the grassy clearing in the woods, no posey of garden flowers will rest on her grave on the 29th.of July—the day of the year she was born and died. Her wildlife visitors will be cruelly snared and killed. Now, saddened, I want to leave the battleground, and everything associated with it, far behind.

2005

It is a fine June morning in England. Yes; I have returned to home soil. There have been bewildering changes since I left close to fifty-nine years ago but, as best I can, I am picking up the threads of the past. I am fortunate to have found a niche in a country district. Man is for ever impacting on his surroundings and his changes can be grotesquely ugly. Thank God, some places escape Man's hand. Except for its quiet rhythm, natural life never changes and to my eyes, is never ugly. Having found some of it close to hand is making readjustment easier. In age I am rediscovering the delights of youth. Trees, birds and wildflowers have by no means been forgotten. They are still here as I remember them, bursting with vitality. Here, of course, the tree species are completely different to those found in my farm forest—as indeed is all the plant life. But there is a connection which I delight in.

On Stockade, in the summer months of the Southern Hemisphere, we were hosts to countless migrant birds. Over the green lands, over the treetops, beneath the clouds, thousands of swallows, martins and swifts hawked for upswept insects the day long. Other migrants would be feeding alongside the local species within the panoply of rich vegetation. The willow warbler, which I heard on my Zimbabwe farm in the canopy of spreading Acacia and msasa trees in January, may be the one I now hear singing as it works through the oak tree's greenery. The reed and sedge warblers singing frantically down at the river bank yesterday could have sojourned by my dam some weeks ago. When winter approaches, they may well return there—seeking the familiar. What will they find? My emotion has followed me. It seems I cannot escape it.

My return to Britain coincided with an election; a non-stop display of democracy in action; freedom of association, free speech, free press, openness of debate, no violence, no vote-rigging; all in all it revealed the workings of a civilized society. Sixty years ago, we had just gone through a long and bitter war in order to save democracy. Africa never understood the concept and still struggles with it. Zimbabwe is going in rapid reverse. When it crashes it will be a nightmare to pick up the pieces.

Here in Britain I observe that there is anxiety about the effects of Carbon emissions on global warming. I see also that there is an awareness of the need to protect and conserve dwindling wildlife and natural resources. Believe me; whatever you do here will be counter- balanced by pollution and annihilation in Africa. Remember; it is one world.

There is a call at the present to provide massive AID to Africa. It worries me.

As usual, I am thinking of the living things with which we share the planet and I fear for them. There are two terrifying words in the English language beloved by politicians; one is Progress and the other is Development. Death and Destruction follow in their wake. Africa will be no exception.

Suffolk 2005 and still planting trees.

ISBN 1-41205584-9